Summits and Secrets

Summits and Secrets

The Kurt Diemberger autobiography

KURT DIEMBERGER
TRANSLATED BY HUGH MERRICK

Vertebrate Publishing, Sheffield
www.v-publishing.co.uk

Summits and Secrets

Kurt Diemberger

 Vertebrate Publishing
Omega Court, 352 Cemetery Road, Sheffield S11 8FT, United Kingdom.
www.v-publishing.co.uk

First published in Germany in 1970 and in Great Britain in 1971.
This edition first published in 2019 by Vertebrate Publishing.

This book is a work of non-fiction based on the life, experiences and
recollections of Kurt Diemberger. In some limited cases the names of people,
places, dates and sequences or the detail of events have been changed solely
to protect the privacy of others. The author has stated to the publishers that,
except in such minor respects not affecting the substantial accuracy of the
work, the contents of the book are true.

A CIP catalogue record for this book is available from the British Library.

ISBN 978-1-912560-03-5 (Paperback)
ISBN 978-1-912560-02-8 (eBook)

Produced by Vertebrate Publishing.

Contents

It is customary for a book to have a beginning and an end. Not this one; and this page could just as well appear in its middle, or before or after, its contents. It is like my life, which runs its course and I know neither its start nor its conclusion.

In a corner of my room there hangs, by a slender thread, a representation of the world. Consisting of two simple circles of straw, it is transparent. Four star-shaped trimmings are a reminder of Christmas; but it has become almost meaningless, and I see that during the course of the years one of the four stars has fallen off. However, the globe keeps on swinging, slowly, now one way, now the other. It hardly ever comes to rest.

I have christened my circles of straw 'The World'. Sometimes I watch it swinging for quite a time and think about it.

For a naught is nothing; but a naught that has started to swing must, after all, be something ...

Part 1

1 The Astronaut

When the first man in space caught sight of the earth, his first conclusion was that it really was round. He next observed that it was surrounded by a shimmering blue cloak, clearly defined against the darkness of the void. Not one of the many stars he could see, not the moon, nor the sun, flaming unnaturally there in the black sky, evinced this fairylike feature. Only the earth – man's heaven.

Day and night succeeded one another swiftly. The speed of the flight was breath-taking, but the astronaut was not conscious of it. In the death-like silence, the earth turned beneath him. Now the strip of atmosphere stretched orange-red about the star, veiled in the darkness of night. Scarcely an hour later, cloud-banks were glittering in sunlight. What had become of time? It was with a sense of irony that the astronaut looked at the face of his watch; except for the capsule – his only fixed point – oceans and continents filed past down below. There were people down there whom he could not see, and those he loved were just as remote. All he knew was that they were thinking of him then – there, under the blue glass-dome.

Someday, somebody, perhaps his great grandson, would fly still farther afield, right through the stars, traversing infinite distances away from the earth. He would know no more of nights and days. With him there would only be the stars, space and the fear of death.

What would be that man's thoughts? Must he not be oppressed merely by the idea of his immeasurable distance from the earth? Would he not live, out there among the myriads of the stars, in the sole hope of a safe return to it? To his earth which, for an inexplicable reason that lay in its very self, had created a paradise in the vast loneliness of space?

Our astronaut looked down again at the ever-receding earth. He too belonged to it; to the narrow, precarious space between zero and 8,000 metres, where man can live – in which all the world's miracles and all its bestialities are enacted – the glittering skin of a drop of water.

Down there under the magic carpet of the clouds, men, were fighting and making love; in the loud din of war, tanks were roaring through the sands of the desert; ships sailed the seas and cities grew to being; here a mother was bringing her child to life, there a professor was cracking his head over the meaning of existence; forests rustled, and a young girl discovered that her breasts had started to form; and somewhere, somebody, cursing the whole world, died soon after. The earth kept on turning, and there was no end to love … for human beings beneath the heavens … who have always longed to go to where earth and sky meet.

And so they set out for the horizon, and climbed the highest peaks. Only wise men and lovers stayed where they were; but no one else understood why they had no need to go so far afield. Not even our astronaut, who had not climbed up to heaven, but burst through it, so that he was now outside, and could see the earth in all its limitations – and space in all its infinity.

A turntable was racing round. There were children, holding hands, cutting capers, dancing in a ring, shouting, laughing, clapping, singing in unison with the loud-speaker: 'Little Marcello has gone up into space in his spaceship with a special mission, and is now happily breaking up the stars with his hammer.' A roll of drums, and the stars splinter in the mirror above the gaily-hued pasteboard-box. Manfredo, aged just two, has fetched a chair and is looking on, entranced. 'Ancora!' howl the others, for the record has run out; the little 'disc-jockey' – yes, he knows how – plants the needle back at the beginning, and for the ninth time the bright-yellow cardboard ship mounts with Marcello to the sky. And the whirling dance goes on …

Out here in space all is silence; the earth down there turns soundlessly. The man in the space-capsule knows that the moment for the descent is near – down through the blue cloak of vapour, which protects the earth from death-dealing space. Meteors are quenched in it, so heavy is it; human beings can breathe and move in it, so light it is. The astronaut knows it: in a few minutes he will himself be hurtling through that sky like a meteor. Then the heat shield will begin to melt, the capsule itself may start to glow … and he, will he be burnt to death?

Everything has been worked out to a hair; he will come down safely to earth.

But will he? Nobody knows. Downward tilts the capsule.

Who knows how many urgent prayers have risen to heaven while men were hurtling back through the atmosphere?

Prayers, yes – but to what heaven? Where is that heaven?

The astronaut has landed safely on earth.

2 Crystals

Suddenly, the first wave of the *föhn* burst upon the silence of the valley. We were on our way to look for crystals, in the night, and the storm howled around us, throwing wave upon shock wave into the vale.

The wind came from the south, roaring over the sub-alpine ridges, swirling far up to the Marmolata's crest, coursing in wild gusts among the pillars of the Drei Zinnen, and finishing by whistling the whole gamut of the scale among the ridges and towers of the Dolomites.

It was as if the whole sky had burst into turmoil, that March night. Was the storm ushering in the spring; in the night, of all things?

The white wall of the Hohe Tauern, confronting the warm southerly gale on its northward path, drove it high up into the sky. But it was not as easy as that to stop the 'snowgobbler', as these storms are called in the Salzburg dialect. True, its cloak of cloud, caught between the ice peaks tarried among the summits – but the storm itself fell with undiminished fury upon the valleys to the north.

There, in the Salzach lowlands, the night-dark meadows stood starred with the first flowers; spring was already here.

Suddenly, the first wave of the *föhn* burst upon the silence of the valley.

We were on our way to look for crystals, and the storm was howling around us. Why had we come here by night?

One of the locals was responsible for that, telling us that he found crystals much more easily by night than by day: they blinked at him from far of in the light of his lantern, as he climbed the gullies in the steep slopes …

The *föhn* threw wave upon shock wave into the vale. They came roaring down from somewhere high up among the glaciers, tearing through the forest, and hastening away from towards the Salzach.

We could see very little, here in the pitch-darkness of the lower Sulzbachtal, which rose, narrowly confined at this point by steep slopes, towards the Gross Venediger – that silvery three-thousander rising above the broad glacier realm of the westerly Hohe Tauern. Even when a gap appeared in the black wall of the forest, we could only guess where the peak stood, high above the head of the valley.

What an idiotic idea, searching for crystals by night ... I should never have thought of it, even in the days when, as a lad, I ranged the valleys with my hammer, dreaming of hidden rifts crammed with crystals. On the other hand if the local was right, it would be like a fairy story. We had thought of that – already imagining the crystals winking at us in the light of the lantern – when we decided to pursue this fairy tale.

So here we were, following the narrow path, which I remembered from my young days as a stone-hunter. There was a place where we had to turn up through the forest to the foot of a cliff. It was at a bend in the path, soon after crossing a brook. Could I find it in this darkness?

'How much farther?'

'I'm not sure. Maybe half an hour, maybe an hour. One moves more slowly by night.'

'Can you remember the place?'

'Yes, I shall find it again.'

Things had changed a good deal. Clearings had disappeared, the forest seemed to have grown denser, or was it just the darkness? The path, definitely the only one in the Untersulzbachtal, had not changed at all. Over there, in the next valley, there is a road now; and in the Felbertal – two or three parallel valleys to the east – today you can drive straight through a tunnel, on a splendid motorway, down to the Dolomites. I am sorry about the Obersulzbachtal – I used to go there on foot ... it was there that, twenty years ago, after a two days' search, I found my first mountain crystal. There it lay on the moss, clear as a drop of dew – just as if everyone knew that crystals always lie on a mossy boulder on a slope. I endowed it with an inner light of its own. Though there was no sun, it was brighter than the snows on the peaks. I can remember how my hand trembled as, at last, I picked it up.

My thoughts were interrupted ...

'Do you think we still need the lamp? The forest isn't so dark here, and you say you know the way. We'll need it when we get there because we can't find crystals without its light.'

'Quite right,' I agreed. I had a reserve flash lamp in my rucksack, but it would be a pity if one of us couldn't see anything, up on the slope. So I turned the lamp off.

That moment, with the crystal lying there on the moss, still shines undimmed whenever I recall it; even though I later found larger and more beautiful ones on the Sonnblick. Not even a shining green emerald in the bed of a stream below an old mine in the Habachtal could oust that small, regular pyramid of quartz from its place in my heart. For it was my first stone.

Today, as I write this, I believe it to be quite wrong simply to believe that the new merely replaces the old. Sometime or other, in some place or other, the past will suddenly surge up – a person, a face, a likeness ... a tune. And when it does, it is there. All of a sudden you relive something you thought long past. Sometimes it is only a recollection ... but sometimes that past begins its own strange existence and grows stronger than the present. And so it becomes a new present.

Consciously or unconsciously? Who can tell, for instance, when a 'successful' man starts slaving away at taking a degree; when a dyed-in-the-wool bachelor marries the girl of his childhood, and a barrister decides to become a mountain guide? And then, it is by no means certain whether they themselves know why.

Even I remember an agonised ropemate, whose ill-fortune it was that crystals suddenly appeared on a ridge we were climbing, and at more than one spot, too. I need hardly say that we did not climb our peak, that day.

'I believe I shall find a great big crystal today ... ' Yes, there was something in the air of this night, but what? I didn't know myself, so I laughed a little and said: 'All crystal hunters believe that – I thought so myself, every single day. A hunter once told me about a wonderful great crystal in a rock fissure in the forest; he used to go back every now and then to look at it. Only he knows where, though ... '

'I can quite understand his keeping it secret. And why shouldn't today be just such a lucky one for us – on my very first search?'

'I hope it will be. It can always happen. But just now it's dark and we have still to find the place. The largest stones found on this face till now were about the length of one's finger – green, brown and sometimes even black ones, of quite unusual brilliance, possibly semi-precious. They are called epidotes, and, so far as I know, no larger ones have been found anywhere; and who knows what else may be hidden in the Tauern, unknown to anyone, even to the old crystal hunters who clambered about up there for decades ... ' (not like me, for only a few days).

'Once – over there in the Habachtal – I had incredible luck myself. The two-man crew of the old emerald mine had been washing for emeralds for days outside the half-silted-up hole in the face, at about 8,000 feet. They had already amassed quite a find of 'collector's stones' – white or pale green crystals, all full of faults and flaws – but were quite contented. Pure, valuable emeralds are, of course, very rare and hardly ever found. The two men were very amiable, and allowed me to disappear, armed with a little luck and a big bucket, into the darkness of the tunnel. I could fill my bucket once, in the hope that, the muddy deposit might hold a collector's stone, in which case it would be mine to keep. I chose a place that looked likely and filled the bucket, at a venture. Once outside, we separated the silvery mud under the jet of water in the sunlight. There, shone a collector's stone ... and another ... evidently my luck was in ... And then, suddenly, we were all three staring in amazement at the mesh: on it lay a glorious emerald, dark green and full of fire, with not a flaw in it ... Nobody spoke; but I knew what was coming next – I should have to surrender the stone. My luck had lasted just that short moment.'

The whole forest seemed to be in motion by now. The dark trunks swayed slowly back and forth, while the branches moved restlessly up and down, as if they did not belong to them.

'I wouldn't have given it back,' said the voice by my side. I did not reply. Odd characters, these trees all around us.

'How did you, a climber, take to searching for crystals?'

I hesitated. 'That's rather a long story,' I said, 'and had nothing to do with climbing, originally. But if you really want to know … ?'

'I do.'

'Well, it started like this. When I was a child, my father took me along one day on to the Kumitzberg near Villach – a little, wooded hill at the gates of my hometown in Carinthia. There were supposed to be red garnets up there whatever they might be; but I realised from the way he spoke that they must be something very special. We got there, after a long time; they weren't anything very special – just red blobs in the rock. What impressed me most was that I had had to walk so far; and my father was very disappointed with me.

'Later, however, at Salzburg, other stones began to mean a great deal to me; there was a big river just outside our windows and its broad rubble-covered flats, which changed in appearance completely after every high-water, seemed to us, when we came out of school, much more important and exciting than all the lovely town, with its parks, churches and fine architecture. On the 'Salzachrubble' nobody read us any lectures; it was our island fastness in the middle of an over-regimented life. No peaceful citizen had ever summoned up the energy to climb down there and interrupt our stony and watery warfare.

'One day I found a fossilised snail as large as a bread plate in a lump of red rock down there. That gave me a new idea; each flood-water of the Salzach brought something new down with it and, gradually, more and more of it was transferred to our house. At first my mother was none too enthusiastic, but she was a woman who loved the sun and the woods and, indeed all nature; and, after I had shown her the snail, she left me to my own devices. I was soon battling for space; for the Salzach brought quite a lot down on its long journey from the Hohe Tauern to Salzburg. My father, just back from the front, sat in a prisoner-of-war camp, and I could not see him. But I could write to him; so, while I was alternately rustling up food from the Americans and hammering away down on the rubble, I kept him posted about my latest finds. He commented back on them and one day, to my great surprise, he sent me a sketch map. It seems he knew where the red snails were to be found! I went there the very next day, going on foot with my map, as I did not then possess a bicycle: it was only three miles to the south of Salzburg. At the bottom of a deep red ravine I found quantities of what I was looking for – a whole seabed of snails, ammonites, crinoid-stems lay there between the ferns and the roots. Every time I found a new creature, the population of that seabed grew in my imagination. Even in the town I went around with staring eyes, and many of those who met me thought I was in a trance. How could they guess that, for me, a nautilus or an ichthyosaurus had just swum across the Residenzplatz? In spite of the heavy traffic, I felt absolutely justified, and certainly no dreamer; it had really happened – only, a couple of million years before. Indeed, someone had once found an ichthyosaurus in my ravine; but that had been a long time ago.

'Every Sunday I scrambled around on the steep cliffs of the gorge; very unsafe ground, slippery with clay, tufted with grass, and at some places dotted with scrubby trees. Twice I lost my hold, but managed each time to grab a branch before going all the way down. As I never met anyone between the walls of the ravine, I soon came to regard it as my own private realm.

'I was wrong, however. I had just gouged an ammonite, the size of my head, out of a newly-discovered ledge – it was narrow and I had to keep my balance by hanging on to a root – just climbed down and stowed it in my rucksack; was just ready, in fact, to whistle my cheerful way home down through the woods, when – as if sprung from the ground, a weather-beaten old boy popped up, not five paces in front of me, regarding me with a knowing kind of look. Unable to find words I just stood and stared at him, as if he were a ghost; but he was very much alive. 'Found owt today, eh?' came the amiable enquiry, emerging from that creased and crinkled face.

'Oh, just a thing or two–' I stammered, diving into my trouser pocket for a couple of crinoid stems.

'So there was someone else! The horrid thought crossed my mind that he might know about my ammonite-place up there. I followed an ancient mushroom hunter's precept: better say nothing. I show him the stems. I could feel the weight of my rucksack tugging at my back.

'Not much luck, then, today!' said the old man, with an amused smile. 'But tha's reet well equipped – so well' (and here he began to chuckle) 'that tha' dids'tna git oop to th' ammonite-layer oop theer cos of t'load tha's wearin' on tha' back …'

'Oh, I see,' said I, greatly relieved; and then we both started to laugh. We collectors had reached an understanding.

'Two days later, I was visiting the old man, to see his collection; and with the undeclared intention of picking his brains to the best of my ability. He lived in a somewhat rickety house at the other end of town. Every corner of the room I entered glittered and sparkled, as if the dwarfs of the Grimm Brothers had brought their whole treasure up from the bowels of the earth. There were blue, red, green minerals; stones of every kind, size and shape, and more remarkable, something not to be found anywhere round Salzburg – marvellous crystals, of every shade and colour. At first the old man was just friendly, but said little: only that the crystals came from the Hohe Tauern. Gradually, I dragged more and more out of him; he told me about the old Roman gold-workings near the Bockhardsee, the emeralds in the Habachtal, all about crystals, dark and light, and also about our own epidotes, here in the Untersulzbachtal. He had suddenly become communicative, and told me a great deal about his expeditions to the rim of the glaciers, about ridges which no one visits. Yes, he said, there must be unimaginable treasures still hidden in the Hohe Tauern. As he spoke, my imagination was increasingly seized by the idea of the giant crystal hidden in some rift and waiting for me to find it. At the end of my visit, when the old man presented me with a coloured map of the Venediger Group, I was for starting out that very instant ...'

'Did you ever find your crystal?'

'No, but only because I did not believe in it long enough. Had I done so, I would simply have gone on till I came across it. But I was lured away by the mountains, the Himalaya, Greenland ... all the same, it might get a grip on me again any day; if so, I shall just grab my hammer, and go after it.'

For a while, the only sound was that of our footsteps. Then I went on:

'Do you know, there is nothing, however big or mad, you cannot achieve, if you believe in it. You can climb an 8,000-metre peak, cross the Atlantic alone in a boat ...'

'If your lungs are up to it, and you have a boat, of course.'

'In the end, you can do anything. The only difficult thing is to get across to people. They have to understand you. Their hearts and souls are no mountains, no oceans; they are islands, waiting and hoping for the moment to come. Sometimes, they do understand you ...

'Of course, not everyone can climb Everest – why should they? They may have discovered quite a different secret: a formula, a work of art – even, perhaps, in so doing – themselves.

'I wonder how many Hillarys and Tensings have never found their way to the heights, simply because they did not believe in them sufficiently? Maybe some descendant of the Vikings, on his Sunday afternoon walk, looks longingly at the waters of some river that winds down to the sea, and knows he is due in the office next morning. That is where he belongs in the "programme" – by his own volition .. . Or *did* he will it? Resigned, he goes home, to watch television, on whose screen he finds what he has lost; the wide, wide sea and far-off, unknown shores. And he waits for something – but what? Finally, he shakes his head, this son of the Vikings, has a look at the papers, and goes to bed. After all, there is always one's leave to look forward to ...'

'Do you climb mountains, then, just because there is no "programme" ?'

'Maybe; but I can't give any precise reason. It is simply that I am happy there, and so have to go back again and again. Sometimes the main attraction is that of the unknown.'

'When did you start?'

'When I was sixteen; soon after I met the old crystal hunter.'

'And why?'

'I don't really know, now. It just happened, on a day when I wanted to hunt for crystals – in fact I was on my way to a source the old man had suggested to me … '

'And then what happened?'

'Nothing – except that I left it unvisited and went straight on to the summit.'

'Do you know why?'

'No.'

The forest had fallen silent. Over on the other side, or down in the valley bed, there was the rushing echo of a torrent.

'If you can't tell me why you went on to your summit, can you describe what it is like to be on a glacier?'

'I love it. For me it is the direct antithesis of a street. It is continually on the move; and you can wander anywhere you like about its ice; for only the glacier itself, with its crevasses and séracs, constrains you. But with enough experience and a good ropemate, you can climb the most savage icefalls and how exciting it is to move among these fantastic structures of green ice, over outsize bridges, past towers the height of a house, through a fan-like tracery of blue crevasses, that changes from day to day! There are times when you hear a muffled crack in the giant's cold body; it has moved a little, again; or the roar of collapsing séracs. And when you are jumping a crevasse, you can hear the water down in its depths …'

'And you haven't fallen into one yet?'

'No – not yet, surprisingly enough, but, of course, one is always roped. So far, at the moment when I felt the ground give under me, I have always been able to crook my knee and throw myself across. Though I did once fall into a waterhole, quite early on, when I was a boy – and I was alone at the time. I had climbed up on to the ice, out of sheer curiosity, to see what it was like up there, and found it quite fantastic. I wandered about between the glacier-streams and huge mushrooms of rock and ice, occasionally throwing a glance over to the boulders on the moraine, in case there might be a crystal lying among them. It was early morning, and the sun had only just arrived; so the waterholes in the glacier were still hard-frozen. They looked like rare flowers – for the long blue-green stems of ice crystals had, during the night, grown inwards from the rim to the centre, star-fashion. The sun mounted in the sky, and for once I suppose I was careless: I stepped on to one of those blue flowers, and found myself standing up to my neck in water. For half an hour afterwards – a shivering Adam – I hopped around and did exercises. Fortunately, there was the sun's warmth.'

'And did you note that "blue flowers" can provide a nice cold ruffle for your throat?' came from my side, in gentle irony.

'Naturally,' I answered, unable to suppress a little smile. 'But is that any reason for my not going where they grow?'

How and why did I climb my first peak? I find it difficult to explain it today.

It was the first time that this lad in the Obersulzbachtal, scrambling around at the edge of the ice and on its moraines, saw the great white summits rising opposite him – those great white, shining peaks. He had never seen anything like it before.

Here he was, hunting for crystals, but stopping again and again to look upwards, into the blinding brightness of the peaks. There they lay under a dark sky, so near and so utterly at rest. The snow up there belonged to a different world.

Suddenly, a dull roar filled the air and, from high up on the ridge, a stream of white poured down on to the glacier bed, shaking it far and wide. No, for this lad, there could be nothing more remote than those white summits. They were different from anything in his experience. He looked at them, deeply conscious of their inaccessibility; yet, at the same time, recognising their beauty of shape – the regular ridges of the Gross Geiger, forming a pyramid – then the iridescent glitter of the Gross Venediger's icefalls, the gentle sweep of its summit, far withdrawn ...

It was all so unearthly and so vast that he could not understand how anyone could go up there; on that dazzling white world there seemed to lie an absolute taboo. And yet people did go up there. The peaks looked down on him and held their peace.

Disturbed, the lad's thoughts went winging to the highest finding place of which the old man had spoken; a saddle in a ridge, nearly 10,000 feet up, in between two summits. On it there were phrenetic-crystals to be found – a glittering pale-green lawn of star-points – and he would very much like to have some. Should he really go up there?

The saddle stood high above the Habachtal's glacier basin and there was a rib running up to quite near it. One evening, he decided to go up. He packed hammer, chisel and some food into his rucksack, and set out at sunrise. The hut keeper had lent him a pair of snow goggles.

The white flank below the ridge was scored by avalanche tracks; the masses of snow had come to rest in the hollow at its foot. Slowly the boy went up towards it. The rib was not very prominent, but looked safe; it consisted more of rock than snow. Right at its start, there lay a lump of crystal, big as a man's head, streaked by little dark-green chlorite blades. What a pity it was broken ... did it come, he wondered, from the vein of quartz up above? But when he got there, there were only scattered spots. He climbed on, over boulders and pitches; till, presently, the sound of the waterfalls at the glacier's tongue grew fainter. And the silence built up around him.

He put on his goggles, for everything was now dazzling bright. The snow diamonds glittered.. He had never been up so high before. To the left, above him rose a summit … lovely, up there in the morning sun, and in some way secretive, though the boy could not say why. He went on up towards the saddle, which drew nearer. So did the summit.

The air about him sparkled. At every step he felt himself penetrating a realm unlike any he had ever visited; everything seemed marvellous ¬the view, the depths below, the very air itself. Far below, now, lay the glaciers, the valley, the forests through which he had come, the broad scree-cones, where he had searched for crystals. On the snow slope down there, he could make out a tiny trail – his own trail.

Yes, he had discovered something, but was not yet sure what. Was it, perhaps, that he could move about up here – move most marvellously? He thought of climbers. Was this it; was he meant to go on up – up into that inaccessible world of summits?

That world of summits … one of them stood there above him; had stood all morning, with its brownish-grey individual structure of bare, shattered rock, rising out of dazzling snowfields. 'A 'three-thousander', this; and, seemingly, quite near …'

As the boy stood there, he could hear water from the melting snow hiccoughing among the boulders. Otherwise there was no sound. Up there, the brown rocks, the highest rocks of the summit, were powdered with the sheen of freshly fallen snow.

There was something very odd about those rocks …

Yes.

Suppose he went on up there?

Yes.

And the phrenites? He looked across at the saddle in confusion. Tomorrow, perhaps–?

Yes.

But me? Me, to go up on to a summit? Me? thought the boy, in amazement.

Yes.

And now he wanted it; now he meant to go. Yes, I meant to, and have meant to ever since.

It was wonderful. I was the only being for miles around, and now I was going up the ridge to my summit. It had not changed an iota; but I had. Suddenly I was full of restless excitement about the unknown quantity of those blocks of rock up there. Rock which could, after all, only be rock – rock, above the snow and beneath the sky. I climbed on up the ridge for more than an hour – the summit was not so near as it had seemed – my joy increasing as I saw the intervening distance diminish.

The initial rib had long ago disappeared into the depths and I was working my way up between airy towers, of the strangest stratification; many of them looked as if they would fall down any minute. Far down on the other side I could now see a blue tarn and, much farther down, the Hollerbachtal. There were many peaks all around me, and clouds – everything had opened out into vast distances …

A step in the ridge pushed me out on to the slope, where there was wet, slushy snow. I traversed cautiously, digging now my hammer and now my chisel into the surface at every step. Suddenly, a little corner of snow broke away under me, grew into a slab of ever-expanding dimensions, broke up and carried away more snow with it. The peace that had reigned was violently replaced by a swelling roar. That is all I saw of it … but from far down below I heard a wild turmoil and uproar … the roar of an avalanche. I stood rooted to the spot, unable to grasp it all.

How glad I was when I felt good sound rock under my fingers again. And the summit had drawn appreciably closer. Suddenly, I came upon a green vein in the brown and grey of the rocks of the ridge – a mass of slender, shining needles, all in confusion, or in little delicate clumps like paint brushes. I wondered what they were, and broke off a lump or two to take along, then continued my climb.

Then came the slab – the slab on which my nailed boots suddenly slipped – and I found myself, I don't know how, sitting a few feet farther down, on the edge of a cliff above the slope. And then I noticed that blood was gushing out of a cut in my wrist – slowly, in spurts, quite a lot of it. There followed long minutes of terrible fear. I lay down and held my hand up high – that might help … It stopped.

I lay there for another quarter of an hour, then I wound a handkerchief round my hand and felt my way forward with the other. I was close to the summit now, and sure that I would get there – a wonderful, overpowering certainty. Nothing could stop me now. A few minutes more and I should be there.

There were rocks, lying piled on each other, against the blue. Silent as heaven itself. Heavenly still …

My excitement was indescribable, transcending everything. I could feel my heart beating. Only those rocks above me, and then …

They were only rocks, after all. But I was up; up on the very top! High above an infinity of air … up on my own summit.

Nobody who has ever stood on the 9,885-foot Larmkogel in the Hohe Tauern can have any idea what it meant to me. For it is an insignificant mountain. But it was for me my first summit, and at that moment it belonged entirely to me.

In the south-west a fairy-like gleam broke through the brown of the cloud-wrack: that must be the Gross Venediger. The sun beat down. The silence was absolute, almost oppressive. Only the melting snow gurgled and guggled. How huge the world must be! Those were some of my thoughts at that moment – they have not changed since. Was that the beginning of it all?

To the north, the blue walls of the Limestone Ranges rose above grey-green, slabby hills of the Pinzgau. I recognised the Hochkonig by the light streak of its summit snowfield. Then there was the Steinerne Meer. At my feet lay the Habach and Hollerbach valleys, and far away to the east bulked a snowy peak, with a sharp, slanting summit – the Gross Glockner?

Clouds kept on hiding the view, clouds that came from the south, sweeping through the sky at about 10,000 feet and getting caught up among the loftier summits. I waited a long time for the Venediger to clear, but in vain.

At times a cloud would approach the Larmkogel itself, and then I sat for a while completely wrapped in white mist, till the wind chased it from the peak and it sailed away again, like a ship, over the deep valleys to the north, farther and farther, till it found some other peak to rest on.

'… peaks, unknown to me,' I entered in my diary.

The stars were sparkling and shimmering. There was the scent of soil and snow. We crossed a little stream, but not the one that led to the crystals. Slowly a fish-shaped cloud swam across the starlit sky, and the darkness deepened.

Just for something to say, I remarked: 'You're not saying much today.'

'No, but I see a great deal; have you noticed the cloud?'

'Yes,' I said.

It lay right overhead now, high over the treetops, like a baldaquin, vaguely defined and yet regular in shape, an odd cloud. Beyond it, the stars were coming out again. There was no sign of my cliff that housed the crystals. We went on. Wherever could that stream have got to? Perhaps it had ceased to exist?

More and more snow patches between the trees … We came out into a clearing, giving us an open view up the valley ahead. We saw the dark rocks of a gorge, pale streaks of snow, peaks rising above, hardly distinguishable. Definitely, no!

'What's up? Anyone gone wrong?' came a worried voice through, the darkness, as I stood irresolute.

'Yes, we've come too far. Perhaps the stream has vanished – I don't understand it,' I had to admit. Ahead of us, in silence, lay the valley …

'And yet you thought you still knew the way – '

Yes, I had thought so. I did not answer. What should I do now?

'Come, let's turn back, and we'll find it. That cliff is above one of those last ravines.'

We *had* to find it. *I* had to find it. Anything else was unthinkable.

Where was that face above the thick forest covering the slope? We went on up a gully in vain. And yet it couldn't help being hereabouts ... or was it only a piece of self-deception, some crazy belief? So far, nothing but darkness and tall tree trunks. Yet something kept on telling me it must be just here. We took to the next slope, a steep groove slashing up through the forest, filled with boulders, piled one on top of the other, often unstable and demanding care. Somewhere I could hear running water – feebly, faintly – a trickle, somewhere up above ...

The silhouette of a cliff loomed slowly out of the darkness, scattered tree-tops, dark against the sky, a cave ... a slope ...

We had found it.

All we needed now was luck.

As we were getting over the last boulders on the slope, we were delighted to find that our old local had been right: for suddenly, between the branches of a bush nearby, there flashed a single splinter of crystal, caught in the hardly noticeable light of our lamp. This was the old man's conjuring-trick ...

Anyone who has ever seen a ring sparkling suddenly in the darkness of a town in this sudden, unexpected way, must have asked himself how it could have happened. It could have been the light of some quite distant street lamp that the jewel picked up and reflected.

And here, on a slope where every separate crystal lying on the surface reflects the light – how many surprises might lurk between soil and sand, stones, plants and the trunks of the trees? A slope full of crystals ... we shed our rucksacks.

Then, without losing another moment, we seized our torches and independently took to the slope. The *föhn* had diminished by now, and only came in occasional waves ...

I was lucky. Flashes and sparks shone at me out of the darkness everywhere, and I hardly moved as I looked all around me. I have never seen anything quite like it. I only had to bend my head a little and in that instant there was the gleam of dozens of crystals, staring dumbly out of the darkness. I took a short stride, and enjoyed a new display of magic fireworks. It was impossible to think of searching. As I went slowly over the soft, springy ground, I was folded in by a void filled with secret sources of light – flashing, occulting, shimmering, increasing in intensity, vanishing, lighting up again – a sequence as fantastic as it was simple, as unearthly, and yet as of the earth, as is space full of the dust of stars, continually newly-born, flaming, dying out, being reborn – mute up there in the darkness. I was as thrilled as if I had found the crystal of crystals, though I was still empty-handed.

When I moved, this universe circled round me; when I stopped, the glittering orbit froze into immobility. Was I not, at the moment, a little God? And so I did not lay a finger on that magic world – it was beautiful as it was ...

When, in the end, I approached one of these flashing lights and picked the crystal up, I found only a tiny splinter between my fingers!

I heard a voice saying: 'It's a little like your dreams.'

I couldn't help smiling. 'Yes,' I thought, but without them I would never have climbed Dhaulagiri's shining glory, nor travelled to Greenland. ...

I now started – with varying success – to approach individual points of light. What happens is this: the crystals glitter much more brightly through the dark from a distance than from nearby in the light of the lamp. Moreover, it only needs one false movement, however slight, and the crystal disappears into the darkness, mostly for keeps. Nevertheless, there are no exact rules and since everything remains uncertain till the very last moment, what happens, again and again, is this:

You move, and suddenly, at a distance of about ten yards, there is a gleam among the leaves, growing swiftly in intensity – you stop dead, certain that this must be a big crystal. Very cautiously, and taking care not to deviate one inch from a straight course, you approach the alluring glint – for if you deviate, instead of a crystal, there will be nothing there but the darkness of the night. Just as you are getting near, a no less mysterious light shines out from somewhere else.

You remember that consistency is a virtue, and go straight ahead. When, at the end of it all, you hold in your hand a single flat object no thicker than your skin, all you can do is to think of a glow-worm robbed by an electric torch of its magic. Meanwhile, the other crystal has disappeared. Is one likely to remain consistent?

However, the chase of these glinting points of light was not always abortive. I finished with a handful of pretty little crystals. Some of them, poison-green, were like delicate needles, some black and step-shaped, others flat olive-brown prisms; all of them alike had a bright sheen. I remembered that people use these epidotes as jewellery, though not very often.

Shortly after – as the result of a further, highly exciting and successful hunt – I had a shining, empty, crystal hunter's beer bottle in my hand, my companion and I were sitting together at the foot of the slope, enjoying an apple or two, bread and bacon, washed down with a carton of milk. Between the silhouettes of the trees a pale glimmer shone down on us from the head of the valley, where rose the Venediger.

'Would you like to see what I found?'

'Yes,' I said, switching the torch on.

There were needles, flakes, prisms – more or less like mine. Not a single large crystal.

'Quite nice,' I conceded, turning a needle in the light of the torch. It shone olive-green and, immediately afterwards, dark-brown.

'Have you noticed how the colour changes?' I asked.

'No – how can it? Let me see!'

'Watch,' I said, holding the needle in the blinding cone of light and turning it ... green ... brown ... brown ... green again.

'How is it possible?'

'It has some connection with the way the light falls on it and through it, and it only happens with very clear crystals – best of all with these small needles. This one will do it too,' I said, handing another one over. 'I have seen much the same thing with icebergs in Greenland; they change colour according to the direction from which the sunlight strikes them.'

The beam of the torch thrust like a finger into the darkness, lighting up a tree, or the ground, without rhyme or reason. Far up the valley we heard the echoing thunder of a springtime avalanche.

'Shall we have a go at the Venediger?'

'Do you think I could do it?'

'Yes, I think so.'

The light of the torch swept the floor almost horizontally. Suddenly there was a movement at my side, a couple of steps and a joyous cry: 'I've got it

I jumped up. 'What – a big crystal?'

'Yes, and so close to us.' I suddenly caught sight of it, half-hidden under a stone ...

'Show me!'

It was a beauty. A dark prism, half the length of one's finger, with smooth, regular surfaces, simply laid against each other – but not symmetrical. A couple of fine lines ran along one edge, underlining its shape. It was a splendid specimen of an epidote.

'You can be unreservedly happy,' I said. 'There isn't a flaw in it.'

'I am,' came the answer.

The find had banished every trace of weariness. Wide awake, we charged up the slope again, as if luck and endurance have anything to do with each other. Or have they?

I have no idea for how many more hours we went up and down that slope. Perhaps it was only a single hour. If you ever ask a crystal hunter how long he spent digging, or climbing up and down in his search, he will look at you with great surprise and give you a vague answer – for, among the boulders, minutes pass like hours and hours like minutes. One simply hasn't any idea ...

It was still dark. I had gone back to the top of the slope and was pursuing my search there. I did not have much luck, but it gradually dawned on me that, on this day, it was of no such great importance. For during this night I had found more than ever before. It was as if the whole showcase full of crystals at home had suddenly sprung to life – in a whirling, glittering orbit on that hillside, an orbit that was still continuing. It was part of me now – my great discovery. It was strong as the air blowing down from the mountains, from their summits;

the air that blows from up there, where everything is so strong and inexplicable – as inexplicable as what was then being wafted to me on that air …

The boy I had once been – it was the same thing as made him go, that first time. A thing indescribable in words. A thing granted me afresh today, as if it had never been before. A thing that had always existed.

Yes, we had both found something – more than ever before. I remembered how I had ranged these valleys, in search of the great unknown. Perhaps a great crystal?

Was that why I had come here today? And you – why have I told you so much already? I hardly know you. Today you found your first crystal. That is almost all I know about you. Down there on the hillside, I can see the light of your torch shining. Why did I bring you here? Is it perhaps that in our very lack of knowledge of each other there lies an element of knowledge?

Down there, on the slope, the light of your torch moves back and forth; a circle of light in which a hand is sorting soil and stones, testing, rejecting, selecting …

Who are you? You, who enfold a thousand possibilities?

The light, its circle, moves and moves, erratically. At a movement of your head, your long hair suddenly falls across the light, a shimmering, shining curtain: Then the circle moves on again.

You remain the enigma.

Or have the crystals taught you some of the truth – about that boy? What would it mean to you if I led you up to some high summit tomorrow?

Will you ever be able to understand that the ridge, the icebergs in Greenland, and the Himalayan snows can mean just as much as these crystals? In that case, we shall not have come here in vain. But, perhaps you, down there on the slope, are only looking for a stone for a ring?

The wind had almost dropped; a chill air rose from the ground. I got up and walked up and down for a while.

'How much longer are you going on looking?' came up from below.

'I have stopped looking,' I answered.

'Then we could move on, couldn't we? I am tired and cold – and I shan't find anything more. Besides that one stone is so lovely – what more could I want?'

I slid down to her over the unstable slope in a couple of strides. 'You are right – let's go. But first show me the stone again … She undid her breast pocket. 'Of course,' she said.

I could feel the nearness of her. The stone was marvellous. I began to think a little less categorically.

'A piece of jewellery,' I remarked; and the description fitted.

'Oh, do you think so?' She held it against her finger, her head tilted sideways, looking at it long and searchingly; and then still longer.

'It would suit you admirably,' I laughed, a little too loudly, and ran my fingers through her hair.

She did not reply. Then a little smile passed over her face. 'Oh no,' she said, looking at me, 'it's not like you think.' Then, suddenly serious and thoughtful, her eyes returning to the stone. It would be a shame. I will keep it as I found it – along with today.'

Dawn filtered between the tree trunks as we came silently out into the Salzach meadows.

Behind us the night seemed far away and yet as real as the grass beneath our feet and the houses we were approaching. Early risers were stirring. The sky was like a turquoise.

We felt, at one and the same time, wide awake and very tired. Down on the road, the ground seemed to give under our feet at every step. I saw crystals – a firmament – full of brilliant flashes. And the day that was coming. The first rays of the sun touching the summit of the Venediger.

A happy certainty. Tomorrow we would be climbing it.

Part 2

3   Grandfather's Bicycle

My grandfather gave me his bicycle, a 1909 'museum-piece'. 'Ride to school on it,' he said; and I can still see the stern but kindly face with its white moustache. He was a headmaster, and headmasters always have to be a little stern …

He had covered the whole of the hilly country around the little village in Lower Austria, where he had worked all his life, year in, year out, either on his bicycle or on foot; for he was a keen hunter.

When he was fifty, he thought he had perhaps done enough pedalling, and acquired a motorcycle; but when the war ended, he had to dispose of it, and started pedalling again. He was still pedalling when he was eighty; and, had not the sight of one eye deteriorated, he would no doubt be pedalling today, when he is over ninety and still facing the world with great confidence.

That bicycle certainly opened up undreamed of possibilities for me. What matter that this 1909 showpiece was one of the first to be made after the famous 'penny-farthings'? Or that it was still rather taller than normal machines, and a little peculiar to ride? That was just its hallmark; and there were definitely three people who knew how to ride it – my grandfather, my father and I. Everyone else – and I had a number of friends who wanted to try it out – dismounted in great haste.

'Either you can or you can't,' thought I, and launched out on great adventures. My bike and I crossed the highest passes in the Alps together, journeyed far and wide through Austria, Switzerland and Italy.

I have it no longer. One day I left it outside the railway station, unpadlocked, as always. When I at last remembered it, two days later, it had disappeared, and it has never been seen again. Even now, I just can't understand it. Certainly, nobody can possibly be riding it. Perhaps it graces the private collection of some connoisseur as a vintage exhibit; or maybe, one of these days, I shall recognise a part of it in an exhibition of pop art sculpture.

Nowadays I belong to the majority of the human race – those who either possess, want to possess or have possessed a car. Nowadays, I too take to the available motorway and think in terms of mileage, petrol, cash, and time. A spin in the car? Yes, of course – why not, on a Sunday afternoon?

Yet I wonder whether mountains, valleys and passes really exist anymore for the motorist? If anyone says they do, I hand him a bicycle and tell him to get cracking. I am sure he will very soon turn back – and will have understood the message. Poor devils! – he will be thinking – meaning the cyclists. Never again will he attempt a pass on a bicycle; but that will only be because he has sat in a car for too long a time.

Rrrums-treng ... foot up, look up to see if the hairpin is clear ... it is ... foot down ... *trrreng* ... then the next hairpin ... *rums-treng* ... through it ... left, *treng* ... right, *treng* ... left, right, left, right, left ... ah, here we are at the top of the pass. The motorist is king of the world. He has done it again ... !

Let's hop out for a couple of minutes and stretch our legs a bit, and look at the view. Noticeably colder up here, but the view is fine, really remarkably fine, the view; a cigarette, eh? Or a quick one at the bar? Yes, the car did very well; the engine still pulls splendidly, well enough, that is – but, of course, such a lot depends on the driver ...

Then down again on the other side, *rums-treng*, the first hairpin, *rums-trrreng* the second ... left, right, left, right, left ... with a new sticker on the windscreen.

What's that I see – a cyclist? And – two more? Dear God, there must still be idealists about the place! The proud motorist at the helm maybe falls silent for a while – or he starts talking about the treadmill of our era, of the shortage of leisure time, of the treadmill from which there is no escape ... the treadmill ...

But perhaps, as I have suggested, he falls silent for a while and does some quiet thinking ...

My grandfather's bicycle was a magnificent treadmill. When you trod on the pedal you took a giant's leap forwards, because the chainwheel was outsize. Later on I changed it for a smaller, more modern one. That produced an additional advantage: for I then had some spare links for my chain again, whereas I had been forced many a time to call in a blacksmith's skill on the old one.

At the outset, I rode to my fossil beds – what an improvement that was! I was there in next to no time. How mechanical transport can alter one's life ... a quarter of an hour's pedalling and I had covered ground which used to take me a long hour on foot, and reached my Glasenbachklamm, the gorge with the ammonites. Farther north, it only took an hour to the sandstone cliffs of the Haunsberg, where long ago the sea used to break against the nearby coast, and where you could find sea urchins as big as your head, mussels and a hundred other creatures. And, just before the end of my fossil-hunting days, fate granted me an unusual and highly impressive find. There, on a boulder below a sandstone cliff, in the middle of the woods, sat a crab, which chance had allowed, almost as if intentionally, to fall from high up in the cliff. I couldn't believe my eyes. There it sat, bolt upright, with half-closed claws, between the ferns and the shrubs, as if waiting for something ... for seventy million years.

That sort of thing had, however, become a Sunday afternoon pastime by now. As soon as I found a little more time, I rode farther afield into the Hohen

Tauern, whose realm of peaks now lay open to me, without an upper limit; but I still kept on disappearing into its remotest corners, to look for crystals, minerals, or even gold – for the Romans had discovered the precious metal in the rocks of the Tauern and had mined it high up among them on the steep shores of the Bockart See. I found the gold-galleries, though they were barely recognisable. I must admit at once that I did not make my fortune, for what I lugged down to the valley was pyrites. Of course, I knew that, but I hoped there might be some gold in it. There wasn't. So, in the end, I dragged half a rucksack-full – and all I could carry – of silver ore out of a gallery which, for a change, had been worked as recently as the Third Reich. I now felt that I had a great deal of silver at home. True, it had not been minted, but that did not seem to me to be important.

Then I climbed up again towards my summits, traversing the Geiselspitze in fog, armed only with a sketch I had made beforehand; for, having no camera, I had started making sketches of my summits. I had already sketched the Gross Venediger and the Gross Geiger, the first, two really white peaks I had ever seen. I was also doing things quite near Salzburg. At Easter, I took a hammer and a chisel, and climbed the north face of the Schafberg, high above the Attersee. There were Christmas roses still blooming down in the woods, snow and ice above that, and finally rock. I felt dreadful, but I could not turn back, and got to the top in the dark. Today I would not dream of tackling it without crampons, and I shudder when I think of it – but young climbers in their early years have all the more need for an outsize guardian angel.

At that moment I discovered for myself a guiding spirit, though a wingless one: it was a book on my father's shelf. He had climbed a little himself in his younger days and later again during his military service. Over and again I had heard the story of his solo climb in army socks – he had left his forage-cap down below – on the Red Tower in the Lienz Dolomites; a story which grew more gripping every time it was repeated. Sometimes, too, when some of his old friends came to see us, I also heard about a certain chimney, up which they had hauled girls from Lienz – by preference fat ones – and how entertainingly Mina had got jammed in it.

The book was called *The Dangers of the Alps* – and it was a fat book at that. There was nothing about Mina in it – but it provided information about absolutely everything else: cornices and avalanches, bad weather, belaying with or without an axe, chimneys and overhangs, snow slopes and glaciers. 'The Dangers of the Alps' said the jacket, 'by Zsigmondy and Paulcke.' Clearly, at that moment, nothing more interesting could have fallen into my hands ... It is a certainty that there could be no book of greater interest, and it happened, not infrequently, at school that the margin of some history book suddenly acquired the picture of a rescue from a crevasse or a snow contour or the strat- ification of some mountain – for it was clearly of decisive importance whether one climbed on the top of the strata or toiled painfully up the outward-sloping pitched roof on the reverse side ...

My history teacher did not approve at all; but what he naturally could not understand was that it is no use being angry with such people, for they cannot be other than they are. And so I got my usual gamma minus for history again. On the credit side, I owed my life to the three-point rule of climbing when, on an easy but exposed pitch, a foothold came away. And it still seemed to me much more interesting to know why a glacier breaks up into crevasses, why in its ice those extraordinary interleavings of blue lie between the paler strata, why and how cornices form, and how to cut a step. When my father presented me with an ice axe and a rope, I was the happiest person alive. For now I had everything I needed.

And what about grandfather's bicycle?

It was still going splendidly. Why shouldn't it visit Austria's highest mountain pass, the Glocknerstrasse, which climbs to over 8,000 feet, and where the sharp peak of the Grossglockner soars another 4,000 above the Pasterze glacier at its base?

The trouble was, I had no mountaineering pal, and I didn't dare go up so high by myself. All the same I set off with a school mate who was at the time a keen cyclist.

We marched and pushed our way up the Mölltal. It rained pitilessly and Erwin and I envied the odd motorist. We were wet to the skin and we never stopped moving all day, so as not to catch cold. In semi-darkness, dead tired, we sought the shelter of an old rick. By morning the hay was wet, and we were dry. When we crept out of our marmot burrows, we found ourselves in brilliant sunshine. True, it was cold and snow had fallen far down the adjacent slopes, but the road soon had us warm again, rising gradually and steadily as it did, finally in wide hairpin turns. We dismounted and reverted to pushing.

Suddenly, at the far head of the valley, a white peak appeared. That must be the Glockner! But it was not long before another and higher one gaining in height as we drew nearer, lifted its head. We swore that one must be the Glockner, but we were wrong again. At last it really came into view, unmistakable in its sharp and slender shape, lifting high above everything else in a dazzling mantle of fresh snow. My heart rejoiced at the very sight of it. Then, mastering my excitement, I thought: 'Suppose I could somehow climb it!'

Next day I persuaded my companion (Erwin came from Hanover, in the plains) to embark on the ascent of a neighbouring 'three-thousander'. We made good progress up it and a tiny glimmer of hope for the Grossglockner awoke in me. Meanwhile, this mountain of ours was appropriately named the 'Sandkopf', which is exactly what it was: miles of debris-slopes and fine scree. Suddenly, I saw a crystal lying in the rubble and progress was abruptly halted. I dug down with both hands, working like a mole, and eventually found a couple more crystals. When I began to dig my fifth 'run', my friend started to show signs of discomfort. I assured him that it was my last but one, and he cheered up a little. After my fifth 'last but one', my fingertips were wide open and Erwin, by my side, was complaining bitterly. It was late in the afternoon, so we turned back. Erwin was quite reconciled to his fate; far up in the rubble, he had found a horseshoe – heaven knows how it had got up there – and today he is a successful veterinary surgeon …

As we left the scree slopes we saw something else for the first time ever: a whole meadow full of edelweiss, white many-starred clusters shining up at us everywhere, covering the whole meadow with a delicate veil of white. That evening I looked up at the Glockner with growing confidence: I didn't know how and with whom but somehow or other I should get there …

That inner feeling about 'yes' or 'no', which I used to have before decisive and often hopeless undertakings, giving me an answer in quite obscure situations, was to remain with me farther and farther into my life. Usually, the answer was 'yes'. Sometimes I did not trust it, and lived to regret my mistrust.

We were still ten miles from the Franz Josefshöhe, ten miles of mountain road at a gradient of twelve per cent. When we got there, we would be 8,000 feet up and looking down on the grey-green ice stream of the Pasterze. The Grossglockner would be opposite us, 12,461 feet high. It would take half a day's shoving our heavily laden bikes, step by step, up those endless hairpins …

Next morning, when we left the little village of Heiligenblut, with its slender spire, we had become a threesome. A Viennese, by name Walter, had latched on to us. The important thing about him was that he belonged to the junior membership of the Alpenverein; so the summit of the Grossglockner had moved sensibly nearer. Proudly I showed Walter our edelweiss. 'Not bad,' he said, 'but they are cow-edelweiss – there are proper ones above the Pasterze.'

Cow-edelweiss, indeed … that same day we clung to the slabs and found the 'proper ones' – wonderful stars with slender white points. They lay like hoar frost above their leaves, above the dull green of their stems, with their little yellow suns at the heart of each flower and the soft felt of their starry points, as clean and fresh as if they had just come from the laundry … then a clump of grass gave way … and I landed backwards on a ledge in the face.

'Stay where you are and don't move,' yelled Walter. I lay gasping for breath, my limbs numbed with fright. In the end, I pulled myself together and climbed up again; but I had had enough of edelweiss. Below where I landed, there was a drop of a hundred feet …

During the next two days, while Erwin went on a bicycle tour over the Hochtor, the 8,200-foot summit of the pass, Walter and I actually climbed the Grossglockner. Even by its normal route it is a regal peak, steep, airy and exposed. No one is ever likely to forget the moment when he stands in the notch between the Klein and Grossglockner, with the Pallavicini Couloir plunging 3,000 feet from his toe caps; and then, turning round, observes that there is a damnable amount of air below him on the southern face.

That was the first time I ever wore crampons, an ancient set of ten-pointers borrowed at the Franz Josefshöhe. 'Keep your legs wide apart!' Walter instructed me, as we worked our way up the steep slope from the Adlersruhe to the sharp-crested pyramid of the Kleinglockner, with the abyss deepening at every step beneath the soles of our boots. Suddenly – a crampon-point had got caught in the meshes of my, stockings. There – oh, hell ! – I stood balancing on one leg. Walter, belaying me undisturbed, laughed and said: 'What a thing! Now straighten yourself out and I think you'll have learned a lesson.' He was right, and yet it can happen to anyone at any moment, and there you are, poised on one leg like a stork. The only difference being that the stork is used to it, while you don't find it amusing. 'Keep calm', is the only answer.

My clothes provided a remarkable contrast to my ice equipment – consisting as they did of a leather jacket and, of all things, leather shorts, to which I was particularly devoted. Later when, at the cross on the summit, cold mists crept around my knees, I insisted on our starting down again at once. Some hours later a swift descent on their seat had restored my faith in that article of apparel. All the same their days were numbered, and it was the Gross Venediger which finally tipped the scales …

Walter disappeared, as he had arrived, and I have never heard a word of him again; but it was he who made a present to me of my Glockner.

I was now seventeen, and my life had undergone a decisive change in a very short time. Ever since, four years earlier, I had found that strange fossil in my trench among the Salzach's rubble, I never let up in my attempts to master more and more of the world. The crystals had led me to the mountains and grandfather's bicycle had laid open for me the road to distant places. I knew I was only at its beginnings, but what joy it was to explore, to guess, to find out everything that might lie along it. The circle in which I knew I had been confined had no limits; it was up to me to extend it ever more widely, to reach out impatiently even beyond it in my imagination, always to be pressing forward to new objectives.

As I rode along the Salzach valley and looked into the lateral valleys opening up to the south, to where the green of the forests took on a bluish tinge, I saw white peaks in the distance. There were more than a dozen such valleys; at the end of each, a high mountain. The road to all of them now lay open to me. I went to one of them, the Gross Venediger, for reasons I need not explain. It was simply the high white peak up above the crystals. There I met some people on their way to the Grosse Geiger and joined up with them. It was an expedition on which I seemed to be breaking out beyond myself, so changed were things since 'a little while ago'.

The Venediger was not at all kind to us. Above 10,000 feet we ran into a blizzard. In spite of all the advice of the nice old keeper at the Kürsinger Hut, I was again wearing my leather shorts – my beloved old gear ... I was already pretty obstinate, even then.

All the same, we went to the summit, where there was nothing but snow and storm; we had no view at all. My elation at getting to the top was soon chilled and killed by the gale which seared my bare knees. I clamoured for the descent. Very soon my legs were entirely covered by a garment of clinking ice tassels. 'My poor calves,' I wrote later in my diary, 'lots of little icicles, one hanging from every hair. A proper pelt.'

I ran as much as was possible and, although they say that ice is an excellent insulator, I made a vow, on the spot, never again to go up high wearing the leathern rig of the chamois-hunter and the poacher.

A few days later, however, we saw the summit of our Venediger as we had looked forward to seeing it. No, it was even better than we had imagined it would be; for that sun-drenched day was a very gift from heaven, up there on the glittering snow, high above the valleys in their autumnal glory. One of those rare days you can hardly dare to hope for, ever again.

Willi, from Vienna, was the leader of our party. I had been deeply impressed, during the preceding days, with his ability to find the way even in the worst weather. He seemed to know exactly what was bound to happen in any given situation. He was pleased with me, the youngest member, who came up last on the rope, because I had twice stopped a fall, over there on the Geiger, by the speed with which I rammed home my ice axe.

Between us went Eva and Trude, two girls from Berlin – and let me add at once that the mountains have nothing on Berlin girls!

Forgotten was the icy storm on the Venediger, forgotten my frozen knees, as if they had never been. We were all hot with excitement and expectation of the magic mountain rising before us. I remember winding my handkerchief around my axe, so cold was it as we moved across the glacier in the twilight of dawn. The Venediger loomed pale overhead, above the slender ribs of its north face and the curling cornices that swept up with its ridges. Under a velvet sky the snow drew a soft line across the broad saddle towards the Klein Venediger – yet another pyramid. The last stars were flickering. Each of us was alone with his thoughts, the rope our only link. And as we climbed slowly up towards the first icefall, my 'voice' of those days recorded:

'Away to the east lay a tumultuous cloud-wrack, coloured from a marvellous orange to red and pale green. The sun was not up yet, the pale and misty sky changed from a steely grey to brilliant green and later to bright red and yellow. A dull sheen lay on the ice armour of the Venediger's summit, lifting above the north face, deeply scored by dark runnels of ice. Where was the sun ...? As though touched by some ghostly finger, the very tip of the Venediger began to gleam a delicate red; slowly the gentle light flowed farther and farther down the face, till the whole peak hung high above us, bathed in the brilliant morning light, while we were still in darkness. 'The glacier looks as if someone had poured raspberry syrup over it,' Trude remarked. The sun was up now; all the summits were now lit by it, only we were still in the shadow of the hollow. Would we too meet light and warmth up there on the saddle? Here it was cracking cold, and my hand and the handkerchief froze to the steel of my axe.

'We were on the last slope leading to the saddle, going slowly up. The angle eased. Thirty yards ahead of me, Willi let out a yell of surprised delight: he was standing in sunshine. As I joined him, I almost had to close my eyes to meet the blinding flood of light that beset me and enveloped me, cancelling out gravity itself. Trude expressed that sensation when she said: 'Now I'm floating away on the sunbeams.' Our dark blue shadows alone broke the shimmer and glitter of that virgin snow slope; for we were the first to come up here since the storm. We were happy beyond description. The remaining peaks of the Venediger group rose out of the flood of light; far away soared the Glockner, and the blue world of spires over there, that must be the Dolomites. A world of savage turrets and walls, with the Drei Zinnen easily recognisable. The shadows, far below us in the valleys, could not even climb up to us; they simply disappeared under the flood of light. We felt weightless as we mounted the summit itself, halting there only briefly. Today there were no limits to the view: one could see right across to the Otztal Alps.'

For us too there were no limits that day, not even for our cautious Willi. A wild euphoria had seized upon us all, as the four of us strolled, arm in arm, down the Venediger to the Rainerhorn, straight into the eye of the sun. The rope behind us dragged on the surface of the snow, but we didn't care. And we sang the song of the Tyrolese girl, which had become our Venediger theme song: 'Hollariariaholadi – holadio … !' There in front of us rose the Rainerhorn. We bagged it, too, and celebrated on its summit with song.

Then across to the Hohen Zaun, the next summit. It was not till we were making our light-hearted way down on the other side to the Defregger Hut that we met people – a whole column of them, coming up, with slow and measured tread, as is right and proper. At least ten of them; a hearty crowd of women climbers of the 'Touristenclub'. They looked askance and shook their heads at our casual procedures, but we were off and away by then.

That was by no means the end of our day – we dined on a few drops of glacier-water, some porridge oats, lumps of sugar, and a swig of lemonade – then rubbed sunburn cream on our lips again, for they were going altogether to pieces today. After lazing about for an hour high above the Defregger Saddle we crossed the Maurertiörl and completed our circuit of the Venediger. By the time we reached the Kursinger Hut, we had been out for fifteen hours. Our

'Hollariaria – holadi – ho – ladiho' in honour of the Gross Venediger sounded a little subdued. After that it began to snow heavily … In my excitement I had quite overlooked the fact that school had started three days ago.

If I have strayed somewhat from the theme of grandfather's bicycle, my excuse must be that so important a mountain as the Gross Venediger was responsible – and the blue world of the Dolomite towers rising above the glittering snow of the saddle …

My friend Peter and I had agreed to leave Salzburg and get to those Dolomites and, once there, to travel the length and breadth of that fairyland of rocky shapes. On our bicycles, of course. Peaks? Yes, some of those too – if possible. I could still see the stark faces of the Lienz Dolomites in my mind's eye.

We were just due to leave, when Peter arrived with death and disaster written all over his face. 'I can't come,' he said. '*She* says I have to choose between her and the mountains!' I was very sorry for him.

He lent me his Leica to take along and I promised to bring back some slides for himself. I had two colour-films – my first – to capture the meadows full of flowers at the foot of the Dolomites and the bright colouring of their rocky walls, as described to me by those who knew.

Milestones, milestones, milestones, rain, rain, rain … wet roads … rain … dense grey clouds, with dark lumps of limestone sticking into them … soaked through … all alone … and the Dolomites as wet as my climbing slippers … push the thing uphill again … would I get to Cortina today? … anyway, what should I do when I got there? So far as I cared, the devil could scoff the lot.

I wondered whether I could latch on to a lorry, if one came past. Latch on, I did, and the driver didn't notice me. Well, now I should at least cover some ground; though what was the use in this filthy weather?

My goodness, he's stepping on it! Of course, it's level here, but it'll soon be going uphill again. Just you hang on! Crash, bang, splinter … I found myself hanging on the lorry's tail-board. It had stopped. My bicycle was somewhere underneath it.

The driver came round and helped me to get it out – I was almost in tears. The front wheel had had it in a big way, otherwise … no damage? Miraculous. What about the main members of the frame? No, only the front wheel. That was bad enough, though.

Two days later I left Cortina, with a bare 3,000 lire in my pocket, and pushed my repaired mount up towards the Falzarego Pass. It was drizzling steadily and the lumps of limestone thrust up into cloud, as usual. The whole of the Dolomites were soaking wet, and so was I.

At last a shape emerged from the veils of cloud – the Cinque Torri. I recognised them from the postcards. At least, and at last, I had seen a peak.

Some hours later, the clouds parted and the gigantic mass of the Tofana rose above them. What a mountain, what a precipice! And then, far to the west, there emerged a white dome. That must be the Marmolata, the only snow peak in this realm of rock-towers.

At the summit of the pass I remounted, and flew down the wonderful road, with its finely built-out hairpins. Down and down I raced – it was quite fantastic. I was heading straight into the sun, now low in the west, under low banks of cloud. The road had flattened out. I met a few people on it, passed a few houses. A deep valley opened up on my left. There, to the south, rose an immense mountain – glowing ghostly red against the dark background of the sky: a dragon's spine, surmounted by spikes, looming longer and longer, a gigantic wall in the red sunset lave. Breath failed me, my brake squealed, as I drew in to the side of the road, bemused. There, to the south, stood that ghostly mountain, a mass of glowing organ-pipes, barring the whole breadth of the valley. An old peasant came trudging slowly by. 'What is that?' I asked him, and pointed to the great red wall. 'E la Civetta,' he replied, as if this were an everyday occurrence, and continued on his way.

The Civetta. I never forgot her. Many years later, I was to return and climb that mighty face; but I will never see her again as I saw her at that moment.

Milestones, one after another, in the sunshine, as I pushed my bicycle up towards the Pordoi Pass, among the flowery meadows of the Dolomites, brightly lit by the sun, with the Tofana's summit now far away behind. There were very few cars; the sunny road belonged to me, as did the gigantic rectangular masses of the Sella group above it. So did the grasshopper which crossed the road in great leaps; and the snail sitting at the edge of the road nearby, pointing its horns. For some unfathomable reason, it wanted to cross the road too. I picked it up and carried it across. Fancy having as much time as a snail! As a matter of fact I had. It was a gorgeous day.

Step by step, I went up on snow, with my ice axe and in my rock-climbing slippers, towards the foot of the Boë-spitze, the highest elevation in the Sella group – a rock peak, with a flat cone lifting above huge rectangular cliffs for its summit. I met more and more snowfields, of hard frozen snow, with wet fresh snow lying on top of it. My leather shoes got wetter and wetter, and larger and larger – I had taken the 'old master' Paulcke too literally and left my heavy climbing-boots in Salzburg – larger and larger grew my shoes …

Finally, having got to the top, I dangled my feet, and my shoes too, in the sunshine. Opposite me, encircled by cloud, flanked by the sharp Vernel ridges, stood the Marmolata, with its broad white glacier, curving steep and massive valley-wards. It was quite irresistible … Below it the road twisted like a worm through the gaily coloured Pordoi meadows.

But what could I do, without boots?

I stood on the Marmolata's summit, in climbing boots as big as those famous Seven League ones. I had simply gone into a little inn down at the Joch and asked the innkeeper if he would lend me his boots for a climb of the Marmolata. Below me, the south face plummeted in a fearsome drop to immeasurable depths. It must be awful to plunge to one's death from a Dolomite face … they were really no place for anyone but a good rock-climber, and even then they were horrific. Very carefully, hold by hold, I felt my way down from that airy viewpoint by the way I had come. In deep thought I went down the glacier and across the meadows, redolent with a cloud of cinnamon scent from the small dark red flowers that covered them, to the Pordoijoch, where I returned his boots to the innkeeper.

The Karersee,[1] that small tarn, a perfect subject for a colour slide. I took one for Peter, too. Crystal-clear turquoise water, its dark pine woods and the grey towers of the Latemar above.

I sat by its shore and gave my machine 'full service', surrounded by my pliers, my 'King Dick', ball-bearing grease, oil can, a cleaning rag, and a sparrow hopping around and complaining because I had nothing more to give him. This was a lovely place; I would push on in the evening – somewhere. Meanwhile, this spoke needed straightening, and there was the rattling mudguard-ring … Somewhere, but where? Perhaps past the Marmolata's southern base … look, here's another spoke … over the Pellegrino Pass to the Civetta … And then the carrier, always getting perilously bent: I should have to load it some other way, or find some additional support for it …

That Latemar, up there … its towers and turrets looking for all the world like recruits, the first time they are told to fall in and dress their ranks, with a certain natural disorder, a sort of irregular regularity, like the rows of pine-trunks rising from the other shore of the lake …

I won't move on tonight. I shall traverse the Latemar tomorrow. I want to see it from nearby.

I did that, and a great many other things besides; and, wherever I went, everyone exhibited an interest in, and enthusiasm for, cycling which was quite new to me. They were very kind, and let me know that a cyclist was a highly respected person in the Dolomites – even a cyclist riding his grandfather's bike. I was even asked for which great race I was in training; and I noted in my diary. – 'Yesterday, as I sped full-tilt through a village, the children shouted at the top of their voices: *"Evviva Bartale! Evviva Coppi! Evviva!"'* I swung into

---

1 In Italian: Lago di Carezza.

the next curves with my chest proudly puffed out, speeding, and feeling, like a champion, only slowing up again as soon as I was out of sight.

Of course, I sent a postcard to my grandfather: ' I have been promoted to the top class. The bicycle is still in one piece. Five Dolomite passes so far, and plan to do three more.' Certainly I had discovered and mastered the Dolomites on a bicycle; experienced, over and over again, the excitement of the unknown view that would unfold beyond the pass – a prize only to be won by long hours of hard work. But then everyone who loves adventure must be prepared to accept hard work – or he will lose both.

And many a motorist – perhaps I should add, many a mountaineer, too? – who thinks on different lines from the cyclist, must none the less realise that he who cheerfully surmounts hairpin after hairpin of a pass under his own steam, yet enjoys a great deal of pleasure in so doing, is totally involved with that 'mountain'; its summit is an aim which he has set himself, and when at last he gets there, great is his joy.

It goes without saying that riding down the other side, free as a bird and motorless, is sheer delight. But that is not all of it. The cyclist has his 'why and wherefore' just as has the mountaineer; though neither of them could explain it. And both earn their 'dimension' again and again.

4 The Matterhorn: An Expedition

The Matterhorn, that slender spire, lifting indescribably above the Zermatt Valley – every climber's dream-wish … sketched, painted, photographed, described in a hundred different accounts, familiar to all … and yet only really known to those who have actually seen it …

Erich, Gundl and I had not seen it yet. For us it was a mysterious mountain, clothed in legends, far, far away, somewhere over the horizon, in an unknown land. To reach it meant, for us, a real expedition. We had never been to the Western Alps. We had no money; but we had our dreams – dreams of unknown peaks, in unknown countries – at least, those we could get to on our bicycles.

The Matterhorn … this legendary Matterhorn … this 'mountain of mountains', over 13,000 feet high; no, nearly 15,000 – it kept on growing, this *Matterhorn*! Why not make straight for it? It drew us irresistibly; though, of course, we didn't know how we should fare at such an altitude – we had never been on a 'four-thousander'.

By now I believed we could climb it. I had heard a lecture by the 'Dachstein Priest'. I did not know exactly who he was, but he didn't look as tough as all that. If he had climbed it, we could!

It was a splendid lecture, entitled 'The Valaisian Peaks'. We were introduced to the white wall of the Lyskamm, with its perilous cornices – not that it looked dangerous, just white and beautiful – but if he said so … Yes, after all, its crest did look dangerous, and it too was over 13,000 feet – yet another four-thousander, surpassing that magic level.

Why not combine the two targets – legendary Matterhorn and our first four-thousander, both at the same time? In short, why not go straight for the Matterhorn? If that cosy looking old gentleman had climbed it, we could. I marvelled at him; as he spoke, the mountain drew ever nearer, acquired rocks, ridges, pitches, arêtes. Yes, we would make a beeline for this Matterhorn, making no detours, paying no attention to other peaks, on the way …

The holidays came round. In front of me the big rollers of a colour machine were grinding away, crushing powder in clouds of green, blue and red dust. I fed the mixture, strictly in accordance with the recipe, and dreamed of the Matterhorn. I had taken this temporary job, so as to earn some much needed money. The firm promptly went into liquidation.

So I went to Aunt Betty, who, I knew, had a kind heart. A hundred schillings from her – well, that was a start. Then to Aunt Traudl ('Hallo, Kurty, glad to see you!'). Enough for the three-speed gear for my bike. Then to Uncle Hans … and … and … to all the relatives I could think of. With very few exceptions – and I suppose, in their cases, my failure to visit them before was responsible – they had all heard of the Matterhorn. Even if it wasn't Mount Everest, the expedition's funds grew satisfactorily. To all of them I promised a picture of the Matterhorn, for their living room, their kitchen, the corridor – it was their problem where to hang it, not mine.

I believe Erich, who was eighteen, a year younger than I, was doing much the same; while our buxom Gundl, with the long plaits, who was only sixteen, was busy working on her mother, in their Styrian home, for the mere permission to come along. It was only when I drew up a detailed list of equipment and provender – 'the thousand minutiae'– that her mother realised on what a serious undertaking we were embarking.

We pedalled and pedalled and pedalled … we got off and pushed … we got on again and tore downhill … then we pedalled, pedalled and pedalled again … still not less than a week to our Matterhorn.

We entered this unknown Switzerland. Spit-and-polish houses, wonderful hotels, everything neat and tidy. Anyone who slept rough got himself fined. The passes were high, the peaks higher still. And the prices … ! We postwar Austrians couldn't believe our eyes. That didn't bother us, however. We lived on our rucksacks, boiled our tea at the roadside; our 'bikes' were amply loaded with what we had brought along – everything we needed.

Push, push, push – all the way up the Furka Pass, which we reached on the stroke of midnight. Our impatience to see the Matterhorn knew no bounds – a shepherd over there on the Oberalp Pass had told us that one can pick out its summit from here in clear weather. Well, we should just have to wait till morning. Now, to find a site for our tent … This was a puzzle, for the heavy rubber-coated 'special' tent my father had given me had no struts – presumably because its designer was an optimist. It had a loop at the top, so that you could hang it up somewhere …

We wandered about the dark summit of the pass – we would gladly have hanged the designer of that loop from the sickle-moon overhead. We found no hooks; so we lay down and crawled into that chilly skin. The only ray of light was Gundl, in between us, comfortable in the fleece sleeping bag. My knees were gradually coated in hoar frost, but my back, at least, was warm. During the early hours, Erich devised several suitable methods for liquidating our clever designer.

Up came the sun … we stood there with chattering teeth, looking at the dark rocky summit in the dim distance, hardly distinguishable between white ridges. There it was, at last, the Matterhorn … still miles away.

'A cup of hot coffee?' This was unbelievable. A friendly man in field-grey uniform had come out of a house at the roadside and invited us in. However, when Gundl asked him if he could shoot as well as he made coffee, he became distinctly less friendly. Swiss soldiers, he explained, were among the best in the world: they even took their rifles home with them and kept them in a cupboard there, always ready to hand. And he showed Gundl his rifle. On that same day she upset a Swiss woman badly, by innocently referring to the Rhône as a 'brook'.

When, at last, we came close to the Matterhorn, it towered to gigantic heights above us, with a banner of cloud flying from its summit.

We had never imagined it could be so high; and we felt like midgets.

We looked up from time to time at the great spike, at its cloud-banner. Did we really mean to go up there? Ought we not first try the gentler Breithorn?

A man with impressive yellow stockings was coming up the path from nearby Zermatt. By way of small talk we told him, without any beating around the bush, what our plans were – and that we intended to stay at least a week or ten days. At which point he declared himself as the collector of the local 'Residence tax' ; and could he please have eight days' worth of it, on the spot ...

'Residence tax?' Surely our ears were deceiving us – this must be some kind of mistake. We were living in a tent – not much 'residence' about that, surely? In any case, we didn't propose to pay a red cent of our precious money. Indignation, anger, heated argument followed on either side. Nothing would move the man with those jolly stockings. So, off the four of us marched to the police station.

We consulted among ourselves – suppose the man was right? At the last moment I had a brainwave. Very politely, we explained to the police inspector that it had all been a misunderstanding – true, we were going to spend a week near the Matterhorn, but on its Italian side. *This* was only a short staging post on our way to the frontier ...

The collector looked murder at me. The last barrier was down. Then we proceeded – still on the Swiss side – up to the hut. How would we fare tomorrow, we wondered?

It was dark. Ahead of us we could see electric torches winking. We could hear ice axes clinking against rock. The shapes of towers in the ridge were silhouetted around us. Overhead, a gigantic dark mass bulked up – the summit.

The cold air was tense with expectation. We must be sure not to lose contact, in the darkness, with the guided parties in front. The three of us were climbing, roped together, up pitches and over shadowy blocks in the gloom. It wasn't particularly difficult, but a little complicated – and endlessly high. There, now we had lost contact, after all ...

Daylight came. We were absolutely on our own. Friable slabs, brittle ledges, everything crumbling, crumbling. Were we still really on the right track, following scratch marks? I had just jumped to safety from a stance that broke away beneath my feet. The blocks went crashing down into the depths … Gundl watched them with startled eyes. Erich shook his head – there goes another! This can't be the right way. Then we heard voices coming down from the right, higher up the ridge. Up that way, then – out on to the east face …

We were at 12,500 feet. There stood the Solvay Hut, an eagle's eyrie clinging to the edge of the rocks; a shelter should the weather change – but at present it was fine. We drew in deep breaths of the thin air of the four-thousanders for the first time – yes, it was rarer, and cleaner. We felt fine.

Over there, that white comb must be the Lyskamm. I remembered the 'Dachstein Priest's' lecture. That was the Weisshorn, and over there the Obergabelhorn, and there the Dent Blanche, and the cluster of Monte Rosa's five summits. How huge and lovely it all was, and how proud we were to be mounting higher and higher on 'our' Matterhorn and not on the gently rounded Breithorn. Grey fog was slowly forming a cowl over the sharp outlines of our summit. It was noon. Another thousand feet to go. Then it was afternoon.

How far now? Everything was dim and grey around us. Everything fell away precipitously, like the pitch of a steep roof. Gasping for breath, we were now working our way up on all fours. We glanced timidly downwards, to the horrific abyss yawning below us – the North Face, directly under us.

The ridge flattened, the snow levelled off. Was that a cross over there? Ye sons of man, we were up! We were on top! On the summit ridge. A few yards more. We embraced, hugged each other, danced with joy. We had captured our Matterhorn – we three had done it!

True, we could see nothing, absolutely nothing – no mountains, no valleys – only one another, some rocks, some snow and a cross, ghostly in the fog. But it was the summit-cross on the Matterhorn.

The wind was howling round the Solvay Refuge, rattling its roof, tugging at its planks, in the night. We felt comfortable and safe, up there at 13,700 feet. Everything had gone smoothly on the descent, except for a mishap on the summit's steep roof, when Erich suddenly found himself hanging on one spike of his crampons and shortly afterwards landed on my shoulders after a short tumble. We looked down the abyss of the north face in terror. Fortunately, I was belayed.

Yes, we had been lucky. Our first four-thousander had entailed some risk, and we hardly knew enough to realise all the dangers involved. But when you are eighteen, you are inclined to go straight for what you want, without lengthy détours.

We lay there in the hut, too tired and happy to make any further plans. One thing was quite certain: this was not the last time we should be coming here.

What is it, then, that turns a dream into an aim? Just those little words: 'I want to.' Let us leave insuperable difficulties to those who believe such things exist.

For me, the Matterhorn was a giant's stride into the future. On it, I learned, for the first time, what one can achieve, if one really wants to.

5 One Step ...

The old churchyard at Courmayeur is different from other churchyards; at least so it seems to me. The wooden war crosses stand there like sinister birds of prey, with anonymous, white marble ones between. Mont Blanc and the Dent du Gèant look down on it all.

Among those curious crosses stands one that doesn't seem to belong there at all – two simple wooden planks, cruciform. Yet it does belong there ... Erich. He fell from the Dent du Gèant.

Whenever Wolfi and I pass through Courmayeur, we usually go down to the old churchyard. Mostly we go separately, just as it happens to come into one or the other's mind. If I find a few wild flowers there, I know Wolfi has been. Though it could have been the amiable, white-haired headmistress of the kindergarten in Entrèves, just as well ...

Four of us had come to Courmayeur together; all of us on our first visit. Mont Blanc towered gigantic over the green of the valley – almost 13,000 feet above us, draped in thin clouds, in banners of snow. We wheeled our push-bikes happily through the narrow alleyways, watching the gaily hued life of the place; buying a few trifles. Erich beamed through his glasses, his whole happy student face alight with pleasure. 'My children,' he said, 'in a few days we shall be standing on that great mountain up there!' And he looked up at Mont Blanc, high over the rooftops.

He had come with his Peilstein climbing partner, Wolfgang Stefan, dark, slight, quiet, though sometimes very funny. He was a student too. They had been training hard recently and had reached a pretty high standard. I had Peter Heilmayer, from Salzburg, with me; he had not been climbing as long as the others, but he was keenness itself. We had all still to get used to the thin air, so we had decided not to make Mont Blanc our first objective.

The first thing we needed was a 'base camp'! We looked around for one, and in due course – in Italy anything can happen – found ourselves sitting in the middle of a kindergarten, cared for and cosseted, adulated and admired – talking broken Italian to the best of our ability. The headmistress, a friendly old lady, saw to our every need; even the kitchen staff was glad to take a look at, and to look after, some of these tough guys, who hang on ropes from icy walls, just in order – God knows why! – to climb some savage peak. We were, of course, delighted, explaining what we meant to do, letting them darn our socks, even allowing them – after a little hesitation – to wash our smalls. We tried to jodel, learned the *'Montanara'*, sang the *'Bergvagabunden'* song to them, and the whole kindergarten then proceeded to serenade us with the 'chiesetta alpina', which moved me (rapidly promoted to the status of professional photographer) to take a group picture. And, of course, we should be coming back to see them, year after year …

Erich was laughing and winking at me, as I had the whole kindergarten lined up in front of us, and unfolded my tripod with true professional skill; a real *fotografo* to the life, posing a few individual figures, with all the vision and assured hand gestures of a true artist – until, finally, I pressed the shutter. We all laughed as I wiped my forehead with my Sunday-best handkerchief. It was all just too good to be true. Not in the wildest dreams of a mountaineer was there ever such a base camp, so many nice people all gathered in one spot!

We had decided to make the Dent du Gèant our first climb. It is a savage rock-tooth, over 13,000 feet high. Well, actually, the figure is a little misleading, for it is the precise altitude reached by the summit. If you approach it by the normal route, all you have to do is less than 3,000 feet of steep but easy snow and rock, to the actual foot of the Tooth itself. Then there is only 700 feet of real climbing, to get to the top. No easy climbing this – Grade III – but we knew there were fixed ropes. We had been told how fearfully airy the climb was; when you clung to the front face of the needle, there was nothing but 3,000 feet or more of thin air under the soles of your boots.

We crossed the bergschrund, and I roped up with Peter, the least experienced member of the party.

'Aren't you going to rope up too?' I asked the others.

'We've got crampons – well get along all right.'

They certainly were getting along all right, obviously in tremendous form. Soon they were up there, on the *'Gengiva'*, the 'Gum', at the foot of the Tooth itself, where they had agreed to wait for us.

Our successive rope's lengths ran out; time moved leisurely by. At last we reached the ridge, close to the huge tower, with its vertical walls of reddish-brown granite. Over there, Wolfi and Erich were traversing the sloping snowfield of the *'Gengiva'*. Then … Erich slipped … threw himself face down on his axe, braking his slide … but, no! … he went on sliding … Why, in heaven's name, didn't the axe grip? … went on sliding … sliding … sliding … out of sight …

Wolfi was standing there, shattered, struck dumb. We rushed across to him, arrived breathless. Quick! There was nothing to be seen, but possibly … Quick! Wolfi was lowering me on the rope.

There was a score in the snow … where he had tried to get a hold with his hands … then a couple of rocks – could he have grabbed them? We shouted: silence from the great white abyss. Could he be hanging, caught up in those rocks, having somehow got a grip, somewhere? Unconscious … ?

Or? Too horrible to contemplate. It *mustn't* have happened!

The farther I moved down that white surface on the rope – it soon became a sheer gully – the more sure I was of the dreadful truth. It was hard, bone-hard down here, not a chance of checking one's fall, nothing to get a hold on, nothing but a slide at increasing speed.

They added another rope, and I reached the rocks. Nothing … no Erich … nowhere … no answer from the bottomless depths. It had really happened.

Wolfi saw me safely up on the rope, threw me a questioning glance. I looked at him, and he knew.

If we came up from the bottom, we should find him – or would we? He might be lying on the top of a pillar, or in a crevice in that 3,000-foot precipice; or even, over there, on the other side. Could he possibly be alive still? We hurried down the normal route, hoping for a miracle in which we no longer had any faith.

There was a party coming up. Had they seen or noticed anything? Heard anything? No, not a thing; had something happened, then? Yes, one of us had gone, fallen down the face. We left them standing there incredulous, and hurried on, down, down into those awful depths. We looked down on to an old cone of avalanche snow, far, far down in a bay at the bottom of the face. We saw an elongated black stain on it. Could it be Erich? That kind of snow is not as hard as rock; he might have been lucky – Dear God, grant he had had luck, like Payer when he fell on the Ortler! – but then, of course, it might not be Erich, after all.

We raced down, panting for breath, never seeming to get any nearer. It was a long, long way down – we had already been more than an hour. The stain was the shape of a man. It didn't move. Could be …

No way down, here – everything fell away savagely into a hollow, more than a thousand feet, below us. We should have to come round from outside and below, skirting the base of the wall.

There was that dark thing down there on the snow – probably Erich. Nearly 3,000 feet below the '*Gengiva*' Dear God!

We circled round the base of the rocks, crossing level snow towards the hollow, where the avalanche cone gradually came into view.

Wolfi ran on ahead up the last 300 feet – I was past following; my knees had gone soft on me. Yes, that bundle up there was a man, was Erich, motionless on the bloodstained snow. Wolfi had reached it. And there he stood, just stood.

At last I arrived. Yes, it was he; his anorak, the grey rift, the …
There was a cry in the silence.

It was Erich, his face shockingly disfigured. Wolfi was still standing there, dumb; motionless. I watched the tears running down his face.

That afternoon, we brought him down to Entrèves. Once again he lay in the triangular tent we had used on the Matterhorn. Then we placed him on a bier in the little chapel, over whose slate roof we had looked up at Mont Blanc a few days before.

What was the point of it all –?

We held a vigil over our dead all through the night. I had never seen the stars so big as they were that night; they flickered as though a storm were passing over heaven itself. Inexplicable.

And most inexplicable of all – there were voices in the air.

Neither Wolfi nor I could give it up. For us the mountains meant everything, as they had for Erich. Not even his death could alter that. Only Peter gave up climbing, later on. Of course we had to ask ourselves whether falling stones, avalanches, a disintegrating hold might not one day dictate an end to it all, however much care we exerted? Could be – but we said 'no' and took great precautions with our belaying. Wolfi and I went climbing together more and more, we were ideally matched, and we became a rope of two – a rope of two equal partners, Diemberger-Stefan or Stefan-Diemberger, each capable of leading it, equally capable of acting as second, according to circumstances. Mostly we led turn and turn about, for our understanding was complete.

Naturally, that did not all come about in a single day. Every mountaineer knows that a real rope partnership is a kind of communal life, in which complete mutual confidence has to be built up. For when one partner, in full knowledge of his own competence, caution or courage, decides to make a move, to use a piton or not, to give up or to go on – his decision absolutely involves the life of the other, bound to him by the same rope. One does not forget that.

One thing is indisputable: everyone you knot-up on a rope with you is different, and on the mountains you will learn to know him. For they reveal each man for what he is.

Without our meticulous and iron-hard training in climbing techniques on Vienna's Peilstein, Wolfi and I could hardly be alive today, after the countless climbs we have done together. And, in spite of everything, it must be admitted that once or twice we both owed our survival to our lucky stars, or to the other's skill. The summer climbing seasons which ensued were long ones: during one, we climbed twenty-five four-thousanders, including some great traverses; the next took us from the Wilde Kaiser to the Bregaglia, on to Mont Blanc, back to the Valais and finally to the Brenta Dolomites. Gradually we grew more and more at home in the whole great sweep of the Alps between Vienna and Marseilles. Then I, too, began to live the greater part of the year in the city of two million inhabitants, which was Wolfi's birthplace.

Fortunately, the Alps begin on its doorstep, in the Wienerwald.

6 Bookkeeping and Pull-Ups

Post-war Vienna. From the 'Piaristenkeller' rises the theme song of 'The Third Man' ; the town is punctuated by Russians and Americans, with a few British and French thrown in. Everyone is on his best behaviour, and fraternises; we have been 'liberated', but unfortunately we are 'occupied'. Some years were still to roll by before Austrian *laissez faire* and Russian Vodka would combine to negotiate a bilateral agreement. 'But,' said the Viennese, well live it out!'

Early each morning, with a thunderous roar, the No 13 came rolling along the Piaristengasse, in District 8; faded red, ancient and rust covered – the tram. Later, at regular intervals, right through till the evening. When it came, the peace of the alley, in which passers-by and pigeons promenaded happily, for few motor cars used it, was rudely shattered. And every time No 13, having completed its approach run the length of the straight road, took the bend opposite the Tröpferlbad, the air was rent by martial sounds – a squealing, a howling, a grating cacophony, which penetrated the topmost storeys as well as the deepest cellars. However, Frau Sedlacek and Herr Navratil, on the ground floor, both dismissed it with the same casual acceptance. 'Only the No. 13,' they thought; for the Viennese can get used to anything.

Indeed, No. 13 belonged to the very life and being of that thoroughfare. Only the tram driver registered a protest every morning against his miserable lot. Since I lived directly above the bend, I was able to observe how he deliberately took a run, the whole length of the Piaristengasse, so that he could thunder into the curve with the greatest possible momentum: there could be no doubt that it was done on purpose. Did he want to arouse the conscience of the world? Because he was unhappy with his job? Had he got a grudge against the bend? Or did he simply want to wake us to a new day?

The rails had to be replaced every six months. Fortunately for us, No. 13 did not run at night. All the same, it was cruelly early in the morning when it thundered past my window for the first time each day, to be followed immediately by that marrow-shattering screech. Then the Piaristengasse was wide awake. So was I …

Surely the man hadn't really meant to be a tram driver at all; he must have had something quite different in mind?

And that thought brought back to my mind my pages of bookkeeping material …

What was to become of me – me, the crystal-hunter, the cyclist, the embryo climber? I knew one could achieve anything one really wanted to – but what was I to want? There was no career to fit me.

If all the millions I was transferring from one account to another were really mine, I knew well enough what my goal would be: exploration … voyages of discovery …

There were Sven Hedin and Heinrich Harrer, for instance; how had they managed it? Riches would be the solution but – by Columbus, as I broke an egg into the frying pan on the electric cooker! – reality was very different. These were the facts of life: a remote back room in a students' hostel in the Piaristengasse – forty schillings a month, three beds, three chests and a heating-stove that didn't work. There the three of us sat, opposite each other, warmly clad against the cold, in fleece jackets, sheepskins and a couple of blankets round our shoulders – the ex-commando parachutist from the North Africa front, now turned sculptor; a bookkeeper who would not be finished with his exams for years, though he was fully competent; and I. Our way of life was rather like that of an expedition's base camp; and female visitors were taboo. (According to the latest reports the ladies of Vienna later occupied the hostel by way of a protest: but not in our time.) The parachutist-sculptor carved religious statues; as he said, you have to earn a living somehow. And then, for his own amusement, he made the most wonderful drawings.

As for me, in spite of everything, I had discovered my own little America, one I could manage – the Peilstein in the Wienerwald – that climbers' practice ground, with its innumerable crannies and climbs. Back there again tomorrow on my bike! According to the Peilstein Song:

> There's fever and fun, and the boys and the girls
> Climbing the rocks like flies up a wall;
> And if, in their sport, should one of them fall …

No, no falling for me, thank you; the one taste of it, recently, had been quite enough of a good thing. Railli, supposed to be belaying me, had taken a beautiful header into thin air; however, the piton had held. Now, let's see how fit I am. Twenty – yes, really, twenty – pull-ups on the door frame! What do I care about non-existent millions in an account book?

I wondered whether the Career-Consultant, who turned up one day at the Graduation-class, was right: he said I hadn't a hope. After I had filled up the questionnaire ('Would you sooner be a chimney sweep or a dentist?') with meticulous care, to the great delight of the class, I developed the curved line on a test sheet, not into a little sponge or even an umbrella, but into a caricature of our careerist – complete with three tiny hairs on his bald cranium. Not even a staggering likeness between the test line and that refulgent dome could persuade him that I had great talent. (God is just: and I too count my ultimate blessings.)

And what else didn't I do? I spent six months intoning, in a bass voice, Schubert's songs and Sarastro, to please the lady who taught me singing and was certain that I was a great 'find', for whom she prophesied a splendid future. Vowel production: 'The rain in Spain falls mainly on the plain' … six months of it. Then I rejected other heavier precipitation on the more level parts of Iberia because they told me to give up climbing, for the good of my voice. And Sarastro was converted to mountain-gypsy tunes on the guitar.

What about rocks? A career as a mining engineer? I left Leoben in a hurry at the end of a single term. Was I to spend the whole of my life sitting near a mine? Quite impossible. Geology? No future in that, they told me in Vienna, at the time. I hesitated and made a big mistake, by not taking up geology. Business? Not exactly exciting. But business instructors were always wanted, and teaching was a family tradition. So I would be a business instructor – that would at least give me time for the mountains. In four years I should have my University of Commerce diploma – and only then could I start to pass the special exams for being a teacher.

Four years sitting in a fleece jacket in an unheated room in Vienna were undoubtedly good training for the icy giants of the Western Alps. Likewise the pull-ups on the frame of the door …

And then, the Peilstein. First with Railli, then with Wolfi, year in, year out, I was always to be found in that exciting realm of smooth towers and walls of superb grey limestone. There, right in the middle of the Wienerwald, amid the first fresh green of early spring on the trees – at first furtively making my trembling way up a Grade IV climb, complaining about one's 'in-and-out' form in April – but happier when I noticed the chap over yonder, who still had that 'sewing machine' shake in his legs – right through to all the little masterpieces of technique, high above the trees aflame with autumn colours.

In between lay our great summer seasons – the Dolomites, the Bregaglia, Mont Blanc. In the autumn we all met again, around campfires or at huts, and told each other what great rock faces we had 'taken apart' – thanks to our iron apprenticeship in the Peilstein school.

Yes, we formed a colourful, venturesome guild, we Peilstein climbers who, Sunday after Sunday, turned up there from Vienna, twenty-five miles away, on our bicycles – till one or other of us filled everyone else with envy by acquiring a 'machine'. Full of relevant humour, too. One loft traverse high above the tree tops was embellished with a tramcar notice, in black-and-white enamel, which read: 'DON'T LEAN OUT.' And, for occasions when, accompanied by good advice from Wienerwald visitors, spiritually involved in our climbing ('there's a handhold, up to the right above you – about seven feet!'), one had safely mastered a difficult overhang and was clinging to nothing more than a few rugosities, 150 feet above the base of the climb, one was greeted by a dentist's placard: 'DON'T SPIT ON THE FLOOR!' Some of the names were very apt, too: you could take your pick from *Suicide Crack* to *Poster Pillar*. The rules, though unwritten, of the Peilstein fraternity were strictly observed. The novice started with the *Balloon* scramble or *The Slab*; our fair Viennese 'Mizzis' were put on to the easy but deep *Schindeltal Chimney*. And one universal rule: woe to him who used a piton on a 'free' climb! The unimaginable creature who started knocking his hooks into the superb handholds of the almost vertical *Vegetarian's Arête* – the origin of the name remains obscure for, though the Peilstein brigade like potato salad, their diet is not exactly meatless – sparked off a minor revolution. From the Jahrerkanzel flowed sounds of local vernacular, boos rose from the couloirs, loud echoes of rage rang from 'Monte Cimone' to the 'Matterhorn', and the sound of many angry voices floated across even to the distant 'Zinnen'; for the Peilsteiners can conceive of no greater crime than to bang a piton into the holds of that arête. Terrified, the ironmonger took to flight (he came, he 'nailed' in the wrong place, and was no more seen). Even so do the Peilsteiners protect the purity of their rocks!

One evening I was poring over my balance sheets, while the sculptor was at his work close by. Presently he plucked at my sleeve and said: 'Come with me, I want to show you something.' He led me to the window above the dark courtyard: 'Something quite unusual,' he declared, staring raptly up at the nocturnal skies. 'Look!' he said, pointing to a dazzling bright star, 'that's Venus; and the one quite close to it, the pale red one, that's Mars. It is very rare to see them in conjunction.' The two utterly different stars blinked; the one a bluish white, the other emitting occasional flashes of red – a magic spectacle. And then Kloska, the sculptor, began to tell me about the nights, out in the Sahara, under the vast vault of the desert sky.

He told me, too, about the telescope mirror he wanted to make ... I remembered a dusty old telescope and microscope lying unused in Salzburg. Suppose we put them together? We did, and it worked. Now we could see Saturn's ring, Jupiter's moons, Andromeda's gorgeous veil of vapours. Kloska, the parachutist in Rommel's army, the sculptor who carved holy figures and drew so beautifully, the human being who pursued his own quiet life and lived only for his art, was completely at home in the depths of the starlit sky, and now he initiated me into its mysteries. I knew nothing of his life, about which he rarely spoke. But one day he told me, as we were once again exploring the heavens, with that very special gift he had of contented relaxation, that the middle star in Orion's belt was not a star at all, but an indescribably distant cloud of shining vapour, which only looked like a star to the naked eye.

I trained the telescope on that tiny point of light, and saw a marvellous feathery, shimmering cloud …

'Its light takes ten years to get across from one end to the other of that cloud,' said Kloska.

And then I understood the peace which radiated from him.

7 Two on a Rope

We had got into a nice mess, damnation take it – properly sewn up and stuck! There we were, hanging like flies on the 3,000-foot face of the Croz dell' Altissimo, in the Brenta Dolomites, and nothing made sense any more. Everything was inimical, resistant, grey, smooth, unclimbable and repulsive: below me, a bottomless abyss …

The face of the Croz dell' Altissimo is the highest in the Brenta, carved as if by a knife out of a mountain accessible, on its other side, to sheep. It forms the lateral wall of a deep gorge. And there, halfway up it, were Wolfi and I, armed with a route description in good clear Italian; our 'rock sense' would, we said, make up for the bits we didn't understand, but since the last passage dictated by that rock sense, it had all become Greek to us. No, not all: it 'strapiombed' everywhere, which meant it overhung. We had found the start of the route easily enough – a ledge with *mughi*, which assuredly meant little bumps, in it (a striking analogy with our Viennese 'Mugl'); since then it had 'placcted', vertically, 'strapiombed', over us, and 'fissured' – cracked or split – all around. And for the last hour I had had a nasty feeling that the description and the route no longer corresponded. At least, so my 'rock sense' told me.

Suddenly, the coin dropped. That rusty piton at the adjectival pitch down below there had lured us on to the wrong traverse. It hadn't been the right adjectival pitch – the right one was much higher up. What kind of an adjectival pitch would that be, we wondered? Now it all depended on our 'rock sense'!

So, now: straight on up, on barely recognisable holds, but fearfully smooth stuff. I banged a piton obliquely into a flake – it wouldn't hold a thing – so, on and up. At last I came to a minute ledge, which might provide a stance. I glued my face against the wall and hammered in another piton. It held!

Wolfi was coming up – clear of the airy slab, like a spider. It looked bizarre; the dark greenish-grey pattern of the wooded gorge, 2,000 feet below, straight under his heels and above his shoulders.

'Watch out for that flake!'

'Yes, but the piton –'

Clatteration! Hold him, you've got to hold him! Agony in my knees, the rope cutting my shoulders, Wolfi's brown shock of hair twirling below me in mid-air, his body out over nothingness … You've got to hold him! I gritted my teeth, while he paddled in the air with his hands, feeling for the rock, finally got a handhold ... – and that took his weight off my shoulders at last. I drew a deep breath; thanks be, the belaying-piton had held firm ... but for the moment my tail was well down ... we hung there on the stance for a few minutes. Then Wolfi led on up.

We did a climb every day. The glowing yellow east face of the Cima di Brenta, the enormous ice-packed chimney of the Cima degli Armi, the stratified mass of the Torre di Brenta, the soaring Campanile Alto, the magnificent rock pillar of the 'Guglia'. Then more climbs: up the giant staircase of the Brenta Alta's south ridge, the 3,000-foot arête of the Crozzon – airy routes in a realm of black and yellow rock castles, high above the green carpet of meadows at their feet. We had got used to it; it no longer surprised us to find only a piton or two on vertical faces several hundred feet high; we had got to know the Brenta's rock, with its thousand rough wrinkles, bollards, spikes – often so needle-sharp that they hurt one's fingers – its caves and its 'hour glasses', behind which one could thread a rope sling: this peculiar Dolomite, whose amazing horizontal holds demanded great finger strength. We could smile, now, at our rock sense of the Croz dell' Altissimo; though we did pursue one more 'Via Fantasia' on the Torre di Brenta.

That same day, on ground not far from the base of the rocks, I found a Roman coin. Had it belonged to a soldier? Or to a hunter? For how long have men climbed up into the mountains?

All that was missing was a Grade VI climb. Cesare Maestri, 'the king of the Brenta', directed us to the Cima d'Ambiez: there was quite a pitch low down on it, he told us – the rest was a dream of a climb. That *was* a rock, a proper rock, he explained, his face lighting up with enthusiasm.

The evening before the climb: the whole face a dim blue shadowy thing, full of questions and surmises. Next morning, 1,200 feet of vertical cliff, brownish-red in the bright sunshine, riddled with holes and crannies. There were coffer-like overhangs, then a crack ... I gasped for breath, spread-eagled on tiny protuberances; moved up a little and threaded through a piton; up again by a series of split second decisions; worked my way farther up the face, which did its best to push me out and off– found a stance where I could take a breather. It was a gigantic free-climbing pitch, then; I wonder whether it still is?

Then followed the dream of a rock climb, vertical, overhanging, pitonless, with innumerable small holes and wrinkles – perfect free-climbing on a sheer wall, with an infinity of air around us. At such moments you are gloriously conscious of your fingers, your muscles; of the toes of your boots winning a hold on the rough Brenta rock; of the wall, close to your face, shining black, brown and bright ochre amid the grey – like flower -patterns in a carpet – and all of it high above the combe down there at the foot of the climb. You are enmeshed in a bright web of thoughts, on which you climb ever higher, pulling yourself upwards from handhold to handhold, foothold to foothold, towards an ever-increasing freedom, while everything below you falls away – as you exalt yourself all the time.

Down there at the bottom, you see the shadows of the towers lengthen, and feel that you belong to your mountain with every fibre of your being and yet, at the same time, here, high above the abyss, utterly free of mind and spirit, you are acutely aware that you have arms and legs – and a body able to waft you upwards, because you have learned to overcome fear.

I belayed Wolfi up to a stance. We hardly spoke, we just climbed. Occasionally one of us remarked how splendid it was, and how right Cesare's assessment of the climb. I leaned my forehead against the rock; it was sunny and warm. What a joy, what a gift of fortune, it was to climb, to be alive in this lovely world! The very rock in front of me seemed a living thing.

A box of colour slides. People coming, after their day's work, people who had perhaps a fortnight or three weeks' leave in a year, people who loved the mountains just as much as we did, many of whom the war had robbed of their best days ... I was giving one of my first lectures. All of a sudden I myself was lost in it all, back in the middle of a summer spent between Mont Blanc and the Drei Zinnen. Everything else was forgotten.

We were at our 'base camp' in the Bregaglia. There were a couple of tents, socks flapping from the rope as they dried in the breeze, flocks of sheep in the distance, 'Peilstein-Joschi' snoozing on the 'post-prandial slab', Friedl sticking some plaster on fingertips worn raw by climbing, Wolfi immersed in contemplation of the great blue face of Piz Badile, Hilde washing yet more socks in the mountain torrent. Here were to be found the loveliest camping sites in the world; the most magnificent arêtes; and the worst behaved sheep. Only yesterday they had devoured some of our savoury West Alpine socks – one couldn't help laughing, much as the climbers sympathised with the sorely tried washer-woman: climbing socks, no mountain stream clear enough to wash them clean, and no representative of the Society for Prevention of Cruelty to Animals within miles!

For a moment I was back in the lecture room, then I was perched once more 2,000 feet above a glacier. 'Come up!' A layback up a 'Piaz'-crack. 'You're there!' A still finer layback. And now it's my turn!' Sunshine, clouds, the *Cengalo Arête*, with the smooth face of the Badile opposite. Every climber knows that 'Bregaglia' is synonymous with 'Bregaglia granite'. Fantastic rock-forms, incredibly sheer peaks, carved by thousands of years out of the living rock, like monsters in the grey dawn of history, with yellow and black lichens on their rough surfaces, towers, thin sword-blades of rock, spearheads the size of a house, the smooth flat scoop of a shovel nearly 3,000 feet high – the Badile itself. And next to it the perfect, regular, gigantic curvature of the Cengalo's outline, loftier still by a few hundred feet, raking the sky. The thousand-foot 'Flat-iron', too, complete with handholds. Arêtes, arêtes and more arêtes ...

Wolfi and I did them all, on alternate days, including the Sciora di Fuori and – it goes without saying – the towering north-east face of the Badile (I had already done that climber's dream, its arête). Then we rode over to the Dolomites, with the *Busazza Arête* in the Civetta group as our target; but when we got there – once again, needless to say – in spite of our thirst for great ridge climbs, we went straight up the north-west face of the Civetta herself, the queen of all Dolomite face climbs, that glowing red screen of organ pipes; soaring high above a southern valley, which a boy with a bicycle had discovered years before.

How many lifetimes do we need to make all our dreams come true?

And now the 'Spigolo Giallo' and all the face climbs on the Zinnen! But when we arrived at the Paternsattel with our last few hellers in our pockets, it rained. We bivouacked in a concrete hut, and sat on our rucksacks, looking at each other, for three days. Then it started to snow.

Autumn had set in. There was nothing for it but to go home.

We always routed our long summer months in the Western Alps from west to east, starting over there in July and finishing up over here in the Dolomites by September. In the end we grew tired of bicycling; hitchhiking was far more comfortable. Finally, Wolfi acquired a small motorcycle, by dint of hard saving and, indeed, at the expense of our basic principle not to lose a day of our treasured summer forays into the mountains by doing a single extra day's work. If it meant living on porridge, it also meant more summits. Meanwhile, I had discovered the 'Grants for Important Ascents', earned lecture fees, and paid regular visits to my generous 'Aunt Betty'. So yet another Alpine summer was assured.

We were at the start of the south face of the Dent du Geant – a rash of karabiners, the jingle of pitons, rope slings for the feet, sunshine; and above us the vertical granite wall, with its overhangs.

I started up the first few feet, with a view to reaching the lowest piton, climbing 'free'. Hell, how the thing overhung! ... No use ... I had to come down again. Suddenly I heard a voice, saying in broken German: 'You should put a starting-piton in – it's the drill here. That one up there is the second one.'

A hop-pole of a long Frenchman had arrived at the starting point, accompanied by a small fat one, and was quietly unpacking his snack-lunch. 'Thanks!' I growled at him, and started up again, ignoring his advice. Nice chap, behaving as if he owned the place – but we would show him! Up I went to within six inches, three inches, of that piton. Blast everything! I had to come down again. There I stood, panting, getting my strength back – I had put everything I had into it, that second time. Wolfi wrinkled his forehead; angrily, I banged in the piton in question; the long slab of a Frenchman sat quietly munching his sandwich. I knew I had seen that type with a woolly cap somewhere before. Never mind that … off I went, not exactly stylishly, but moving quickly – now we would get clear of the two sandwich munchers!

I found a stance on an airy pulpit. 'Up you come!' I shouted down, to Wolfi, out of sight. The rope told me how smoothly and swiftly he was coming up; I could see his brown mop appearing around the corner, and – by Friday the thirteenth! – a woolly cap, too. That long slab had arrived at the same time, and was laughing, between a fine set of teeth: '*Alors*, the piton was all right, wasn't it?' – so paternal! – 'You see, I know my way about here; this is the seventh time I've done it.' *Seventh time!* He hauled in his rope – we were hanging out into thin air from that pulpit in all directions – and once again those teeth flashed above a tough chin. 'You don't mind if I go on ahead?' he asked. 'By the way – may I introduce myself? I'm Rébuffat …' So it was Gaston Rébuffat, the world-famous climber – admittedly the king of the castle in his Mont Blanc group: why, he must know every hold in it! Humbly, we mumbled our names, shook him by the hand – clinging with the other to the rock; then we leaned out even farther into the air to let him pass. Down below us the ropes swung slowly to and fro. Certainly an odd place for such an introduction.

For a while our human bunch of grapes – we were now four – hung out from the sun-baked face, nearly 13,000 feet up; then elegant French étriers jingled in space and Rébuffat disappeared from sight above an overhang.

A storm was raging on the Peuterey Ridge – the weather had broken suddenly. We knew how many had died on the White Mountain, thirty to forty in some seasons – and how often the weather had been responsible for their failing to return from the peaks and faces of the massif.

Snow, and more snow – we had to get down before it was too late. We only had two days' provisions left, a stupid mistake. We groped our way down the Couloir, then through the ice towers of the Fresnay glacier, valleywards. At last we were down safely, though minus our Peuterey Ridge; but we had at least the turreted south ridge of the Aiguille Noire to show for it.

This damned weather! We had lived up there for a fortnight in the bivouac-box under the sharp tooth of the Fourche de la Brenva, before we could finally do the *Arête du Diable* on the Tacul and the south face of the Dent du Geant …

Every day, as we sat there, the gigantic White Brenva face had shimmered down on us, mostly out of the clouds; and the north face of the Aiguille Blanche de Peuterey, with the ice avalanches roaring down it to shatter the silence.

A thought entered our minds: it must be marvellous to climb those white walls, that difficult ice – those unique ice faces, huge, forbidding, holdlessly smooth, with their blue bulges, their crystalline towers. For, although we were already committed to rock of every grade of difficulty, we had not yet taken a single step in the world of cold, ice-armoured faces.

Was there something keeping us away? Was rock climbing to be our whole life? Or was the other thing just something which would come in good time?

When I look back today, the following thoughts spring to my mind: Wolfi had come to the mountains from an apprenticeship on rock, I, who had started as a crystal hunter, from the white world of snow. All the same, once the day dawned when to climb a peak by the normal route, or in the course of a long traverse, failed any longer to satisfy, I had become a rock climber, like Wolfi. Rock – with all the difficulties of extreme climbing – that was the thing: cliffs, ridges, arêtes of rock.

Now, in our third Alpine season, we both thought for the first time about an ice climb: the Brenva Face of Mont Blanc. The thought was stifled by masses of snow, falling day after day. Our first intrusion into the world of ice climbs, into the realm of mountaineering of every grade of difficulty in the white element – never of course, to the exclusion of rock climbing – would have to wait till next summer.

This process of development in the whole wide field of Alpinism over a life-time will doubtless repeat itself for many a climber. There is a biological parallel here: in the grey prehistoric days, we all swung from branch to branch. The laws of heredity have repeated the process in our own day. The develop-ment is simply that the naked 'hairy ape' has at last invaded the ice-world.

'The standard of a nation's cultural development is recognisable by its table manners', I read on the page of newspaper in which I had wrapped our toma-toes. Well, well! And we Austrians are supposed to be civilised people. Yet, there, opposite me, Wolfi was sitting on the grass, barefoot, cooking polenta. Were we really a good advertisement for our country? At that moment Wolfi pushed a tomato into his mouth and for several minutes gave a good imper-sonation of someone trying to swallow a tennis ball.

'Have you ever considered,' I ask him, 'what kind of an impression of Austria we present when we are abroad?'

Wolfi made a puzzled internal noise corresponding to '*mmmmmh*', the expression in his eyes exactly matching the tennis ball in his mouth. Then, after swallowing: 'What's wrong with it?' he enquired.

'This paper says you can recognise the standard of a nation's cultural develop-ment by its table manners,' I explained, looking pointedly at the tomatoes. Wolfi laughed, picked another one out of the paper and shoved it into his mouth. It appeared that the recognition of cultural standards lay behind the next tomato. I gave up my attempts at education, fetched my spoon out of my trouser pocket and immersed myself in polenta. Wolfi did likewise – it is just one of those freaks of chance: he is left-handed, I am right-handed, so we can spoon things out of the same pot at the same time. (This is known as rational-isation: arriving at an end by the simplest means.) Anyway, we only had one pot. Wolfi put a finger in his mouth and cleaned his teeth. 'You should use a toothpick,' I reminded him, licking my spoon clean, 'and do it in the loo! You aren't civilised.' (A bronze coloured millipede was climbing over the polenta bag.) Wolfi spat scornfully: 'That I suppose is why I developed the system for making do with only one cooking pot – and with no need for washing up, at that?' (Sequence: polenta or porridge, then a soup-cube, finally tea – and then turn the pot upside down and leave it in the sun.) 'Any objections?'

'None,' I admitted, having exhausted all my arguments. After all, inventive powers are part of civilisation, too.

Wolfi looked at me pensively and fired his final shot: 'This seems to be your day for moralising. Do you know, it's a long time since you trimmed the ragged edges of the holes in your trousers – shall I lend you my knife?'

I did not reply, but, using a piece of newspaper for a napkin, wiped my mouth and raised the aluminium saucer of tea to my lips. After all one must start from small beginnings, and good intentions have their value. See! Wolfi was following my example … !

Of the newspaper, there was nothing left.

8 Twenty-Thousand Feet in Twenty-Four Hours

Had we been seized by some form of madness? Or had we joined the tribe of mere record-hunters? No: we were simply itching to know whether we had the necessary stamina to climb the Obergabelhorn with its crystal-white north face, so difficult of access – as it were, in the original conditions, before there were any club huts – direct from the valley level.

We were in splendid shape. After various other climbs, we had just done the 4,000-foot north face of the Dent d'Hèrens in eight hours. What a gem of an ice chimney – the crucial key pitch of the *Welzenbach Route* (how often had it been borne in on us that the name of that great ice expert stood for climbs of exceptional beauty of form and quality)!

Our fourth and fifth summer seasons in the Western Alps had afforded us an initiation into this new realm of the great ice faces. We had savoured the crystalline element, in various degrees of steepness and severity, on the Dent d'Hèrens, the Obergabelhorn, Breithorn, Lyskamm, Aiguille Blanche and Grands Charmoz; and finally the great Brenva face of Mont Blanc. On our way to the gigantic north face of the Dent d'Hèrens, we had cast longing eyes up at one of the greatest 'combined' rock and ice climbs in the Alps – the north face of the Matterhorn. We had both got over the days of our rock climbing intoxication in the Brenta Dolomites; we knew now that one could not do everything. Whether on rock or on ice, our minds were turning more and more to the really big climbs. If the actual climbing was less attractive than on many a smaller peak, we now found the very size of the undertaking more impressive and exciting.

Twenty-thousand feet without a break: from our tent outside Steinauer's shack at Winkelmatten, near Zermatt, to the top of the 3,365-foot Obergabelhorn, and back down again to our tent. In between lay various ascents and descents; the climax, of course, being the mountain's delicately ribbed north-west face, an ice wall whose base is so difficult to approach that, to the best of our knowledge, it had only been climbed five times. Each party had tried to reach its foot, which rises from a savage glacier cauldron, by a different route. One of them had actually climbed *down* a ridge from the summit in order to get there. And we, starting out from Zermatt, had somehow to find a way over the high intervening range of rock to the west, so as to get down into the cauldron beyond it. Once there, the face is a smooth, finely drawn slope with an inclination of fifty-five degrees. The whole thing would normally take three days.

One o'clock in the morning. We fastened the tent door behind us and left Winkelmatten, its huts shadowy shapes in the moonlight. We went up into the night, past the benches thoughtfully placed by the tourist board between the dark trunks of the pines, past the sleeping steinbocks in their enclosure.

By dawn we had negotiated the boulders of the moraine and reached the Rothorn Hut, at 10,500 feet, having come up fully 5,000 feet. The sky was an extraordinary apple green, above the pale glimmer of the Wellenkuppe's snow-cap. We felt marvellous, and stopped for a cup of tea before continuing the ascent.

The sun came up, painting the rocks a reddish-brown. Our breath turned to a vapour-cloud. What a glorious day this was! Over there rose the Triftjoch, a rocky saddle high above the glacier, our next objective. Up here there was a great deal of fresh snow. The question was whether we should be able to get down from the saddle into that cauldron of ice lying in the valley beyond it, and so reach the foot of our north face?

Nine o'clock, on the saddle … opposite us, the Obergabelhorn, shining like a crystal, seamed with bluish-white flutings, still a mile away beyond that deep and ice-filled glacier-bowl, involving a descent of hundreds of feet to its bed of green shadows, blue séracs, huge crevasses and – beyond all doubt – masses of freshly fallen snow, promising much hard labour. The great white face of our peak flung back the light like a mirror, across the deep ice-blue of the dark net-work of rock-slopes below us on our side – a miracle of loveliness!

There was certainly no direct way over to it from here. Wolfi bit his lip, as he scanned the surging, long drawn-out corniced ridge to the left, the north-east ridge of our four-thousander. Could we reach the foot of our face by following it, say, as far as the great *gendarme*, and then cutting diagonally downwards? A steep and most unusual route, surely involving the longest traverse we had ever met? But first we had to turn back and climb the Wellenkuppe.

Late in the morning we were on the 12,796-foot summit of the Wellenkuppe, where the north-east ridge of the Obergabelhorn begins – an undulating edge, swinging up above the abyss in a long curve, like some narrow suspension bridge, to the sharp summit of the peak.

By midday we had got to the *gendarme*, and started on our diagonal downward traverse. God, how that slope went plummeting down!

We went on traversing diagonally downwards well into the afternoon, clinging to a sixty degree wall of ice for one hour, two hours; climbing like two tiny spiders across that huge white slope, traversing and traversing diagonally downwards …

At last, the bergschrund at the bottom lay only a rope's length below us. Who was going to climb down into it and up out of it again, for the sake of the record, to regularise our ascent of the face? You perhaps, Wolfi? No, not Wolfi. Perhaps you will oblige, Kurt? No, not Kurt … we decided that our climb would have to count without that small formality.

So, at last, we could start on our ascent of that enormous crystal, straight up the middle, from its base to its summit, up a face something like 500 yards high. It would be rather nice to have a camp bed along for rests at the stances!

An endless succession of white ribs, sweeping upwards at fifty-five degrees, uniform, similar, symmetrical, regular … peaceful, and soothing to the mind … with a gossamer film of ice dust rippling down over them.

It was a positive dream of loveliness. One of us moved up, belayed by the other; then the other one moved up, belayed in his turn. Our belaying pitons went in solidly at the stances.

Yes, a camp bed would have been rather nice …

That went on for three hours. Overhead, the ridges were closing in to meet at the summit. Just below it, we were suddenly aware that we had defeated the crucial challenge of that vast white uniformity. Now, straight up and out by the *direttissima* (as a gesture)! Fearfully steep, absolutely smooth ice, with a seventy-degree pitch, then a few rocks – and there we were, on our summit. So much for that!

We sat there for a quarter of an hour, while sun-shot mists drifted about us. It was a lovely world! It was also past four o'clock – fifteen hours since we had started out across the meadow down there in Zermatt. We had completed more than half our journey. Somehow, all sense of time seemed to have deserted us. There was the sun, of course, and our watches …

We were on our way down, moving steadily along that corniced suspension bridge of a ridge. Suddenly, the lower half of the Matterhorn's north face loomed out of the mists, glittering in a mantle of freshly fallen snow. Before us rose our *gendarme*, with thick grey fog all around.

The fog turned yellow, and began to simmer. Light was coming through it – brighter and still brighter, finally dazzling. There was a stir in the air; then, as if by magic, the whole world lay clear. There stood the Dent Blanche and the Obergabelhorn, drenched in the liquid gold of the sunset. Everything was golden-yellow – the mists below us, the mountain face, our tracks in the snow. The hours had suddenly dissipated into thin air. The sun was going down. We were tired and transfigured – we felt as if we could go on like this for ever. Everything about the day was odd – and now night was drawing in again.

7 p.m.: back at the Rothorn Hut, after eighteen hours and some 13,000 feet of up and down to plague our limbs. How pleasant it would be to stay here at a comfortable hut! Resisting the temptation, we staggered on down towards Zermatt – we *had* to know whether we could achieve the aim we had set ourselves. Boulders, the zigzag path, darkness, thoughts – I never wanted to be on that mountain face any more, all I wanted was to be in our tent: in Wolfi's Alpine-Association-Section-Austria double-lined tent, made of material tested in the Himalaya, which always let the rain in, because it doesn't rain in the Himalaya, it snows …

Wolfi had stopped. 'I'm waiting for the moon to come up,' he said, and lay down among the boulders. I was waiting for the next bench, above Zermatt, and went on my way towards it … *tarum-tumtum … tarum-tumtum … tarum tumtum … hoppla!*

There it was, my bench. Praise be to God and the tourist board. Now the moon could come up, if it wanted to.

A pretty young lady with an odd looking handbag and stiletto heeled shoes was coming up the meadows towards me – a sight to cheer one: big almond eyes, long, dark shining hair, slim legs. She sat down by me and opened her pretty mouth. 'Would you care to take me up with you to the Finch Terrace?' she enquired.

Would I, a guide in this year 2000, care to – not likely! There was a batting of blue eyelashes. I thought it over: a promenade like that on a chilly ice terrace? Hadn't people in this day and age anything better to think about, than that one-track North Face of the Dent d'Hérens?

Out loud, I said: The coffee isn't at all good up there and they haven't finished the surface lighting of the crevasses. The kiosk over there on the Tyndall ridge serves a much better mocca. Of course, we could just eat a Cassata and then climb a few feet, if you really want to; or we could take the dear old lift to the summit – though I'm afraid it's a bit ancient now.' (Even in 2000 AD, a guide must show at once that he knows his area, if he expects further assignments.)

The sweet young lady got a mirror out of her handbag and redrew her mouth with a lipstick. 'What would you charge?' she asked.

'Hm!' I temporised. Dear old Fiechtl, in whose day everything was so simple, had been dead a long time. I rummaged between punched cards in my rucksack for the latest punched computer-card, which now takes into account, day by day, not only the temperature, air pressure, wind force and the state of the weather, but also the guide's fitness. (I had been relegated to Grade I – so many flights up to the terraces had properly grounded me; and all those summit parties up to the new chapel on top of the Breithorn– these occupational hazards!) If Welzenbach only knew that nowadays one flies up to enjoy a small black coffee in the middle of his ice wall …

But wait a moment; something very odd was happening. The lovely one was pulling an ice piton out of her little bag, karabiners, rock pitons and – by Fiechtl and Welzenbach! – a gossamer-thin storm suit of the new Mars-tested super-skin. Surely she couldn't actually want to *climb* the old route up to the Terrace? Impossible … Kurt, pinch your arm, you must be dreaming …

I could hear someone running in the woods. Wolfi came past at a jogtrot. The moon was up, too. Down below, a few lights were winking – Zermatt. We stumped on down, and finally – 'by the skin of our teeth' – up the slope that rises to Winkelmatten.

At 1 a.m. we collapsed into the tent like two felled trees – almost exactly twenty-four hours after leaving it, and after 20,000 feet of height differential. (Later I worked it over again, and it proved to be only 19,300 feet. Nothing is ever complete, not even the most beautiful chapter heading. We ought, after all, to have done that little extra bit down into the bottom of the bowl.)

We woke up at three o'clock the next afternoon and stretched ourselves in the sun outside the tent. Someone was coming up from Zermatt, through the meadows.

Yellow mists were still floating before my eyes – but now I was suddenly very wide awake. Yellow stockings: the local collector of the 'residential tax', no doubt about it! I took one big leap into the tent, to resume my residence there. Wolfi continued to lie on the grass, smiling happily. Now for a local gala!

The taxman arrived. Soon Wolfi was babbling amiably about the Matterhorn and how long he and his buddy, asleep there in the tent, proposed to stay around that lovely mountain. It was quite a pleasure to listen to him, now he was coming to the point. 'In any case,' he said, making a significant pause – 'we're starting for the Theoduljoch today and going over on to the Italian side …'

Perhaps I had not quite slept off the effects of yesterday, but the yellow knee-hose seemed to change colour. I gave a loud yawn, opened the tent flap and blinked at my old acquaintance. It was worth two whole days of residential tax. He actually recognised me.

We were sitting in the Hörnli Hut, filing the points of our crampons as sharp as possible, for the North Face. Old Kronigk, the hut keeper, winked at us. He knew us by now and had guessed our intentions; but then he shook his head. 'The weather,' he said. It was beautifully sunny outside. We went on filing. Wolfi had just come back from a solo climb of the Zmutt ridge, from which he had taken a good look at the face. It was in excellent condition: this time we would do it.

By midnight a storm was raging and it was snowing hard – unbelievable masses of snow. Everything had turned white, and the warm wind was coming from the south-west. Not a hope, this time. Next year, perhaps.

Not long afterwards, we were pedalling, as so often before, out into the woods in their autumn glory, to the familiar grey walls and towers of our Peilstein practice ground, where the local 'Matterhorn' and 'Monte Cimone' stand side by side. Wolfi had acquired a girlfriend. It was really charming to see how careful he was that she didn't fall off – how devotedly he showed her every hand and foothold. But – thought I, what about … ? Wolfi reassured me about my 'but': he would not let her come along on our next summer's north-face campaign, he promised.

I breathed again, rejoicing. That was how it should be! When one went to the mountains, one should think about mountains and nothing but the mountains. There spoke the true, the genuine mountaineer; he was one of the real ones – *un des purs*, as Samivel has called them. (Anyway, nothing to be surprised about; wasn't he my ropemate?)

I, of course, had no idea then what fate had in store for me. I did not know that, next summer, I would continually be persuading Wolfi that we needed further supplies of fresh food for our ice climbs; and that each time, as soon as he had blessed me resignedly with his agreement, I would be hurrying down hot-footed to Zermatt …

Just to fetch apples, of course.

9 Daisies, a Cat and the North Face of the Matterhorn

'She loves me … she loves me not … '

Daisies on the North Face of the Matterhorn – on its stances?

Shining dark rock, blue glittering ice, light in the bursting bubbles of glassy mountain waters – marsh-marigolds – veils of ice rippling down the face –

Rébuffat said it: 'A marvellous heap of stones, the Matterhorn.'

Sunshine on the North Face. Hot sun. Ice blossoms, tinkling down from the rocks, out into the darkness of the valley, flashing yellow and white …

Daisies? Anything is possible – if one thinks of it.

Anything is possible, when a determined, resolute Swiss girl packs her bag and says: 'I've got a dog already – now I want a husband!' Especially if she knows where to find him: in Vienna. So she travels to Vienna.

Obviously, we Austrians must have a wonderful reputation in foreign parts as husbands; we are supposed to be faithful, reliable, happy-go-lucky, sociable, comfortable and hard working; if we happen to be a bit slovenly, well, they hope that can always be cured.

I forgot a most important thing: love asks no questions. I asked questions: What is this that comes rolling down on me by Transalpine Express right across the Alps? Apart from what, why just on Vienna (fateful thought!)? I wonder what she looks like … ?

Wolfi and I were on the Peilstein. Your mind doesn't seem to be on climbing today,' he suggested. No, I was thinking about quite a different matter.

It was in the Bernina, three years before. White peaks above the Tschierva Hut; the Biancograt, Piz Roseg opposite, Scerscen in between. Huge cascades of ice. But I, lying totally snow-blind in the darkened dormitory of the hut, could see none of these things. My fate arrived after a six-hour trek up the Rosegtal on pliant espadrilles, with blisters on her soles, gritted teeth, a hard head and a very sweet soul. She wanted, for once, to see the homeland peaks from nearby – not only the distant lands in the wide, wide north.

Grit under my eyelids. Dark, confused contours. My lids felt swollen, and now and then came stabbing pain. Damn it, don't rub them! Hardly able to open my eyes, I lay quietly … waiting … in the darkness …

That was the door … quiet footfalls … someone was there.

A voice said: 'I'll put a couple of bandages on your eyes – cool – it'll do them good.' A damp cloth descended on my eyes and two hands adjusted it gently. What angel was this? The clear voice of a girl, with a Swiss accent, rolled r, hard k and all …

'Thanks a lot,' I said. Who was she? The cloth was cool and comforting. Passing my hand pensively over my beard, I considered: one of the hut staff? Definitely not. No sound; but I knew she had sat down somewhere nearby.

'Thanks very much – please tell me – '

'Is it really better?'

'Oh – yes – comfortable.'

Silence. What was there about that voice – clear and gentle at the same time? Of course, a man should not be inquisitive; especially when he can't see.

I could not leave it, though. 'Tell me, who are you?'

She laughed. 'They call me Busle[1] – the Cat,' she said, in that highly appropriate voice.

That put an end to any thought of further rest. Before my mind's eye, far from blinded, there trooped, on delicate feet, a whole menagerie of cats: grey, tabby, red, blue with greenish markings and humped backs, all on velvet paws.

'I need a fresh bandage,' I said.

The hand was long and slender, I discovered; for, as it adjusted the folds, I held it for a moment.

One thing I knew, now – I must get my sight back immediately. And for that, I definitely needed more bandages. Busle had gone out of the room, but she had promised to come back.

It was dark, and I could see blue, metallic peaks, shimmering outlines of glaciers. I had removed my sunglasses – things were silhouettes and shadows. However, I was able to establish this much. Busle was tall. Slim down below and rounded high up. Her hair had a bluish gleam in it; it was probably brown, or perhaps darkish-blonde. She had described it as: 'Busle-colour, my own colour.' Her face presented itself as a rounded disc with dark eyes in it. Tomorrow she had to go.

I asked her to go to the ice falls with me, though I could only show them to her, now, in the dark; for by daylight I could see nothing.

The séracs glimmered. Her lips were soft. She was full of warmth and imagination. There could only be one Busle like her, even if I could not see the colour of her eyes.

Three years ago, now.

---

1 Busle is a pet name, widely used in Switzerland and really means 'kitten'.

The train arrived during the evening. Why was I so excited? The neon tubes of the Westbahnhof vibrated shrilly. I hardly recognised her.

'Really you?'

Up and down the city we went. She was nervous, and walked, as I did, at full tilt. She had a saucy nose and a pony-fringe, and unbelievably long legs.

A cafe: her hand, her voice. Warmth, clarity, imagination.

Yes, it was really Busle.

Here we were in the grey city by the Danube, with its anonymous masses of people – the blue city by the Danube, with its flowering trees, the Prater, the great wheel; with schnitzel overflowing the plate, with the Wienerwald, its gentle outlines overlapping like stage settings, right out to the Schneeberg. Trees like in a Japanese painting. And the orange-red sickle of the moon, setting now behind the blue-Danube city's sea of lights.

'How old are you?'

We were under the last of gas lamps, their gently hissing light a yellowish-green, on our way down to the city. How old was I? 'Twenty-six,' I said, carefully adding two years to my age; I am usually truthful, but we happened to be the same age, and a man is only a man if he has an age advantage. Anyway, why ask?

We walked the streets till the sun rose. I knew something more, then. Her eyes were grey-blue-grey-brown. That matched her general colouring – grey-blue-brown-green. Busle-colour. She knew three languages. What a good idea of hers, to come to Vienna!

The sculptor, sculpting, remarked: 'Mars is in conjunction! That's three times I've said it, and you haven't heard me. What ails you?' SO … Mars … ah, yes. 'Excuse me,' I said. But surely it will last for quite a while?' And I went.

She had twenty pairs of high-heeled shoes and travelled all over Europe alone … she had an unusually keen colour-sense and collected beer-bottle caps … she was always full of unexpected ideas … oh, she was lovely … and at home she had her own library, she said, fluttering her eyelashes learnedly, full of great, fat books …

I leaned forward: there were three buttons to her blouse, one of them was open – by Lollo – !

'You aren't paying attention, Kurt. I was telling you about my library,' said she, reproachfully, her face taking on the look of a dyed-in-the-wool state school-mam. I cleared my throat. 'Yes,' I said. 'Lessing was a great man.' That was a big mistake; with a face set in deadly earnest, she promptly gave me a meticulous briefing on Lessing – or was there perhaps a tiny glint of roguishness at the corner of her eyes? I pulled myself together (so was the blouse by now), with great difficulty producing a variety of consenting and disagreeing answers, which laid woefully bare my knowledge of German literature. Why were her eyes so bright? Why did she suddenly smile? Self destructively contrite, I accused myself: 'Kurt, you are a cultural-defective – that has got to be changed.'

'You are a wonderful librarian ... I said. And what a fantastic library you are! I thought.

I bought myself a *Signpost to Literature.*

Meanwhile, Busle was gone away.

Situation Report:

1. Season of the year: trees and finances, green (al verde[2]).
2. The Bookkeeper: misses my daily pull-ups on the doorjamb.
3. The Sculptor: carving a statue of St Antony (though he has seen Busle and knows Wilhelm Busch, who described the terrible 'temptations of that holy man').
4. Wolfi: regards me as if I were a sick horse when, at the '*Vegetarians' Arete*', armed with my new learning, I gave him a lecture on Lessing's plays. 'Don't forget the North Face,' he says. 'Don't you let me down over that one!'
5. Me: I regret nothing. The North Face? I shall apply to the Alpine Association for a grant. After all, the North Face is a top-ranking climb.

A letter from Switzerland! It says Busle can come along to the Matterhorn. When I told Wolfi so, on the Peilstein, he groaned.

There was this letter. And another, and another. While the sculptor hewed, I lay on my bed, my face covered with a sheet of business figures, and dreamed – a climber caught between 'ought' and 'has'. Oh, Busle how you have changed the life of this bookkeeper summit-stormer! 'Ought and Has'? One has what one has.

Eyes deep as the blue-green lakes of the glaciers ... an ice wall with a pony-fringe ... but no, the temperature's all wrong ... Vesuvius ... Sophia Loren ... the desert ... camels with their rocking gait ... camels with resolute gait? In high-heeled shoes? That was the trouble, she never walks the same way. *Tarab!* – trot! Daisies, nodding, nodding.

The North Face of the Matterhorn, with its nodding gait ...

The North Face!

My request to the Alpine Association!

I almost choked for want of breath.

---

2 I.e. 'the money is finished'.

Final instalment … 'request a grant from the fund for top-ranking climbs'. Well, I had done that.

The North Face of the Matterhorn, with its nodding …

Hey! No arguments about its top ranking; it ranked much higher now – wasn't Busle corning along?

Fate moved on rapid feet, now. *Signpost to Literature* in my baggage, off I went to Switzerland.

It all moved so quickly. Helvetia is used to victories. Moorgarten and Sempach: that is where the Austrians were beaten, as every Swiss child knows. Eyelashes flutter knowledgeably, but very sweetly.

There was no doubt about it. She meant it, in good earnest. So, I suppose, did I. None the less a kind of wonder, a sort of amazement fell upon me. I, to marry? That was the question I asked myself; with the instinctive recoil experienced by all sharers of the same fate, down whose back the thought of that unfamiliar legal status has sent coursing a light shudder.

It passed. Remember Moorgarten and Sempach? And now '*Tu, Felix Austria, nube!*' Austria the fortunate, go marry!

I was as radiant as Jove and sent a card to my tame astrologer. As a prudent Austrian, I stipulated a breathing-space – two years. Time to finish my studies.

After that … what rapture! What a lovely world! (Only first I shall have to make friends with that dog.)

Permission to make our attempt. Financial aid guaranteed. Our summer of the North Face is guaranteed.

This time we shall get our North Face, you Matterhorn: your top-ranking North Face!

Foaming breakers; cliffs rising sheer from them. When the waves suck back, all the shingle in the bay rustles. Great and eternal is the Ocean.

I wrote to Wolfi: 'Busle and I will explore the conditions on the North Face and, until you come, I shall get acclimatised to altitude.'

The sweet-scented trees were in blossom and the sun shone. Altitude: zero – a good place to start from. On our napkin-holders was written: '*Signor Lui*' and '*Signora Lei*'. We fed on mussels, Asti Spumante, top-grade *fritto misto*': top-ranking …

Silent stood the Matterhorn and said nothing. Sure, Wolfi and I would climb the North Face.

Dandelions and daisies. Our tent stood close to the glacier's edge, at nearly 10,000 feet. Wolfi was still on a training course with his Section. A wintry-looking Matterhorn peered through the clouds.

You needn't come for another ten days,' I wrote to Wolfi. 'There's a horrible mass of fresh snow on all the faces.' All I had left was a big bag of polenta. Top-ranking polenta. And the treasury? Down at sea level.

That night I dreamed for the first time of the Central Administrative Committee of the Alpine Association. There was a green-clothed table and a great many silent faces around it, looking at me, and still looking at me … edelweiss, lulled beneath a black storm cloud. Postponement of sentence.

A green meadow; dandelions and daisies!

You moaned something awful in the night – is anything wrong?' Busle questioned me, genuinely worried.

'I dreamed of my record of tours – I think we ought to climb something, you know.'

'Oh, yes – how thrilling – lees go straight for a four-thousander!' she cried, her eyes shining.

'The Breithorn.'

We did it by the ordinary route: six hours of solid slogging.

That night I dreamed of the association again; the expression on the faces round the table had not altered. They looked sad and troubled. One head was being shaken. Wisps of blue cigarette smoke formed the word: 'top-ranking?'

But I don't smoke; my solicitor can confirm it!' Busle was shaking me by the arm. Have you a lawsuit running?' she enquired.

Yellow blew the dandelions – exactly the same colour as the polenta. Yellow, yellow and again yellow.

'I can't look at that stuff you're cooking, ever again. I shall die of starvation' … and two great tears welled out of those glacier-lakes. I was at my wit's end. 'I'll make you some porridge' … 'Well, that would be a change,' she sobbed. Something made me cast a glance forward into the future.

'You know, you'll have to learn how to economise,' I said.

'Oh! … xhuatzl ch – Ch – Ch …

Bluish-green flashes of lightning, and a yellow one, as the polenta-spoon flew towards me …

'Chaibech – ch – ch …' (Please stop it, Busle dear. You are absolutely right. It was *not* the right moment … I'll fetch the spoon) … ch.

We made our peace.

'I'll go and get a job,' she said, 'down in Zermatt, when Wolfi comes and you start up the face – so we won't have to economise so much.' Oh, you wonderful, wonderful Busle!

But that wasn't enough. Another dream: through yellow polenta a radiant vision of Wolfi in golden corduroys, ringed by a maharajah's aureole. He still had his grant.

He would be arriving in three or four days.

The broad ice-block of the summit, the sheer precipice falling from its skull-cap. There it hung, two thousand feet above our heads, crowning shadows, slabby rock, terrifying grey ice, a whole façade of houses up there, blue, chill, shining in the early light – dangerous …

To think that Welzenbach survived all his ice climbs,' growled Wolfi. Under a hanging glacier one isn't safe even at night. Now was the most dangerous time – soon the sun would have warmed the ice up there, playing havoc with the tensions. Suppose one of those streetcar trains came thundering down …

We panted on up the tortuous couloir of the Breithorn's north-west face, crawling on all fours, ice hammer in one hand, piton in the other, moving simultaneously, not belaying, Wolfi and I, moving as quickly as we knew how. This broke all our rules, but here the danger of a slip was less than that menacing us overhead.

'Look out!' A shadow flew past us, slicing the air quite close to us. Then silence.

It was our first training climb for the North Face enterprise. We climbed Willo Welzenbach's great route through the north-west face of the Breithorn in eight hours. Not bad time, but then, not particularly good, either.

Situation report:
1. Wolfi: We aren't in top form – more especially you!'
2. Wolfi again: 'Move the tent up from the beautiful meadow another thousand feet on to rough slabs,' adding, with a meaning glance at me; 'that's the place for an Alpine tent!' No dandelions. No daisies. Polenta.
3. Busle: Selling apples and pears in a Zermatt fruit-shop. Such is life.
4. Me: Such is life.
5. The North Face: still full of powder snow. Our next objective would be the Lyskamm.

'Wolfi, believe me, polenta tastes better and is healthier if you add paprika and onions, also apples and pears. Hasn't anyone told you how important fresh foods are for climbers, according to the latest researches?'
'Yes, but …'
'Oh, you needn't worry.'
'Listen to me …'
'All the same …'
'But …'
'Nevertheless …'
The opposition weakened; silence reigned.
'Agreed, then?' 'Agreed!' 'Wolfi you are a decent climbing partner. I award you the Golden Edelweiss and bars. I'll hurry down to Zermatt … I know the way …'

'Goodbye, Busle!' I said, as, my rucksack stuffed with Zermatt apples, I hurried off again, up to the Bétemps Hut, in the shadow of the Lyskamm; there was also a sweet melon for Wolfi, No disappointments for him; here I was, though I am not sure that he was convinced by my theory of condition-training, adapted from that of the marathon runner to the mountaineer.

The icy upsurge of the Lyskamm. Huge white balconies, their surfaces marvellously sculptured. Above them, corniced ridges, against the blue. A thrilling peak!

The north-east face of the west summit is 3,000 feet high. We climbed it, arrow-straight, by the most direct line we could find. It was a first ascent, and only seven and a half hours.

A marvellous climb. Wolfi was radiant and so was I. Now we could really think about our Matterhorn North Face!

It was evening, we were down in Zermatt. Busle had gone on ahead, up to Schwarzsee, underneath the Matterhorn. 'You go up to the hut,' I had told her, 'I'll be following quite soon.' That iron man, Wolfi, on the other hand, was lying in the tent somewhere, breathing mountain air. Wolfi – *un des purs* as Samivel has it – one of the 'real' ones: every fibre of body and brain now concentrated on the North Face, speaking of nothing else. Two days from now we would be starting up it …

I had told Busle I would be coming soon. So I bought a few small things for the North Face; and then, unexpectedly, ran into some old friends. It got late, and later: no question of 'soon' any more. But it is nice to feel comfortably sure that, whatever happens, one is being waited for.

It was midnight when I knocked at the but door. The place was shut, every bit of it. 'Busle!' I called, in a half-voice. No answer. 'Busle!' – a little louder this time. There were plenty of windows (but which one?); they were all dark, and the wall of the but smooth.

Surely she must be awake? How could she be sleeping peacefully while I was standing out here in the cold? A dog trotted across the meadow; I did a few knee-bends. She must be sufficiently worried about me to open the window at least every quarter of an hour, to see whether I had arrived? Well, say, at least every half hour! Really, one shouldn't put one's faith in women …

In the moonlight a striped cat was promenading through the grass; it sat down to gaze at me with a kind of scornful nonchalance. 'Busle!' The cat gave a jump. My fury kept me warm for another quarter of an hour; then I set about finding a place to bivouac in. No anorak, no bivouac bag, nothing. What a pitiful object! Wolfi, of course, always has something along with him.

Cardboard-boxes, lumber, pitch darkness – I had got into the woodshed. Hard beechwood logs, of course … how unkind can Providence be?

I couldn't aspire to any higher storey. The outline of the cat showed up again in the door-frame. 'Gschschsch!' It made another jump. No, really – before I let myself remember the whole long night … yet freezing isn't much fun either …

What about the boxes?

'Oh, Busle' – I wrap myself in corrugated cardboard – 'how can you bear' – I wedge myself into a big rectangular box – 'my getting frozen feet' – a dust of pudding powder, smelling of strawberries comes out of the box, as I push my feet through its bottom and stick my legs into the next carton – 'instead of staying awake' – I cram a reasonably soft macaroni box over my head – 'unable to sleep, and only waiting for me to come?'

Hard and horrible are the dictates of fate. But I am beginning to believe it was done on purpose. 'Gschschsch!' Is that brute there again?

Hop it – my requirement for cats is fully catered for. I am a climber, in training for the North Face. One of the 'real' ones, at that …!

What? Can't even turn round anymore? This blasted pudding box! I've grown four-cornered. What if I force it? That's just about all that was needed. What a smell of strawberries …

Life is very hard – hard and four-cornered.

Comes the dawn. Bitterly cold. The surroundings begin to take shape and colour … SWISS NOODLE PRODUCTS: UNSURPASSABLE … In large letters before my eyes. I try to wriggle my toes. OVOMALTINE, THE NATURAL BRINGER OF STRENGTH … I have discovered a kind of rocking motion, inside my cardboard fortress, which provides calories. The morning hours are the chilliest. Ah, a ray of sunlight, falling square across the beech-logs, with little points of light dancing in it. Look at those boxes and logs! You just wait, my Busle, for today's thunderstorm, Austrian pattern!

Half a moment, though. No, I must never give her the pleasure of amusing herself at my expense, about my bivouac! Why, I met friends down in Zermatt, and so I stayed there. So sorry, Sweetie, that you waited for me … A much better version than my first idea. Ha! Ha!

I climb out of my boxes and emerge. There is Busle, sitting in the sun outside the door. 'Good morning,' says she, quietly, her eyes shining. My words stuck in my throat. Should it be version One or Two?

Have you developed a sudden passion for Macaroni?' she asked, amiably. I removed the box from my head. Moorgarten …

'Sweetie,' she smiled, 'how you do pong of strawberries!'

Sempach …

I took my drubbing as well as I could. (No wonder: for the Swiss army is one of the best in the world; but Helvetia decides which corner of the home shall house the rifle.)

It was midday. I was affectionately occupied with sun spray and Busle's back (we Austrians are reckoned as helpful, unselfish, always ready to atone for a little slovenliness by attention to detail). Suddenly Wolfi came on the scene, clinking with pitons – actually our 'real' one had the pitons in his rucksack, but I could hear their spiritual clatter, as he found me occupied in such unalpine activities, the day before our face climb – so excuse the poetic licence.

Said Wolfi, wearing his North Face expression: You do know we are starting tomorrow?'

I nodded and went on creaming.

Wolfi threw a first warning look at me, then a second slightly oblique one just brushing Busle's back (she never got a mention in his written accounts). 'I think,' he said, we should be getting on up to the Hörnli Hut.'

Busle beamed at him. 'Good luck, Wolfi,' she smiled (not without emphasis) 'my Sweetie will soon be finished, and then he'll come.' Wolfi drew a deep breath and looked up at the North Face. Then he sat down.

And now let him carry on with the story:

'... at our feet lay the little mountain lake in which this proud peak mirrors itself. It was not very late yet, so we stretched out in the sun and enjoyed the beauty of the afternoon.

'The mountain soared majestic above us. Its sharply-defined ridges and flanks fall steeply away on all sides. But the most savage and withdrawn of them all is the North Face. The sun only penetrates that wall, almost 4,500 feet high, for four hours a day. There is not much hard snow on that face; for the most part only treacherous powder snow covers the smooth rock. Two frightening questions kept on recurring to our minds: would we be above the ice field before the sun loosened the stones, held fast by the frost? Would there be heavy icing on the rocks?

'Time passed. We shouldered our rucksacks. We met people who took smiling stock of us. Our small climbing rucksacks were topped by a mountain of clothing and other things carefully tied on with line; and a miner's helmet shone from Kurt's. (Wolfi was always highly scornful about it, likening it to a useful porcelain article – never would he don such a thing in his lifetime! He was to change his mind later on.) Once again we approached the Hörnli Hut looking like two mountain tramps. Everything good happens in threes. (Wolfi, of course, means that this was our third attempt on the North Face; we had been there twice before, during the_ previous summer.) All around the Hörnli Hut, close to the foot of the Matterhorn, one can hear every language under the sun. There are people examining the Hörnli Ridge through the telescope, trying to discover today what awaits them up there tomorrow. Tired climbers with happy faces passed us on their way down to the valley. They had had their wish. We did not want to attract any attention and did our best to get our equipment into the sleeping quarters unnoticed. The guardian of the hut came up to us and asked us straight out whether we intended to try the North Face in the morning. It was late, and I tried to sleep, but I couldn't; I was far too excited. I kept on looking at my watch, hour by hour. Once Kurt said to me: 'Oh, do stop being so strung-up!' But he must have been feeling just the same.

'At last it was midnight. A glance out at the wonderful sky, full of stars, encouraged us not to lose a moment. We climbed cautiously up old, eroded avalanche-cones, with the North Face, deep in shadow, looking eerily down on us, like a ghost. From below, our route had looked unmistakable; now, we had to search around for quite a time before we found our bearings. At about 2.30 a.m. we reached the lower edge of the bergschrund. It was still so dark that we could not see for certain where it was easiest to get across. Kurt settled it by going straight for it, up the cliff. We came to the ice slope. A stone whistled past us like a bullet, then utter silence again; the only sound was the crunch of the frozen snow under the pressure of our crampons, and the occasional sharp ring of one piton striking against another.

'Above us, the first rays of the sun were already falling on the rocks. Rope's length by rope's length we climbed on steepening ice at an even pace. Up here our twelve-point irons got little purchase on the hard ice. And now we were getting the first morning salute from overhead. Small fragments of ice, loosened by the sun, went humming past our heads. (The daisies! It really looked like a shower of flowers; but then, of course, I was wearing my miner's helmet.) We had to watch out for them very carefully. We kept on diagonally to the right, towards the great concavity in the middle of the face, which provided our route for the next 1,400 feet. We changed the lead after nearly every rope's length. The next time I wanted to bang in a piton as a belay, it struck rock after only a few centimetres. I tried another spot, but there was simply nothing to be done. I shouted to Kurt to take great care. Presently we came to a steep rock-step below the great bay in the wall. I tied myself to a piton, took off my crampons and climbed a rope's length up steep rock. Kurt kept his crampons on. In this way we contrived that one of us was always ready for difficult rock, the other equipped for ice.

'In due course, the stratification of the rock became very awkward and there was a heavy layer of ice on it, so I had to put my crampons on again. Although we were warmly clad, the cold up here was biting, for not a ray of sun had yet penetrated this huge, slanting, open gully. To our right, the wall went winging sheer into the depths to where the crevasses in the Matterhorn glacier looked like tiny cracks. Above us to the left it loomed up, starkly unclimbable. Against these measurements of terrifying might and size, a human being feels very small and forsaken.

'We pressed on, slowly but steadily, upwards. The climbing became very unpleasant, on a regular, thin sheet of ice, frozen bone-hard, overlaying a mass of loose stones. (Hiebeler commented later that the photographs made it look like winter conditions.) I looked longingly up at a little rock-spur, up there in the sun, where the Schmid brothers had bivouacked.

'At eleven o'clock, we tied on to two belaying pitons and swallowed a couple of lumps of sugar and a lemon. The way ahead did not look too bad at first. The best of it was that the angle seemed at last to be easing off a little. But how wrong we were! Ahead lay smooth slabs, without a single hand or foothold, furnished with minute irregularities and heavily iced over. As I none the less started another stroke with my ice hammer, the slip-ring slipped off the shaft, and the whole hammer out of my frozen mitten. A cold shiver ran down my spine and I held my breath. The hammer was caught by a minute projection and hung there, just below my feet. I climbed down three feet and, to my delight, got a grip on it ...

(After that exciting mishap, we reached a traverse in deep powder snow, which brought us on to that part of the wall which is known as the Roof. We were now well above 13,000 feet.)

'The big snowfield lay ahead of us. Just above us the face looked savagely shattered and rocky. We could already make out the fixed ropes on the Hörnli Ridge, over there. The terrain became more broken and therefore easier. Towards the top the rock became so good that, in spite of our great exertions, we really enjoyed the climbing. We could hear voices on the Zmutt Ridge ...

'We climbed a last steep gully of shattered, rough rock, and then over a short snow slope, straight up to the cross on the summit. It was 7.30p.m. and the sun was very low. Together on the Matterhorn's summit, we revelled in an unforgettable sunset. An enormous sense of joy enveloped me ...

Those minutes enveloped all three of us in it. Busle, who had lost sight of us against the sheer size of the face, now spotted us all the way from Schwarzsee as tiny spotlighted figures on the summit. After seventeen hours on the face, we unroped and in the dying light of an undying day started down towards the Solvay Refuge. All our dreams had been fulfilled – we could hardly believe or grasp it yet – for, three times before, I had been on the Matterhorn in cloud. Today everything was clear. At last we had got our North Face. No bivouac, not a cloud in the sky all day ... Yes, today, all our dreams had come true.

I did an idiotic thing. Dark though it already was, with the lights of Zermatt quivering down in the valley, there in the darkness of the dark rock-world, I leaned against a black boulder with my camera and pointed it towards the horizon. My hand was shaking, the camera slipped on the rock: over the double-edged silhouette of the Dent Blanche, the colours fuse in a wide band of dark blue, red and yellow.

'Cheerio, Busle!'

The little red train was pulling out of Zermatt and moving away along the valley slope, a small red streak … then a dot.

The platform … suddenly I was surrounded by nothing but strange faces. I grabbed my ice hammer and started off for the Theodul Pass, in Wolfi's wake, bound for far off Mont Blanc.

Nobody else climbed the North Face that year. The slopes below the Matterhorn slowly turned brown. One day the soft, broad, white blankets of the snow unfolded itself on them and on the mountain above them. It was winter once more.

The following summer did not see me in Zermatt. I was living in a tent on the rubble-covered Baltoro Glacier, far away in the Karakorum. Another summer came; I was at the foot of the Eiger's North Wall. Yet another and another summer, as the Earth kept turning … I never came back to Zermatt.

There is a meadow, packed with daisies. The sky above it is clear and the air is deep, and transfused with light. The wind caresses the slopes. The daisies lift and droop their little heads. They say 'Yes'.

It is … it is … it is …

I wonder, will anyone else ever again discover flowers on the North Face? The daisies lift and droop their little heads.

They say 'Yes'.

And yet, in a thousand years, no single day passes away.

Himalaya: 'The Gift of the Gods' … so said Herbert Tichy, as he and his friends stood on Cho Oyu's summit.

It is in truth, a gift of the Gods to stand so high above the world. I ask myself this: does the intrusion into those ultimate heights change a man? Do the Gods, in return for what they grant, exact something from the best-beloved?

No one knows the answer.

10   The Giant Meringue

Once in his life – irrespective of age – everyone suddenly does something quite crazy; nor does he normally regret it.

The direttissima of the Königswand, the hardest of my first ascents was a fantastically crazy performance, which still gives me pleasure today, though I would not care to repeat it. But then, I couldn't, for it is no longer possible; the key pitch has since collapsed into the abyss.

That is not to say one couldn't do the *direttissima*, without the 'meringue', today. It could be easier, but I am not sure. For that summit is a sphinx; and that enormous cornice of ice, into which they carved a complete defence position during the First World War, and which fell off the mountain after the second climb, is building up again. Who knows what it will look like tomorrow, or in twenty years' time?

Before the cornice fell, my route was repeated, by none other than Wolfgang Stephan, my regular climbing partner, who for once was missing on the first occasion. For him, that absence had been too much to stomach …

He and two others had an even more disturbing passage than we did. One of them came off, though without hurting himself. The following few sentences from my friend's report of their climb will give some small idea of their venture close to the limits of the possible:

'The "Meringue" loomed like a giant balcony above us … the nearer we moved to it, the more impossible it looked… we couldn't hide our anxiety from one another … in the end, a perfect hedgehog of pitons … sheer over the abyss; an amazing sensation to be hanging there from those tiny iron shafts, 12,500 feet up, above nothing … getting more and more impossible to communicate with the others, planted below the overhang … at last my hand was able to touch the rim of the cornice.'

They had climbed the face and reached the bottom of the barrier, that is the 'Meringue', at about midday. Not till seven hours later, about 6 p.m., did they set foot on the summit. It had taken all that time to master the key pitch. The third man came off while retrieving the pitons, and found himself hanging in thin air, 2,600 feet above the Königswand glacier …

'There was our companion, swinging far out from the face, remote from all possible contact with it. So we threw a rope across to him and tried, without the least success, to haul him up. Then Gotz hastily constructed a block and tackle hoist.' Thus Wolfgang's report.

I do not know whether anyone attempted it again after that; certainly, no one succeeded. A few parties have climbed the face and reached the summit by a traverse to one of the ridges on either hand.

And how did we fare? I have an ancient account in front of me. Let it take us back to those fantastic September days, when that blue pavilion of ice still thrust far out over the gulf below, when the summit was still 'in one piece', and I myself all of twenty-four years old. I was both a dreamer and a realist then: bewitched by those white lines of crystal, ready to take any risk to realise the route my imagination showed me, up that loveliest of ice faces in the Alps. At least, that is how I – lured by a mountain's magic – saw it.

A soft wind caresses the summit of the Königsspitze, soughing among the rocks, sporting with the powdery snow, now and then whirling it in glittering banners skywards, then falling again to leave the mountain quiet in the still air.

It is very quiet up here now. It is autumn, with a hint of winter on many a day. Very rarely does anyone come up here. It is late in the afternoon: the wide blue vault of the heavens arches overhead, from the distant cluster of the Dolomite spires to the white heads of the Bernina. Far down below, in the Sulden valley, the fires of day are quenched and a dim twilight reigns. The icy sweep of the Königswand, too, grows darker, that face plunging away from here to the north-east, overhung by the blue shimmer of untrodden ice bulges. Slowly the mountain's shadow grows out into the east. The gnomon of the sundial. Minutes on the horizon …

The wind starts up again, keen in the stillness, plays about the slender topmost seam of the cornice, leaving a line of glittering dust, outlining the huge buttress of ice and snow. The sun's rays slant to the summit. What was that? From the inner recesses of the mountain comes a soft, almost inaudible thumping. Again, clearer this time, coming from the north-east, where the giant roll bulks far out over the face. Then silence again; till, suddenly, glistening white at the farthest rim, the snow whirls up, farther over now, quite close to the highest point. Lumps of snow go flying, an ice axe flashes in the sun … a head appears, joy written large on its countenance. Up into the sunlight, and on to the summit!

For two hours there is no rest up here, on top. The air is full of shouts, deep holes are carved out of the snow, ropes run out and taken in; till only the last red gleam of the sun lingers on the summit and the darkness of night comes creeping up those mighty flanks. It is all over: here the three of us sit in the snow, exhausted, dead tired.

And the *direttissima* up the Königswand is fact, now!

I had discovered the mountain years before, when I was still a boy. We were standing on the summit of the Weisskugel in the Otztal Alps – I had just acted as guide for a Viennese and two girls from Berlin (the latter we already know; but the man from Vienna was, incidentally, not Willi, the hero of our Venediger story); and we were quite excited because we wouldn't make out what the odd-looking peak, sticking out of the clouds to the south, could be. In the end someone told us: 'It's the Königsspitze.' The name is apt, for the peak is regal, and 12,655 feet high.

My next view was a close-up from the top of the Ortler. I was on my own, having just come across the Stelvio on my grandfather's old boneshaker, making my way home from the Western Alps. There she stood in the morning sun, in all her magic beauty. The light fell slantwise on the delicately fluted crystal smoothness of the north face. 'That man Ertl,' I thought to myself, 'had a pretty fair idea of what to tackle!' For it was in the thirties that the Munich 'Mountain Vagabond', Hans Ertl, with Hansl Brehm for partner, had made the first direct ascent of the face. High up on the climb, the huge summit ice bulge had forced him away on to the left-hand ridge. This ridge had been reached, as long ago as 1881, though lower down, by another victim of the spell cast by that face – for once that overdone word is justified in this context; this was Graf Minnegerode, who achieved the first ascent with the brothers Piggera and Peter Reinstadler, three of the best guides in Sulden. They climbed the left-hand side of the face, a less direct route; but without crampons, without pitons – simply in nailed boots and with an ice axe clutched in their fists. Fifteen hundred steps they cut. And they were the first to climb it.

Albert and I were standing at the foot of the Königswand in the broad, white cauldron of the upper Königswand glacier. It is difficult of access, for huge crevasses and walls of séracs bar the way from below. That is why we had come by daylight, so as to mark our night-time route in advance, for we wanted to be well on to the face by sunrise.

We were tired, and sat down at the edge of a crevasse. We had been stumbling around on the debris of the moraine for hours in the noonday heat, sweating as we built one cairn after another; perhaps a hundred, particularly important among the rocks at the base of the wall, where the route goes up and down, back and forth, in this confusing approach to the white cauldron and above the sérac walls. We had finally got in from the side. Now we sat, letting the September sunshine scorch our hides – a treat after the snowfalls of the previous days – and taking a look at the face.

Yes, that Ertl, the mountain vagabond, a man of Nanga Parbat, explorer of jungles, he knew a thing or two ...

Then we went into details. A couloir, flanked on either side by rocks, leads up the lower part of the face; above it, a diagonal rib sweeps far up towards the ice buttresses of the summit region. Hans Ertl had gone up it; we intended to climb straight up from the top of the couloir, following a narrow rib of snow which, mounting in a soft curve and growing even more slender as it mounts, soars right up to the first balcony of blue ice, plumb in the middle of the face.

And then, what?

What a route that would be, straight up to the top over the bulge and the cornice! A dream route, forbidden, impossible … fascinating. Could we do it? Boring a way through, like moles? Perhaps there was a secret crack? Or a way right over its outside? A way over that giant roll of frozen snow – straight from the confectioner's – a 'meringue'! And so the name was born.

Hans Ertl, too, had wanted to go straight on up. But he had only four pitons, and then – he fell off, as can, alas, so easily happen. The fall quenched the joy of climbing, blunted the drive to press on; and so they turned aside. 'Glued to the smooth, cold wall of ice,' he reported, 'it took us four hours to master this very difficult pitch, the traverse below the summit overhang.' They reached the left-hand ridge quite near the summit, but the great bulging obstacles remained unclimbed. Never yet had a man reached the summit straight up the face. The King's crown was still untouched.

Albert was no less enthusiastic about the idea of the *direttissima* than I. He was one of those 'old hands', an experienced ice-man, a blue-eyed giant – one of those who surprised us youngsters by not 'doing' anything for long periods and then suddenly, with no fuss at all, tackling something really difficult, as if it were the most natural thing in the world. How then did I suddenly team up with him? This throws some light on the working of our vagabond nature, which is not always the result of planning ahead. A whole summer's climbing in the Western Alps had gone by, and Wolfgang's time had simply run out; he just had to go home. And so, all at once, there I was, partnerless. Should I go home? Well – no. I spent a couple of days messing about on the Drei Zinnen with a young man from Tyrol – Karl Schonthaler, later to be known as 'Charlie'. Then I was on my own again. Should I go home? Instead, I telegraphed the Edelweissklub in Salzburg: 'Send me someone at least up to *Pallavicini Couloir* standard.' Albert Morocutti mounted his motorbike – and now he is sitting next to me, quiet, thoughtful, blinking up at the slopes. He is one hundred per cent committed. Yesterday we put in some training on the icefall. Tomorrow we are going to start up the face … though we did not know it would be in vain.

Someone knocked. It must be the hut keeper. 'Thanks!' Two-thirty. One leap out of my bunk and across to the window. Yes, the stars are out. Fine weather.

Then the familiar humming of the Primus stove, the flicker of the candle, breakfast. The last items go into the pack. That's the lot!

Out we go into the clear night, where not a breath stirs. In the cold out there, our footsteps are the only sound. Abnormally tense, we kept on glancing up at the mountain's dark silhouette. Then the glow of our lamp showed up our first cairn; there it stood on the grass, built of red and blue jam tins, slightly crooked and helpless-looking, but a masterpiece of our own making. We had to laugh. 'Now for the genuine Chianti flask, which we finished yesterday!' 'Oh, I thought the next one was the tin of donkey in oil?' Over there, something was fluttering, almost ghostly, in the darkness: the economics section of yesterday's paper – in black and white, such a help towards spotting a cairn in the middle of the night! Slowly we lost height, till we met the glacier's level. There, on a particularly lovely cairn, was the Lollobrigida in all her beauty. We began to move upwards again, finding our way easily enough, thanks to the decorated cairns, drawing ever nearer to the mass of dark rocks on the other side. We reached them in about an hour from the hut. It was still pitch-dark.

We stumble upwards in rubble and sand, finally roping up on a small shoulder of rock. In the first pale light of dawn I start up a brittle chimney, feeling my way up, my pocket lamp in my mouth. Almost at once, out comes a handhold. 'Look out!' I yell; but it had already reached the bottom with a crash. Luckily, Albert was safely under cover and there was no damage to the rope.

Up on the glacier there was already a fair amount of light. The whole face of the Königswand rose bathed in a peculiar greenish-yellow hue. On we went, across the smooth, hard surface; when it steepened, we stopped to put on our crampons. A shout from my companion drew my glance upwards – the sun was coming up. The icy summit ramparts glowed a brilliant red; slowly, softly, the lave flowed down from rib to rib, from hump to hump, leaving only the deep runnels in greenish blue shadow. Even around us, down below, the slopes and séracs caught a faint shimmer, reflected from the shining wall above. Presently the first rays met us, as we were busy adjusting our crampon straps, and a golden, glittering stream of thousands of tiny crystals shot up towards the sun …

A puff of wind came across the glacier. The air was set in motion, gently stroking the slopes – and it was daylight. As we traversed below the Mitscherkopf, the first stones began to fall, counselling us to keep on the move. Threading our way through huge crevasses, we reached the foot of the wall, at the base of the couloir; nothing to be seen above it from where we stood.

At 7 a.m., later than we had hoped, we were at the bergschrund. We stopped to empty a tin of milk, chewed a couple of dried prunes, and got the ironmongery ready. The upper lip overhung a long way, protecting us; but only a little snow came trickling down, not a stone, not a fragment of ice. It was all lovely and quiet? Well, we should see, later on.

I went at the slope above the gash, with an ice piton in my left hand, the ice hammer in my right; to get over the bergschrund I cut some steps and handholds. Then came the first surprise: 'Washboard snow!' It was fantastic: the surface consisted of innumerable little transverse ripples, hard as bone, some white, some blue, forming a pattern like Grandma's washing board. Something between snow and ice, sometimes both. What mattered was that this concoction provided a veritable Jacob's ladder to the sky. What incredible luck! Never before in my life …

We gained height rapidly, in those ideal conditions. Those blue and white ripples were so fashioned as to afford ample foot and handholds. It was only at stances that we hacked out a step. Albert beamed, and I beamed back at him. There were a few vertical pitches – rock islands hidden beneath the ice – quite a lumpy world. But what a joy! For several rope's lengths we forgot any question marks hanging over this marvellous blue September day.

There was a yellow knob of rock above me; to its right, in the sunshine, everything above shone white. The couloir above us was barred by insurmountable pitches; we had to move across, up that way. I worked my way up towards the knob, zigzagging between sheer ice, snow and passages of rock. The face had become pretty steep hereabouts: I looked diagonally down the couloir below me. I stopped to knock a piton in and snapped a karabiner into it … At that moment the 'meringue' came into view – way above us, 1,500 feet or more overhead, a great pavilion, hanging repulsively in thin air, tons of ice balanced out in the blue of the sky, so simple, so motionless – and oh, how it overhung! It seemed quite crazy that it could hold firm, that not a morsel of it came down; but then, it was autumn.

One summer's day it swept two to their death just here, when some of it broke away. I thought of the seconds while they waited helplessly. Today only a few small snow crystals came dancing down the slope. Today there was magic in the air – and that giant bulge hung up there, as if under some spell.

Are we climbers' fatalists? I suppose, in certain situations, we sometimes come fairly near it …

Meanwhile, 1,500 feet above our heads, the thing still hung quietly in thin air.

Hours went by. We were in the midst of an extraordinary world of ribs and more ribs and flutings, all going upwards. We chose one and crawled up it, as usual, on all fours; two tiny black dots on that vast face.

Now and then we glanced up at the ice ramparts above: over the first blue bulge, to the 'meringue' itself. We had got used to it by now, but the nearer we drew to it, the more dauntingly the question hung over us—where was there a way through? A fine powdering of snow and ice came rippling down, but nothing worse; the sun had disappeared behind our mountain and we were in shadow, as we pushed on up towards that first blue bulge. It seemed close enough to grasp, but we never seemed to get noticeably nearer to it. Rope's length after rope's length ran out. Time had lost all meaning. Below us our snow rib lost itself in the gulf, our footsteps up it looking like a column of windows in a skyscraper. Everywhere around us, similar slender ribs swept down into the depths, concentric, like the rays of some gigantic fan, whose top we were trying to reach. Down at the very bottom flashed the mirror of the Königswand glacier's sunlit floor, the overhangs above our heads reflecting its sunny brightness.

At last the snow on our seemingly endless rib grew thinner. Then it petered out into sheer ice. Now down below, I hadn't really bothered my head very much about that first ice bulge. Just an ice bulge – so what? Here, the old story was repeating itself: an ice pitch, at a distance, is just that; close to, it is something quite different, something that only shows its teeth when your nose is literally jammed against it. And what teeth! This has happened over and over again to every ice climber who ever lived. A little farther over there, Hans Ertl once had had to fight it out with this self-same bulge …

I worked my way up towards the bulge with the utmost caution over a steep slab of black water-ice, of execrable toughness. It took all I knew to cut holds in it. High time, now, to bang a piton in. I tried; but before it even held, there was a sudden crack and an ice-cake a yard long went hurtling down into the depths, almost upsetting my balance. A damned near thing that! At last I managed to get it in with innumerable tiny strokes of the hammer; but on the bulge itself; no matter how I tried, no piton would hold: not the thin flat ones, not the hollow-stemmed ones, not even the extra short ones … Resigned as a burglar might be, finding himself unable to force the glassy security of the König's impregnable keep, I felt my way, with a clatter of ironmongery, back down the smooth slab again. 'No use!' I reported. Our first attack had been repulsed.

It was noon. There we sat on two nicks we had hacked out of the ice, chewing a couple of dry biscuits. What now? Should we take Ertl's route, leftwards, up to the ridge, abandoning the *direttissima*? Or should we have a go, in spite of the wretched ice there, a little to the right, where the bulge broke up into a succession of little pitches, like a blue-tiled roof?

The biscuits tasted horrible. We were only 350 feet from the summit. Three hundred and fifty feet that were the crux of the whole climb … Why had the ice to be so bad, just at the crucial point!

Down below, the light was gone from the burnished mirror of the glacier, the shadow of our peak had begun to reach out across the valley. Down there, in the shadowy green, the tiny houses of Sulden shone bright with small points of light. Look, let's get on with it! I got up, slightly stiff from sitting, and started to traverse slowly out to the right …

Down in the valley the Sulden guides were astir, and a few end-of-season visitors with them.

'You've lost the litre of red you bet me – they're going up to the right, the Devil they are, as I said; and now it's going to be tough!' Alfred Pinggera bit his lip, jammed his eye to the telescope and nodded. A dyed-in-the-wool mountain guide like him knew just what a hazardous game was starting, up there. And Alfred grinned with pleasure all over his sun-browned face, because he had been sure that those chaps wouldn't turn it in. The other one, who had lost his bet, nodded, too, a little more doubtfully. 'There's something tough doing up there today, all right! The Giant Roll on the König, of all things! Wonder if the pair will do it – the one with the beard, whom you call "The Spirit of the Hills" and that long slab of an Albert, who only blew in here a couple of days ago? It looks barmy to me – those two little dots below the summit.'

As I began my traverse out to the right, I could not guess how many ice-bosses I was going to meet, nor did I know how many litres of 'red' had been wagered … It seemed better that way, at any rate, for I was still choking with those dry biscuits.

There, in the shadow, a shining tablet of ice, high above the sunlit world, and steep as a church roof! Never in my life had I hung on such a slab. It affronted my nose, shimmering blue everywhere, all round me, broken up by almost vertical pitches several feet high.

Taking the greatest care of my equilibrium – not a place to come off, this – I leaned against the wall and hacked out a couple of handholds in front of my face: very cautiously, so as not to shatter the brittle ice. A couple more, higher up for my hands. Gripping them, I lifted a foot and climbed gingerly with the front teeth of its crampons into one of the first two nicks, now transformed to a foothold, threw my weight on the top two, then on my foot. It held, and so I pushed upwards, straightening myself slowly against the face, and started to gouge out another handhold. Over and over again, with the need for the occasional piton; but only Albert's special short ones were any good here, the others simply bent. And so, hold by hold, I wormed my way upwards, nearer and nearer to the great Roll of the 'Meringue' …

The tension increased. I hadn't the least idea where we could get through, nor could Albert see a way. All we knew was that those horrid tons of ice hung just above our heads, poised motionless. The excrescence barred the whole face with its stratified layers, an insurmountable obstacle, some eighty feet high, either vertical or overhanging. And so it stretched away, unbroken, to the Sulden ridge, away to the right: only there it was a shade less high.

The main overhang, the penthouse of the 'meringue', was directly to our left, with further balconies behind it, not so easy to see from here. And just behind the great protrusion there was a slight re-entrant. Could it be a shallow groove which would offer a route through those overhangs? Well, it seemed the only faint hope. So: up through the 'meringue' itself ...'

Easier said than done ... Handholds, belaying pitons, the lot. At last I am directly below the huge wall, with a balcony chest-high in front of me. Very cautiously I push my arms over it to full stretch, and what do I find – a column of ice, with a gap behind it, a real stroke of luck! With cold fingers, I thread a sling through it, snap in a karabiner and, thanks to a pull on the rope and a couple of snake-like wriggles, there I am sitting in a niche above the balcony. The next bit isn't very amusing: headfirst, on my stomach, I wallow my snowy way along a closely overhung ledge. A few more strides, and I am right inside the 'meringue' itself!

All blue. Extraordinary traceries, their curving lines making a graceful sweep. I stand, looking up. The vertical has become a meaningless word ...

The great roof of ice goes winging over my head like some huge dome, jutting out fully twenty feet, then rolling gradually into the depths, drawn downwards by its own weight. I can almost touch the icicles hanging from its lower rim. I stand there, gazing, for minutes on end, overwhelmed by this miraculous blue dome, inside which I am, at the world's most inaccessible place; this dome, a fantastic creation of the winds and of gravity. All the day's targets are forgotten. I am the first to penetrate this shrine.

Albert followed me up, experiencing much the same difficulties as I had. Then off I moved again, tense beyond words as to the possibilities of finding any way ahead. The corner, the 'groove', might be the key; but after a very few steps I could see that our dream of the summit prize was over. Another balcony, of mushy yellow snow, in which no piton could possibly hold, barred any hope of further progress. The pity of it! Looking up, I could see – hardly fifty feet above me – a narrow seam of gold, the sun lighting the rim of the summit.

We turned back without a word, repeating the crawl along the snow ledge, the balcony and the traverse to our stance, in silence. Then, foot by foot, as the shadow of the 'König' lengthened over the valleys far below, we worked our way across to the Sulden ridge, looking back again and again.

And then, all of a sudden, I spotted it ... surely, there, just above the snow crawl, one small weakness in the ice armour, and the only one! Three bulging overhangs, but definitely of good ice; higher up, it deteriorated, but only where it was no longer overhanging. Yes – just at the most improbable spot – there was a way up under the beetling roof of the 'meringue'; then a traverse on a repulsive-looking ledge below the overhangs, a diagonal climb over them to the upper rim of the dome itself, a narrow seam of snow – and the summit could be won!

I knew I should have to try it, however long I might have to hang in the ice; that last link in the *direttissima*. But not today. It had been a day in a thousand. There we stood on the Sulden ridge, looking back, across to the 'meringue', looking down the immense sweep of the Königswand. And there, immune, stood the summit ...

More showy days, putting the 'meringue' out of court; at least, in my opinion. And Albert and I had already climbed the North Face of the Order. His leave was over, and home he had to go.

And I was alone again. Go home? Impossible. Not without my 'meringue'. Besides, I had the cash for a week more. 'The "meringue", the "meringue", the "meringue"': round and round in my mind. The weather was perfect. The König soared crystal clear to the sky. Everything was set for the last, decisive effort to make him mine. But I was alone, and the 'meringue' could not be done solo. I simply didn't trust myself. On the other hand, I couldn't leave without it: *suppose someone else were to come and bag it!* I should never forgive myself! It just wasn't on. It was I who had to bag that 'meringue'. Furiously, I washed last summer's socks, trimmed my beard, darned the holes in my pants and sat down beside the path to the hut.

'How about a climb?' I asked the first one to come that way, who looked at all qualified – having first exchanged a few opening gambits about the weather and the surrounding mountains. No joy at all. As soon as I began to unfold my plan in detail, my opposite number lost all interest, or remembered a previous assignment, or had to look after his girlfriend's interests. I started to seethe: 'These damned women in the mountains! How many first ascents have been scrapped on their account?' It was beyond endurance – though, of course, only an excuse. And this 'meringue' was such an obvious thing!

I went back to Sulden in despair. Alfred was my last hope – the guide. Alfred promptly agreed; indeed, he was enthusiastic. But Alfred's wife, in the next room, had overheard, and invited him to a tête-à-tête. I began to see red – flaming, crimson red.

I am sure Alfred would have come along just the same; but I was not prepared to let my 'meringue' shatter the peace of a whole, long family happiness. So I passed on – up to the Hintergrat Hut. I knew Fritz Dangl, the guardian up there, a tough nut and a guide, too. Perhaps he would join me?

Up there, a vision of utter peace met my eyes. There on the bench outside the but sat Fritz, smoking his pipe, with his grandfather beside him. The children and a dog were playing around the place. No wife in sight.

Fritz agreed at once; but he couldn't leave the but for a few days, till his wife got back. 'Can't you come sooner?' I urged. No, not till then. Abandoning myself to my fate, next day I climbed the North Face of the Little Zebru, so as to keep my hand in. I soon realized that, in spite of my days of enforced idleness – or because of them? – I was at the top of my form. So I opened up a new route to the north-western peak of the main summit and, after a restful little nap up on the south summit, came down by its north face. That turned out to be a rather dicey trip, and I was glad when I got to the bottom. I got back to the but in the evening, with two solo 'first ascents' – one up, one down – in the bag. Enough to make one happy. But I hadn't bagged that 'meringue' yet ...

By now, I knew every inch of it by heart – Fritz has a super-telescope – and I was banging the pitons home where they belonged, in my dreams.

I heard that a couple of youngsters – probably 'extremists' – with heavy rucksacks, were on their way from Sulden to the hut. I went to look, and came upon a tent. Here they were, two Austrians. We reached agreement in no time. Tomorrow we would meet on the summit and attack the 'meringue', approaching it from the Sulden ridge, by which they intended to reach the top. I informed Fritz Dangl of the latest turn of events. Then I went over to the Schaubach Hut.

Some reader or other may confront me with the proposition that a true first ascent should be made in one piece, all the way up from the bottom. Ideally, that would, of course, be the most satisfactory way. However, on some first ascents of extreme difficulty, one dispenses with a repetition of the pitches one has already successfully pioneered oneself, as superfluous; and traverses in again on another day, to start at the point where one left off before. That is how the West Face of the Dru was first mastered, the *Gemelli Arête*, the North Face of the Eiger in winter conditions. Nor had I any doubts about the practice, having regard to the extreme difficulties of my *direttissima*. Only the last bit was missing, and it was that bit which still had to be done.

The Königswand was bathed in morning sunshine. I had packed all my ice equipment and was sitting quietly outside the Schaubach Hut, enjoying a rare little moment of idleness. By rights, those two ought to be in sight on the Sulden Ridge by now ...

Not a sign of anyone. Had they been taken ill, or could there be some misunderstanding? Or had they, after all, changed their minds at the last moment – everyone is entitled to. In thoughtful mood, I looked up at our own route on the Königswand, where I knew each separate boulder. Suddenly, I saw two new ones ... there they were, my young friends ...

Nobody has ever got up to the summit of the König as quickly as I did then.

When I reached it, my pair were already just under the 'meringue', having made good use of the steps we had left. But something had happened somewhere on the way up – a hammer had broken and was quite useless. Moreover, they had only five pitons. Hans Ertl himself couldn't have got up here with those. At shouting distance we joined up. I would bring my equipment across to them. One condition: I was going to lead on that 'meringue' – *my* 'meringue!'

Down in Sulden, the guides' hearts missed a beat. That tiny black dot up there was slowly pushing its way across the face – up there, under the giant bulge, 2,500 feet above the foot of the wall …

That appalling gulf below my feet! I had dithered before taking the first steps out on to the precipice. However, a look across at the 'meringue' drove me on.

Ice in front of my face. Two thousand five hundred feet of emptiness under me. I dare not look down. Utterly alone. Sheer madness, this.

I am stuck; my nerves have let me down. Trembling, I bang a piton in and hang myself on to a line. Deep breaths. My God! Out with the spare rope, and into the piton, hanging on it, and moving on again …

The rope has run out. I have got to untie. The rope goes rolling slowly across the sheer face to the piton, with the lazy swing of a pendulum; obedient to the laws of gravity, it hangs straight down the precipice now, over there, like the second hand of a stopped wristwatch.

All on my own again. Only my fingers to rely on, and my nerves. Mustn't think. One step, and a compulsory rest. Another. My life depends on the precision with which I make them.

I have got there. Above me, on a narrow ledge, stands Hannes, airborne, it seems. A fine piece of work, his traverse across, under the overhangs. At all events he has retrieved the pitons behind him. How could a second follow him now, unless he 'pendulumed' across? Unnecessary, now, anyway. Much better like this.

I sent a couple of extra long pitons up the rope to Hannes. No one could say what his stance might still have to put up with. We both felt a lot better after that. Very soon I attached myself to the rope again, belayed this time by Herbert. Here I am, at last, under that immense roof again. This time, it has simply got to go!

The first thing was to get up to Hannes, and, seeing what this involved, I plumped for the double-rope. Herbert belayed me along the ledge – thirty feet of traverse with a cold, overhanging swell of ice at chest level, pushing the upper part of my body out into the void. With the aid of a couple of pitons I reached Hannes on his incredibly airy stance. Now Herbert could let my doubled rope run out, swinging across to us pendulum-fashion. There it hung loose below us, moving slowly back and forth. We looked at the overhangs and I fetched a lemon out of my pocket. 'Have a bit?' I asked. 'Thanks,' came the slightly grudging answer: for these two had really wanted to complete the climb on their own, and had, like as not, sat below the 'meringue' for a while, contemplating it. Anyway, here the three of us were now, and none of us would get up without help from the others. For better or worse, we were all in it together – as in some familiar political situations. There Hannes and I sat sucking our lemon, each his own half; looking up at where we wanted to be, guessing where the top might be, hidden behind an ice bulge. How glad I was to have *étriers* with me; free climbing on the outward pull of the rope on this mighty cornice could only lead, sooner or later, to falling off. It was bitterly cold up here at 12,500, in the September shadow. With a clatter of pitons, I was off again, and banged the first one in. Hannes kept on belaying me to perfection, which cheered me up. No one wanted to become airborne – down that face – at this point. I kept on hammering away at that piton. The minutes prolonged themselves into hours. This was the toughest ice climb I had yet met …

To me, dependent from the overhang, everything looked crazy! The sun stood crooked above, hidden from sight. In went the next piton: now for the étrier.

As I lifted my foot, I could for a split second glimpse the spare rope, far down below, on the slanting face of the wall, seen diagonally below my crampon points, a thin line like a forgotten shoelace. I felt for the étrier with my points – the thin sliver of my wristwatch's second hand circling before my eyes. I got hold of the rope again, found a new footing in a space above the slant below me. Thin air, ice waves, everything at a tilt. Gravity alone told me where the vertical was. Another piton; another ice-cake went clattering down into the deeps. At a certain point I realised that I hadn't enough pitons. With the greatest difficulty I retrieved those behind me, only to bang them in again above.

A pull on the doubled rope! Worn out, I rest for a moment against the slope. Then up again over a bulge, a small one this time. What a grind! But I feel good all the same. I have got so far, and now it is only a question of time. There is only one more vertical pitch ahead, then the slope eases back.

Blue flakes of ice. One of them goes shattering down into the gulf. A fine cake, this! I had thought the pastry up here would be solider stuff. But, even if I wanted to, I could no longer go back now. So, now for a short breather.

I take a look under my arm at the slope below, deep in shade. One huge funnel of ribs and runnels, a gigantic blue fan. And there in the middle of it Hannes' face, drawn with the icy cold. Time to move on! In goes another long piton, at an angle, between two flakes. Cautiously, I trust my weight to it, and it holds. In goes an étrier, and I am dangling clear, relying entirely on two small flakes, damn it! But it's no better *inside* the bulge; I know because I've tried it. This is the wind's handiwork. So, on with the dance …

God, the piton's … coming out … !

Down! Seconds prolong themselves into an eternity. I gasp for breath, cling madly to the piton below, hanging crookedly, and start to lower myself. More second, long ones. Fighting … hanging … standing. Standing arched in space, but standing again. That was close to the ultimate limit, that was! Curse those bellying flakes, curse them! I lean my head against the wall. There, dangling from the karabiner, swings the faithless piton.

Now things are getting really difficult. The ice here begins to be rotten. And it is still vertical, too; the last swell of the face, before it eases of Here I am pushed out farther than ever, trying to lean as little as possible on the pitons and still somehow to keep contact with the wall on hand- or finger-holes. Presently I find I can occasionally force the shaft of my axe in, and, with a circular motion, hollow out a wedge-shaped hole. Into it I plunge my arm up to the elbow, put my whole weight on it, then repeat the movement on the other side. It is terribly exhausting and I am pretty near the end of my tether. Panting, I lay my face against the vertical snow cliff Careful, though! I feel as if I might go flying down any moment. No chance of turning round, either, any more. It's either up, or the long, airy flight, now …

On again. Six feet more and I am over that flaky belly. At last the slope begins to ease. At last I can't see anything down below me anymore. Less agitated, I lean my face against the slope again.

Hannes was shouting up from below: Why wasn't the rope moving anymore? Did I know it was perishing cold? All this in a beseeching tone. After all, he had been hanging from his piton for more than two hours, hardly daring to move, alone on that ice ledge. He must be shivering to death. Of Herbert, not a sound for long ages, now.

I screamed down to him that the worst was over.

Of my dozen pitons, I have only one left. This one is not for the hammering, I use it in order to make progress. I grip it in my fist, this my sole life insurance. And now for the diagonal move up to the rim of the cornice. Above me there, a snow overhang, with sunlight playing at its edge – the summit.

Tougher again, as I hack out a few holds in the seam of the cornice. I try to beat a way through it; great masses of white, ice cold, powdery snow crash on to my face. Spitting and gasping for air, I can feel the strength ebbing from my arms. The blade of my axe flashes in the sunlight above me … but, hell and damnation, I'm all in …

Try farther out to the left, on the very crest of the 'meringue' … Pull yourself together; you know your last belay is miles away down below there! I move across, plunging my piton into the snow at every step – my very last piton, my lucky mascot …

Now I am on the very crest of the 'meringue'. The summit must be close overhead. With great care I batter down the last small rim of snow. Just above me, the wind is whirling glittering snow dust high into the air. I ram my axe in and haul myself up. One last little bit, one last output of strength and then – I am up on the summit in the full blaze of the sun!

Later, we were all three together up there. We did not hurry away, for our coming descent in the darkness gave us no qualms; we were much too strongly under the influence of the events of the past few hours. We sat in the snow, eating a bit, talking – always coming back to those incredible hours, to the same marvellous thing …

The summit is empty now, quiet as it was before we came. True, the snowy surface is disturbed, and there is a deep breach in the narrow outer hem of the cornice. But the wind will come rustling there again, stroking the snow, softly smoothing the hollows, and getting on with his eternal architectural work. And in time he will efface every trace of us.

11 Tempest

Today the giant banners of the storm are flying from the Lyskamm's summit; the cornices asmoke with blown snow. Pressure waves go buffeting through the air, there is a rattle of ice darts, pain numbs your face. The blue, blue sky is filled with the organ-notes of some mighty symphony. This is the soaring tempest of the high places!

One of nature's most stupendous manifestations, it clutches at your very heart. Bent double, you almost float on the waves of air, staggering to keep your balance, covering your face against the stinging volleys of those icy particles ...

This may all be happening on the Lyskamm – but today's fury is the great storm of the Himalaya: the mighty tempest of the high places, ice-cold, merciless, tremendous, under the wide blue vault of the sky.

See to it that you don't lose your gloves! Take care not to be blown bodily of the ridge into limbo!

Safely back in the valley, the rushing roar of the air is still in your ears and the joy of it remains with you: for that is just how it must be in the far-off Himalaya – as tremendous as it was up there today ...

12 My First Eight-Thousander; To Broad Peak with Hermann Buhl

Day was drawing to its close over the Baltoro peaks. The shadows of the giants lengthened slowly across the broad floor of the glacier, merging to form a silent sea of darkness, from which the mountains rose like fiery islands. The sun drew down in its quivering, flaming glory towards the horizon. Then – in a magical interplay of lovely colour– only the summits of the eight-thousanders shone high above the world, their snows glowing a deep orange hue, their rocks brownish-red, lit with an unearthly brilliance. Two men were standing on a peak, still breathing heavily from the ascent, their limbs weary – but they did not notice it; for the all-enveloping glory of the sun's low light had encompassed them, too.

Deeper and deeper grew the colours. The last rays of light now rested only on the topmost summit crests. Then, suddenly, as they looked eastwards beyond the rim of snow at their feet, they saw the wide shadow of the mountain cut a swathe out into space, till it lay as an immense pyramid athwart the Tibetan haze and thrust beyond it, far out into the infinite.

No dream-picture, this. It was real enough, and it happened on the 26,404-foot summit of Broad Peak.

I owe it to Kurt Maix, the writer about mountains, the climber, the man who understood the young and had himself remained young – as anyone who has read his book about the South face of the Dachstein knows – that Hermann Buhl invited me to join his 1958 Karakorum Expedition. Maix was president of the 'Reichensteiners', that small, intimate Viennese section of the Alpine Association, of which I was already a member; and when I came back from doing the 'Giant Meringue' on the Königsspitze, it was he who said: 'You ought to go to the Himalaya, that's where you belong.'

The peaks of the Himalaya – they had always been my dream.

So they had, too, for Hermann Buhl, the man who had climbed Nanga Parbat solo, the man who looked so small and light, not in the least like one's idea of a mountaineer. At first sight, one hardly noticed his tremendous will-power; yet he had set out alone from the last high camp below the Silbersattel to climb the summit of that ice-clad giant, on which attempt after attempt had failed over the years and which had already claimed more than thirty lives. Without oxygen, taking only his rucksack, an ice axe and ski sticks, he went up alone into the dark skies of the death zone, into a world where none can exist for long. Hermann Buhl, the 'loner', got to the summit and came back; badly frostbitten, after unimaginable efforts and perils; after spending a night, at over 26,000 feet, standing erect on a narrow stance; hearing weird voices, tottering with exhaustion, at the very limits of his being. For his safe return to the valley-levels he had to thank, first and foremost, his incredible willpower. So long as a spark of life was left in him, he would never give in.

I only knew him from a distance – I had seen him once or twice at lectures, and heard much about him. He had some of the quality of the great Himalayan peaks – for me there was something unapproachable about him. Once, after a lecture, he wrote 'Berg Heil!' on my Alpine identity card, and from that day I regarded it as a mascot.

So Kurt Maix introduced me to his friend, Hermann Buhl, and suggested me as a candidate for his expedition, which was due to leave in a few months, in the following March. I shall never forget that moment in the room where Kurt Maix wrote his books, when for the first time I stood face to face with Hermann, fearing the wrong answer to the dream of my life, opposite the slim, light-limbed mountaineer with the lively, dark eyes, the thick mop of hair, the prominent nose – and, in the background, Kurt Maix's cheerful, weather-beaten face. It all happened so quickly. Buhl talked to me briefly ... the North Face of the Matterhorn, eh? ... so you are a student; do you think you could act as an expedition doctor? ... that 'Giant Meringue' was a bit dicey, wasn't it? I agreed: it hadn't been easy, but magnificent stuff. He gave me a cursory but friendly glance; then he said, 'All right, you must join us.' Cloud-capped ridges, an endless ocean of peaks burst on my eyes – what had happened to the walls of that room ... ?

Maix was already telephoning through to the press. The Austrian Karakoram Expedition had acquired a fourth member. Name: Kurt Diemberger. All right: D for Dora ... and berger like Berg – mountain. Yes, in March ...

Again, no dream, this; it had really happened.

We went by sea, all round Africa, for the Suez canal was shut. To Fritz Wintersteller and myself it made no difference, the ticket was good for either way; we were accompanying the two tons of our expedition's baggage to Karachi. Fritz came from Salzburg and was a first class climber, as was Markus Schmuck, the fourth leaf in our four-leaved clover. At twenty-five I was the Benjamin of the party by some years. Fritz, a quiet easy-going type, who rolled his own cigarettes even on the summit of Mont Blanc, was our 'Minister of Food'. The smaller, quick, wiry Markus possessed a first-rate administrative talent – in the end, Hermann had handed the overall leadership of the expedition to him. He himself remained in charge of all climbing matters, and while actually at work on the mountain; then, even the leader of the expedition became subordinate to him. Hermann and Markus were to follow us by air; in the meantime they were still busy at home whipping up the last money that had not come in yet.

So we sailed on – right round Africa – soaking in a thousand impressions – the sea, an occasional glimpse of the coast, the colourful life on board, the wide horizons, a visit to the top of Table Mountain. Every day, for a whole month, the ship travelled the length of Austria – it made one realise the immensity of the Dark Continent. Secretly, when there was no special celebration aboard, we toasted Nasser – for having closed the canal. Then we did another thirty laps of the main deck, at a trot, so as to keep fit.

Our approach route lay through the valleys of Kashmir's Baltistan. Each day we and our sixty-eight porters covered a stage of about ten miles, sometimes even less. The tempo was typically Asian; we were destined to get used to it during the next three weeks. The porters normally carried a sixty pound load, though a few of them humped slightly larger ones. Every mile or so, sometimes even sooner, they took quite a long rest. Then the word 'Shabash!' ran down the long, irregularly dispersed groups of our column of bearded men, and they set down their loads supported by cords running across their shoulders, either on some wayside boulder or on a thigh-high, T-shaped wooden prop – a kind of rudimentary walking stick – which each of them carried. Or else they sat down, made tea, heated stone slabs and baked chapattis on them – unsalted flat-cakes consisting simply of flour and water – sang and danced to a rhythmic clapping of hands.

We had travelled north from Karachi by train, through the wide, endless plain of Pakistan. From Rawalpindi we continued our journey by air, across the main Himalayan chain. We flew past Nanga Parbat, but saw nothing of that mighty peak, for clouds enveloped it entirely. After a flight of two hours we touched down on a runway of sand at Skardu, capital of Baltistan, a place which boasted 5,000 inhabitants. There we waited some days for the porters to put in an appearance, which they did eventually; we were assured that this represented a fair degree of punctuality. Then we set off northwards, on our way to the great ice fortresses of the Karakorum, whose distant gleam Hermann had glimpsed from the summit of Nanga Parbat ...

'Shabash!', the slogan of our 130 mile-long approach march. However, one acquired the virtue of patience, shedding the vice of Europe's frantic haste. From the Indus we followed the Shigar, and after that the Braldu, through desert-like, arid valleys, barely reached by the monsoon that breaks on the main chain of the Himalaya (actually their water comes down from high and distant glaciers) ; valleys full of sand- and debris-flats, shimmering in the heat of the noonday sun, while unnamed white peaks floated in the sky like some mirage.

Then, suddenly, we would come on an oasis, rich with early green and pink clouds of apricot trees in blossom – hundreds of them, foreshadowing the ripe fruit we should find on our return journey. It was spring now, early April; we should not be passing this way again till summer.

The broad valley of the Shigar gave way to the savage gorges of the Braldu. The picture of a suspension bridge consisting of three interwoven plaits of willow branches still reminds me of the following conversation between a traveller in the Himalaya, well known to me, and the mayor of a local village ...

'We shall be crossing that bridge tomorrow. Is it safe?'

'Perfectly safe. You need not worry: it will hold.'

'How often do you rebuild it?'

Quoth the mayor, after a short pause: 'There is no need to worry. We always rebuild it just before it gives way.'

A lover of the truth, at all events.

At every place we came to, I found myself fully occupied – in my capacity as 'doctor'.

Doctor? 'Well, you have been a student,' Hermann Buhl had said. 'Someone has got to act as our doctor!'

I had indeed studied – international trade. So I bought a book called '*Vademecum*' (literally, 'come along with me'), took a short course in administering injections, persuaded a doctor to explain the more important diseases, and presently found myself the proud possessor of sixty pounds. of medical supplies, neatly done up in bags labelled: 'Nose, ears, eyes, frostbite, pneumonia', and so on. For dentistry I was equipped' with a single pair of all-purpose forceps. I never used it.

Now, my poor confiding patients waited in a queue – the healthy and the sick – while I punctured blisters, squeezed drops into eyes and ears, sounded chests. Fortunately, I had a good supply of pain-killing tablets, for doubtful cases. You see, unlike at home, nothing could be allowed to go wrong, and I had to exert special care in my therapy – for I knew we had to come out again by this same route.

There were, however, occasions when I really could do some good.

After marching nearly a hundred miles, we arrived at Paiju, the last pathetic clump of trees and flowers. Before us, huge and rubble-covered, lay the tongue of the Baltoro glacier, bordered by its sharp containing peaks.

Alpine Technique on an Eight-Thousander

Hermann Buhl was well-disposed towards me. I knew it from frequent small touches, such as suggestions he might throw out, and I was glad. He would sometimes explain to me, in a paternal manner, things I knew perfectly well already; but when I saw what pleasure he took in imparting the knowledge, I refrained (sometimes with difficulty) from saying anything. Certainly, I came to know Hermann in a very different light from that in which many of those with whom he 'crossed swords' picture him. Of course he was a difficult man – that did not escape me, either – an extrovert individualist, thin-skinned, and sensitive as a mimosa – but a man in whom there burned an eternal flame for his mountains. Many who did not possess the same degree of burning vision tried in their own fashion to explain things that were crystal clear to a Hermann Buhl. He never compromised. His zeal knew no limits – and in pursuing his aims he could be unbelievably tough with himself and with others. Not everybody understands such a man.

I wrote, and dedicated to him, a final chapter for his book 'Achttausend, drüber and drunter'.

One morning, at Paiju, Hermann issued me a light-hearted invitation to go on a reconnaissance with him, and I gladly agreed … We stood on a high shoulder of the savage granite pinnacles of the Uli-Biaho group, looking up at the huge Paiju Peak, across at the rusty-brown cathedrals of the Trango Towers, and up the Baltoro glacier's immeasurable length, farther and ever farther – to where, twenty-five miles away, soaring above the stratifications and bosses of its rubble-covered ice stream, the eight-thousanders stood ghostly, unapproachable, incredibly high, not of this world. And there we saw our mountain, our Broad Peak. And two hearts leaped for the joy of such a day.

Now we began talk about our mountain much more frequently. We were all full of enthusiasm and zeal, as was indeed essential, for the undertaking which lay before us would demand the last ungrudging effort each of us could contribute. No one had yet succeeded in climbing an eight-thousander without using high-altitude porters; this is what Hermann wanted to attempt. His plan was that from base camp onwards there would only be climbers on the mountain; they would do everything, load carrying, establishment of camps and, finally, the assault on the summit. And it was all to be done without the use of oxygen; we were all to achieve high-altitude acclimatization during our load carrying up to the high camps.

It was certainly a novel concept, tough and not without its risks; but we all looked forward confidently to the day that would see all four of us on our summit. Hermann, the only one of us with previous experience in the Himalaya, thought it could be done, and he must be right. At home the plan had led to the shaking of many a head; but then, Buhl's plans and achievements had always been more daring than anyone else's. No one knew where, for him, lay the limits of the possible; nor had he yet found out for himself. Broad Peak, without high-altitude porters, without oxygen: 'The ascent of an eight-thousander, using the technique of the Western Alps,' he had called it. It was a typical Hermann Buhl plan.

And the route to the summit? It was just as daring as the plan itself: it would simply go straight up the steep ten thousand-foot face of the mountain, over a col at 25,600 feet and thence up a short terminal ridge to the summit crest. It was a splendid, direct route, which had already been recognized as possible and described in the 'thirties by that famous Himalayan explorer, Prof. G.O. Dyhrenfurth. Buhl had chosen that route up the 'West Spur' not only for its directness, but because it was less dangerous than the route by which Herrligkoffer had attempted the peak some years before, leading as it did for quite a long stretch, known as the 'Gun-barrel', through the tracks of ice avalanches. To be sure, Herrligkoffer's expedition had had no choice, because the West Spur was as good as impassable for its laden high-altitude porters – a consideration which of course caused us no worries. Farther up, our route, and his ran together for a little way; but above 23,600 feet, ours broke absolutely fresh ground, on which nobody had ever set foot.

As to the high camps, the intention was to equip them relatively lightly and with no view to lengthy occupation, in keeping with the character of the summit assaults, which were to start as rapid thrusts from base camp, as soon as the 'ladder' of camps was complete.

One day followed another. We and our porters moved on and on over the Baltoro's world of humps. We were now more than 13,000 feet up, and the halts multiplied increasingly. It snowed during the nights and the cold was icy. We had already survived one strike on the part of the porters; it was clear that the next one was not far off. The shape of the peaks on either hand was beyond all imagination: the needle-sharpness of Mitre Peak, the fantastic surge of the Mustagh Tower, the huge, shining rhombus of Gasherbrum IV, only just short of the eight-thousand metre line – Gasherbrum, appropriately means 'the gleaming wall' – and, last of all, Chogori, 'the great mountain' – known to the world is K2. I have not calculated it exactly, but I am sure that this gigantic pyramid could contain a dozen Matterhorns. Our Broad Peak, the Breithorn of the Baltoro, with its three summits of 24,935, 26,248 and 26,414 feet, bulked ever more massive ahead of us. Ever colder and more hostile loomed its huge west face; it had been the cold and the storms which had forced Herrligkoffer's expedition, in spite of the presence of such experienced men as Kuno Rainer and Ernst Senn, to abandon the attempt. (Senn had gone flying down over the mirror-smooth 'ice wall', halfway up the face, for about 700 feet, and would not still be climbing had there not been the soft snow of the 'high plateau' to check his fall at about 21,000 feet.)

At 'Concordia', in fresh snow up to our knees, we met with the expected strike on the part of our porters. All attempts at negotiation proved abortive;

this time no pay rise could shake their decision to go home. Too cold, too much snow, they said.

So there we were sitting on our cases – we four climbers, two mail-runners and Captain Quader Saeed, our liaison officer, left, at this moment, with very little to *liaise*. From now on, we were all porters – shuttling our baggage and finally establishing our base camp, at 16,000 feet. 'Very good training for later on,' remarked Hermann.

Four Men on the Spur

Get yourself fit by carrying loads, and get acclimatised in the process ... in other words, accustom yourself to the altitude by humping a fully-laden ruck-sack up the mountain so often, and for such long hours, that eventually it does not grind you into the ground, your headaches disappear and you cease to gasp for every breath. At that point you will be going like a bomb; and incidentally the high-altitude camps will also have been established.

On 13 May, a lovely morning, we set foot on the face of our mountain for the first time and pushed on up the gullies and slopes of the West Spur to about 19,000 feet, where we discovered an airy but otherwise fairly suitable platform in the ridge, just roomy enough to take a tent. It lay about 3,000 feet above base camp, and three days later our camp I was in being. We found the long stint up to it easier each day and the process of acclimatization was noticeable; all the same we high-altitude porter-sahibs all agreed that the West Spur was a pretty steep assignment, and our relief was obvious each time we dumped our thirty-five to fifty-pound loads at the platform. At that stage, however, the advantage of climbing on so steep a spur became manifest; for, instead of a slow, laborious descent, we were able to go tearing down to the bottom, some 2,500 feet, in a sitting glissade on the seat of our pants, a method which took only half an hour and saved us much time and expenditure of effort.

By 19 May we had established camp II at about 20,992 feet, under the icy overhang of the high plateau's giant cornice. Hermann and Fritz pitched the tent, while Markus and I brought up the supplies from base camp. During this operation, Hermann and Fritz made a valuable discovery: in the natural refrigerator of the 1,500-foot high 'ice wall' above the plateau they caught the glint of a salami, a bottle of egg-liquor and a tin of bacon belonging to the Italian K2 expedition; the last item having been fetched by Herrligkoffer's team from the Italians' base camp. Surely it was by an unexampled circular tour that the bacon found its way into our cook pot; the liquid was still excellent and even the three-year-old salami had been perfectly preserved up there, as we confirmed after our first hesitation. At our 'ice palace' (camp II), below the cornice, we later on replaced a tent which had been crushed by snow pressure by one belonging to the earlier expedition, found by us on the ice wall; and we built their fixed ropes into our veritable handrail between high-camps II and III, on that very cliff.

We were still short of one camp, the assault camp from which our attempt on the summit would be launched, a camp III at about 23,000 feet: the last rung in the ladder of camps we were in this way pushing up the face. Unfortunately, on 21 May, the weather broke, with devastating days of blizzards and gales. We sat in our base camp and waited; but on the 26th we were all four on our way up the Spur again in beautiful weather. Although camp III had not yet been established, we had decided to go for the summit. After Hermann and I had prepared the slope of polished ice above the Plateau so that loads could be brought up it, while Markus and Fritz looked after the supplies, we finally joined up and established our assault-camp, at just under 23,000 feet, on the evening of the 28th. Fearing that the weather might turn bad again soon, we dispensed with a rest-day and started out at first light the next morning.

We made good progress at first, but higher up we were greatly troubled by the deep powder snow lying on the steep face and, above all, by the fearsome cold. When the sun's rays at last reached us, we all felt as if we had undergone some kind of a redemption; but this was followed by an ever growing, leaden sense of lassitude as we gained height. Were we suffering from lack of oxygen? Or was it the effect of the cold we had suffered earlier? Whatever the cause, we moved more slowly all the time. During the afternoon we reached the saddle between the central and main summits, 25,600 feet up! Before us lay a steep ridge of snow and rock. We felt it could not be very far now; perhaps we should still pull it off By now, however, each step demanded four or five breaths. A couple of rock pitches called for our last reserves of strength; only willpower forced our weary bodies up, foot by foot, and time was passing at an unbelievable speed.

Fritz was just ahead of me, Hermann and Markus about 150 feet behind us. At last! There, in the level rays of the late sun, above a steep snow slope, we could see dark rocks clean-cut against the sky. There was nothing higher. We made a last effort. Fritz and I stood on the rocks, with clouds drifting around us. There was really nothing more above us …

In front of us, to the south, Broad Peak's summit-crest fell away in gentle curves, swung away widely beyond them – and then – yes – started to rise again! Went on rising, up and up, to form a shining cone of snow, way over there, probably an hour away – the true summit! Perhaps fifty or sixty feet higher than our vantage-point, no more than that … but an hour away, over there. It was 6 p.m. – much too late to go on now. Bright mists enveloped the ridge, darkness came climbing out of the abysmal depths. If anyone went on over there now, the odds were against his ever getting back …

Down we plodded, 3,000 feet down, back to our assault camp. By the time we reached it we were all in, utterly spent. Two days later we were all down at base again.

There we were, repeating to each other, over and over again: 'Sixty miserable feet short … only sixty vertical feet in height … but those sixty feet were at the other end of the mountain!'

Well, we would just have to capture them next time.

Markus and Hermann had suffered a degree of frostbite in their toes. We ate heartily and recovered from our exertions. Then the weather turned marvellous again, clear and beautiful, but icy cold. We dashed up the spur again, leapfrogging camp I and sleeping at II, below the plateau. The following afternoon, 8 June, we were up at our assault camp once more, just below 23,000 feet.

'Tomorrow, and tomorrow and tomorrow …'

To the Summit

It was unusually light in the tent; the moon was up outside. I kept on thinking about the morning and couldn't sleep much. Hermann kept on turning over next to me. The hours simply crawled. We dozed off for a while …

Hermann woke up at 2.30. So did life in the tents. Just getting up was a job, for there isn't much room. Nor was there much time for breakfast. Thermos containers changed hands from tent to tent. Then at last we were off!

It was unbelievably cold. Our fingers stuck to our crampons. Ice fragments went clattering down the slope outside the tent. The thermometer at the tent door read –25° C. So it must be –30° outside. But it was a fine morning.

We went up over ice and wind-packed snow in the half-light. Not a breath of wind was stirring. Every now and then our crampons grated on the hard ice. Soon it grew lighter; the first gleam lit the high summit of K2. As if by magic, a little later, hundreds of peaks all around us had caught the new day.

High overhead, the Broad Peak summits stood dark, seamed here and there with bright patches. We looked longingly up, to where there was light and there must be warmth, too. The whole of our western slope lay in deep shadow, and the cold increased every minute.

Down there the tents grew smaller at every step, as we moved into deeper powder snow alternating with wind-caked hard surface. The cold was pitiless, penetrating everything – our huge Himalayan boots, our fur socks, paper linings, everything. Nothing could stop our toes from losing all feeling. The only thing to do was to halt every zoo feet, and swing our legs for a couple of minutes as hard as we could – an exhausting exercise at that altitude. For all our early progress we were now moving forward very slowly. Hermann, who lost two toes on Nanga Parbat, soon had no sensation at all in his right foot. I wasn't quite so badly affected, yet we had been climbing for four hours in this murderous cold. It was eight o'clock before the first rays of the sun came to us over the col. High time, too; especially for Hermann, though by now I couldn't feel my toes at all, either. The only thing now was to get out of our boots and resort to massage. Presently Markus and Fritz, who had taken a line rather to the left for the last part, joined us and we were all sitting in the morning sun at 25,000 feet. Hermann and I went on rubbing our feet, but it took a long time to get any feeling back into them. Markus and Fritz were the first to get sensation restored, so they took over the lead from us. Eventually we put our boots on and started up after them. My own feet were perfectly all right again and I felt in good form. Not so Hermann's – he had fierce pains in his right one and went more slowly every minute. His old Nanga Parbat injuries were throbbing unbearably in his veins.

The last 700 feet up the final slope to the col is steep, bare ice; the end bit, consisting of some rocks, is very hard work indeed. We got to the col at 1.30, half an hour behind the others. Hermann was in such a bad state that he had to lie down. He didn't think he could get to the top in his condition. I suggested a rest and some food, which might help; but he only took a handful of dried prunes, some glucose and a drop of tea. His foot was hurting him fearfully.

I stared out far into the west. There in the distance rose that solitary giant, which we had already seen from the plateau, the peak where Hermann had been frostbitten, during his bivouac at 26,000 feet. But he had been to the summit first: all by himself, to that 26,620-foot summit of Nanga Parbat. He had paid a great price …

There was hardly a breath of air moving over the col, nor a tiny cloud anywhere in the sky. The sun struck down with full force. We had been there an hour, and Hermann felt a little better.

So off we went again.

We hadn't much time left, but it ought to be enough, if we didn't have to stop too often. Our only chance of getting to the top was a steady, unbroken pace. At all events, there was no doubt that our other pair would get there; for, a little earlier, we had seen the tiny figures of Markus and Fritz disappearing high up on the ridge into the almost black blueness of the sky.

Very slowly we moved on up the steep rock-and snow-ridge leading to the subsidiary summit. The ridge was plastered with huge mushroom-like cornices. The horrific precipices plunging from the east side of the central and main summits were clothed in similar amazing snow structures – mushrooms, ribs, enormous pilasters of snow. The great wall along whose top we were moving dives fully 10,000 feet into the abyss. It almost made one giddy to look down on unnamed peaks 20,000 feet high and the broad rivers of glaciers flowing away to the far horizon. We had the sensation of being incredibly high in the earth's surface. But it was still a long way to the summit …

We stopped again to rest. We went on again, fighting for oxygen for our lungs. A few yards farther on, we stopped again. Then, on again. The intervals between rests grew shorter and shorter. Our neighbour, the Central Summit, roughly 26,250 feet high, showed us how slowly we were gaining height, for it was still well above us. At last we reached the rocky step in the ridge. The chimney by which it is climbed demands an output of effort. Hermann braced himself and got up it, but after that we hardly moved forward at all. And we had still not got up to the 26,000-foot level.

We stopped on a little shoulder of snow. It was a quarter to five. Two more hours before the sun goes down. And we had been more than two hours over the short bit from the col up here. The summit was still a long way away. If we ever got to it, it would be in the dark. And then what?

We admitted then that it was too late, and it was a sad and bitter realisation. The fact was that it would be lunacy to go on, at our pace.

Could I do it alone? I wondered. I asked Hermann's permission to have a go. He knew how set I was on it, and said yes. I thanked him, promising he wouldn't have to wait very long. I would be back as soon as possible and then we could go down together.

I wanted to say something to cheer him up, but knew there was nothing to be said. There he sat in silence on the snow, staring out into the distance, staring at Nanga Parbat – and, as he sat staring at his own mountain, I knew what he was thinking …

If I was to get to the top, I must move quickly; there might just be time. I felt pretty good, as I started off up the ridge again, alone.

That slope up to the subsidiary summit is steep. I was soon gasping for breath. But presently I was above the central summit. I gritted my teeth, climbing much too quickly; but I couldn't afford to go slower. I stopped, leaning on my sticks, panting. For a moment everything went round and round. Then I saw Hermann sitting down there, still gazing out into nothingness. Never mind, I thought, I'll soon be back with you again. But now, there's the top up there, and I must get on with it. I wonder how far it is – maybe an hour? I wonder where Fritz and Markus have got to? Perhaps I shall be meeting them soon, now …

There they were, two dots on the snow of the summit slope. That's them, and they're still going up. It was a little after 5 o'clock. Come on, I said, don't hang about, there's no time to spare, and Hermann's waiting for you down there. I went at the first great humps like a madman. Then the ridge flattened out, giving way to a mixture of rock and snow. I moved as 'quickly as I could, shoving myself forwards with my ski sticks, my eyes fixed on the next two yards ahead. No time now for looking to right or to left. Now at last the summit was coming down to me at a fair pace. My breath was coming in great gusts. I was puffing like an engine. I knew I mustn't stop, or everything would go swimming around me, like a little while ago. Then I was at the last little rise to the summit. My knees wanted to sag. On you go! Only a few yards more. Steep now.

My heart thumping like mad. But there are the last few rocks, the summit snow slope, just over there ... and Markus and Fritz ...

They had just finished taking their summit photographs and were on the point of starting down. A few steps in the summit snows and they had reached me at the highest rocks. 'Could we make a summit picture?' I asked while greeting my companions. 'No time - it's too late' was the surprising answer – and not even a minute later, after another couple of words, off they went ... So strange did hit me such refusal, that in a matter of seconds I shot two instant pictures of my descending companions together with the highest rocks of our mountain, in black and white and colour ... then a third one, still wondering about this encounter. A minute later I was alone. I stood there, utterly exhausted, and looked back to the subsidiary summit. I had only taken half an hour to come up from it, so I felt I had earned a short rest. I moved up the few yards to the last steps in the trail, at the edge of the mighty summit cornice, and dropped my rucksack on the snow. What a relief to be sitting down again! My breathing soon settled down to normal and in a very short time the atmosphere didn't even seem thin any more.

Wherever I looked, a sea of peaks met my eye. Far away, over there, the Pamirs; farther to the left, all by itself, Nanga Parbat, 125 miles away as the crow flies. K2 bulked enormous, just above the subsidiary summit – 28,250 feet of it. I looked up at it in awe, realizing that my 26,400-foot perch was so noticeably lower. To balance that, I looked down and far, far below me recognised a fairly hefty dwarf; it was, in fact, the proud sharp head of Mitre Peak, 20,000 feet high. Beyond, soared Masherbrum, which had lost nothing of its magnificence. Close at the feet of Mitre Peak lay 'Concordia', my eye plunging almost 12,000 feet down upon it. Then I began to look for our route up the long waves of the Baltoro. That browny-green spot at its far end must be Paiju, the last little oasis before we took to the ice. I couldn't take my eyes off it; I hadn't seen a living green thing for six weeks ... Why, today must be Whit Sunday! At home, now, the trees must be in blossom, the meadows green with lush spring grass; at home, they will be thinking of us. All about me the great peaks stood in an immense silence. I suddenly felt terribly lonely ...

I got up. From behind the cornice those two magnificent eight-thousanders, Gasherbrum II and Hidden Peak, lifted their heads. Then I looked out to the left of the cornice, eastwards, where the ranges were lower: brown ridges with snow on them, giving way to greyish-brown plateaux, stretching away into the distance – Tibet? That cornice in front of me annoyed me. Hone could look out over it without hindrance, it would feel just like looking down out of the sky; a unique sensation, to be up above everything, with nothing but air and empty, infinite space round and about. I wondered whether it would be safe? When I tested it, I found the cornice was solid névé, a nice permanent structure. Finally I stood clear, with nothing between me and the view, nothing but thin air all round me. I gazed eastwards for a long time over those extraordinary depths, far into the unknown, which must be Tibet. An unbounded loneliness lay on that landscape. There was something incomprehensible about it, though what, I could not say. Then I brought my eyes down to the glittering rim of snow at my feet, which was the ultimate edge of Broad Peak. I let my ski stick roam over the curve of it, but that was the limit of my climbing.

It was time to go. Hermann would be waiting down there. I was on my way down the summit snow slope, when I stopped in my tracks and took another look around. What more could I want? I had seen everything. I had been on the summit. What was I waiting for? I didn't even know myself.

I hurried on down, leaving the topmost rocks and the summit snows farther and farther behind. At my feet lay the undulations of the long, almost level crest. It was all over. Was I really happy? Was that the hour of which I had dreamed ever since I first set foot on a mountain? Down there on the ridge, my ropemate was sitting, the man with whom I had hoped to climb the summit. And what about the summit itself? It had been impressive, the prospect from it overpowering; but the picture in my imagination, my fantasy summit, outshone it by far.

I stopped again and looked back towards the top, with the trail clearly etched in the snow. Yes, it was all over. I had been up there. It was the climax of a climbing-life – it was the Thing itself. But how utterly different. What a pity! My dream picture was fading into paleness. It is so still and silent up here, and I am tired and very lonely …

I hurried down as fast as I could go; but I was no longer moving as quickly as I should have liked. All the same, half of the crest was behind me now; in a moment the subsidiary summit must pop up behind a rib of rock. Hermann wouldn't have too long to wait now. We should be able to get well below the precipice under the col before daylight failed for he would be rested now …

Hermann had remained sitting on the shoulder for a while, then he had felt better; so he took an expert's survey of the steep slope to the subsidiary summit. It didn't look so bad, after all. Yes, he must get up as far as that, at all costs. And after that? Suddenly he knew he would go on beyond it too. Slowly, with all that incredible strength of his will, he started to move, very slowly, upwards. The slope was inhuman and never seemed to end. But Hermann's willpower was even more endlessly in conquerable. Yard by yard he drew nearer to the subsidiary summit, and there on its crest he met his two teammates, Fritz and Markus, coming down. 'How much farther? 'Oh, a good hour.' And so, trusting to his Nanga Parbat luck, Hermann went on. He was determined to get to the top now, even if it was in the dark.

The Summit of Dreams

I was still up at 26,000 feet, breathing several times to each step I took. It was slightly uphill again. There were the now familiar rocks. Then the subsidiary summit came into view again, with K2 bulking high above it. I took note of it vaguely and looked down over the hump in the ridge ahead of me. What on earth was that? I stood rooted to the spot. A yellow dot? It must be a hallucination. But it was moving, and it was an anorak. It was Hermann. 'Hermann!' I shouted.

How on earth had he managed it? In the state he was in? Nobody else could have done it. I was amazed, no almost shattered, by such an incredible exhibition of willpower. And now, surely, we would be able to go up to the summit together …

Hermann kept on coming up, slowly, step by step, his face drawn, his eyes set straight ahead. Then he was with me. I wanted to say what I felt, but the words wouldn't come. I was just glad that he was here, with me.

It was close on half past six. The sun's light lay quite flat on the crest of the ridge. The Baltoro lay swamped in shadow. The peaks below us seemed incredibly plastic in the horizontal illumination. The sun would be down any minute now.

Surely it would be madness to go on to the summit now? I started worrying about it. Our assault camp was 3,600 feet down there; and here we were climbing up into the night. But Hermann Buhl was going on ahead of me. Hermann, who had already once spent a night at 26,000 feet. Why not this one, too? True enough, he had had unbelievable luck that time. Would we have the same good fortune now? And if we didn't – what matter? I spent a moment savouring the thought; then an extraordinary thing happened.

Suddenly everything was so natural that I could laugh about it all; about the fears of all the others down below there, their fears about their lives, my own fear of a little moment ago. Now, for the first time, I was truly at one with the heights up here. The world down there lay bottomlessly far below, and utterly devoid of meaning. I no longer belonged to it. Even my first climb to the summit was already remote beyond words. What had it brought me? Boundless astonishment that it had all been so different from my anticipation, utter disappointment. That was all, and it was all forgotten already. But now the true summit was up there, bathed in unearthly light, as in a dream.

The shapes of the huge snow mushrooms grew ever more ghostly, their shadows strangely like faces. Everything seemed alive; and there in front of me on the level snow went Hermann's long shadow, bending, straightening, even jumping. It was deathly still. The sun was almost down. Could anything in life be so beautiful?

I stopped for a moment, leaning heavily on my sticks, then moved on, smiling to myself. There was Hermann going on ahead. We were going on to the top together. Yes, we were going to it in the dark; but ahead of us gleamed a radiance, enfolding every wish life could conjure, enfolding life itself.

Now was the moment of ineffable truth – the silence of space around us, ourselves silent. This was utter fulfilment. The sun bent trembling to the horizon. Down there was the night, and under it the world. Only up here, and for us, was there light. Close over yonder the Gasherbrum summits glittered in all their magic; a little farther away, Chogolisa's heavenly roof-tree. Straight ahead, against the last light, K2 reared its dark and massive head. Soft as velvet, all colours merging into a single dark gleam. The snow was suffused with a deep orange tint, while the sky was a remarkable azure. As I looked out, an enormous pyramid of darkness projected itself over the limitless wastes of Tibet, to lose itself in the haze of impalpable distance – the shadow of Broad Peak.

There we stood, speechless, and shook hands in silence. Down on the horizon a narrow strip of sunlight flickered – a beam of light reached out above and across the darkness towards us, just caressing the last few feet of our summit. We looked down at the snow underfoot, and to our amazement it seemed to be aglow.

Then the light went out.

The west face of Broad Peak lay drenched in the pale illumination of the moon. There were deep shadows among the rocky steps of the subsidiary summit. Presently we were among them, looking for the way down. It was not easy and we roped up for safety. The chimney was particularly difficult in the darkness, but just before the col we were out in the full light of the moon. Then we started down the steep face.

Camp was still nearly 3,000 feet below. Hermann felt a little better now, but we were both dog-tired; too tired to risk a bivouac. So, on we went, down and down.

We must have been going for untold aeons. We halted at the edge of a crevasse, nodding. The ascent was a dark memory now. There was still half the descent to be negotiated. Down in the depths there was a vague gleam, which must be the plateau. It gave us the rough direction, but it never seemed to come any nearer. It seemed quite impossible to get any nearer to it.

'What are we sitting here for? We ought to go on down. It would be lovely to go to sleep.' Somehow we staggered to our feet and started down again. Down and down. Endlessly, eternally down …

It was half past midnight before we got to the tents. We opened the flap and crawled in. In, and into the blessed haven of our sleeping bags. 'Oh, sleep it is a gentle thing … '

Safely back at base camp together, we were all looking up at our mountain, as the evening sun turned its high summit to molten gold. And I gave thanks to fortune for the fulfilment of the greatest wish in my life.

The shining radiance of that great peak will be with me all my days.

Chogolisa

It was by now mid-June. There was a fly sitting on the tent roof and a spider mountaineering on a boulder. The ice had melted steadily and our Base Camp tents were perched on lofty plinths. We were slowly recovering from our exertions and spent the time writing reports and letters: 'All four members of the expedition reached the summit of Broad Peak on 9 June by the shortest and best route, employing neither high-altitude porters nor oxygen equipment ...' The sun was beating down on the roof of our tent. We were surrounded by the white glitter of high peaks. 'We intend to stay here a little longer and do a few gentle climbs – maybe one or other of the six- or seven-thousanders ...'

Down there in the valleys it must be high summer. It even makes itself felt a little up here. I lay in my sun-warmed tent and, while the melting ice streams gurgled away outside, I kept on picking out from among my home mail (we were so much at world's end that the latest the mail-runners had brought up the glacier were six weeks' old) a picture postcard, with a meadow, a tree and, in the background, a little lake on it. On the back was written: 'I am here on a little walking-tour. Tchau!' The card was from Busle, and the tree was a real tree. (How long since I saw a real tree?) Then I re-read her last letter, which came from Norway. 'I have come to the far north,' she wrote, 'I can't describe to you how big that world is – something that I can't explain.' She could not describe that great world of the north, which I had never seen. An odd idea occurred to me. Hadn't I, too, penetrated a great world which I could not describe to anyone, not even to her? Up there on the summit ridge of an eight-thousander? When I got home would I be the same person I was before I came out here? I took another thoughtful look at that tree. Oh, I should like to be going home this very minute! I looked up and saw the great peaks that ringed us, Chogolisa's heavenly roof-tree, the séracs of the Baltoro glacier. Here I was, once in a lifetime. I wrote her a letter from one remote world to another.

Chogolisa is a magic mountain.

It is so lovely that the statistic of its height, 25,110 feet, seems irrelevant. The British had long ago christened it 'Bride Peak', because it is always entirely clad in white. A white rhombus, an icy roof, high up in the heavens. Dyhrenfurth, when he wrote his book about the Baltoro, remarked: 'Its classic beauty of form and the repose of its outlines stamp it as the ideal ice mountain.' Only when seen from a distance of some twenty miles does it reveal, at the left-hand end of its great pitched roof, a minute dark tooth, the small rock turret of its summit. The mighty south-east ridge, sweeping up for something like three miles, catches the full sun from early morning onwards – a great advantage – and it was as long ago as 1909 that the Duke of the Abruzzi's expedition attempted to reach the summit by it. At 24,600 feet, only 500 below the top of that immense roof, they were forced by a storm to retreat; and, for a long, long time that remained the greatest height achieved by man. Nor had anyone reached the summit since.

On our ascent of Broad Peak we had all marvelled at that beautiful mountain to the south of us; but much nearer, to the west, there had been splendid peaks in the Savoia group which had caught our eye as possible secondary objectives. In the end Hermann, who like the rest of us had made a good recovery while resting at base camp, was especially attracted by Mitre Peak and the Trango Tower; besides which we also wanted to visit the Gasherbrum glacier and reconnoitre Gasherbrum IV – or at least take a close look at it from there.

However, the first consideration was to evacuate the Broad Peak camps. Markus and Fritz, taking Captain Quader with them, cleared camp I; and while Hermann and I went all the way up again to deal with II and III, Markus and Fritz, on short skis, went over to the Savoia glacier and climbed the group's highest peak, a fine summit over 23,000 feet high. This lightning foray came as a great surprise to Hermann and myself, who had no idea they had such a venture in mind. We turned our eyes southwards: we would make Chogolisa and the Gasherbrum glacier our programme. And we, too, would carry it out as a two-man expedition. Regarding the Pakistani government rules for expeditions such an enterprise could not be done without a special permission, but Hermann Buhl and I, after asking our Liaison officer for it got the kind and clear assurance: 'they got their peak – you have your peak' – with Chogolisa as an icy roof visible from the kitchen tent, where we asked him. After the tragedy – and ever since then – our Liaison Officer denied and denies to have ever given us such permission … but one should keep in mind, that the consequence for him would for sure have been terrible.

The One-Runged Ladder

Chogolisa would demand several high camps, that was obvious. Yet we could not carry more than one tent. The solution was daring: a single transportable high camp – a ladder of camps consisting of a single tent. Herbert Tichy and his Sherpa had worked their way up Gurla Mandhata in Tibet that way. So our single tent should serve as our base camp and all succeeding camps, I, II and III, as necessary; a single rung in a ladder which we would push up the mountain day by day.

After Hermann and I had decided, during the course of 10 June, exactly what we should need for our attempt on the peak, I went on ahead that evening towards Concordia, carrying about eighty pounds. Hermann who still had some things to fetch from the foot of Broad Peak, followed me early next morning, humping a similar load. Thanks to the marker-pennants I had planted, there was no difficulty about re-joining one another, and we were able to push on together, late in the afternoon, over the endless humps of the Baltoro's central moraine. By evening we had found a marvellous site for our base camp close to the enormous ice falls at the bottom of Chogolisa, and there we pitched our tent. High overhead soared the mountain's fantastic roof; wherever we looked, we saw nothing but ice and snow.

In spite of that, Hermann thought our climb would only take a few days; after it, we might still turn our attentions to Mitre Peak. The Gasherbrum glacier and more especially Gasherbrum IV were perhaps rather too far to contemplate.

On the 22nd we were already halfway up Chogolisa's ice falls and laid a depot down on a ridge of hard snow we found there. The next day, the weather was bad; we decided not to wait too long, but to push on as far as we could get.

'24 June: 4.30 a.m. off with tent; snowing gently; weather nothing special; going very well; 7.30 a.m. depot at 18,000 feet; rucksack, with depot material, about fifty-five pounds; on up the Spur in knee-deep snow; trail broken all the way to the Kaberi Saddle; about 5 p.m., pitched camp at 20,900 feet; whole route marked with pennants.'

What was the story behind these cryptic entries of Hermann's? First of all, that he was in splendid condition. In spite of the deep snow, he broke the trail all the way up to the Kaberi Saddle and would not hear of my relieving him in the lead. Secondly, that on that first day of ours we climbed 4,600 feet. (These facts should, I hope, convince anyone who imagines that it was an enfeebled Hermann Buhl who tackled Chogolisa, beyond any doubt, that the contrary was the case. Certainly every mountaineer will recognise it.) Moreover we were carrying anything up to sixty-five pounds on our backs and, in view of our rapid progress in spite of poor weather, our spirits were very high. After heating a drink on our hissing cooker with great difficulty, we went happily to sleep in our first Chogolisa camp.

Next day, Tuesday the 25th, the weather was bad again. We stayed in our sleeping bags till ten o'clock, cooked a meal and, at 1 p.m. struck our tent and, in spite of knee-deep snow, climbed to the shoulder in Chogolisa's South-east Ridge, at a height of 22,000 feet. There we erected our tent again, this time as camp II. We were now high enough to warrant a direct attempt on the summit. All we had to do was to wait for fine weather ...

Towards dawn on the 26th a furious storm blew up. It leaned against the outside of the tent and we against its inside. Luckily we had anchored it well. A few feet higher up, bedlam had broken loose. The wind was screaming over the shoulder with unremitting fury. When at last, after several hours, the walls of the tent stopped flapping, we went out, intending to go up a little way towards the crest we called 'Ridge Peak' and stretch our legs. It was only then that we realised how sheltered our tent site was. Up on the shoulder we were almost blown away. The rope curved out in a wide festoon, parallel with the ground, weightless, airborne. Ridge Peak looked down on us through clouds of blown snow, flecked here and there by the sun, and the air was full of the howling of the storm, a mighty symphony.

We were soon back in our sleeping bags, hatching out future plans. In the autumn, Hermann wanted me to come with him on a double traverse of Mont Blanc, by all its great ridges. Then, the following year, perhaps, we would have a go at Rakaposhi ...

Towards evening the barometer began to rise again and we cheerfully fell to packing our things for the morrow. Then it suddenly cleared, and through the entrance to the tent we saw Baltoro Kangri, sublime in the light of the evening sun ... we might climb it after Chogolisa ...

The Last Day

27 June dawned clear, fine and calm, a veritable gift of the Gods. We were happy beyond words. Our rest day had done us good, and we felt brimming over with fitness, and a burning zeal to bag the summit.

We were off at about a quarter to five. It was still very cold, but we knew it couldn't be for very long. The sky grew lighter and lighter above Baltoro Kangri. To the south lay a sea of summits, peaks about 20,000 to 23,000 feet high, and hardly even explored. To the north the sun was already touching K2. Between us and it, Broad Peak displayed only its main summit, masking the other two.

Almost as soon as we had got our legs moving, the warmth of the sun reached us. We tramped happily up over the glittering snow. Free of our loads, we made unbelievably easy progress. The going was excellent on the very crest of the ridge, but the snow was deep and trying on either side; besides which, the wind had formed dangerous wind-slabs on the slope. One of them broke away quite close to us and went thundering down in a fair sized avalanche to the level plateau of the Kaberi Saddle below. It made quite an impression on us and we stuck carefully to the crest of the ridge, which was so far uncorniced. But how would things go up there on Ridge Peak, where we could see cornices several yards wide projecting unpleasantly in a continuous hem? No doubt the storm of the previous day had notably increased their size.

At 23,000 feet we left the ridge, by now corniced, and traversed a little way across a smooth ice slope to reach a projection farther up. There were actually a few rocks here, quite a curiosity on this mountain. And what about the route above? Ye Gods! There was the summit, just over there! It couldn't be any great distance and it certainly didn't look difficult. We ought to be up on it by midday, we thought.

Indeed, the next bit was easy; the slope flattened out appreciably and all we had to do was to keep along it to the deep notch beyond Ridge Peak. We made light of turning the huge cornices which towered over us to the right. Chogolisa's immense roof drew rapidly nearer, but after a quarter of an hour we had to admit it wasn't going to be easy. The slope grew steeper and the sector of ridge rising behind it had a distinctly airy look. Then suddenly we could see the whole route, and there was nothing about it to be lightly dismissed. The ridge down to the notch was as sharp as a knife blade, its left-hand side a giddily steep precipice of rock and ice, to its right great cornices hanging far out over the North Face. We should have to be very careful there. The rock precipices below us kept on forcing us farther up towards the jagged white crest. We belayed carefully with the rope, watching for avalanches. A small wind-slab did in fact break away and went sliding away into the abyss. The snow conditions were really a curse. Just as we got to the rocks, Hermann went through to his waist, and hardly had he scrambled out when he was sitting in another hole. Damn it, the slope was a positive honeycomb! Hermann balanced his way forward as if walking on eggshells – lucky man, he didn't weigh much. He reached ice-plastered rocks and moved from foothold to foothold with incredible delicacy of balance, hardly touching the holds as he moved. A moment later he disappeared over a rib. 'Up you come!' I could hear him calling.

Rope's length by rope's length, we worked our way along the ridge, sometimes on the slope, sometimes right up at the edge of the cornices. Steadily, the wind passed over the crest; glittering snow rose towards the deep blue dome of the sky. Down in the south there were huge clouds now. But they did not move.

We had made good time in spite of the unexpected difficulties. It was only 9 o'clock when we reached the saddle at 23,000 feet. And there, only 2,000 feet above us, was the sharp tip of the turret on the long crest of the summit ridge. A steep, but for the most part broad, ridge of snow led up to it.

We sat down in a sheltered hollow, in glorious warm sunshine, and took off the rope. We were ravenous; what about a drop of tea and those delicacies we had saved up for our trip to the top? 'This is the best day for me since I came out with the expedition,' mused Hermann. How well I understood him. Climbing a seven-thousander in three days ... not in three weeks!' This was just his pigeon – very different from what he went through on Broad Peak. I shared his obvious delight.

We didn't move on for a whole long hour. When we did, we took alternate leads in deep snow. We were unroped now. It was enough to carry the rope with us in the rucksack, Hermann said, so I did not think much about it. A steep pitch with a short ice cliff called for work with the axe; after that it was easy again. Occasional cracks in the slope spelled avalanche danger. They pushed us out farther on to the brink of the precipice than we had intended.

Ridge Peak was gradually sinking below and behind us. To the south, the great mountainous banks of cloud were moving very slowly nearer. The sky was calm and of a deep, deep blue. The banner of snow blowing from Ridge Peak seemed to have grown a little. To the north lay a tremendous prospect: all the giants of the Baltoro lined up in a row, a whole chain of peaks 26,000 feet high or only just less. We let our gaze range in wonderment from K2 to Hidden Peak. We took photographs and then moved on again.

How quickly the clouds were coming towards us now! We hoped they wouldn't interfere With our view from the top. We quickened our pace. The last steep pitch began a little way up there, and close above it we could see the tower that was the summit – 1,500 feet at the most – *that* couldn't take so very long.

Presently a little cloud came climbing up the slope below us. It grew larger, enveloping us, enveloping the peak. Without any warning, all hell broke loose. Grey veils of mist scurried across the ridge. Unnatural darkness swamped us. We fought our way forward through clouds of blown snow, bending double to meet the fury of the gale. On the crest of the ridge it flung itself upon us in full blast, snatching at our clothes, trying to claw us from our footing. It was terribly cold and the needles of ice blowing down into our faces hurt savagely. We could only see the next yard or two ahead. We kept on changing the lead, struggling grimly upwards.

It didn't seem possible. I thought of the blue sky such a short time back. It had all been so quick. I had an uncanny feeling – hadn't exactly the same thing happened to the Duke of the Abruzzi, quite close to the summit? Were we going to be robbed, too? Away with such stupid thoughts; it was only a few hundred feet, and we had got to do it.

It grew lighter for a moment, as the wind parted the driving clouds. We stood rooted, looking up to where the summit must be. There it was, near enough to touch, looming darkly above us. An instant later the wrack had swallowed it up again.

The storm continued its horrific din. Laboriously we moved up, with a steep, bottomless precipice below us, keeping close to the ridge crest. Everything was white now and we could hardly see.

We were at about 24,000 feet. Only another thousand to the summit tower. Suddenly Hermann spoke: 'We've got to turn back at once, or the wind will cover our tracks up, and then we shall stray out on to the cornices!' He was quite right. We hadn't given a thought to it; and now visibility was almost nil.

We should have to hurry. We turned then and there. Hermann had been leading, so I was in front now. He followed at a safe distance of ten to fifteen yards, which was all that visibility would permit.

Bent double, I felt my way downwards. It was incredible – only 150 feet down, there was no trace to be seen of our upward trail, except the deep holes made by our axes. Very soon there wouldn't be very many of *them*. And still the tempest kept up its infernal din.

I reckoned we must be at about 23,600 feet, and that we must be near the steep avalanche slope which had pushed us so close to the cornices. If only one could see a bit more! I turned and saw Hermann coming after me, keeping the distance unaltered, following in my actual steps. As I moved down, I kept on looking across to the left, trying to see through the mist. All I could see was that it was getting a bit darker overhead and a bit lighter below. That must be the edge of the cornices. It seemed a safe distance away, but in mist distances can be deceptive. Perhaps it would be better to keep a bit to the right, but then I should have to look out for the precipice. It ought to be here by now. Ah, there's another axe hole …

I looked anxiously to the left and then down to the surface at my feet. I was at a loss; it was almost impossible to see anything at all. *Crack!* Something shot through me like a shock. Everything shook, and for a second the surface of the snow seemed to shrink. Blindly, I jumped sideways to the right – an instantaneous reflex action – two, three great strides, and followed the steep slope downwards a little way, shattered by what I had seen at my feet – the rim of the cornice, with little jagged bits breaking away from it. My luck had been in, all right! I had been clean out on the cornice. What would Hermann have to say about that, I wondered? I stopped and turned, but the curve of the slope prevented my seeing over the crest as I looked up. The light was improving a little. Hermann must bob up any moment up there. I still couldn't fathom that extraordinary shaking sensation; had the snow really settled under my weight?

Still no Hermann. 'Hermann!' I shouted. 'For God's sake, what's up? Hermann!' I rushed, gasping up the slope. There it was, the crest … and beyond it, smooth snow … and it was empty … Hermann … You! …

Done for …

I dragged myself up a little farther. I could see his last footmarks in the snow, then the jagged edge of the broken cornice, yawning. Then the black depths.

The broken cornice – that had been the quaking beneath my feet, then.

I couldn't get a sight of the North Face from anywhere near. I should have to get down to Ridge Peak for that. As I went down, the storm gradually abated, and the mists lifted from time to time. I was utterly stunned. How could that have happened just behind me? I had the greatest difficulty in getting up the short rise to Ridge Peak, but even before I got there it had cleared up. I hurried out to the farthest edge of the cliffs.

The storm was hunting the clouds high into the heavens. Above the veils of mist and through them a ridge loomed up – a tower – a great roof with tremendous banners of blown snow streaming from it. Chogolisa, the horrible. I could see the spot where we had turned at about 24,000 feet. Our trail down the broad snowfield below was crystal clear. Then that fearsome drop to the north – into the clouds. And there, even closer to our tracks as they ran straight downwards, the encroaching precipice. And then I could see it all with stark and terrible clarity. Just at that point, Hermann had left my tracks at a slight bend, where I was hugging the rim of the precipice, and gone straight on ahead, only three or four yards – straight out on to the tottering rim of the cornice – straight out into nothingness. Of the foot of the wall I could see nothing. Stupidly, I stared upwards again.

If we had been roped …

I looked down along the face, shuddering …

No, I should never have been able to hold him there; at the moment of his fall I myself was too far out on the overhanging snow.[1]

At last I could see clearly down below, where the broad snow-masses of an avalanche fanned out. The crashing cornice had set it off and it had swept the face clean. Hermann was nowhere to be seen. He must have fallen at least 1,000, maybe 2,000 feet and was lying there buried under the piled-up snow. Could he have survived that? There was no answer to my shouts and I had no way of getting down there. I should have to fetch the others and we should have to come from below. That was the only faint possibility. I strained my eyes, searching every cranny, searching for a rucksack, a ski stick, a dark blob. But there was nothing to be seen – absolutely nothing. Only our tracks – up there …

Clouds blotted the mountain out again. I was alone.

Mists and a high wind were sweeping the corniced ridge as I tried to find the way down. At times I could see nothing at all and could only tell from rifts in the snow that I had strayed too far down the slope. After what seemed an age, I found our tent. It was a horror of emptiness. I took the absolute essentials for the descent and went on down. At the Kaberi Saddle there was knee-deep fresh snow, through which only a tiny corner of the marker-pennants showed. I probed with my feet under that smooth expanse of white to find out from which side our ascent route had come, then went straight on into the whiteness … to the next pennant. I wandered vaguely down endless hollows, over crevasses, through fog, then into the darkness of night. For long, indescribable hours of horror – during which I at times had a feeling that Hermann was still with me – I managed, by some miracle, to find my way, onwards, downwards. Then, just before the great icefalls, my pocket-lamp failed; so I had to bivouac

---

1 Though, perhaps, the pull of the rope would have kept him in my tracks, and he might never have strayed from the right line of descent. – K.D.

A similar thought was expressed by Othmar Gurtner, commenting on the author's account in *The Mountain World*, 1958–1959. – Translator's note.

at 18,000 feet. In the first pale light of dawn I made my way down the icefalls. On and on … endlessly on … till, twenty-seven hours after Hermann's fall, I tottered into base camp.

The search which followed found absolutely nothing.

Once again, the monstrous rubble-covered river of ice lay freed of all human presence. The sun burned down on it with scorching intensity. The snow was rapidly vanishing, melting into the waters of gurgling glacier streams. Chogolisa's white roof-tree seemed to lift into the very sky itself. The great peaks stood silently all around. Were they, too, mourning? Or was this only the great healing silence which eternally enfolds all living and dying?

The engines droned as we flew down the Indus Valley, with mountains close on either hand, sharp spires past which we floated. Steep ridges thrusting up; an occasional glimpse back to the giant Baltoro peaks … K2, Broad Peak … already distant, as the minutes sundered us from the months. We should soon be seeing Nanga Parbat.

My thoughts went back to our inward flight, when the weather had been bad. I could see Hermann's face, as his eyes bored into the grey clouds for a sight of his mountain. At last he had spoken. 'We'll only fly back on a fine day,' he said.

Today was a fine day.

The savage peaks ahead parted, and only then did we realise that they were only low wing-pieces to that great stage setting. High above them there was a shimmer of white; snow banners rose to the heavens. There it stood, the mountain – immutable, immense, imperishable – Nanga Parbat.

We could see its dazzling glaciers, and the summit crowning them. Above it the sky stretched blue-black and deep – as if yet another sky were climbing, incessantly, over and up it – up to an infinity of heights and depths.

Hermann Buhl.

Silver banners, ever-growing up into that dark vault.

Part 3

13   The North Face of the Eiger

A child was playing snowballs.

It was dirty, grey snow, the last relics of winter on the flower-strewn meadows of a slope, high in the Bernese Oberland. The child ran from one patch of snow to the next, made snowballs and threw them into the flowers, where they broke into glittering dust.

We went on, up over the meadows. Tona, Hilde and I had come up from Grindelwald by chairlift. It was a gloriously fine day.

Tona is my fair-haired wife. I met her in Milan on a lecture tour; she was studying geology then. We went up into the mountains, we fell in love, we married – three years after my Broad Peak adventure. And now we were taking Hildegard, our equally blonde daughter, on an excursion.

Over there, across the valley, the Eiger stood sombre, only the long sweep of the Mittelegi Ridge and the snow on the very summit brightly lit by the sun's rays, dazzling white, making the North Face seem darker still by contrast.

I would not try it again; once was enough. Yet I understood well enough why I had done it, as I looked up at the Mittelegi, glittering white, and the dark North Face winging upwards.

'Papa – why did you climb the Eiger?' Hilde asked me. Tona was smiling; the green slopes lay warm under the sun. What should I say?

'I can't explain it exactly,' I replied. 'But the Eiger is big and high.'

'M'm ... ' She did not seem very convinced, and nor was I. Then she laughed and started all over again to run from one patch of snow to another, making snowballs, throwing them into the green grass. Ah, thought I, she can't be racking her brains about it any longer ...

Then, suddenly, she came back, stopped, and looked at me with a little smile. 'Do you know'; she asked, 'why I should like to climb the Eiger?'

'No'; I said, deeply curious now to know. 'Tell me, then.'

She laid that fair head of hers a little on one side, crushed the last remnants of a snowball in her palms, and looking up at the summit with her bright eyes, spoke deliberately, pausing several times, as if carefully weighing the meaning of her words.

'I ... the Eiger ... I should go up ... to make snowballs ... you see ... the snow is much whiter up there.'

That is just how she said it.

Why do we do these things? Because we enjoy them? Standing at the foot of the Eiger's North Face, I very much doubted it.

A huge, dark triangle rises sheer above the meadows of Alpiglen. There is no life in it, only cold rock. A monstrous slab composed of stone; of grey, riven ice fields, of crumbling bastions … a labyrinth of glassy runnels and ice-encrusted niches between polished steps of rock, rising vertical – like storeys of a house set one on top of the other – right up into the clouds.

That is the Eiger – a world of shadow, ice and silence: a silence broken occasionally by the rattle of falling stones, audible right down to the meadows at its foot.

Rébuffat once described it as 'a stone standing in a flower garden'. It has never been better described. The base of the 'stone' is two and a half miles long, about half of which is occupied by the North Face. As to its height – if you could lodge the three Zinnen like a child's bricks, one on top of the other, the Western on the Grosse, and the Kleine on top of that – they would still fail to reach the Eiger's summit by hundreds of feet. So it is not surprising that, when you look up it from its base, the ground seems to give way beneath you – for that face is 6,000 feet high.

Six thousand feet … between the meadows at its feet and the clouds on its 13,000-foot summit rises a surface which, on the flat, could accommodate a city. Yet, a city is an expression of man's life and activity; the Eiger was not made for human beings. Because it stands entirely on its own and wide open to the west, every break in the weather smites it first and with insensate fury. Its inward-curving cavity is like a dark, empty shell tilted against the sky. The clouds which get trapped in it cannot get out again; they cling to the face, circling endlessly between the tremendous ribs enclosing that hollow space, until they eventually dissipate or are sucked up over the summit by the north-westerly gale. Even when the face is clear and windless again, everyone who stands at its foot and looks up into the curved recess feels that something defying all description lies locked in that hushed amphitheatre. Does that concave face embrace the dimension of death itself; of the negation of everything?

The Eiger's face was not made for human beings; its artillery of falling stones strikes blindly. That wall transcends all concepts of battle and victory, of life and death. At least it did till men came and imported them. Men who lived and thought there under that hail of stones, in the whirling fury of the tempest, at the very limits of their being. Men who sought to penetrate that inhuman dimension of the North Face, by trying to climb it …

It is an unnatural, outsize dimension, beyond human ken. It is also a dimension whose secret no one can resist.

Certainly I, for one, could not.

Wolfi and I were determined to climb the North Face – we two together, and alone together; neither of us wanted to do it with anyone else. For if we understood anything it was that this would stretch us to the utmost.

During the years when succeeding summers had seen us climbing together in the Western and Eastern Alps, we had become a partnership on the rope in which each of us knew he could depend utterly on the other, no matter what situation might arise. A rope like that can tackle anything ...

We had become friends.

When we arrived to try our luck, there had been twelve successful attempts. It might have been thirteen, but no one knew for certain – Notdurft and Mayer were 'presumed dead' in the exit cracks. Gonda and Wyss, too, had all but got to the top, when a small snow slide swept them to their death from the last few easy feet of the summit slope. The historians had disallowed the climb because they had not actually stood on the summit of the mountain. So the total remained at twelve, during which thirty-eight people had reached the summit; seventeen had died in the attempt. For the last five years before we came, one vain attempt after another had been made to achieve the thirteenth successful climb. Stefano Longhi's body was still hanging roped to the face. Nobody had been able to reach him, for he had died in a rather inaccessible place, way off the normal route, high up on the level of the 'Spider', that notorious ice funnel, from which curving gullies, likewise filled with ice, reach out into the dark face in all directions like the legs of an insect.

Obviously, Wolfi and I could not shut our eyes to all those facts, and we were just as anxious to go on living as anyone else. Nor did we want to take any risks – so far as it is possible to avoid them on the Eiger's North Face. We had always climbed with the greatest care, and now we intended to apply an even greater degree of caution to our formidable task. What we did not intend to do, was to abandon our plan – nor, we knew, would the others who were here with the same objective in mind ...

And who were these others?

One of the great attractions, when one arrives at the foot of the Matterhorn or Mont Blanc, the Civetta's gigantic wall, the Drei Zinnen or the Bregaglia peaks; as one strolls through the streets of Chamonix or Courmayeur – or, in this case, Grindelwald – is to see who is there; for one knows that one may at any moment meet old acquaintances, climbers with whom one has stood on some peak or other, or even friends whom one has not seen for years past.

So we were soon exchanging greetings with Ante Makohta and the slim, fair-haired Nadja from Ljubljana – Nadja Fajdiga, one of the best women climbers anywhere, not only in Jugoslavia. They too were waiting for their great chance – settled weather conditions. Their much-patched, sun-bleached tent was meanwhile pitched on an alp high up near Alpiglen. The only things that could disturb a climber's idyllic peace up there at the foot of the Eiger were cows, and inquisitive people, who wanted to know what the rope was for. And so, as every summer, there were quite a few tents to be seen about the place.

One of them belonged to Hias Noichl, that indestructible guide and proprietor of a ski-school at St Johann-in-Tirol. He and those two cheerful cosmopolitans, Herbert Raditschnig and Lothar Brandler had also set their sights on the Eiger. At the moment, Herbert and Lothar were busy serving savoury rarebits, good solid *Berner Röschti* or a Swiss fondue to the guests of the Hotel Gletschergarten in Grindelwald. To see them in their white jackets and black bowties hurrying hither and thither, light-footed – with a smiling 'of course' … 'thank you' … 'immediately' … 'ready now!' on their lips, you would have thought they had never done anything else in their lives. Today Lothar is a film producer and Herbert travels the world year in, year out, as a cameraman.

They too were waiting to tackle the Eiger. Their rucksacks were ready, packed; they could exchange their white jackets for anoraks any day, but the weather gave them no encouragement. It had not only to be fine; it had to be settled. For they too wanted to take as few risks as possible – the Eiger was dangerous enough under a blue sky; and even if you wore a helmet, you couldn't crawl under it for complete protection. So they were biding their time and had gone into the hotel business for a change.

I saw a quiet middle-aged man sitting in a corner, writing. He had high forehead and craggy features. It was Heini Harrer, who in the summer of 1938, with his friends, Anderl Heckmair, Wiggerl Vorg and Fritz Kasparek, had been the first to find the way to the summit up the North Face, after a bitter struggle lasting three days – the last part in appalling weather, but then the Eiger has spared nobody so far in that respect. Now he was working on his history of the North Face, which turned out to be a splendid book and a bestseller, not only in mountaineering circles; for today Frau Schulze in Hamburg and Signor Rossi in Milan have read all about the North Face[1]. It is not without good cause that so many telescopes are to be seen everywhere around Grindelwald, trained on the Eiger, and surrounded by the gay tribe of holidaymakers.

Does that bother the climbers on the face, as he crouches against the rock, his nose pressed against cold ice, with the stones hailing down on him? Not in the least: he has plenty of other things to worry about.

Our base camp was in the cellar of a carpenter's shop at Grund, just below Grindelwald.

---

1 So has John Smith in Birmingham. In 1959, the translator of this book had the great pleasure of converting Harrer's *Die Weisse Spinne* into *The White Spider*, widely read by the general public here too. – H.M.

It was an ideal lodging; we were wonderfully comfortable among empty packing cases and racks, which enabled us to sort and separate to our heart's content the considerable baggage our small expedition had brought along. But first we did something even better; we carried an old armchair, a packing case and a table out into the garden. There, surrounded by flowers and a variety of vegetables, we could sit in the sun, with the Eiger high overhead. Then we bought a few postcards with harmless views of the neighbourhood – huts up on the Alps, the gentlemen who blow the alpine horn, a stream with clouds above it and – yes, we even found one in the end! – Grindelwald minus the Eiger. These we dispatched to uncles and aunts, and to all our near and dear ones who, we knew, might worry if they heard that anyone was on the North Face again. 'We are having a lovely time,' we wrote. 'We have done a couple of amusing climbs and are now resting here. After that we want to do the traverse of a splendid ridge. Don't worry about us.' It was all perfectly true, even the bit about the Schreckhorn-Lauteraarhorn traverse. This was to be our final training climb before we committed ourselves to the face; a fact we naturally didn't mention.

With us at the time were our friends, Franz Lindner and 'Charlie' Schonthaler. Franz, that calm, imperturbable character, we shall meet again in this book, on the Peuterey Ridge of Mont Blanc. Charlie, a carefree enthusiast in every aspect of life, who came from the Tyrol, has just returned with me from the great faces of the Bernina Group. After his very first experience of digging crampons into the sheer ice of the *Klucker Route* on the North East Face of Piz Roseg, he had struck brilliant form, as we did the North Face of Piz Palu, the North East Face of Piz Bernina, the ice nose on Piz Scerscen and, to crown everything, the first ascent of the *direttissima* on the North East Face of Piz Roseg's main summit. He was fully qualified for the Eiger, but he knew I wanted to go with Wolfi and fully understood. During the following days he helped me, in the most unselfish manner, to transport all our equipment up to our 'high camp' at the foot of the face, while Wolfi was doing one more climb with Franz. Today Charlie is a ski instructor, alternating between Australia, Squaw Valley and Kitzbühel and, if you are lucky, you may even meet him in Munich, which is supposed to be his hometown.

There was not much more to be done, now. The rocks of the Wetterhorn glowed reddish-brown in the sunset, but a huge fish-shaped cloud was drifting through the pale sky. Still anything but 'Eiger-weather' …

All the same, I wanted to go up with Charlie next day to the foot of the face.

The Bernese Oberland, with its streaming glaciers and proud four-thousanders – Finsteraarhorn, Mönch and Jungfrau – lay under a clear blue sky. The weather looked really good at last.

The long line of the huge Mittelegi Ridge was bathed in sunshine; from the massive rock buttresses at its start in the valley to the shining white of the

Eiger's summit, where it ends. A few little tufts of cotton wool were playing tag in the dark hollow of the North Face. The little red cars of the Jungfrau railway climbed the steep rack and pinion track between the meadows …

'Alpiglen!'

Out with my pack … and then another sack, and the cardboard box, and the long sailor's sack, and the carrier frame … the conductor was getting impatient. How could anyone be carting so much stuff with him in a summer holiday resort?

Luckily, the stationmaster seemed to understand perfectly; for we certainly couldn't take everything up with us at one go. While the bustle of the trippers faded away and the little train climbed on its way, he stood there, taking stock of our pile of goods. Then he looked at us and muttered: 'The Eiger, of course!' and shook his head. 'If you like, you can park some of it here,' he said. 'I have often done it before.' He straightened his cap and pointed to a door: 'In the corner, on the right there,' he advised. We were only too pleased at the offer; we had been on the point of asking for it. Charlie carried everything we could not manage to the place indicated, while I was tying one sack to the wire frame.

The stationmaster was still standing there, watching us. He was a slow, comfortable, pleasant Bernese type. 'Many thanks,' we said, when we had finished: 'We'll be back for the rest today.'

'Today or tomorrow, whenever you like,' he nodded. Then he suddenly knitted his brows and looked hard at me. Just as I was beginning to wonder what was coming, he said, very quietly: 'Do you have to do that thing?'

I searched around for words. 'Yes,' I said, … you see …

'Nowt happened to us as yet!' said Charlie with a cheerful grin. 'Come on,' he said, tapping me on the shoulder.

I was still thinking of the man as we slowly climbed far up the green, flowery slopes; and once, when I turned to look back, I felt sure he was still standing down there, looking up at us.

The sacks weighed a ton, and the ascent was a long one: But what a morning it was: sunny and green, everywhere. This Alpiglen was a lovely corner of the world! In front of us rose a broad tongue of forest; above it the North Face hung like a blue shadow. Not till just under the summit did the sun gild a snowfield, the white veins of ice in dark rock – the very last bit of the climb. There didn't seem to be any distance between it and the sky above.

Lothar, Hias and Herbert must have pitched their tent somewhere in this wood, but we couldn't see it. We meant to site ours much higher up, indeed as high as possible; for it was still a long way from here to the start of the climb, at least an hour by night. We were resting again and, with all this gear to cart, we should have found it much more comfortable to stop here. Then we remembered our friends, whom the vicar of Grindelwald came up to visit one day, with the idea of trying to talk them out of the Eiger. So on we went, up the hill.

We found a tiny, steep-sided patch of grass just below the first slabby steps of the face. This was at 6,600 feet, and no one could get a tent farther up. When we looked up, with our heads tilted right back, we could see, way up there, the big icicles hanging down the greyish-brown wall below the 'Spider'. The summit itself was out of sight, high above.

We used moss and slates to build a level platform into the slope and planted our fabric house on it. We were protected from any odd stones falling from above by a projecting rock. From here it was no distance to the start of the climb; we could get there without expending any effort.

A few days later, after Wolfi had rejoined me in our 'Alpine Weekend Cottage', as we called it, we enjoyed a really priceless experience. We had just been checking our supply of pitons, when he suddenly nudged me and said: 'Look! There's someone coming up!'

I saw a dark figure coming slowly up the slopes, still a long way down. I recognised a uniform. 'A policeman,' I said. We looked around us, but there was no other tent, nobody else; there could be no doubt he was coming to see us. All the way up from Alpiglen, an hour away down there ...

'Any guesses, Wolfi?'

'Not a thing.'

The uniformed figure continued to climb resolutely, straight for us. 'Anything to do with your motorbike?' I suggested.

Certainly not!' replied Wolfi with an ugly look. 'My motorbike, indeed!' Wolfi is very touchy about his skill as a rider.

The facings on the uniform were now clearly recognisable. Another quarter of an hour or so ...

Wolfi had an idea. 'Do you think they have put the North Face out of bounds?' he asked.

'Nonsense!' I retorted. 'Anyway, we'll soon know now.'

Then I had a bright idea. 'Do you think we look like someone else?'

'Possibly,' said Wolfi glancing at me and grinning amiably. 'They may have seen your passport photo, taken on that machine at the railway station.' Tit-for-tat, for the motorbike, eh? I thought of that photo. Never again would I try to save money.

'In any case, don't look so agitated,' said Wolfi. 'Sit down and relax.'

We relaxed, in that expectant frame of mind in which everyone waits, when the eye of the law falls on them.

Here he was at last, sweating heavily, touching his cap and assuming an official attitude.

'Your passports, please, gentlemen!'

Oh, so that was it. We handed him our passports.

He ran his fingers through the pages, looked briefly at me, then at Wolfi, addressing his question to him: 'You're going up there, eh?' he asked. He pointed up at the shining curtains, which had been moving slowly up the face all morning.

'Hm,' said Wolfi. What *can* one say when one has planted a tent at the foot of the wall?

'It depends on the weather,' I interposed.

Our policemen nodded. 'Yes, I know,' he said and pocketed our passports. 'You can fetch them down in Grindelwald,' he explained, 'afterwards – when you have got back safely.' He paused for a moment, before adding: 'You see, we always do that nowadays – it often helps us with the question of identification.'

He wished us good day most amiably, touched his cap again and turned to go, visibly relieved that it would now be all downhill.

'H'm,' said Wolfi, and made his 'funny face' – thrusting out his lower lip, biting it and creasing his face, as if to laugh. But when he does that it usually means he is not at all happy.

A wild gale was raging across the Oberland. Ice blossoms formed on the ridges, but it was a glorious day, with the sun flashing on the rocks, marvellously beautiful to look at in the magic clothing conjured by the storm.

We were on the ridge leading from the Schreckhorn to the Lauteraahorn, in the course of our last training climb before tackling the face. Franz was still with us, but Charlie had gone home. Wolfi and I had decided to start up at the first opportunity, once we were back in Grindelwald.

When we got there, we heard that Hias, Lothar and Herbert had made an attempt while we were away. They were down below again, after an indescribably difficult retreat, without any assistance from anyone almost all the way. The photographs in the papers showed Hias's face drawn with pain; he had one arm in a sling. They had reached the 'Flatiron', when a small stone falling clear from the Spider a thousand feet above struck him on his hand as he gripped a hold.

Poor Hias – what devilish luck! Now he was in hospital at Interlaken, where they were trying to save what remained of his hand. The hardships of that retreat had left their mark on Herbert and Lothar's faces. They had had enough of the Eiger for the time being. Later on, they worked out a plan to climb the face in winter, when there are no falling stones, when the cold freezes everything into immobility. But Hiebeler and three others beat them to it.

We visited Hias in hospital; it was all we could do for him.

At last the weather had turned fine. The snow high up was melting. The North Face looked even darker than usual, a sure sign that the rock pitches would be dry, free from snow and ice, and that much easier at least. To balance that, the ice fields in the middle section would be glassy and tough, with no snow crust; and more stones would come down by day – the bombardment would only cease at night and into the early morning.

I called up Zurich on the telephone and asked the met station if one could trust the weather. 'Well, it was a temporary "high" – not too bad.' Could it last a couple of days? It might …' What were we to do? Yesterday's report from the Tourist Office had sounded much more promising, and the weather certainly looked good. We decided to go up to our 'high camp' and see what happened. Two days ought to see us through our climb.

We packed up. Everything lay strewn on the grass round the tent: pitons, provisions, ropes. We were starting this very night, so as to be climbing tomorrow. Should we take that ring piton, it was a bit heavy? How much petrol? The small tin. Tut you *must* take your big gauntlets.'

The result? Enormous rucksacks – much too heavy for Grade V severities; but holding everything necessary for a week on the face – one never can tell …

No use: it was simply too much. We stood the rucksacks on their heads and started sifting everything all over again.

The slight, blonde Nadja had come up from her tent. 'I see you're busy packing. Starting up tomorrow, then?' she enquired.

'Yes,' said Wolfi, laconically, and went on rolling up the bivouac bag. It just had to get smaller, somehow.

'OK,' said Nadja. 'Then I'll go and cook you a real meal.'

Darkness and silence. Somewhere up there the face frowned on our tent, unseen, but seeming to claw down into it with invisible fingers. We had set the alarm for midnight – for we wanted to be early on our way. Slowly, the minutes ebbed.

We were taking twenty pitons, five of them for ice; an equal number of karabiners; two 130-foot ropes, one of them a light reserve one, in case a retreat was forced on us; a quarter of a pint of petrol, for the small extra-lightweight cooker – enough for five days if it came to the worst; also the rest of bur equipment, well tested on any number of face climbs. Our provisions, weighed to the last ounce, concentrated and worked out more than ever on this occasion, consisted of a small bag of corn-flakes, baked in sugar, nuts and raisins – about two pounds in all. A handful of this special food keeps one satisfied for quite a time – possibly it swells in one's stomach. For the rest – fruit juice, chocolate, glucose and quite a hunk of smoked bacon, filling and satisfying; add a little bread, a luxury if one considers its weight, but a necessity. Then bivouac candles for the night; for if anything was certain, we should have to bivouac. A few other trifles …

I had fallen into a deep and dreamless sleep. I woke and looked at the dial. Still an hour to go. Well, I was hardly likely to sleep any more, now.

I got out the sketch of our route and quietly turned on my torch, laying my hand over it with great care, for Wolfi was still asleep. A narrow crack of light glowed red between my fingers …

It was a fairly large photograph of the face, on which we had pencilled in the route. I skipped the first 2,600 feet of the plinth, with its horizontal stratification. It was not difficult, and we wanted to deal with it before daybreak; Wolfi had been up it during an attempt last summer; he knew the way. After that massive stratified plinth, there are 3,000 feet of sheer and at times vertical rock face, with long traverses to be made, gaining little height and costing much time and labour. In the central section we would have to cross the three ice fields, steep as church roofs, each of them poised above vertical cliffs, and with their ice pitched at from fifty-five degrees to sixty degrees. The traverse of the second ice field in itself is a matter of twenty rope's-lengths. During all this, the main danger is from falling stones, from which there is no respite till, after the third ice field, one reaches the 'Ramp'; there they fall clear through thin air, missing it in their flight. After that, we should have to take great care not to continue too straight up the face, as Mayer and Notdurft did last year, and Longhi and Corti too, a mistake to be avoided at all costs. Our job would be to find the 'Traverse of the Gods', a crumbling ledge leading to the Spider's huge funnel. Once through that, another place demanding the greatest care; for, above the Spider there are countless runnels, cracks, twisting gullies, not all of which take one out to the summit.

Yes, we would be taking that photograph with us and looking after it as if it were a talisman; for if mists and blizzards robbed us of all visibility, it would be our only guide to escape from the face. On it we could measure rope's lengths with our fingers, find the route, either up or down; for there is no way of getting out of that enormous shell to left or to right. I folded the picture up carefully and put it away.

A quarter of an hour to go. In the red light glowing through my fingers I held a small medal, its dull gleam bitten into by tiny lettering. Busle had given it to me when we parted. The Protestant Paternoster in English: For thine is the kingdom, the power and the glory, for ever … Her prayer– she was a Protestant. To me it was not less precious for that; in this whole world there is only one of it.

Overhead, in the darkness, soared the North Face.

Almost midnight, now. I pushed my head out of the tent entrance to see what the weather was doing. Stars and more stars; not a cloud in the sky; dew on the grass. The Eiger in impenetrable darkness.

Crawling in again, I shook Wolfi. 'Just on twelve!' I said.

'OK – OK I know. Just five more minutes … '

Presently: 'Is it fine outside?' he asked.

'Yes, a clear sky and dew on the grass.'

'Well, I suppose that means we go. What does the altimeter say?'

'You've got it in your pocket,' I replied, handing him the torch. The brilliance of its beam made me shut my eyes for a moment. 'Well, what does it say?'

'Very odd,' said Wolfi, tapping its dial. 'Ten feet higher than yesterday, and that should mean bad weather. Yet it's really fine, and cold, outside – couldn't look better.' The dial could have slipped round in my pocket, _or it might just have gone wrong.' We had had trouble with it once before. 'Anyway, I say we should go … '

1 a.m. Up over the patches of grass, towards the start of the climb, traversing, going up and down, to the debris cone we knew rose above us. Every now and then we caught sight of the first crags, in the light of our torches. Above them stretched an impenetrable curtain of darkness, a black mass, whose upper edge cut into the starry sky – immense and unknown. What had we to offer against that? All I knew was that I would not want to tackle it with anyone but Wolfi.

'Here we are!' He had recognised the place from his attempt the year before, when I was in the Karakorum. We climbed the debris cone and a crag or two till a patch of snow shone white in the beam of the torch.

'There's a slab off to the right, here,' said Wolfi, locating it presently, as the beam moved over the rock. 'Only Grade III!'

I followed him as he crossed the little schrund, where the snow had melted, and disappeared up the rocks above. All right! Only Grade III it might be, but with a rucksack weighing a ton … no ballet dancing here.

On we went, up crumbling rock pitches, ledges, precipitous sandy rubble. It wasn't difficult, but it was damnably tricky work, for we could only see the next few feet ahead in the light of our torches. By three o'clock, we were at the foot of the First Pillar, up on our left; we couldn't see it, but Wolfi knew it was there. No moon, only the light of the stars; the mountain was asleep, utter silence reigned on its face. We continued our strange, ghost-like ascent, hardly exchanging a word. Every now and then the beam of one headlamp or the other slashed through the darkness. Occasionally a stone went clocketing down into the void, reminding us, surprisingly, that the face did not consist merely of a few feet of rock on which one happened to be climbing at the moment, but that there was already a great deal of it below us.

We climbed unroped, each of us alone with the light of his lamp, the sound of his boots on the rock, the feel of his hands on it. From time to time, a flash of light, or a word – the only communication with the other man.

It was 4 a.m. and still dark. 2,000 feet of the face lay behind us. Wolfi stopped at the foot of a step, barring the way, not very high but vertical. 'I don't remember that one,' he said. 'Never mind, let's get up it, and not waste time searching around. Make a back for me.' I planted myself firmly on the ledge. Oops! – and again: we were up, not exactly elegantly, but what did style matter, if we could save time and strength? What mattered was getting as high up as possible before the sun was on the rocks.

Another step, another back up, this time superfluous.

'Up to the left,' said Wolfi. 'We're above the "Shattered Pillar" now.' And he pointed across to where a profile was looming vaguely out of the first grey light of dawn, the shadowy, threatening overhangs of the 'Rote Fluh'. The stars were paling now – fewer and fewer, till there were only three big ones.

'We'll be at the "Difficult Crack" in a moment,' said Wolfi, as we traversed to the left up the slabs.

The sky turned blue above a red streak on the horizon; not the tiniest of clouds in it. The rocks around us were beginning to reflect the new day. And what a marvellous one!

Wolfi was beaming: 'Suppose we had believed the altimeter!'

'Yes,' I answered. 'It's just like our Matterhorn day!'

What a day that had been! The sun had met us on the ice field, dazzling bright, to shine on us all the rest of the day. And as the points of our crampons bit into the snow, we kept on thinking: 'Here we are on the North Face of the Matterhorn, *our* North Face … at last … and on just such a day as this … on the North Face …

And now we were on the North Face of the Eiger.

You see if we're not the first to get right up the face in fine weather,'

I shouted across to Wolfi, who was traversing along a ledge in the rock, now brightly lit by the reflected daylight. Above us towered the face, smooth and overhanging. It would not be long before we were in deep shadow again.

We came to the Difficult Crack, one of the Grade V pitches. Ten feet straight up, there was a piton below a projecting roof. Wolfi clipped himself on and straddled out on to the slab to its left – cautiously, slowly not altogether easily, for his rucksack was heavy. This was no place for ballet dancing, no matter how good the climber. By now Wolfi had got to the overhang thirty feet farther up, not a very big one, but …

Wolfi was cursing his rucksack: 'Damnable, the way this lump pulls one outwards!' He was panting, and I kept a close eye on his every movement. There, he's done it, he's up! I have never seen Wolfi 'come off' yet; he doesn't like the idea, so he never takes a risk. Of course I belay him carefully in spite of that, but it is a comfortable feeling to be on the rope with him. That is probably why we have climbed together so often.

As it happens I don't like the idea of 'coming off' either.

Wolfi had moved on up, straddling widely in a groove, his red anorak a bright spot in the morning sunlight. I took a picture of him, with the overhangs of the 'Rote Fluh' overhead. The Rote Fluh – a face in its own right, a face in the Eiger's great face, leaning far out over our heads, unclimbable by normal means, impossible.

What must Hinterstoisser and his friends have felt that day, years ago, when they looked up from this point? ... Would it be possible to traverse below that smooth, solid wall, across to the first ice field; could they get there without having to climb that first enormous cliff? Would the Eiger unlock its gate for them?

The Eiger unlocked the gate. They found the traverse, that 'Hinterstoisser Traverse', which is the gate to the North Face. And then it locked it again behind them.

For, when they were forced to retreat, they found the traverse – heavily iced by the break in the weather – impossible to negotiate; a withdrawal over its glassy slabs is only feasible if the traversing rope is left in position ... and they had taken it with them ...

Very soon we should have dealt with the first 2,600 feet of this gigantic face. It was by now 7 a.m. Everything down in the valley was bathed in sunshine, the meadows shone green, the houses in Grindelwald small and cosy. Where we were, it was cold and grim. We were out of the sun now, and there was ice wedged between the rocks in places. The climbing was not hard and we gained height rapidly; but the area of what was climbable was continually shrinking, swallowed up by the might of the Rote Fluh above us and ahead of us and by the rim of the fearsome precipice pushing up on our left. Finally, it narrowed to a wedge of a snow crest and then – petered out.

We were out on the smooth sweep of the face, surrounded everywhere by almost vertical slabs. The first few feet were covered by a veneer of ice, above which we could see a piton and an old hemp rope, curving out in a wide loop, then disappearing from view. 'One of its strands is broken,' growled Wolfi.

That rope had been hanging there for a week, ever since the retreat of the Hias, Lothar, Herbert trio. Poor Hias ... all because of these blasted stones! All hell must break loose here when the sun is shining on the upper part of the face; the slabs and the rounded limestone cliffs are in places scored with a network of white scars where the stones have struck. At the moment all was quiet. 'A somewhat hostile district,' growled Wolfi, and moved off with great care out on to the slabs.

The Hinterstoisser Traverse is 130 feet long. Wolfi had disappeared from view. Out ran the rope in little jerks, quicker than I had expected, but then the rock was dry and in excellent condition. It was a hot summer and so the Eiger was 'dark' for us, and I have already explained the advantages and drawbacks of that – easier climbing on the difficult rock sectors because they are free from snow and ice, but heavier falls of stone, and tough polished ice, hard as glass, on the ice fields above.

I could just catch Wolfi's 'come on!' from the far end of the traverse. It is a most impressive place. Below me was an appalling drop of 2,600 feet to the meadows, above me 3,000 feet more of the face. Between the two there was a rope, a piton and a small stance, on which I re-joined Wolfi.

He looked at me and said: 'I'll go on, as far as the "Swallows' Nest".' It was almost a question, but he had already hung a sling into the next piton. 'All right,' I said. 'I'll take over from there.' He moved up on the piton, while I belayed him.

'Don't forget to retrieve the sling – it's ours. I don't want to waste any time here,' he called down, almost as if apologising for his technical inelegance; the pitch really didn't call for a sling, he could have climbed it 'free'. But now time was of the essence …

The Swallows' Nest. There we sat, with our legs dangling over nothingness. I tried to spot our tent, without success. Anyway, we had to be moving on. So, on with crampons, for the ice field. It was my turn to lead now, even if it would have been pleasant to sit in this nice, comfortable niche a little longer …

'It's as exposed as any face in the Dolomites,' Wolfi remarked, adding: 'Rebitsch was the first to get down safely from here.'

I tightened my crampon straps a little, looking down into those blue depths at the same time. It was from somewhere round here, it occurred to me, that Toni Kurz had made his last despairing effort to reach the rescue party below. From here he had let himself down, with the last failing remnants of his strength, on the rope, still ready – the only survivor of a party of four – to fight for his life; let himself down (and I leaning out as far as I dared, could see no end to it, for down there the face overhung) to within six feet of his rescuers, where the knotted rope jammed in the karabiner …

Six feet from succour and life … and there it all ended … there Toni Kurz fell backwards on the rope and died.

Wolfi was addressing me: 'I thought you said you wanted to take over the lead?'

'So I do,' I said. 'I'm off– but watch me carefully up the first few feet.'

Those first few feet were steep slabs of limestone scoured absolutely smooth; the ice field must have been much bigger at one time and this was its old, polished floor. I remembered the description: 'Millimetre precision work for a pedant'; it really was abominably smooth hereabouts. I breathed a sigh of relief when at last I was able to dig my points into grey ice. It was tough and in places smooth as a mirror, but they managed to grip. Bless the blacksmith down in Grindelwald who let us use his emery-wheel!

If only we had not got to climb rock to get up to the second ice field, and so blunt the new, keen edges on our spikes! Yet it didn't look very promising without crampons; a barrier of solid rock, down part of which comes pouring a kind of frozen waterfall – a glistening curtain of black, glassy bubbles – the 'Ice hose'.

We decided it was better to try the dry end of the barrier, without crampons. Wolfi started up it, climbed the first few feet, disappeared over an edge, said something about slabs, then complete silence. It must have got hellishly difficult up there. The rope kept on coming down, going up again, down again, up again. Somewhere up on that roof Wolfi was obviously hard at it, but the waiting seemed endless. There was, of course, the view to look at, nice green meadows down below; but what in God's name was going on up above? Wolfi had stopped moving altogether; only a few fragments of ice came tinkling down. The sun was gradually invading the rocks high up near the West Ridge, but as yet not a stone had fallen, though it was half past eight. What on earth could be the matter with Wolfi?

As I went up, five minutes later, I found out. It was a thing like a steep roof, covered in places by a thin skin of polished ice. I looked diagonally downwards … not a pleasant place to go sliding down … At last I got up to Wolfi, on a bad stance, with a fairly useless belay – but the only one available. 'I shall be glad when we're away from here,' he confided.

We could see the second ice field above us, a gleam of greyish-green. All I could think of at the moment was that, up there, one could bang pitons in anywhere one liked. But we had to get there first …

A tongue of ice stretched down towards us, but at least thirty feet overhead. Till then there was only a glittering, glassy layer of black water ice, less than an inch thick, on the solid rock. Not a hope of fixing a piton or cutting a step in that. As I put my crampons on again I couldn't help thinking how stupid we had been to get ourselves into this hole: if we had only kept on, up to the right! Well this is where we were, so thinking wouldn't do any good …

'I'm off,' I said.

'Yes – and you know … Wolfi indicated the rope, lying loose in his hand, by a movement of his head.

Yes, I knew well enough what kind of a belay it was.

I placed my crampon against the glassy surface. Could I get a purchase? No, not here. What about there? Yes, there. Now for the next step: I had managed to clear a grip for my left hand. I moved up. The layer of ice was a little thicker, and I moved a step higher on it. I found another place where my spikes gave me a purchase. The seconds went ticking away, each of them vital, none of them bring any respite. Each of them might have been an hour, or more. Here was the slab, the little hollow in the ice, and here was my foot. The only thought in one's mind, how to put it down properly. Good: that one had got a firm hold!

After an eternity there was proper thick ice, good enough to cut a handhold, but lying hollow over the rock, giving out a dull sound; not thick enough for a piton, it would simply shatter. Up again, another handhold – getting better now.

And then, at last, decent ice. In went a piton. I gave a sigh of relief, so did Wolfi. The world immediately looked a friendlier place.

'Just a moment's rest,' I said, 'then I'll move on.'

'Yes, you take a rest, by all means.'

I took a rest, looking at the piton, the ring, the snap-link, the rope and the grey ice before me. God, those last minutes had been quite a thing!

I went on resting. There was a niche in the ice up above, followed by a crack at the side of a rock rib. That must be the best line to take. Off I went again.

I reached the niche, a hole in the ice, through which I hung a sling – an additional belay; then came the crack, which went easily, backing up between ice and rock. As I emerged, I could see the steep slope of the second ice field just ahead.

Only another twenty feet,' I shouted down to Wolfi.

There was a little rock island just above me, which I should be able to use as a stance. I treated myself to the luxury of cutting a couple of steps, great big comfortable steps ... the ice splintered, the fragments clinked as they flew, till their sound died away down below; potsherds, tough and glassy, toughened by the cold and the eternal shadow which enveloped us.

Sssssssssss ... !

A stone whizzing past, not very far off– the first sign of life on the face. Then all quiet again, here in the shadow; utter silence. High above, rock and snow lay bright in the sunshine, quiet, peaceful, warm looking. And that was precisely where the menace hung – the menace that could at any moment shatter the cold silence down here, the menace of that beautiful warm glow.

Tick ... tick ... ssst. Just a baby stone, hopping harmlessly, dancing down the rocks, whispering past like an insect, small and no danger to anyone. But how long before the cannonade would start, to shatter the peace and quiet down here? It could be minutes, it could be half an hour ... It was 9 a.m.

I looked up at the warm, even light on those rocks. Then I started cutting steps again, smaller ones, quicker than before. I was up. In went a piton and then I hacked out a stance.

I shouted down to Wolfi: 'You can come now – but look out! The first stones are arriving.'

'So I noticed,' came up from below. 'One has just gone past me.'

Wolfi was coming up – the traverse, the piton, retrieving the sling, pushing a leg into the crack, reaching up with his arm. At that moment there was a 'click' on my helmet, and I enjoyed an instant's satisfaction at the thought that I was wearing it. Then Wolfi joined me.

'We'll have to get up there before it really starts,' he said, pointing to the upper rim of the huge ice field. He was right; there seemed to be at least a measure of cover under the jutting cliffs up there. We should take much longer by following that long curving rim than if we traversed diagonally, but – 'Look out! Something's coming!' Wolfi, six feet above me, reacted instantly, pressing himself hard into the ice. A host of little dots was coming down in a grotesque dance across the grey surface 300 feet higher up. They grew larger, bounding down towards us in great leaps, a grey army of them. Now! ... that one's missed me, and that one, but what about this one? ... sssst, ssst ... Suddenly everything was quiet again. It was all over.

Wolfi straightened up slowly. 'Benediction over?' he asked. 'Then I'll lead on again. You keep watch and shout if you see anything coming.'

I cast an anxious eye up the face, the surface of the ice, the groove running up to the rocks above. Nothing stirred. The rope ran out quickly, as Wolfi went diagonally up the next 130 feet. He dispensed with step cutting; we had to get out of the line of fire as quickly as possible. Tack ... tack ... tack, his crampons bit into the smooth surface, tilted at fifty degrees or more. It looked uncanny.

The view down the face had completely disappeared; all we could see was the lower edge of the second ice field projecting over the abyss like a ski-jumping platform, with green ground beyond it, sending up a pale green reflection, mirrored by the surface up here, making the blue shadows look even colder.

We wondered whether we had been spotted yet. Not that it makes the slightest difference. There is no place on earth where one is so utterly alone. I squinted up the runnel to where Wolfi stood, with only the frontal points of his crampons biting into the steep, bone-hard surface. I stooped and took a tighter hold on the rope.

Everything else had lost all meaning. Wolfi was standing up there on four steel spikes. Whether they held or slipped depended on his next movement ...

We were alone ... alone with the North Face of the Eiger. At that moment even our friends had ceased to exist for us.

Down at the Kleine Scheidegg, Herbert had his eye to the big telescope. 'I've got them,' he shouted. There, in the black circle of the lens, small and forlorn against the huge face, with a few cloud-tatters floating around it, he had seen two tiny dots against the grey belt of the second ice field.

Fritz von Allmen, the hotel proprietor, one of the greatest Eiger experts, who had followed our climb for a long time past, joined him. 'Midday – much the worst time for falling stones,' he commented.

'Yes, it's sensible of them to be keeping to the upper rim, in the shelter of the rocks, till they get out on to the Flatiron,' said Herbert, adding ruefully: 'I wish them better luck than we had!' Lothar was with him; they had come up from the valley as soon as they heard somebody was on the face. They did not know, of course, when we intended to start, but they were pretty sure that we were the two dots they had detected on the face ...

We were now deep inside the great shell, working our way up to the end of the ice field; in sunshine now, and it was warm. Water was trickling down the rocks, the ice was softer and had acquired a crust.

The hail of stones was nerve-racking, coming irregularly: short gaps, positive barrages, isolated salvoes, then utter silence once more; one never knew what to expect. We made use of every available inch of cover, pillars, pitches of rock, overhangs, crannies. Looking up for a moment at the crumbling bastions high overhead during some interval in the bombardment, we felt little surprise at the unnerving whistle of the falling stones, the sharp crack as they struck on rock, the dull thud when they hit the ice.

At this point the dirty grey surface of the ice field looked like the face of a man scarred by smallpox. During the fearful minutes of the unprotected moves from one source of cover to another, we were painfully aware of every inch of our bodies. If it had been possible to hide ourselves completely under our helmets we would have felt a great deal better.

Our method of progress was an unusual one – a gigantic hanging traverse of ice, on a rounded edge formed by the melting away of the ice field's upper rim from the rock above it. For the most part we only supported ourselves against it, for it was by no means all of it solid enough to stand anyone leaning out from it. That traverse across the second ice field is twenty rope's lengths – more than 800 yards long. You have to grab it a hundred times, move up a hundred times, always with the same extreme care.

I looked up. Bang! Something hit me in the face, blinding me. By sheer instinct I leaned forward against the face. 'It's finished', I thought. My eyes opened again. There was blood running down my anorak. I put my hand tentatively to my face…..

Wolfi had me on the taut rope, as I worked my way, bemused, up to a safe stance. Nothing much, he assured me, only a scratch. A small stone had hit me on the bridge of the nose. Just a small stone …

My head was buzzing. 'Come on! Off this damned ice field!' I was still digesting my shock, but Wolfi was already balancing over the irregularities of the icy edge. No time for rest and recuperation sessions here, he said; it was the last thing I wanted, anyway! Wolfi led the next two rope's lengths.

By the time we were traversing out on to the Flatiron, I was quite myself again. At last we were off the second ice field. For which relief much thanks.

The arête of the Flatiron, 250 feet high, jutting out like a regularly curved nose from the furrowed face, lies directly beneath the Spider and is, consequently, more than usually exposed to the hail of stones. Climbing simultaneously, we hurried up its easy rock and sat down, to get our breath back, under a small overhang near the top. Here we were really safe, and we could actually sit. We had now been engaged in fourteen unbroken hours of climbing.

We were ravenous, as we got bacon and bread out of the rucksack. There was even water, dripping down the rock. Now that we were sitting here and the tension was lifted, we could feel the weariness penetrating our bones. We had been on our feet since 1 a.m. and now it was half past four in the afternoon. We were not likely to get much farther today, but there seemed nothing to stop our reaching the summit tomorrow, if only the weather held.

That was the only question in our minds as we watched the little puffs of cloud all around us, climbing up the face, growing in size, disappearing – dissolving into thin air.

Shimmering curtains – as if the spirits of the air were engaged in a grotesque, swirling dance in the void all around us, accompanied by the thousand voices of the North Face, from the high, almost barking whirr of the smaller stones to the less frequent dull growling and roaring of the big lumps. And, somewhere, there was the sound of water pattering down the face.

We were climbing the steep Ramp, which slashes a way up the un-broken cliffs, anything from vertical to overhanging, below the Spider. It was getting late; soon it would be dark. We wanted to get to the good bivouac site we had heard of, above the most difficult pitch in the Ramp, the famous chimney, which was either filled by a waterfall or by its frozen counterpart. It seemed a doubtful project. Behind us, through the mists, we looked across the tilted roofs of the two ice fields to a fabulous view; but beyond it lay the veils of dusk. Here, on the steep Ramp, with nothing but sheer cliffs and a snow gully all around us there wasn't even room to sit down. We should have to push on till we found a place. We got out our headlamps and our torches. By a stroke of luck we found a small hollow in the rock at the end of the first rope's length; there was just room for two people to sit, close together.

We made our preparations for the night very slowly and methodically (this is a long-standing item of bivouac-lore: the longer you take over the preliminaries, the shorter the night) hammered a couple of pitons firmly into the rock, bashed the sharper projections till they were more rounded, melted snow for a hot drink of fruit juice. Ironically, there was water pattering down, a few feet above us in the darkness; but neither of us felt like climbing another inch. Before pulling the bag over our heads, we took a last look at the lights sparkling down in Grunewald, more than 8,000 feet below; we agreed that it must be much more comfortable down there and wondered whether we should be looking down on it from the summit tomorrow. Mists were creeping up from below; the lights wavered, grew dim, disappeared. The night air breathed coldly on us. We sat down and pulled our protective tent-covering over us.

The first light of a new day was filtering through our Perlon shell. The night had been quite bearable, in spite of the stones which had refused to surrender their sharpness and the smallness of the sitting room. Only once did I have to wake Wolfi up, when I heard him say: 'Uncomfortable here, I'm going out where it's level ground,' and saw him preparing to stand up. Otherwise, we slept almost all the time.

I lifted the Perlon casing a little and looked out. Fog! Everything was grey, water dripped down the rocks, a dull silence enveloped us. Water – not ice! No early morning frost, then. I didn't like it at all and woke Wolfi up at once. We had to get on without wasting a moment. In all probability, the weather had broken.

All the same, we allowed ourselves a hot fruit juice breakfast; then we started to climb again, stiff in every limb. In the very first chimney we ran into a lively waterfall. Damnable discomfort! The water got in everywhere, down our necks, up our sleeves, no matter how carefully we went. Our fleece jackets became cold compresses …

It grew darker and darker. At the top of the chimney, it began to snow. So the weather had broken, after all; for us, as for everyone before us. After this last chimney at the top that could be fatal. Visibility diminished and diminished. We simply must not miss the access to the *Traverse of the Gods*. We got our photograph out, measured rope's lengths on it with the width of our fingers, remembering what Heini Harrer had told us: not to go all the way up the narrow ice field above the Ramp, but out to the right, by the first opportunity offered – the only one that led to the traverse. We just *had* to find it; for we knew what lay above, if we went wrong, and what had happened there to others before us …

Clouds of powdery blown snow enveloped us. It must be that dark gap over there. We hurried across to it, to find that beyond it lay the crumbling black slates of a precipitous rock band – yes, that must be the Brittle Band leading to the traverse itself. It tallied perfectly with the photograph, too.

Very cautiously, we worked our way across that ledge, bestrewn with loose slates and falling away precipitously below. There were one or two rock pitches going straight up – and there we were, at the start of the traverse.

This could only be the famous *Traverse of the Gods*, but it did not look in the least like what we had expected. 'A route high above monstrous abysses, and giddying precipices,' said the description. We could see none of this – fog lay close to our right, above our heads and on this band ahead of us; a band covered with debris, sloping slightly outwards, not always clearly defined, and partly clothed in a grey, loose, soft crust. Not at all inviting.

We moved step by step, with the utmost caution, always carefully belayed by one another. Could we possibly get to the top today? It seemed essential that we should, for we shuddered at the thought of a second bivouac on the face. But it was already almost midday …

A solitary stone swished past and disappeared into the grey. We did not hear it strike down below. The depths to our right, hidden in the fog were bottomless. Suddenly we are at the end of the band; a steep ice slope loomed ahead of us, a gigantic many-armed funnel … we were at the Spider.

Down at the Kleine Scheidegg everyone was getting worried. There was nothing to be seen but clouds and storm; the mountain had drawn its curtains. Was there yet another disaster brewing?

Meanwhile, Salzburg and Vienna had become aware of what was going on, and who was involved. The papers were full of pessimistic comment: once on the face, rescue was impossible – the only chance was right at the top or right at the bottom. Anywhere in between, it all depended on the climbers themselves – a lesson painfully drummed in over the twenty years since the first successful ascent. Even Herbert and Lothar were worried. Fritz Von Allmen had telephoned them in Grindelwald to say visibility was nil: occasionally a strip of rock, a ledge, a patch of ice broke through the clouds … beyond that, not a trace …

Again and again Von Allmen trained the telescope on the pother of cloud in the boiling cauldron, between the Ramp, the Spider and the summit.

Stones came whistling down, but fewer than yesterday. On the other hand, we could see nothing. At the upper rim of the Spider's gigantic funnel we were met by the problem of a maze of interlacing gullies in the grey fog of cloud. Which of these exit cracks was the right one? Not even our photograph of the face provided a definite answer.

At last we came across a piton; that must be it. We made good progress and found a second piton, so we carried on.

There was plenty of cover from 'shots'; but shots were few and far between and one could hear them coming from a long way off. The silence was mostly unbroken, and yesterday's showers of small stones seemed to have dried up. Perhaps the snow was immobilising them. Anyway, it was all quite different from yesterday.

It had grown appreciably colder since noon. Could it be just because we were higher up, or merely because we were tired? The face seemed absolutely endless, this face that ends in a summit 13,000 feet high. Here we were in the fog and the clouds of the exit cracks. Would we ever get out of them and up to the top?

Suddenly, there was no way of any kind to be seen ahead. An enormous overhang bulged out like a giant's forehead; farther to the left, a fearsome looking crack shot up next to a rock buttress. Were we expected to go up there? According to the route description there ought to be a yellow crack, a 'rather difficult' pitch. Could this be it? But there was another one beyond it, which might be the way out of this blind corner; and yet another beyond that. They all looked exceedingly savage. It began to snow again.

Straight ahead of us, in the snow, we discovered a weathered rope. Could it have come down from above? We wondered what its history might be: Well, it couldn't reveal its secret; and Wolfi was already hanging from the yellow overhang of one of the cracks. 'Hopeless!' he panted and came down again. Then he tried again, only to fail a second time. In the end we were both standing together, utterly at a loss, in that horrible corner, with the wind whistling around the pillar above us. Suddenly I had an idea that something didn't make sense here … that old rope was a clue …

'Look after my rope,' I told Wolfi, 'I'm going to explore down below.'

It was pretty dicey; the rock was very brittle. A big lump hit me on the helmet, but luckily it hadn't come very far. I stopped for a moment, then traversed out to the right and immediately recognised the main couloir. Owing to the fog, we had strayed into a *cul-de-sac* – and lost two precious hours!

It seemed hardly possible that we should still get up to the top today; a bitterly disappointing thought. Everything was freezing up in the storm; everything was white now, cold and hostile. The cracks in the rock were filling up, our anoraks were covered in ice, and it was cruelly cold on the stances. Evening was drawing in.

We embarked on a race against time. We fought our desperate way up, foot by foot, our crampons digging into the ice in the bed of the gully, searching for a grip on the slabs of its containing walls. We gasped our way up an overhang. Suddenly there was nothing under my feet, and the rope ran taut; a moment later I felt lifted gently upwards and clawed on to a handhold. The piton had come adrift. I cast a grateful glance up at Wolfi, who had held my fall.

No time to waste! Which way now? Straight up, or over to that pulpit on our left? We could not afford to make another mistake; better examine the pulpit, to make sure. Cheers! A piton, an abseil piton … and below it, to the left, a narrow platform, an icy, splintered rock bulge, and a steep gully shooting up from it …

Somehow the pitch seemed familiar … a picture in some book or other, with a man standing there. Down on the rope – this was it – now or never. This would settle the question: to bivouac or not to bivouac, indeed to get to the top still, or not, today. To get there, or not …

Down we went on the rope. Now, up and on again: up through the couloir, full of water, up on stiff fingers. All of a sudden great loads of hail came rattling down, covering foot- and hand-holds, fusing with the water to form a slithery film. It was 7 o'clock by now and getting uncomfortably dark.

Some kind of a ridge loomed up. We climbed out of the gully and on over slabby rock and snow. Wolfi had just climbed a rocky knob when -

A shout from above? Voices? People? A hallucination, of course, born of fog and weariness. There it was again: Herbert's voice …

Sure enough, it was our friends, shouting down through the storm; and, though we could not see them, we were overjoyed. We shouted back, and simply rushed up the dusk-dark slope of white above us. But remember to belay, said something in our minds, remember to belay! Then a figure loomed out of the fog – Herbert's figure, a rope's length below the ridge, from which the snow banners were streaming. Up we went, on all fours, our axes in one hand, a piton in the other, drawing nearer and nearer to him up the steep slope. First one of us, then the other. Would the seconds never finish ticking?

We were on the last few feet of the Eiger's North Face.

We were shaking hands, embracing … the rim of the cornice … back-patting … the last step across it … 'Thank God you're here!' … Yes, off the North Face, up out of the bottomless abyss … And thank *you*, too.'

It was over, thirty-three hours of it. Over, at a quarter to eight on the evening of 6 August. Over, at nightfall, after thirty-three hours of climbing and one bivouac, after two days all alone with that giant Face. We were safely up here and talking to people again; here with Lothar, Herbert and Winkler, the Swiss climber, who had come up to wait for us, not knowing when – or whether – we should arrive. Simply because we might need help …

Oh, how glad we were that they were there! Not that we needed anything; but just because they *were* there.

Very soon we should have to settle down to a bivouac, somewhere on the descent, in wet clothes and ice-clad anoraks. But it wouldn't be on the North Face any more; and everything is more bearable if you are with friends.

In less than an hour it would be pitch dark. While the others were packing up their gear, Wolfi and I went on up the narrow, almost level crest of the final ridge, till a hummock of snow loomed up at our feet.

We were on the summit of the Eiger.

It was the first time we had really grasped the full implications. We stopped and shook hands again. Our Eiger! Wolfi, we have done it. You and I.

Postscript

The descent was no cake-walk, but nothing could bother us any more, now that Eiger was in our pockets. The thermometer fell to –12 °C during the night, and it snowed right down into the valley. The gale screamed around the rocks and jammed every cranny with ice. We sat under our bivouac sack and sang, almost all through the night, with breaks for brewing tea. In the morning, our friends, who had sat close by in the other sack, cast some very odd looks at us. Herbert confessed later that they had the impression that we might be just the least bit – you know! – light-headed. Not a bit; we simply sang to keep the cold out – it is warmer if you sing.

Moreover, we sat bolt upright and with our muscles tensed, for then you don't feel the wet shirt on your back nearly so much. And every now and then we brewed tea.

In the morning our anoraks rattled like cuirasses – everything was frozen solid. As we went down the West Face, we lost our way and found ourselves on limestone slabs; not very steep, but smooth and snow covered. We were wearing crampons, and it was not particularly difficult; but there was the danger of a slip. So we thought it best to turn back, and that meant climbing up 300 feet we had just come down. However, we got down to the bottom at last and – remembering Wolfi's dream at the bivouac on the face – found ourselves going out 'to where it was level'.

How wonderful it was to be splashing in a hot, green foam-bath, to be lying in a newly made bed, to be alive, and to be able to enjoy life – this wonderful life of ours ...

Everything was splendid at the Kleine Scheidegg, and Fritz von Allmen saw to it that we lacked nothing; but we were soon busy packing up our tent, our sleeping bags, a cardboard box and everything. The great Walker Spur on the Grandes Jorasses was luring us away – and why not, in a summer which had brought so much luck?

There is not much more to say about our Eiger climb. Some people were angry with us because we did not give our photographs and reports away, free, gratis and for nothing, like good idealists. It is only now that I actually realise what bad businessmen we were: the sales did not cover a third of our climbing expenses that summer.

It was the others who did good business; the European Press made a picking. There was not a paper which did not carry a report, not a periodical which failed to produce a page of pictures. Perhaps that was because there had been so many failures and losses for years past and we were the first pair to come through safe and sound.

A climb like that can have the most unpredictable consequences. I discovered that the production of protective helmets had stopped or was on the point of stopping before our ascent. Now, all of a sudden, every picture paper, for the first time, showed helmeted heads, our heads and those of our friends. Production started up again with a great, unexpected leap. Financially, we got nothing out of it; but if many of the 'extreme' climbers have seen fit to protect their skulls with PVC ever since 1958, it was definitely our climb which set the fashion. For nobody, not even climbers, can escape the stealthy, subliminal influence of the advertising media. So, maybe, in the long run, the Eiger has saved as many lives as it has claimed !

I have been looking in the cabinet which houses all the old letters of that time; some of them were beyond price. Next to a letter of congratulations from the Austrian Embassy, I found a card from the Rechter Bauer Skittle

Club of Dusseldorf. It reads: 'You idiots, do you really think you have done something remarkable, by climbing like monkeys on a stick?' This has the ring of true conviction about it.

Again: a textile firm in the Vorarlberg expresses its astonishment that when I was discussing the question of corduroy trousers as Eiger-wear, I said something about a 'sponge', which soaks up everything and never dries out again. I said it with deep conviction, too; for climbers and skittlers alike are no beaters about the bush. What I did not know then was that this firm had a very special corduroy cloth – a waterproof one, extremely solid, in all colours.

I clothed all my friends in the patterns.

And then there was my helmet. What became of my dear old helmet, which took such a drubbing on the Eiger, after seeing me up the North Face of the Matterhorn? Alas, it is no more. It disintegrated under the weight of a boulder somewhere in Turkey. That was its last service, and the head beneath it went unscathed … Bianca's head.

Bianca di Beaco from Trieste is one of Italy's finest women climbers. When, on the way up to the but on the Aiguille Noire, I suddenly fell backwards off an easy but exposed pitch, because a handhold gave way, she gave me a 'shove' and remarked: 'un litro di vino!' – as is customary in Triestine climbing circles on such occasions.

She had undoubtedly saved my life; so I gave her my helmet.

That great Eiger summer was not over yet. We stood at the foot of the massive Walker Spur of the Grandes Jorasses, 4,000 feet of granite, hard as steel, bristling with difficulties up to Grade VI; a marvellous ladder leading to the mountain's highest summit, more than 13,000 feet high.

It is technically the severest of the three great north faces in the Alps, harder than the Eiger or the Matterhorn; but on it there are no falling stones, a most important difference. The slightly greater severity is thus much more acceptable in a climber's eyes, and it is indeed a climb one might even care to repeat.

The combined Eiger team had sprung into being. Wolfi and I, Herbert and Lothar did the buttress climb as a foursome – three long days of sunshine, cloud and blizzard, up that ladder to heaven, bivouacking on narrow ledges, with climbing passages where we looked down as much as 3,000 feet between our legs; enormously impressive, as we all agreed. As Wolfi and I shook hands at the top, we recalled how we had done the three great faces in partnership …

Fate soon set our feet on different paths; Wolfi's engineering jobs took him first to Switzerland, then to Pakistan, but our times together are not finished. I look forward to the day when we shall tie up on the same rope again – even if it was only for a short climb on some practice ground. Lothar lives in Munich and makes films – mountain films and crime films – you cannot make a living, he says, out of mountain films alone. And Herbert, cameraman and world-tramp, is not very far away, for he married my sister. So one or other of us at least is at home from time to time …

Back for a moment to the summit of the Jorasses – that great summer of the Bernina ice faces, the Eiger, the Walker Spur. Wasn't that enough?

I looked out over the cornice and away to my dream climb, the great ridge over there, for me something even greater than the Eiger and the Jorasses – to where the glorious Peuterey Ridge swept up from the blue-green depths of the Val Veni, the greatest of all Alpine ridges. Hardly ever climbed in its entire length – five miles of rock climbing, gigantic abseils, rock pinnacles, ice arêtes, mixed snow and rock work, every kind of difficulty, breaks in the weather, icy cold – climbing higher, day after day, above shimmering abysses, through cloud, storm and sunshine, up – up, to the summit of Mont Blanc.

The mightiest and finest climb in the Alps. Was I at last ready to try my luck on it?

In the autumn, maybe, when the weather is better and more dependable …

14 A Lesson in French

The Calanques – a Garden of Eden

What does an Alpine climber do when it is raining in Chamonix? He drives to Georges Livanos in Marseilles, or rather to his practice climbing ground. Practice ground? An understatement for the Calanques; they are a climber's paradise. For these are limestone cliffs, some of them hundreds of feet high, rising sheer from the sea; and there are some you can only get to in a boat.

In addition to all this, there are Morgiou and Sorrniou, two small fishing villages, with idyllic and alluring names; the only two places, locked in their dreams, on that twelve-mile-long coast – a hem of the land which is uncrossed by any road, and deeply indented by innumerable bays. Cactuses blossom there, and the hot sun beats down on a turquoise sky, perfectly mirrored in a seabed covered with red starfish, while shoals of glittering fishes flash in the crystal-clear water above it. There is no road to those two hamlets, only two pot-holed tracks, extremely difficult to find. This is a landscape in its original, primeval state.

Who would not wish to pitch his tent there? So – let us go.

We were at Livanos' home in Marseilles. We had actually tracked it down, and even found him there – a miracle, in view of our scanty acquaintance with the language, and a miracle in respect of the man himself, for he is never at home. This salesman, always on his travels, this specialist in Grade VI climbs, always on 'extreme' faces, takes his wife with him when he goes. Yet here they were, both of them, lively, gay, relaxed, as if we had always known them. Very soon eggs and tomatoes were sizzling in the kitchen, while Livanos cracked jokes and talked about the Calanques.

Later, over a strong cup of espresso coffee, he asked us what exactly we were looking for. Sipping the aromatic beverage reflectively, I told him: a climb on firm limestone, with a view of the sea, in some deserted corner, and redolent of the warm south. Livanos grinned. 'You German romantics!' he said and promptly drew a bold sketch, laughing happily as he did so, really enjoying himself. 'It's Morgiou you want,' he said. 'The Grande Chandèle, our tall candle. That's the best climb round there; highly romantic. And don't forget to do it by its Marseilles ridge – it's much the best thing on the Chandèle.' He hummed a few bars – could it have been the Marseillaise? – handed over the sketch, and off we went.

We had a job to find Morgiou, but we did, thanks to the sketch map. One can rely on Livanos: from the Marseilles suburbs onwards, every road was correctly marked. We would have been completely lost without it, for I know about twenty words of French and Wolfi commands less. So we would have been hard put to it to find a recondite fishing harbour.

Morgiou, a bay with brightly coloured boats in it, under the hot sun. We decided to have a look at the Chandèle straight away and find a place for our tent. The scenery was savage, a coast of precipitous cliffs, below which we made our way; there were shrubs and trees growing out of the rock, and the air was keen with the tang of the sea.

It grew more and more lonely; the sea was glittering and moving; there were cactus flowers – and nobody. Just a small fishing boat out there between the islands. In the middle of all this solitude, stood a noticeboard – how very odd! It said: *'Occupé – les naturalistes de Marseille.'* It was all French to us, so we went on. Then we turned a corner. 'Oh … !' we said, and fell into a temporary silence.

The accent was unmistakably French: stalking gazelle-legs, swinging hips, and a lot of other things besides … at a distance, but not so far away as all that.

'H'm!' I remarked and looked at Wolfi, whose mouth was still wide open, whose eyes shone with the light of a boyfriend in a television commercial. … 'H'm,' he said, clearing his throat, for he had taken note of my look and had immediately assumed his toughest north face expression: 'The "naturalistes" must be nudists, then …' Was it only my fancy, or had his Viennese accent suddenly acquired a French *timbre*? 'Obviously,' I replied and, unhurriedly, took stock of the impressive landscape. It was a marvellous bay.

'What do we do now?' asked Wolfi as the next contribution to our voluble dialogue; moved no doubt by his mountaineering conscience, and pointing to the rock tower of the Chandèle, beyond the marvellous bay …

'A typical Calanques feature, on superb rock, with views far out to sea, a magnificent climb': thus Livanos' description before handing the route guide over to us. Oh, that Livanos!

So much for the description. (This is where it ended.) Now what? Before our eyes, lovely, happy nudity … and, by heaven, this was obviously France!

'It's the only way through,' I said, summing up the situation, and trying to sound objective. To our left was a cliff, barring the way, with the breakers creaming at its feet – then a strip of sand, and sharp-edged, sloping slabs – the only sharp-edged objects to be seen in that direction …

That Livanos! I could just imagine him grinning over his 'route description', specially designed for 'Romantics'.

'We must get across – but how?' growled Wolfi, wrinkling his forehead. We had never met a mountaineering difficulty of this kind before, and there is no mention of it in Paulcke's textbook on alpine dangers. But it has never been our habit to beat a retreat.

'There are only two ways about it,' I philosophised. 'To be noticeable or not to be noticeable. With, or without … '

Wolfi scratched his head. 'Oh, well,' he said, smiling contentedly. We decided for 'with'. The alternative would really have been too much bother, with all this climbing gear of ours …

We were certainly noticed. The first looks cast upon us went through us like gimlets. We thought hard of the *Grande Chandèle* and continued on our way.

Now everybody was staring at us, the intruders, with many an inquisitive glance. Could we be members? Blushing, we looked, as indifferently as possible, away beyond slim shoulders, feeling the while appallingly 'dressed up'. None the less we accomplished that exciting traverse. With stride unfaltering, our pitons clinking among French bosoms, our bodies hung about with ropes and climbing hammers among French buttocks, dazzled by graceful contours, our pulses racing, but undeterred, we made our way through that shapely panorama set in the graceful coastal scenery of the Calanques; two tough sinewy alpine figures, their thoughts fixed only on the summits, the cynosure of all eyes, like models on a catwalk … Suddenly, Wolfi begun to hum a Parisian ditty, unmusically, out of tune. I too slowed my pace as I crossed the big, sharp-edged, sun-drenched limestone slabs, with their outcrop of sheer loveliness. I had to, of course, because of the sharp edges …

I wondered if mountaineers could qualify for membership? My pace grew still slower. After all, Paulcke's book on alpine dangers says: 'Go slowly and you go well, and if you go well you go far.'[1] And if you go well … ! Ye gods, I was fairly dazzled the next moment; if I could only address that gorgeous creature! I groaned – oh, these language difficulties! – and passed on in silence, broken hearted. Passed on, left her … and if you go well – that ass Paulcke had no idea what well means. Well didn't mean the same thing, here and now. No, here, if you go slowly, all that happens – unfortunately – is that you still get on far too quickly. At this moment a deep sigh next to me announced the end of the 'Song of Paris'. If you go slowly, you get along too quickly and much too far; there was no doubt that we had irretrievably completed the traverse. I sat down, exhausted, on a boulder. Wolfi said not a word and passed the flask of peppermint tea across to me; then he took a swig himself. From the last slab of paradise the strains of the Marseillaise came wafting over to us.

---

1 *'Ce va piano, va sano: the va sano va lontano.'*

It was only later, from much higher up, that we observed quite a different approach route to the Grande Chandèle. Livanos again – he never mentioned it!

Oh, well …

Sun, sea and sand – and, of course, rock. The weather had long ago turned fine again on Mont Blanc; but it was fine here too, and here stood our tent, on the seashore.

We balanced our delicate way up that lovely ridge. Down below lay the island-studded sea; a gentle breeze blew in from the distant horizon, the rock was firm, the water rippled and glinted, more than 1,500 feet beneath our feet. A splendid cliff, this Grande Chandèle, a marvellous tower, set in an enviably beautiful practice ground, in the midst of a region that has neither roads nor houses – almost as it was in the beginning of things …

We sat on top, blinking up at the sun, down to the sea.

'*C'est très joli ici*,' remarked Wolfi, for once in unexceptionable French.

'*Tu as raison*,' I replied. Then we went off for a swim.

15   The Great Peuterey Ridge

First: a black and white title, then a deep orange one, across a black and white picture. After that, grass, green or brownish in colour; a little lake, high above the Val Veni; the shining dome of Mont Blanc ...

Words: *'A silence – almost absurd – a silence built of substance and tiny seconds ... fashioned by this autumn sunshine ...'*

Terenzio's voice quavered a little. Renato sat there, leaning forward, headphones on his ears, his hand on the volume control – a dark silhouette, like the others. Not a sound except Terenzio's speech. Not a movement, for the microphone picks up everything. There, on the top floor of our house in the Via Crispi, on the outskirts of Varese, at two in the morning, we were recording our film: 'The Great Ridge'. Action! Silently, I touch Terenzio's shoulder – the signal for him to start speaking: *'Every really great peak ... demands its aura of silence ...'*

It was going like a bomb, this time; we hoped it would be the last night of our recording sessions for Renato, Tona, Terenzio, Adriano, Gianluigi – the little team which could really take the credit if the film ever reached the Trento Festival. I had spent the whole summer cutting, joining sequence to sequence, excising again, swapping them round – arguing, defending, quarrelling, viewing, planning and reconsidering – with Tona and, particularly, with Renato. Anyone can shoot a film; to bring its idea to eventual fruition, to the point where the perforated reels constitute a film which projects what one had in mind, so that others can share in the experience, is quite another matter. I would never have succeeded but for my friends, but for Tona and, of course, my own obstinate head; for this was my first attempt at a film. I listened to Terenzio's rough, dark voice – so appropriate to this odyssey on the Great Ridge; his elocution might at times be imperfect, but what mattered was that he was a climber, and therefore knew exactly what I wanted. So had they all – and they had all, long ago, lived through that adventure on the Great Ridge, high above the Val Veni ... in September, with hardly a breath ruffling the grasses, the air unimaginably clear, and not a sound invading it ...

Words, once more: *'Space ... seems to lose a dimension here ... a flower, the summit of Mont Blanc ... both infinitely near ... or infinitely, far ...'*

The camera zooms slowly upwards – up the Aiguille Noire – the Aiguille Blanche – three seconds of Mont Blanc's summit (everything has to be timed to a split second) – now … I press Terenzio's shoulder again.

'*Trrreeeeng– Wumm– Trrreee … !*'

'Curse all motorcyclists ! At two in the morning, of all things !'

Trrrreng – we could still hear it, disappearing in the distance. Everything washed out! This rider of a moped, at two in the morning, who had nothing better to do than choose the Via Crispi for his homeward journey, and with his throttle wide open at that, had wrecked everything. We had taken everything into account – even the bells of the nearby church – and now this … he had even broken the temporary padding of our 'recording studio' under the roof. A good thing for him that we couldn't lay hands on him!

Adriano rewound the spool, cursing. Then we started all over again: '*A silence … almost absurd … '*

A glitter of snow diamonds, a pale glimmer on the crest of Mont Blanc, under a yellowy-orange sky, and a figure moving up from the depths …

Words again: '*Aims, eyes, spirit – all focused on infinity … '*

As the figure came closer, Gianluigi plucked deep open-string notes, like the sound of bells, haphazard, and as he thought fitting for this moment, as if he himself were the central feature of the film. It could have been his dark blue figure, moving across the glittering lights in the snow …

'*Buongiorno – and a good morrow be yours, too!*'

Well done, Terenzio. He had said it so feelingly – and how important that was, when there were a hundred ways of saying it; why, he might have said it in a voice that conveyed, 'to hell with it – I've had enough of this!' No, he had spoken the last words of the film in exactly the right way. Renato took off his headphones.

'My blessed infants,' he said, 'we've done it!'

We toasted Trento, the film, the ridge, anything and everything. Anyone in the Via Crispi at four o'clock that morning might well have wondered what kind of a party was going on under the tiled roof up there.

We hardly dared to hope that the film would win a prize at Trento – where, this time, space would provide competition.

The longest ridge traverse in the Alps is no simple tour, but a great mountaineering expedition. It was Tona who put the question which was in all our minds:

'Will the viewer understand the unfolding of this huge traverse, up over the ridges, up and down over towers and peaks? Above all, have we succeeded in conveying the spirit in which the climb was carried through? Have we been able – in three-quarters of an hour and 1,500 feet of film – to capture, for others, five miles of climbing, five days of it, the nightly bivouacs, the marvellous feeling of being up there, high above the world and outside time, the joy of it all … ?'

She was right. The idea of making a film up there had meant a complete divorce from time; a traverse of that great ridge almost in the spirit of a hiker, day after day, content to wait in one place till the light and the clouds were right for the picture – even on so mighty a ridge.

We had, of course, no idea whether we could do it. Hermann Buhl and Gaston Rèbuffat had tried before us to traverse the ridge in its entirety; both had failed, driven down by bad weather. The traverse had only been completed twice, once by a German party, once by a Polish. Of all the great climbs in the Alps, this one will remain the least often accomplished; for here the probabilities of success are lower than on the North Face of the Eiger or the Walker Spur of the Jorasses, both of which it exceeds in size and length – five miles of climbing, roping down, then climbing again, on the most varied of ground, as against about two miles on those famous Alpine north faces. The first sector alone, the South Ridge of the Noire, involves a mile and a half of climbing between Grades III and V, the second consists of a 1,600-foot abseil down that peak's vertical North Arête – a large imponderable in bad weather!

The final sector, the traverse of the Aiguille Blanche, the descent on to the broad saddle of the Col de Peuterey and the 3,000 foot ascent from there to the summit of Mont Blanc – this sector by itself is often called the Peuterey Ridge, though it only, constitutes its upper half – is technically easier, but just as grand and impressive; here too a change in the weather has often dictated a retreat.

To make the route up this 'upper half' of the ridge easier, the Italian Alpine Club has established a small bivouac box on the Brèche Nord at about 11,500 feet; many have spent storm-bound days in it, glad that it was there to give them shelter. (The ascent to it is a big climb in its own right – it is reached from the Fresnay Glacier up a couloir, after picking a route to its foot between veritable palaces of ice).

Franz Lindner and I estimated that our traverse of the ridge, including all the preparations and a return to the Val Veni – where we had set up a kind of base camp – from the summit of Mont Blanc would require at least a fortnight. (Wolfi wasn't very keen on the proposition on account of the gigantic abseil from the Noire. Not long before, during a winter attempt on the South Face of the Dachstein, a piton had come away as he was roping down, and he had fallen nearly ten feet; by a miracle, and thanks to the depth of the snow, he had suffered nothing more than a horrid fright, but, understandably, he had ever since evinced a slight bias against abseils.) Franz and I established a first ever supply dump close to the bivouac box in the Brèche Nord; we also left the ice equipment up there, so as to carry less weight during the rock work on the

Noire. Using two 'museum' ice axes from the days of our grandfathers, and without crampons, we worked our way down to the Fresnay Glacier and back to the valley, across the Col Innominata. There we replaced the axes on the Guides' Monument (from which we had borrowed them in the first place), and climbed back to our base camp. Everything was now ready.

It was on a wonderful September afternoon that we set out for the little untended Noire hut, near the Fauteuil des Allemands.

Soundtrack: 'This scent of autumn pervading the air, this gentle sunshine, almost warm, augured good luck for our climb ... how near was Mont Blanc's summit ... how far, the summit of Mont Blanc ... '

The Great Ridge. For me this was much more than a climb, this ridge at which I had looked up so often. Today I still count it as the biggest and most reward-ing of all the great alpine routes. It will remain so; for in it there lies combined, everything that can make a climber's heart beat faster.

We were roping up. All our night thoughts, our mountain doubts, melted away. Only the present counted now. The pinnacles of the south ridge were already touched by the fingers of the dawn.

The South Ridge of the Noire ...

The rock under our hands was gloriously rough, every hold, solid as steel. Up it went, up and up, slab after slab, cliff upon cliff, tower after tower, all of it steep, and always above the sheer abyss on either side. Mists came drifting up from the séracs of the Fresnay Glacier, to dance around the pinnacles and about us as we climbed on, drinking in the fresh clean autumn air.

All around us lay sunlight and valley and vast distances; the banks of cloud building slowly in the sky, the turquoise eye of the little Checrouit lake far below, and the warm scent of autumn rising from the foothill meadows; the grey rubble stream of the Miage Glacier, snaking deep down into the valley, right into the green of the forests and the fields; the tiny houses along the Dora's banks – all far, far below.

The rock was beautifully varied. We met slabs whose rounded surfaces were covered with greyish-green lichens; white felspar crystals stuck out here and there, asking to be pocketed. There were ledges offering firm foothold for a groping boot, wrinkles in the rock inviting one to entrust the whole of one's body weight to them and heave it up with one's arms. We came to a huge over-hang and used each other's shoulders to overcome it. Then we were over the second tower and on our way to the next, the Pointe Welzenbach. We traversed out on to the right-hand face over ledges and slabs.

So we went on and up along the granite Jacob's ladder of the south ridge. And while our arms and legs were busy with the mechanics of climbing and our eyes engaged in searching out the way ahead, our thoughts went out over all the depths and distances around and about us. It goes without saying that we were happy beyond measure on our south ridge.

By the afternoon we were on the summit of the Pointe Welzenbach. There we sat down to rest and eat, and looked down on the way we had come. The first tower, the Pointe Gamba, looked like a small tooth, the pinnacles of the second lay far below us, and here we were, sitting on the third. Willo Welzenbach once got as far as this; it was some time after that before a way was found to the summit over the Pointe Brendel and the Bich. Looking up at the yellow and rust-coloured walls, we rated them at fully V – perhaps a bit more than that, though there is only one short traverse on the vertical face of the Bich, which is supposed to be from V to VI.

We were at a little flat place with a bivouac wall all round it, a reminder that not everyone can do the South Ridge in a single day, and that we would probably find quite a few 'parapets' higher up.

We wondered whether we could still get to the top of the Pointe Brendel before nightfall. 'Let's get on with it,' said Franz, and we started off again. We now came to the first abseil, where we soon found a suitable block; the rope went whistling down and we followed comfortably enough in our 'Dülfer' seats. There followed a gently sloping step and a traverse to the left before we were at the foot of the Brendel's severe upthrust.

We craned our heads backwards to look up it, and spotted the route up the almost perpendicular slabs to the left, leading to the overhang above. This was another of the many things we wanted to film, but the difficulty was how to look after the rope at the same time? 'Leave it to me,' said Franz, taking the camera, and off I went. After a slightly overhanging start, I reached the first piton and could see the second, ahead of me. Of course, the rope had to jam plumb in between the two, just when I was not exactly comfortably placed. 'What's up?' I shouted down to Franz, 'give me some rope !' 'Lovely shooting,' he replied calmly and put the camera away. 'Now you'll have to wait a bit while I get the knot undone.' It didn't really take very long but, getting my breath back at the second piton, I thought to myself: 'No more safety knots in the rope, thank you. It's better just to rely on climbing carefully!'

Unfortunately the sun chose that moment to disappear behind a big cloud, so I had to wait. Not that it mattered, for we didn't care how far we got that day; but as the blessed light of the sun seemed to have gone for good, I decided to get on with the traverse. The moment I was across, of course the sun came out again. Up came Franz's voice : 'Get back again!' I couldn't very well refuse, and in any case, it was a nice traverse; so back I went and did it again. It all took ages, but I had to chuckle at the thought that for once we didn't mind about time, and what huge fun it was not to have to. Our journey up the great ridge would go on for days – just as many days as needed – all of them glorious days, as we simply climbed higher and higher up it.

We climbed the second pitch of the Brendel in the dusk. Presently it was quite dark, as we felt our way over easier rock to the spacious summit. There we found a splendid place for an overnight bivouac, in a hollow, where we could lie down and stretch full length, side by side; once again it was equipped with a protecting wall to break the wind. There was only one fly in the ointment; we were dreadfully thirsty. Naturally there isn't any water laid on the south ridge, and nowhere on the way had we seen so much as a spot of snow. There was nothing to be done about it, and one can't have everything; perhaps we would find some tomorrow, on the summit.

The night was still, with only an occasional feeble stirring of the air about the peak, both only to die away almost at once. We were very happy with the day's work and looked forward to a night in the open worth remembering. It was very clear, and a thousand stars shone down on us with a rare brilliance. Soon I was welcoming my old friend Orion, as he came up over the horizon.

Then I suddenly noticed a patch of light shimmering between the rocks. I switched my torch on and there, miraculously, in autumn time, up here, was some old snow. It must have been the only fragment of snow on the whole of the South Ridge. We took it in turns, without more ado, to lie on our stomachs sucking in the little trickle of melting water from that old snow, repeating the performance again and again. It was bliss, and now our happiness was complete. The only thing missing had been water.

It was a lovely night. We slept full length on our rocky bed, wrapped warmly in our fleece bags, covered by the tent sack. Every now and then I woke up to look up at the stars, to the glittering scarf of the Milky Way, and to watch the leisurely progress of Orion; happy in the knowledge that we would be continuing our journey up this great ridge for many another similar day.

Being autumn, it got a little chilly towards dawn. Slowly the sky lightened, yellow at first, then blue to eastwards; then the sun shot up and it was day again. The granite towers of our ridge were swathed in mists, turning our little summit to an island in the monotony of grey, through which the sun glimmered from time to time. At times the wind parted the curtains and we looked up at Mont Blanc, still remote and high above us. Down below, the cloud shadows were chasing across the crevassed surface of the Fresnay Glacier. We made breakfast and did some filming, before we realised it was eleven o'clock and time to be on the move.

Ahead of us lay the hardest sector on the whole climb, the precipitous surge up to the Pointe Bich, whose arête and ensuing traverse had moved even Hermann Buhl to respectful utterance. We wondered a little how we would fare on it with all our baggage. The passage of a few pinnacles in the next col brought us to the foot of the pitch. Baggage and all, it went better than we had expected; admittedly, we were reaping the fruits of an unbroken summer's climbing, and that helped a lot. Once up the steep arête, we tackled the traverse, which goes off to the right along a short airy rock ledge above an overhang, offering only tiny fingerholds and forcing one's body out over nothingness. Short as it is, it made extreme demands on our fingers, while our packs did their best to pull us outwards off the mountain. It was soon over and we stopped for a breather before continuing for quite a time over easier ground. Now it would not be long before we were on the Noire's subsidiary summit. Then came another difficult rope's length, involving slabs and a small overhang. While Franz worked his way up from piton to piton, I filmed him and looked after his rope. Then we decided to put the camera away for a while, for it was time to be getting on to the summit of the Noire. On we went, over easy rock, to the subsidiary summit, and looked across to the true summit, on which the metal statue of the Madonna was reflecting the light of the setting sun. Below it, blazed the gigantic slabs of the West Face; and there, far down behind the Noire, where it was now getting dark, we thought we could make out the bivouac box, and wondered whether we would get there tomorrow. We only stopped long enough to look at the vast panorama spread about us, then roped down into the next gap. Soon we were climbing over easy boulders, sometimes on the ridge, sometimes on the face, towards the summit.

A red sunset was flushing the sky as we reached the Madonna. There were isolated clouds floating above the mountaintops, shaped like big fishes, raising sudden misgivings in our minds. What would we do if the weather chose this moment to turn sour on us? Ahead lay the tremendous abseil down the northern arête of the Noire, an undertaking to be treated with the greatest respect. It would be a serious blow if the weather broke here and now. We could only hope it would hold till the day after tomorrow and that we should be able to reach our provisions at the bivouac box first. We found a sheltered place below the summit, with plenty of room to lie full length, and made everything snug for our second night out. The lights of Courmayeur twinkled up from the valley as the night passed slowly by.

A Break in the Weather

The summit of the Noire put on a halo of gold. A sky of unusual beauty, shot with every imaginable colour, heralded the rising of the sun. And the weather was still good.

We breakfasted on porridge, and packed up. We knew that very few parties had roped down the North Arête, and had brought plenty of pitons in case we went wrong. The abseil facilities at the summit did not look very safe to us, so we banged a heavy ring piton into the rock just below its northern side; as it went in more firmly at every stroke, my grateful thoughts went out to Wolfgang Stefan, my companion through years of climbing, who had given it to me for this very purpose. We had climbed the South Ridge several years earlier up to this point, but no farther, thinking ourselves not yet ripe for the whole Peuterey Ridge.

The piton was home, down went our two 130-foot ropes, and I was soon on my way down over sloping slabs, and straight into thick fog, a not very helpful feature, which would make route finding very much harder. However, the weather was still fine, even if things seemed to counsel greater speed than before. At the bottom of the rope I found some more pitons in the rock, and made myself fast, leaving the rope free for Franz's descent. We were soon heaving the ropes out into a white emptiness again and listening for them to 'slap' down below. For a few moments we caught a glimpse of the inclined slabs which would be our next landing-ground; then we tested the pitons and followed one another down through thin air. We were delighted to find the next launching platform, after swinging to and fro a little in our 'chairs'; there were three differently coloured loops of rope hanging there ... All we had to do was to retrieve our own rope, thread it and go on down.

We could have done without the fog, though. Finding the right place for the next stage in the descent at the end of each rope's length was becoming quite a problem.

After another 'air lift' we found ourselves jammed together on an exiguous stance in the crest of the arête. We could see a shelf thirty feet below us, with pitons and wood pegs coming up towards us, new ones; so we must be bang on Jean Couzy's direct route. We heaved the ropes over the edge; they disappeared silently, drew taut, without so much as a 'slap'. All the indications were that we should be sitting suspended over the void at the end of our 130 feet. We dropped a stone and – after a longish time – could barely hear the sound of its impact; so there must be 200 to 250 feet of vertical and partly undercut rock beneath us. We had better go down the thirty feet to the shelf. We reached it soon enough and when I pushed myself along it, still in my sling, at last I came upon an abseil piton, from which our ropes would touch the bottom.

That airy descent landed us on the great shoulder of the Noire's North Arête. From there we were left with the same distance down a chimney as we had already come from the summit. The first thing to do was to retrieve the rope. We tugged with all our strength, it wouldn't budge. It had stuck somewhere up there.

Stupid! We changed positions and tugged some more. Both of us, with might and main. All in vain: the rope just hung there, hopelessly stuck up above – 130 feet above, right at the top, of course. A nice kettle of fish, to be sure. The only solution was to climb all the way up in prusik slings and straighten things out.

Franz volunteered for that thankless job, saying he had been practising the technique only a little while ago. To some purpose, I must admit, when I saw him get up in under a quarter of an hour. Meanwhile it had started to snow. The weather had broken. Franz arranged the ropes in a different direction, tested their mobility and came down again. We both hauled anxiously on the rope, this time with better results than before. Cheers – the thing was moving!

The gigantic chimney, with its thousand feet of roping-down, was unmistakable in spite of the mist, and when, at the end of the first abseil we came upon a chock stone with a rope ring, we knew we were on the right road. Rope after rope, down and down we went. At times stones whistled past, dangerously near. After a time it stopped snowing. The chimney became a steep groove which we only left almost at its bottom, traversing out to the right between abseil stages every now and then, so as to reduce the height differential between us and the rift falling from the Brèche Sud to the Fresnay Glacier as much as possible.

It was halfway through the afternoon before we finally got into the rift. There was no time to waste if we were still to get to the bivouac box on the Brèche Nord. We packed up the ropes and climbed up over slabby debris to the Brèche Sud. There we had to turn the pinnacles of the Dames Anglaises, rising in an irregular cluster ahead of us, on their left flank. We climbed a little way, then traversed slightly downwards, with frequent changes of direction, dictated by the nature of the ground. We had to go very carefully, for the rock, while not difficult, was unreliable and there were snow patches in between. After much up and down and to and fro on the unstable stuff, we were very glad to reach the couloir leading up to the Brèche Nord. All that lay between us and the bivouac box now was the upper arm of the couloir, consisting, unfortunately, of sheer smooth ice.

So near and yet so far! We were dog-tired, hungry, and it was growing dark. Otherwise we were perfectly happy. In spite of a day of bad weather, we had managed to traverse the Noire and reach our objective. The rest of the ridge was practically in the bag, for with enough provisions up there at the bivouac box to enable us to face even a prolonged spell of bad weather, what could now prevent one going on, to the top of Mont Blanc?

I led, using the only crampon we had with us, while Franz belayed me with due care. While I was beating step on step in the smooth surface with my ice hammer, it was suddenly pitch dark. At long last we got off the ice and reached the slabby saddle of the Brèche Nord, with the bivouac box close at hand. Outside, the snowflakes were whirling as we lay down, there and then, to sleep. How long, we wondered drowsily, before it turns fine again?

Our fourth day on the ridge dawned. We snuggled closer in our blankets with only one resolution in our minds – to have a day off. All the same, we took a look at the weather through the door of the box; fresh snow was lying outside, but the sun was shining, newly risen. The fine weather was back again after the break. We would certainly have to wait a day for the layer of snow to settle. So we fetched everything out of the depot and had a good tuck-in after our days of scanty fare. We reconnoitred the next day's route for a short way and took a few feet of film. Our load for the following day was hugely inflated by provisions, ice equipment, extra film gear, a tripod and all the rest, but we felt very fit. Still, if we were going to climb from 11,500 feet, where we stood, over the Aiguille Blanche and on to Mont Blanc's 15,782-feet summit, we should have to make an early start. A fine day gave way to a clear evening. We knew then that we could be sure of fine weather for the last stage of our long trek.

The Final Day

Autumn, in tune with our most secret desires, gave us, for our last day, her most perfect of all perfect days. As we climbed the Aiguille Blanche, our eyes ranged far and wide over innumerable peaks, in the warmth of the morning sun, under an immaculate blue sky. Down in the green valleys the houses of Entrèves and Courmayeur were small, beyond belief. It was sheer bliss to be alive.

Behind us the Noire diminished rapidly. We kept on thinking about its South Ridge, the night we had spent out on it, the exciting endless abseil down its northern arête, till at last the traverse of the triple-headed Blanche began to demand all our care and attention. From the summit we looked down on the huge saddle of the Col de Peuterey, lying nearly 1,000 feet below us – another long abseil. Once down, we jumped the bergschrund and tramped across the broad, smooth saddle; up over the opposing schrund, and then a short rest. The sun was already slanting down, so short are these September days. On, we went up the long, long 3,000 feet which separate the col from Mont Blanc's summit. Once on the ridge again, we were met by an icy blast, though the view and the sky remained clear. We made slow progress, taking care that the bitter gusts didn't unbalance us on the narrow white edge. Suddenly the great white mountains around us glowed red and Mont Blanc's monstrous shadow streamed out across the world. It was an overwhelming sight, even if the gale called for all our attention and our fingers had grown numb.

Presently there was nothing except a livid twilight. Moving together, we worked our way up without a pause. We did not belay, but each of us was on the alert, knowing that a slip on that narrow ladder to the sky could hardly be held. Then it was night. The abyss fell away beneath us, impalpable, illimitable, invisible. We only knew that it was there below us. Neither of us could see the other, obliterated by the uncanny darkness. And so we climbed, endlessly, onwards. Endlessly, straight up – up into the vague, dark nothingness overhead; but now we were belaying one another, rope after rope. The ridge gave way to a rounded slope, a kind of broad rib, getting steeper and steeper. The gigantic cornice of Mont Blanc de Courmayeur never seemed to want to put in an appearance.

We could see a sharp silhouette against the stars. It was the cornice, and soon we had found a way through a breach in it. We sat down thankfully in the snow. We had done it. We were up. What was left to do would be nothing by contrast with the last few hours.

We moved on again through the marvellous night. This was the last stage on the long journey from the valley to Mont Blanc's summit; and as we went, our thoughts were centred on the days behind us.

(Tona) 'To our surprise, the hall was full of applause. So the public had understood and identified itself with that long journey on which Kurt, Franz and all the rest of us had worked so hard! We were at the Eleventh Mountain Film Festival at Trento. Kurt was going up the step to receive the prize. I was full of joy for him, for our friends, for everyone who may in future traverse the great Peuterey Ridge. To have brought it off was a marvellous feeling. I had had the luck to contribute something – helping Kurt to share something of his passion, his mountain magic, with others.

'He looks at his ridge with loving eyes, and it was perhaps a part of that love he had succeeded in giving us.'

The Great Ridge …

16   Alpine Geometry

Mont Blanc de Cheilon

'Mathematics are marvellous!' our maths master used to pontificate, a sublime expression transfiguring his thin face.

We knew he meant it, and none of us dared to refute him; we nodded silently and thought about the next exercise we should have to do. He was very strict. Today I am sure he was right: mathematics are wonderful. They are clear and incorruptible – especially in exercises, at school. I even taught mathematics myself for a year or two.

However what I set out to talk about is 'Alpine Geometry' – a very specialised subject. Every climber knows the thrill of his own trail up a face – the pleasure in its regularity (the final consequence of which idea is, of course, the *direttissima*). He knows the thrill, the unique inexplicable tension, which the regular shapes of the mountain world awake in him: huge pyramids, enormous rectangular slabs, piled-up triangles of rock, white circles, immense squares – the thrill of simplicity of shape and outline (and the excitement of mastering them, to an unbelievable extent, by his own efforts, his own power), the thrill of the straight line upwards … in fact, the Alpine geometry … a thrill impossible to explain.

The first time I discovered something of the fascination of form was when, suddenly in a practical geometry session, cylinders, cones and pyramids started to turn on the papers, rolled through different 'eye levels', threw their shadows on it. I was doing much more than required at the time, cutting imaginary pyramids open, letting the light fall into them, turning them, making clusters of triangles penetrate one another and throw shadows on each other. Often I was not at all sure if I would get a result, or what it would be, there on the white expanse of paper. It was often hard work, but highly fanciful.

Yes, I was doing more than required – for I started to draw the figures for some of my classmates; and the professor was very pleased with us. A few errors, corresponding to the particular party, prevented him from noticing it. True, he seemed a little surprised when it came to oral tests – fortunately infrequent, but when they came fraught with minutes of shivering anxiety for those taking part. By doing practical geometry in this way I, again, avoided working on my thesis, a tedious essay in German on the 'treasures of the homeland'. We were a good team.

After I graduated I confessed to him. I admired him greatly not only because, in his own sphere, he was a past master, but because I like people who not only have an enthusiasm, but actually put it into practice.

Remote, in the ranges of the lower Valais, at the end of the lofty Val des Dix, a tributary valley of the Val d'Herens, stands a very unusual mountain. Seen from the north, it exhibits the shape of a huge pyramid, mathematical in its regularity. Its steep north face is, by one of nature's freaks, an exactly constructed equilateral triangle. It is called the Mont Blanc de Cheilon.

One day in the thirties two daring young men stood at the foot of the face, sampling it – Ludwig Steinauer and Wolfgang Gorter. Then they climbed it, by a route as straight as Steinauer's braces and Gorter's natty tie – up the plumb line. It was the first ascent of what was still now the single, finest and most direct line up that mighty triangle.

My 'geometrical' feelings sensed a challenge.

For thirty years there had been only one repetition of that first ascent – for obvious reasons. Not only was the face far from anywhere, but it was exceedingly steep, as witness the crowded contour lines on the map. In fact, the slabs of smooth ice and the rock shields of the final wall achieve a seventy-degree pitch in places. The second climb had not been carried through to the summit, but had finished with a traverse out on to the ridge. There had been good reasons for that: right at the top, the crust – as elsewhere, too – is very thin, and getting thinner year by year; so the risk is increased and, at places, where polished rock has now made an appearance, so have the technical difficulties. It seems incredible, but Gorter and Steinauer on their first ascent managed to find a bivouac place up there, on that final wall. It must have been very uncomfortable.

Max and I had once again had our fill of desks and window views on to a garden, of the harassing day-to-day preparatory work for our expedition to Dhaulagiri. This had meant hundreds of letters; arrangements for a glacier aircraft; and, to raise the necessary funds, one of the biggest greetings card operations ever mounted (we were later to dispatch 16,000 of them from Katmandu). The organisation of an expedition demands strong nerves. We felt that if we didn't tackle a climb soon, we would cease to be human beings. So we got into the car and headed for the Valais.

The guardian of the Cabane de Dix came into the dormitory and woke us at 2 a.m. Half asleep we staggered down to the common room, packed the last essentials and had a hot drink. Then we stepped outside.

It was very cold and there was not even the tiniest of clouds in the sky. In the light of the full moon we did not need to switch on a lamp. Our mountain bulked up enormous ahead of us, seemingly quite inaccessible, and ghostly in the moonlight. We crossed the glacier in a wide curve from the right, making for a prominent pulpit of rock, projecting from the right-hand end of the mountain's base. It was the only place from which we could hope to gain access to the foot of the face, for to the left every approach was barred by a high barrier of séracs.

It was still dark when we got there, to find that it was hardly any distance down into the hollow beyond. We decided it would be best to rope up, and while we were doing so, the eastern sky began to brighten. A cutting wind had risen, stiffening our fingers; but it was an east wind – a good omen. For a little while Max had some trouble with a too short crampon strap. Daylight was coming swiftly now; we could see the mighty upsurge of our triangle, felt the thrill of the clean straight line, the excitement of following it up there, step by step …

We got down into the hollow and went up, over small avalanche cones, to the bergschrund. It gaped wide open, but we found a place where it could be crossed quite easily. And then we were on the face.

There was hard grey ice in the avalanche tracks, but we always found snow-covered ribs on which we could make upward progress. When, occasionally, they petered out all of a sudden, we had to traverse on to the next rib, now to the left, now to the right. It was quite an amusing game, picking out the best line. At the end of each rope's length we hammered in a belaying piton. The second would then come up, climb through, and assume the lead till the next stance – fully 200 feet each time. So we gained height rapidly.

Meanwhile, the sun had come up, its light appropriately matching our joy at this gorgeous climb. We felt sure that, with everything going so well down here, things wouldn't be half so bad as expected when it came to climbing out, up above. We might even be on the summit by midday!

Each time the leader hacked out a stance, a cloud of glittering crystals came tinkling down the face, raced past and disappeared in a rapidly thinning veil towards the abyss. There, on a hillock at the glacier's rim, stood the hut, small and forlorn. The light pricked out every wrinkle in the moraine. A few insignificant splinters of rock on the east bank had grown into gigantic shadow fingers, clutching far across the glacier's surface. 'Like looking down from the rim of some moon crater,' I couldn't help thinking: or like the echo mountains of Saint Exupery's Little Prince, when he came to visit the Earth.' Yes, pictures of Mont Blanc de Cheilon hold something more than that for me: an utter feeling of release. The breath-taking sensation, the joy, of denying the vertical its verticality; of hanging poised between huge and different eye levels; the experience of watching the earth's greatest shapes 'turning', beginning to change, raising up, sinking down into the depths – as if by some conjuring trick – simply because a small human being, taking thousands of strides, alters for himself that 'eye level', freeing himself from the one basic eye level of the plains.

The experience the climber and the man at the drawing board share is the same sense of freedom and power, many times multiplied: a sense of mastery over all planes, the horizontal, the vertical and all the others, but in their actual reality. A gigantic practical geometry. The climber can make the greatest objects in the world turn for his inspection, so that he is able to grasp their form, simply because he has climbed above the usual plane on to a mountain. And once he has done that, all planes are his …

The higher we got, the more mightily did the Dent Blanche tower up to the east, its North Ridge savagely crenelated.

Our wall continued to get steeper and steeper. When we looked down to the bergschrund, the slope down there looked flat; yet we remembered clearly how, for the two hours spent on it, we had regarded its inclination as 'quite something'.

When Max was leading, all I could see of him as I looked up were his legs, his rucksack and the rope, falling free for a long way before it touched the snow. We were now on a white rib, barely a yard wide, which swept unbroken to the foot of the rocks above. With an ice piton in our left hand and the hammer in our right, we made good progress up it. The snow, however, grew progressively more unstable and it was with mixed feelings that we gazed up at a tortuous couloir, overhead to the right, which led through the armour plating of the summit wall's slabs and seemed to offer the only route. Now, too, as we approached the rocks, our ice slope steepened again considerably. At every step we noticed that smooth ice lay under the continually thinning snow. The underlying layer often changed in the course of a few yards, and we tried to make the most of what offered by zigzagging upwards.

At about 9 a.m. we reached the foot of a slabby rock buttress, interrupted by small snow patches, which rose towards the summit. At this point we had come up more than half the face, and its right-hand containing ridge was much nearer now – the one whose shadow falls far across the face in the afternoon, just as now, in the morning, the buttress casts its shade from the other direction. If only we didn't run into bad snow just here …

We stopped, close to the right-hand base of the pillar, at a great block jutting out like a balcony, near a frozen waterfall. We were sure that there would be a practicable pillar of snow above it, though we could not see it from where we were. Then we moved very slowly upwards, to meet exactly what we had feared – loose powder snow lying on polished ice.

At each step my left hand drove the piton, gripped very short, into tiny crevices in the steep face as hard as I could; my right hand, holding the ice hammer propped my body away from the wall, and the front teeth of my twelve-pointer crampons dug into the ice – not very far, but just enough.

'Six feet more!' came up from below. Aha! At last the rope was running out. I hacked out a handhold and banged in a piton. Then I cleared a stance in the ice with my axe; the fragments went hurtling down to where Max, a rope's length lower down, pressed his body into the face, so as to escape them as much as possible. How glad he'll be that he has a helmet on, I thought.

Max came up and joined me at the stance. Where do we go now? Perhaps the rock above us to the left would go? The only other alternative was a dicey-looking traverse up to the right, to where the couloir began again. Let's try up to the left – after an overhanging rock pitch there seemed to be a ledge running up to the pillar.

The ledge was an illusion; it turned out to be a steep slab with snow lying on it. However, after about thirty feet it looked much better than expected, for the next bit, anyway. I had to clear away whole masses of snow to get any kind of a handhold, then I moved a foot cautiously, my crampons found some kind of a purchase – but I couldn't see where, and was glad to get a belaying piton in at once. On with the grind! No stance yet, but a crack, into which I could get my arms, and then a foot. So far, so good; but still no stance. I pressed on – it must get better soon. 'What's up?' Max called from below. 'Nothing,' I shouted back, gasping for breath and taking great care not to slide out of my snowed-up crack. At last I reached a knob of rock; I had arrived at the pillar. But where in heaven's name had I landed myself? Nothing but snowed-up slabs, seventy degrees steep, ahead. Suppose I took my crampons off? That would be lunacy, for there were continual snow-patches between the places where the wind had blown it away. No, my lad, you have committed a hopeless blunder this time!

I looked around me, resignedly. Over there on the right lay the traverse we had been so keen to avoid. From here it looked a novice's delight! True enough, it often happens that everything looks easier than just where one happens to be – but there was definitely no future where I was. So back we go again!

It took a long time to get down, and as soon as I got there Max tackled the traverse. I was somewhat depressed; our 'howler' had cost us a great deal of time. We would have to make up for it now, if we could– easier said than done … I could already hear Max's irons scratching on sheer rock under the snow. So there were slabs there too. Max came back a little way, climbed down about six feet and tried again. Anxiously I followed his every movement. I was able to give a little diagonal support with the rope, but it wasn't much help to him out there. He went down another three feet, then started to traverse. I held my breath, taking every step he took with him in my mind. Grab that boulder sticking out of the snow! He had hold of it. I breathed again; he was over the worst bit. Then he began to climb again. 'Fifteen feet more!' I shouted across to him. Very soon Max was hacking out a stance in the ice of the couloir and belaying with two pitons. I rejoined him on a comfortable stance, where he had made an extra step for me, and leaned against the wall. As it was by now midday we ate a snack; standing in our steps, and took a good swig at the tea flask. The pencilled shadows had vanished from the glacier; only the crevasses – we were looking straight down into them – showed dark.

Thank goodness, we were now on ice again. We hoped it would continue for a long way up. We were certain of one thing: even the steepest of smooth ice was here preferable to the snow-covered rock, with its downward stratification.

Max went on, and cut a few steps. 'The ice is getting thinner again,' he called down, 'and pretty putrid into the bargain!' The rope ran out a foot at a time and there were long pauses in between. Small wonder, for the pitch of the couloir was fearsome and the crust of ice had dried out and become so thin that the hammer kept on striking through to the underlying rock; and the rock, thanks to the action of the ice was mostly smooth and totally inimical to pitons. Another rope's length farther up things didn't look quite so bad, however.

Max went on working his way up for nearly half an hour. His belaying piton, dug into the rock, was not very reliable. I moved forward with the utmost caution, and didn't get on much better. Nothing but black ice, powder snow, rock continually thrusting through. Meanwhile time simply raced away without our noticing it. It was well into the afternoon. The view into the abyss was fearsome. Slowly, terribly slowly, we gained height. Irritatingly, the summit's sharp ridge overhead seemed so close at hand. It could only be a couple of rope's lengths more …

Damn this final wall! Were we going to get stuck in it?

The sun was slanting down on the face, now. Clouds were slowly creeping up it from far down below. Evening was drawing in. We climbed on undeterred, but our progress could be measured in feet. The crest above our heads, which we had thought to be so near, drew nearer again. We must get there soon, now …

Yes, we had thought the same thing before – I don't know how long ago. Somewhere here those two bivouacked on the first ascent. I could not imagine where; for I could not see a level patch even the length of one's foot – everything was precipitous here … perhaps it had been still higher up.

Well, we had to get on. There were a couple of ice hoses, some three feet wide, reaching up into the rocks of the final wall like spider's legs. It could only be three more rope's lengths and that should be possible before it got dark. A bivouac here on the slabs would be a penance – like monkeys on a stick. We chose the right-hand hose, but after about fifty feet further progress in it was impossible. I wallowed my way forward through powder snow, unable to find a handhold anywhere. Then I found a crack for one foothold, but that exhausted all the possibilities. Well, there was a parallel groove over to the left;

nothing but to traverse into it. To my astonishment, miraculously, there was a good crack facing me – just what was needed for a fine belay! I hammered a piton in and it held firm. Now to get into the groove …

Thirty feet up it, I was able to manufacture a stance. Just as Max joined me there, the sun finally disappeared behind a bright bank of clouds. We hoped our luck would hold. Max climbed on and disappeared above me behind a rock arête. I could only pay out the rope foot by foot … evidently it hadn't got any easier.

I could no longer hear Max, though every now and then a shower of ice chippings and snow came hurtling down over that rocky edge. A lump of ice hit me on the shoulder, but I was past caring; I crouched against the face and waited.

Slowly the twilight seeped in, with clouds mounting high into the sky. Suddenly I was back in one of my first geometry lessons. Our maths master, full of enthusiasm, had just constructed an equilateral triangle on the blackboard, for us to copy into our exercise books. Spring was coming in, and I was watching the white clouds outside the window as they moved slowly towards the mountains. Next moment, those clouds were in my exercise book, floating round my triangle, quickly converted by a little shading into the semblance of a mountain. I was just considering how to sketch in the immediate neighbourhood when the whole thing came to a sudden end … it seems that our mathematician had no feeling for 'art' …

The glacier, far below at the foot of the face, was a blue-grey shadow. Down in the valley, the first lights were twinkling.

There was another hailstorm of ice chippings, followed by a load of powder snow. As they disappeared into the depths, Max called down to me. I was very glad to be on the move again.

The next rope's length brought me into darkness; the only glimmer of light was a pale streak in the western sky. 'There's a bivouac place up to the left,' shouted Max. I climbed a slab and a few feet of smooth ice, and reached the top of a rocky knob. It wasn't even big enough for one man to sit on! It was now pitch-dark, and I could only make out my immediate surroundings. The pinnacles of the summit ridge looked like a cardboard cut-out. Bivouac – but where? Climb on by the light of our helmet lamp?

I could not make out how far it still was; I only knew I was at the start of another gully. I felt my way gingerly up it. Snow – good, holding snow! I worked my way carefully upwards; it was loose, but perfectly sound climbing. I called to Max to come up, for he had the lamp. It *must* go now.

Max came up, climbed past me to a better stance. Here, it was possible to undo a rucksack. We turned the lamp on; its beam captured a big round spot on one of the pinnacles of the summit ridge – quite near, not more than 130 feet, and the rock up to it not at all difficult! We had won our fight. I could hardly wait to fasten the lamp to my helmet. As one rocky knob after another caught its glare, I pictured to myself what our feelings would have been in the morning, if we had settled for a miserable bivouac a rope's length farther down.

We were on top. 'No bivouac!' we said. We could sit down comfortably at last. Here on the summit of Mont Blanc de Cheilon, with its mighty face down there below us. We rummaged in the rucksack for everything eatable; there was even some tea left in the flask – a welcome surprise. And the light of our lamp threw a cosy circle around us.

Then we climbed slowly down through the night. It was 2 a.m. when we sat on the wall outside the but and took our boots off.

We woke to a brilliant morning; more truthfully a brilliant forenoon, when we stepped outside the hut. Under a clear blue sky stretched the long snowy comb of the Pigne d'Arolla; in the east, small and neat, rose the Aguille de la Tza, and down the valley ranged the shattered pinnacles of the Aiguilles Rouges. Far away to the east we could still see the tip of the Matterhorn. A gentle breeze was sighing round the hut, and the yellow and orange coloured alpine poppies, growing thick on the knoll which houses the hut, were nodding their heads. A bee was humming hither and thither. We watched it and, every now and then, cast a glance up at our wall, humming – we too – any old song. On this glorious day, we felt as if everything – the air, the peaks and the glittering glacier – should join in.

We looked again to see whether the rope had dried out. Yes, it had. And what about our pitons, many of which had acquired a peculiar shape, like cracknels, since yesterday? They would need a bang or two with the hammer.

We packed our rucksacks and bade the hut keeper 'Au revoir !' Then we strolled along the lake, turning and turning again to where, at the valley's far head, Mont Blanc de Cheilon greeted our eyes. The Triangle.

17   The White Mountain of the Himalaya: Dhaulagiri

High above the foothills of the Terai, flashes an enormous pyramid. From time immemorial the Nepalese have called it Dhaulagiri (Dawalagiri): *Dawala* is the Sanskrit for white, and *giri* is a mountain. So: 'The White Mountain.' Its gigantic flanks of rock and ice, high as the clouds which daily march on its ridges, gleam in a perpetual mantle of newly fallen snow; they have done so just as long as clouds have been rising from Nepal's primeval forests, to envelop the mountain towards midday and then build up and up, to more than 26,000 feet, where they finally meet above the summit. Then that great mountain floats high above the world, in a cone of clouds.

This icy giant, standing solitary and unsheltered, might just as well have been called 'Peak of Storms', but no one thought of the name till, much later, men came to climb it, experienced its terrifying tempests and remembered them for the rest of their lives.

Dhaulagiri (26,795 feet) was the first of the fourteen eight-thousanders to be attempted by a modern expedition, the last but one to be climbed. Its fortress-keep defended itself for ten long years and fought off seven expeditions before finally falling to the eighth.

When the strolling minstrels, who have frequented the valleys of Nepal with their fiddles for hundreds of years, sing their famous ballad of Tensing – '*hamro Tensing Sherpa le tsaru himal tsutsura*' – they may by now have added a lay in honour of those two lucky 'Sunday's children', Nawang Dorje and Nima Dorje, who went to the summit of the great White Mountain.

Let me sketch the history of this great peak, the story of years of effort on the part of men who wanted to stand – for one short moment – high up there, 'where the Gods live'.

1949

An aeroplane was buzzing like a tiny insect among the icy giants of the Himalaya, one day in 1949 ... A well-known scientist, Arnold Heim, boarded a Dakota at Delhi. He was a Swiss, a geologist, interested rather in the structures and composition of the mountains than in routes and campsites on them. It was a flight of great importance, just as the year itself was an important landmark; for the gates of Nepal, so long barred to foreigners, had at last been thrown open.

The Dakota took off, gradually gained altitude, and, over Butwal, swung away to the north. Flying above the Terai plains, still in darkness, then over the low forest-clad ranges of the Siwaliks, it then followed the sombre trench of the Kali river, cutting deep into the glittering wall to the north – the untrodden thrones of the Gods. The plane flew on, between Dhaulagiri to the west and Annapurna to the east, out over Tibet and then back again. Arnold Heim was the first man to enjoy that pioneer's view of all the great summits, and he used his cameras to full advantage. The pictures he brought back were a unique documentation of the glory of those Himalayan giants. He was happy to reflect they would doubtless fire the imagination of countless climbers, to whom Nepal had for so long been forbidden territory.

1950: The French Reconnaissance

In the very next year, a great snake of some 200 porters could be seen writhing its way over the Siwalik ranges into the Kali Gandaki valley, following the traditional trade route to Tibet, along which flour and tea used to travel northwards, salt and borax down in the opposite direction. They were bound for Tukucha, a sizeable village of low, flat-roofed houses and inns, to the south-west of which Dhaulagiri towers some 20,000 feet above the valley level. Here the expedition, consisting of the élite of the French Alpine Club – Lachenal, Ichac, Terray, Oudot, Rébuffat and Schatz, under the leadership of Maurice Herzog – were to establish their main base. For Tukucha, at 8,500 feet, half way between the Dhaulagiri and Annapurna massifs, was the ideal starting point for reconnaissances in all directions.

The objective was to climb the first eight-thousander ever. The French had not yet decided which of the two – Dhaulagiri or Annapurna. Reconnaissance parties went out daily and returned with their reports. Several of them explored Dhaulagiri's east glacier, streaming down to the valley straight ahead of them. 'Not exactly a stroll!' Rébuffat reported after the first visit. Later, they forced a way to within 1,000 feet of the ice plateau which crowned the huge icefall. There, a thunderstorm, accompanied by heavy snow and the clatter of disintegrating séracs, drove them back to camp. In the end, Terray and Oudot reached the rim of the plateau, where they could see the North-East spur leaning like a white ladder against the sky. There was, however, no way of reaching its foot – it was as impossible for laden porters to cross the heavily crevassed field of ice as to scale the icefall itself.

Yet another thrust brought the French to the foot of the enormous, crenellated South-East Ridge, or what they named 'the Frenchmen's ridge', whence they gazed up at the South Face, fully 13,000 feet high, one of the loftiest in the world.

The map furnished by the Survey of India aroused great hopes; it showed an easy access route to Dhaulagiri's North Face up the valley of the Dambush Khola, a small tributary of the Kali. Herzog and Ichac went up to reconnoitre it on 24 April. The valley rose far too steeply and held far too little water for one that was fed by the north glacier. Presently, a steep-sided cirque of cliffs terminating the valley put paid to the theory of an easy approach to the north face. Obviously, the map was wrong. Back they went to Tukucha.

This is an example of how, in the Himalaya, one might have to try desperately to locate and approach an unknown mountain before even getting to where the climb starts. And, even if things have since then improved vastly, it is something which the reader should be made aware of.

Reconnaissances continued – of Annapurna as well as Dhaulagiri. It was decided to try the Dambush valley again, and on 26 April Herzog and Ichac, joined this time by Terray, camped twice before reaching a pass, followed by a cauldron of snow and yet another pass, from which they could see an arid valley, with snow patches in it, opening up towards the north. Once again Dhaulagiri was nowhere to be seen. So back once again to Tukucha.

It was not till 5 May that Oudot and Terray entered the 'Unknown Valley', as they called it. From this wide basin they climbed a 17,000 foot pass leading southwards, later to become permanently known as 'The French Col'. From it they obtained their first view of Dhaulagiri's North Face in all its immensity. They saw, too, that the glacier below them clearly fed the Mayangdi Khola which flowed south. The Cartographers' theory that the northern glaciers drained down the Tukucha side was scotched, once and for all.

And what about the prospects?

'I won't set another foot on this mountain,' Terray declared tersely at the council of war held at Tukucha on 14 May, which finally decided for Annapurna and against Dhaulagiri. 'Nobody will ever climb Dhaula … !'

1953: The Swiss attempt by way of the Mayangdi Valley and the 'Pear'

The French success in 1950 on Annapurna, the first eight-thousander to be climbed, turned the thoughts of Swiss climbers to the giant ice peaks of Nepal. In spite of all, Oudot's picture of Dhaulagiri's north face inspired moderate hopes; accordingly, a very strong team was assembled under Bernhard Lauterburg.

They approached the mountain by the Mayangdi Khola, with its paddy-terraces, little hamlets, undulating track and suspension bridges. Farther up, the dense bamboo thickets of the rain-fed jungle forced them to hack away with mattocks; they were continually pushed up on to the slopes where, above a colourful rhododendron belt and the dark Himalayan pines, gleamed Dhaulagiri's flanks. Later, when there was nothing worse than a few birch trees on a tongue of moraine, they set up their base camp. To obtain a view, it was necessary to move farther, around a projecting spur. Before them lay the huge north glacier – known ever since as the Mayangdi Glacier. And, high up above, they saw the brown, debris-covered slopes of the 'French Col', but now of course, from its other side.

Straight opposite them rose the North Face of Dhaulagiri, some 11,000 feet high, with the icefalls, ribs and couloirs that form its plinth. Above the mighty barrier of séracs, at about 20,000 feet, they could see a long glacier terrace, on which a high-altitude camp could perhaps be sited. Above that, soared the gigantic smooth, unbroken face, which has fascinated and lured all those who have ever seen it – that mighty wall, pencilled with fine hatchings, as by some great artist, from which a few extraordinary islands of rock belly out, looking like monstrous pears.

The Swiss thought they could find a route up the 'pear' which reaches farthest down the face. The angle seemed to ease off above its upper rim, though the wall between it and the West Ridge was dauntingly steep. If they could only get up on to that ridge, the way to the summit must lie open to them.

They found a way through the savage ice towers of the sérac zone. They needed two camps before reaching the terrace and there, at 20,000 feet, they established their assault base. Another camp was somehow clawed on to the rock below the 'pear'; but the horrific sweep of that feature from the terrace to the ridge above measured well over 5,000 feet !

Every attempt to find another campsite failed; the rocks of that immense wall were too steep and too polished. Yet they managed to push forward to within 200 feet of the ridge. They could find no way of climbing the final cliff.

They rounded off their gallant attempt with two reconnaissances, to the South and North-East cols respectively. In the course of these they made one important discovery: Pfisterer established that an aircraft could land on the broad snow plateau of the North-East Col, or at least drop material on it. Years later, the last Swiss Dhaulagiri expedition was to profit by this knowledge.

1954: The Argentine Expedition – a near miss

On 21 May of that year a most unusual thing happened on the 'Pear' face: the report of a blasting charge shook the cliffs, re-echoing like a thunderclap among them. Twenty-seven more followed. After the very first detonation, Felipe Godoy, an army sergeant major, hurried from under cover nearby to assess the results: the mountain had not disintegrated, no avalanche had been started, only a few lumps of rock were scattered around. It took three days to blast out a platform large enough to take two tents – Camp VI of the Argentine expedition to Dhaulagiri.

This was an enormous expedition. Its fourteen tons of baggage amounted to about 600 porter loads; but pack-animals were also used as far as they could go. For the actual climb there were fourteen experienced Sherpas, under Pasang Dawa Lama, the Sirdar. The leader of the expedition was Lieut. Francisco Ibanez, who had made a name for himself in the Andes, and had learned much about Dhaulagiri while acting as liaison officer on Lionel Terray's French expedition to Fitzroy. At the farewell party at the Casa Rosada, President Peron agreed to a proposal to sponsor an Argentine Dhaulagiri expedition, with the full support of the government and the army. The climbing party also included the Slovak Dinko Bertoncelj and Gerhard Watzl from the Tyrol, both naturalised Argentinians.

From Godoy's camp on the platform four parties started the climb towards the West Ridge on 30 May. The monsoon, which would put a stop to all activity on the mountain with its blizzards, was due very soon. By way of a gulley and a difficult chimney of loose rock they reached the ridge and at 25,000 feet sited their last and highest camp on it. Savage pinnacles barred the way ahead, towers which reminded them of those on the 'Catedral' at home; towers which masked the view forward to the summit and looked terribly difficult to turn.

Bertoncelj and Ibanez had come up, but Ibanez decided to wait in that high camp till a summit party consisting of Magnani, Watzl, Pasang and his brother came back from their attempt. Bertoncelj and the remaining Sherpas went down again. 1 June proved to be the decisive day, when a mixture of courage and luck, both good and bad, brought the assault party past all the difficulties, and still robbed them, by a trick of fate, of the summit they felt was 'in the bag'.

Nobody foresaw the chain of events. The summit party set out simply to reconnoitre the route ahead, leaving their loads and sleeping bags in camp. 'I only had with me some chocolate and a tin of condensed milk,' said Watzl afterwards. Yet they succeeded in doing what nobody was ever to do again: moving on tiny ledges of extreme difficulty, with a drop of anything up to 13,000 feet below them, they turned the pinnacles.

By 4 p.m. they found themselves on a snow ridge, put on their crampons and stamped their way up and up it till they were almost at the magic 8,000-metre level, over 26,000 feet. There they met with two great boulders with a small ice cliff between them. Watzl climbed it and this is what he saw: 'A gently rising crest about a mile long, without any difficulties in it.' The route to the summit lay at their mercy.

As the weather was unusually fine, they decided to bivouac and make the most of their unexpected luck. They finished digging an ice cave by the last glimmer of daylight; the night they spent in it was a cold one and conversation turned time and again to Argentina's famous steaks. Well, they had none of those, but in the morning they would have something much more valuable – the summit of Dhaulagiri … !

At 5.30 a.m. they crawled out of their cave – to find two feet of freshly fallen snow outside … no hope of the summit now without at least a second bivouac; and the descent of the smooth ledges behind them, newly covered in snow, as perilous as problematic …

Watzl took the cruel decision to retreat. The descent turned into a fight for their very lives. Pasang's brother was seriously injured when he fell and was checked by the rope, but in the end they all got safely back to camp.

Ibanez hoped to mount a second attempt, but it never materialised. He himself fell a victim to this series of misfortunes. By the time they managed to get him down several days later, from those icy altitudes to base camp, he was so severely frostbitten that it was clear there was no hope. After the long weeks of an agonising journey back to Katmandu, he died there.

1955-58: Germans, Swiss and Argentines

Nobody ever got as high again on the 'Pear' route as that first Argentinian venture. Certainly not the so-called 'Vegetarian Expedition' of Swiss and German climbers in 1955, under Martin Maier. One of the conditions of their financial support was a prescribed diet, in which meat played no part. Their official report stated that blizzards prevented their getting higher than 24,300 feet.

In 1956, the second Argentine expedition occupied the historic camp on the ridge as early as 11 May, but got very little farther. This time the monsoon arrived a month early and Col. Huerta, the leader, ordered a retreat. There were also complications caused by the fall of President Peron, who had promoted the expedition. For better or worse, his name was erased on the expedition's packing cases. I have a photograph in my collection of a window shutter in the Mayangdi valley fashioned from one such case. *Sic transit gloria mundi!*

Again, in 1958, the Swiss, under Werner Stauble, got no farther. Detlef Hecker and a Sherpa made a last vain attempt on the pinnacles, then bad weather forced them down. The descent of the Pear face involved them in a dramatic avalanche incident, but happily without serious damage.

The Swiss camp V was a unique development in Himalayan history. Fearing that Godoy's platform would no longer be recognisable, the Swiss had, with their well-known attention to detail, built a contraption – a kind of grid-iron – rather like a bedstead with long legs, but only two of them. This they fixed to the steep slabs of the Pear at 23,600 feet. On that lofty frame they erected a tent. Two of these structures, swaying fearfully in Dhaulagiri's gales, mostly dictated sleepless nights. One can only imagine what it was like: the darkness, the fierce gusts of wind, the grating of the stilt-like legs on the slabs, and a precipice thousands of feet deep below the 'bedclothes'. '*Viel luft unterm födli*', in good Schwyzerdütsch: 'Plenty of air under your backside!'

Flinging great snow banners into the sky as the gales raged, Dhaulagiri again won the verdict. The whole world waited for the expedition which would at last succeed in defeating the White Mountain. Many by now called it the most difficult of the eight-thousanders; for, one after another, the other great Himalayan giants had conceded defeat, while year by year, climbers of different nationalities came to the gigantic face of the 'Pear', to fail dismally. And still everybody clung to the same thought … the next one must be successful.

1959: The Austrian Expedition

This expedition, organised by the Austrian Himalayan Association, was under the leadership of Fritz Moravec, a bearded high-school teacher, who had already led a successful expedition of this kind when he climbed Gasherbrum II.

The Austrians were the first to tackle the mountain by its North-East Spur, that steep, straight route to the summit snow cap of Dhaulagiri, which starts in the great hollow of the North-East Col. The French had already looked up at it during their reconnaissances of the east glacier; so had Pfisterer, the Swiss, when he pushed forward to the col from its other side. From there, westwards, a glacier arm, broken up by steep cliffs, falls to meet the broad floor of the Mayangdi Glacier at about 14,400 feet. Passing beneath an enormous rock triangle, which they named 'the Eiger', the Austrians forced a way, menaced at all times by falls of ice and rock, up towards the North-East Col. Camp II, sited on the col itself, was then equipped as their advanced base. There, they were still more than 8,000 feet below the summit.

From the saddle's wide snow plateau, there first rises an ice crest, after which the spur goes soaring straight up. Its steep, sharp crest is supported on the left by a colossal ice face with an angle of from forty to sixty degrees; on the right, by a narrow upturned triangle of rock. And so it rises steeply to 23,000 feet, where a rock cliff at least 300 feet high and in places almost vertical, marks its termination. After that, the slope eases considerably till, at 24,300 feet, the snow- and rock-steps in the ridge steepen again, before, at 25,600 feet, it meets the Frenchman's marvellously crenellated, long-drawn South-East ridge (a 'dream route', but endlessly long!). From the point where they fuse, the main ridge curves up towards the summit's final crest, broken only by a few isolated rock patches.

Of course, the Austrians could not see the route in its entirety from the outset; the mountain would only reveal its secrets as they advanced step by step up it. However, they had seen enough to justify the following comparison of the two routes.

'The Pear': its main difficulties high up on the mountain, particularly at the start of the summit ridge; the whole face exposed to avalanche threats; camps mostly difficult to site.

The North-East Spur: technical difficulties in the steep ice below the spur and at the rock cliff 23,000 feet up – in other words much lower down; no difficulty about campsites; avalanche dangers far less; and delays on account of bad weather more acceptable on its ice than on rock.

Pasang Dawa Lama, whom we have already seen on the Pear, considered that the chances on the spur were better. The Swiss Eiselin, and the German Hecker, had already expressed that opinion. So Moravec decided for the North-East Spur.

Progress was swift: by 21 April, camp III was in being at 20,200 feet and on the 24th they started to establish camp IV at the foot of the ice wall, a thousand feet higher up. The intention was to site a further camp at 23,000 feet on a high platform at the top of the rock triangle.

It was at that moment that fate struck. 29 April had been decreed as a rest day. Everybody in the little huddle of tents on the vast white expanse of the North-East Col was occupied in reading, writing letters or playing cards. Suddenly, someone noticed that Heini Roiss was missing; he had gone outside a little while earlier and now he could not be found in any of the tents. They followed his track away from the camp for about fifty yards, where it ended in a dark hole in the surface of the snow. There he had fallen into a crevasse; he was still alive, wedged far down in its depths. They worked frantically to widen the narrow rift, the only hope of getting him out alive; at last they managed to bring him to the surface, but he was dead.

A cross on a slope below the 'French Col' marks his resting place.

The expedition was never able to recover completely from the severe loss of one of its best members, which overshadowed everything that was to follow. All the same, they made a gallant attempt, digging themselves in, high up on the spur, where the gales had in the meantime ripped the tents to tatters, in an 'ice parlour'. They safeguarded the whole 1,600 foot ice and rock-arête above camp IV with a chain of fixed ropes, toiling prodigiously, continually hampered by bad weather. When, on 22 May, they at last established camp V at 23,000 feet on the tip of the rock triangle, they went straight on to prepare the difficult 300 foot wall which barred the way above. The monsoon was by now very near. On 24 May they pitched their last and highest camp, a little below 24,300 feet, hoping that there would still be time to tackle the summit. Next day, Karl Prein and Pasang Dawa Lama started out for it from that last high tent.

Up rock pitches and snow gullys they went, under a blue sky. Shining in the morning sun lay the ranges of the Dhaula-Himal, Tukucha Peak and the 'Breithorn', farther away, the icy peaks of the Nilgiri chain – the 'Blue Mountains' – and Annapurna's towering summits. To the north, a frozen brown sea of lower peaks stretched away into illimitable distance – Tibet. It was a marvellous view, and for a minute or two they were able to forget the terrible, icy fight to gain height, for, that day, Dhaulagiri's raging wind nearly uprooted them, robbing them of breath, freezing their stiff faces and the very blood in their veins. It was an appalling ordeal, as step by step, bent double against the blast, they struggled on upwards.

At about 25,600 feet they saw a ridge joining them from the left; to the right they thought they could make out the summit over the intervening humps. They were not far off now – another five or six hours should do it, if they could survive the murderous cold and the icy tempest.

It was an impossible task. They would have to try again tomorrow. So, back they went, down to the tent, only to find the gale had ripped open one side of it. They spent an icy night, with drifting snow building up inside the tent, till, by morning, their sleeping bags were covered in a two-inch blanket of snow. However, Karl Prein was as tough as they come, and Pasang who had been up to 26,000 feet on the 'Pear', and who had stood on Cho Oyu's summit with Herbert Tichy and Sepp Jochler, had dreamed for years of the summit of the White Mountain.

They tried again, and were beaten back again by the wind. They could not believe that all their efforts were in vain. After another night in their tattered tent, they tried a third time. All in vain – defeated again by that roaring tempest. Then it began to snow; the monsoon was knocking at the gates of the Himalaya. It had all been for nothing.

'We have no key to this mountain,' said Pasang Dawa Lama, with tears in his eyes, as they turned to go down. 'This is the third time I have reached so great a height on it, but the Gods are not willing for us to enter into their habitation.'

So far there had not been tragedies of a Nanga Parbat scale on the 'White Mountain'. They came, later, when in 1969 an ice avalanche buried five Americans and two Sherpas in the icefall below that long, crenellated South-East Ridge and, a few months later, five members of an Austrian expedition perished on Dhaulagiri IV.

What made me go out there again, to attempt another eight-thousander, particularly this one – Dhaulagiri?

The hour I had spent on the summit of Broad Peak had made an ineradicable impression on my heart and mind. I often felt that nothing could happen to me again which could match it, not even on Himalayan heights. One cannot repeat such things – and yet …

Once one has climbed those distant white peaks, high as the clouds, remote even when you are close to their feet, their lure endures for ever, there is no escape, one dreams of them, of moving towards the summit, high above the outspread world, through a wide and frontierless sky, trusting that no storm will break that day – even though it should break.

Hermann Buhl went on from his Nanga Parbat to another eight-thousander, Broad Peak; then, on Chogolisa, he strayed out over the cornice in a blizzard. Gyaltsen Norbu, who had also stood on the summits of two eight-thousanders, perished under an ice avalanche on Langtang Lirung. Was I too, who could still not fully grasp that Chogolisa had not meant the end of everything for me, to try another of those mighty peaks at whose gleaming, all-compelling feet you feel their sheer inaccessibility?

Even today, with all the technical progress that has been made, no one can foretell the outcome of one of those attempts. Terrifying is the breath of those icy giants, when they awake, and man becomes a little living something, due to perish somewhere. They are still the 'Thrones of the Gods'. Nobody who has seen them can doubt it.

Yet, when Max Eiselin invited me to join his Dhaulagiri expedition, I could not possibly have refused. Was this not Nepal's glorious White Mountain – still untrodden by man – one of the world's highest peaks?

Sufficient was the very thought of being up there on that crest, high in the sky, more than 26,000 feet up, among the clouds themselves, unfettered and without an oxygen mask, just as I am, moving towards an unknown frontier close above my head – a mere human being high up in space, whose feet are still – unbelievably – in contact with the earth ... moving on and up ... till he stands on the summit.

Only to imagine it excited me hugely, for that is how I am. Yes, I would go and climb, and that mountain would belong to me. Would it, though? All I knew was that I would give my last ounce of effort to stand on its summit.

I knew the Gods might ... maybe ... but I had seen a picture of that mountain; what an indescribable thrill to be going to it.

The Gods ... maybe ... but I would have one more try.

When Herbert Tichy said goodbye to me in Vienna – that Herbert Tichy, who had journeyed through China, Nepal, Alaska, all over the earth's surface; who had once had his fingers frostbitten on Cho Oyu and still gone on to the summit; my friend who was holding my hand – he looked at me for a long time, before saying: 'I wish you all the best.'

Then he added this : 'And even if you should not come back, I still wish you joy of it.'

The International Swiss Expedition to Dhaulagiri, of which I was a member, started out in the spring of 1960. It was a huge expedition – thirteen climbers whose target was the ascent of the thirteenth eight-thousander; for only it and Shisha Pangma remained unclimbed. Max Eiselin's team included five other Swiss, Ernst Forrer, Albin Schelbert, Michel Vaucher, Hugo Weber and Jeanjacques Roussi, Peter Diener, a German, and two Poles, Adam Skoczylas and Dr Jerzy Hajdukiewicz, the expedition's doctor; like Max, a Dhaulagiri veteran of 1958; Norman Dyhrenfurth, who had come all the way from the USA to film and photograph the climb; and, finally, two very important people: Ernst Saxer, the glacier pilot of the expedition's aircraft, and Emil Wick, his mechanic.

We were committed to the world's highest unclimbed peak, and prepared to do our utmost. This time we just had to pull it off. For our route we chose the North-East Spur.

Yeti's Flight to Dhaulagiri

Yeti was no abominable snowman, but our gaily-coloured glacier aircraft; an amiable gnat, striped red and yellow, which floated tiny and forlorn, above the mighty valleys of the wide Himalaya, and hung between their great summits like some buzzing insect. Yeti had lifted us all from the depths of the Terai to the 16,500 foot snow saddle of the Dapa Col, at the rim of the French explorers' 'Unknown Valley'. This was intended only as an intermediate station – for acclimatisation purposes – en route to the proposed landing of the whole party on the North-East Col, 1,800 feet higher up. We could hardly wait for what would be the highest glacier touchdown ever made.

It was, of course, an experiment, just as everything we were doing was a unique 'first time ever' conception: nobody had ever tried to use a 'gnat' to leap-frog all the valleys in one swift bound and fly every man-jack of an expedition, baggage and all, up to over 16,000 feet on a Himalayan giant, and so avoid the long weeks of an approach march with hundreds of porters. Nor had we forgotten Pfisterer's report on the North-East Col's saddle, half a mile wide: 'an ideal landing place'. Even so it would be no child's play, for it lay at a height of more than 18,700 feet. We wondered how that would work out.

Ernst Forrer, the great gangling country postman from the Toggenburg, who was used to a daily round of twelve miles at home, and I, who had previously gone up to great altitudes, were chosen as the first two to be landed up there, with a tent. We had both stood the first experimental leap of 16,500 feet from Bhairava very well, although we were at first confined to our tent with fearsome headaches and other unpleasant side effects.

Eleven years had passed since Arnold Heim's memorable flight. Now an aircraft was once again to play its part in Dhaulagiri's history; and this time we were going to land! One of the greatest adventures in the opening up of the Himalaya was under way, though we could of course not foresee that we were destined to return home minus our Yeti; that our bright butterfly, in which we had known the fantastic thrill of flying between those mighty peaks, would lie abandoned, its wings broken, half-tilted towards the rocks, at the edge of a glacier torrent high up in the 'Unknown Valley', having crashed during take-off, owing to a minor technical failure.

I think everyone of us has a bit of yellow or red metal hanging on a wall at home, as a memento of our Yeti …

On 3 April the weather at the Dapa Col was glorious. Not a breath of wind stirred on its broad saddle of snow. The tents stood bright yellow and gay in the sunshine. Far away in the blue distance rose Annapurna; close at hand the ice slopes of Tukucha Peak swept up to the sky. It really looked as if the hour, so long and impatiently awaited, for Forrer and me to be airlifted to the South-East Col, had at last struck. Certainly Ernst Saxer was 'raring to go'; in weather like today's, in these air conditions, the first attempt to land on the col should definitely be 'on'.

First, however, he took-off in our wide-winged four-seater, unladen, and with only himself, the expedition's leader Max Eiselin, and his mechanic, Emil Wick, aboard, to test the wind conditions at the col. We watched them go, then packed our belongings, praying inwardly that there would be no reason to postpone our flight. We could hardly control our impatience to be up there at the foot of the gigantic North-East Spur. From here, we could not see it, nor the vast snow saddle of the col, nor even the summit of our eight-thousander; for, right in front of us, ice armoured, scored by flutings, Tukucha Peak went winging to the sky – at 22,650 feet, far lower than Dhaulagiri, but effectively masking the whole view in that direction.

After a long time, Yeti was in sight again. Soon it was banking in a wide curve and landing elegantly close to the camp. We rushed across, eager to know if the flight was on. Definitely! 'In with all your gear and quick about it,' said Saxer. Equipment, food, gas for the cooker, a tent, more equipment, more provisions … then we ourselves got in and shut the door behind us. Good – all set to go!

A moment or two later our plane's broad runners were gliding down the slope, and down we tore at full throttle into the broad hollow, which seemed to come rushing up at us. Now … we had parted from the slope, airborne, in full flight, looking down at the wide floor of the hollow as it slipped quietly away beneath us.

We had taken off on the Tukucha side of the col, and suddenly we were out beyond the rim of the hollow. Deep gorges went plunging abysmally below us, grey, black, their gullies filled with snow, all looking fearsomely steep. The 8,000-foot leap from the Kali Valley to Dapa Col looked like a ladder to the sky, first green, then grey and brown, finally white. We slid across a rocky, slabby buttress in Tukucha Peak's lower structure, and there we were hanging, far and free, out in thin air. Saxer was bent over the controls, we lay over sideways as we looked horizontally across to Annapurna while, on the other side, the steep slopes leading to the col swung across the windscreen and we felt pressed down into our seats – then the plane levelled out and we were flying back in the direction of Dapa Col. It all happened so quickly; I just caught sight of Dapa Peak, which Albin Schelbert and I had reconnoitred together;

we were going too fast for me to be able to identify the tents of our camp; then we were over the huge snow-flecked groove of the 'Unknown Valley'. We were flying at about 100 mph. The engine droned, we hardly exchanged a word. A whole veined network of water-courses and snow gullies passed under us.

And then – there it was: *Dhaulagiri!* I touched Ernst on the shoulder and pointed up to the cloud banners, the giant form straight ahead of us – exactly like the pictures from which I knew it – simple beyond words, mighty, unbelievably beautiful – Dhaulagiri. No, it was more than that; this enormous thing towering above us was more wonderful than the vision any mere picture could conjure up. This was the tremendous, the inaccessible mountain. I was shattered by what I saw. And the nearer we got to it, the smaller we felt.

Easily recognisable were the characteristic bands in its rocky faces, rising steeply next to one another, pear-shaped, from the white expanse of the snow-fields and glaciers. There stood the dark, riven plinth, the smooth white belt of the middle zone above it, then the savage cliffs below the hanging glacier high up, under the summit's huge crest.

That was our target – though at that moment I hardly dared to admit it to myself. All the same I sent a silent greeting up to the broad summit of that giant peak. Thaulagiri, here I come!' I was possessed by a great joy.

Beneath us now lay the slopes leading up to the 'French Col', where ten years ago they had struggled before halting, staggered by their first sight of the 11,500 feet North Face of the White Mountain, as they stood down there on the saddle now rushing up to meet us … almost close enough to touch … across which we had already leaped, out and away. Next moment we were looking far down on to enormous debris slopes pouring downwards into a glacier cauldron – the Mayangdi Glacier, of course. And now we were flying straight as a dart towards the rocky base of our mountain. Great God! It was growing and growing, till it filled the whole of the sky. And still we flew on, straight into it. Dhaulagiri! It was absolutely horrifying. Surely we must be going to hit those rocks, so close ahead?

But Yeti was already banking steeply. I drew a deep breath as I looked through the window up to the clouds and snow scarves high up on the summit, while on the other side of our plane, now tilted at forty-five degrees, there shot up, beyond the wing, a grim chaos of shattered ice, séracs, yawning crevasses – dear heaven, that was one of the icefalls in the glacier which falls from the North-East Col! Before we could take a good look, Saxer was heading straight for the mountain again, only much higher this time, having gained altitude during that first wide sweep. This time the broad snowfields of the middle zone were facing us, more or less flat. Even the stratified rocks of the 'Pear' looked less difficult now; though the cliff above them must be quite a problem. I took a quick look past my companion into the depths below, for we were banking again. A savage rock spire swept up and past, then monstrous slabs, and far below, the icefall. Seconds later, Ernst and I were staring as if transfixed at the North-East Spur, now shooting up prodigiously straight before our eyes. We were flying almost straight into it, bearing a shade to its left. Good God! That was the thing we were proposing to climb? A Jacob's ladder, disappearing into grey clouds; perhaps that was what made it look so steep. In any case it looked savage – more of a buttress than a spur.

I leaned far over to my right. There lay the North-East Col – broad, white and soft. An enormous dip, or rather a plateau, miles wide. We were coming in very quickly, now.

To the left rose some rounded ice summits and a sharp white snow peak – the 'Breithorn' and Tukucha Peak, probably – with broad white glacier hollows between them. Beneath us, the crevasses grew fewer and fewer, then we were over smooth white snow; we were flying over the saddle, straight towards Dhaulagiri's lovely, crenellated South-East Ridge. It was almost impossible to believe that anything like this vast natural arena could exist – it was so big that the plane could fly into it and then bank round in a wide curve without ever getting too near the South-East Ridge. The right wing lifted slowly skywards, revealing a horizontal view across to distant Annapurna's many summits; then, suddenly, we were close to mounds of snow, the wing dipped gently and we were flying straight in, to touch down .

Nothing but snow below us, nearer and nearer, quite close, now. Tack! We were sliding on it, the engine roared, we lost speed, we stopped. A touchdown as soft as butter, as if on a feather bed. We had arrived!

'Gorgeous, Ernst! Thanks a lot!' we cried. I would have liked to embrace him for sheer joy at that incomparable flight. And we had got here safely! He too was delighted, and no wonder; this marvellous landing place, a perfect touchdown, and finally his: 'Altitude, 18,300 feet!' For our friend Ernst today had brought off the highest glacier landing yet achieved; a source of great joy to our pilot. Wick was beaming, too, though he was, as usual, quiet and relaxed.

We jumped out on to the snow. It was unlikely that there were crevasses here, but we got the ropes out, just in case. The first thing I did was to tie Ernst Saxer to Yeti's front wheel spar, greatly to the amusement of the other Ernst – the climbing one, who was going to share the tent with me up here. Saxer took pictures of his Yeti, then asked to go farther afield. I let some rope out, untied him from the wheel, pushed an ice axe into his hand, grabbed one myself – and off went Ernst, at a murderous pace for such an altitude, straight across the wide, level saddle. It must have been half an hour before we got back to the plane.

It was time for them to take off again. Saxer and Wick climbed up into the cockpit, resuming oxygen masks. Forrer and I planted ourselves to right and left under the wings and grasped the struts. The engine sprang to life, singing, screaming, droning; and at a signal from Saxer we rocked the aircraft up and down. The skis began to slide, we were caught in a whirlwind of blown snow dust. We threw ourselves down, still in the whirling cloud of snow for some seconds, on our knees; then we got up, somewhat out of breath, and waved to Yeti, humming away rapidly into the distance. We were all alone.

It was by now mid-afternoon. We looked around for a suitable site for our high base camp, and very soon we had agreed on it. Then we dragged the sacks of equipment and food across to it and, as an icy wind got up and we were already in the shadow thrown by the peaks, we set up the camp's first tent and anchored it firmly. We panted a good deal for though this second flight in Yeti had, in spite of the distance covered, only brought us up some 1,800 feet, the difference was noticeable and we had still to get used to the new altitude. However, neither of us felt at all bad; but we were glad to crawl into our fleece bags quite early.

By the time night fell, even the smallest of cloudlets had vanished, and the cold had grown intense. We leaned out of the tent door, looking up at the gigantic dark mass of our mountain, with Orion shining directly above its summit. And, all around, thousands of stars sparkled in a beauty beyond all bounds of reality.

The Plateau in the Clouds

This vast natural arena, and the Jacob's ladder of the spur shooting up from it … everything was on so immense a scale that it almost passed belief.

Our little gnat visited us every day – announcing itself first of all by a gentle buzzing, then becoming visible as a tiny dot between those massive walls. It was usually quite near by the time we had spotted it and grew swiftly, to become recognisable as our bright-hued Yeti, roaring overhead and away, to dwindle again to a yellow streak against the ice ribs of the 3,000-foot high, pinnacled wall of the South-East Ridge. Surely it must crash into it? But, no: it disappears somewhere into the white glare of the saddles mile-wide curve. For a moment even its sound is lost; then, equally suddenly, it is here again as large as life, and touching down. Saxer and Wick jump out, waving; or, if we are still resting in the tent, they shout across to us.

We had settled down into a regular routine; dragging cases, sliding sacks over the snow, rocking Yeti. This exhausting exercise was indispensable on take-off, if our gnat was to become airborne in the rare atmosphere, for the friction of its two skis in the snow at the start could be considerable.

We could not risk leaving the cases and sacks scattered about the place; there were almost such masses of fresh snow that by next morning we might be unable to find them. North-East Col and Dapa Col were two very different places; up here the mountain made its icy breath felt. Besides, a packing case buried in the snow could spell dire disaster to Yeti, as it came in to land.

Taking everything into account, life up here at 18,700 feet was a strenuous affair.

At first, we could not even spare a thought for the great white spur winging up above us.

We were glad when, on the day after our arrival, two Sherpas were flown up to assist us, but the older of the two was taken ill during the very first night, and Saxer had to fly him down all the way to Pokhara, in the plains. The younger one, Nawang Dorje, stayed up with us. Those first few days in the white desert of the col taught us what Dhaulagiri's might and mass, its cruelty and its beauty held in store for us.

Occasionally I scribbled a few notes in my diary, reflecting our feelings …

3 April (two days after landing on the col)

Yeti came up, bringing Georg, but he went down again. He complained of the length of time it takes to acclimatise. I am still very weak on my pins. I often sit down on a case and let my loads fall into the snow, without having to bend. A big drum calls for our united efforts.

'Much tougher than Dapa Col. Ernst stayed in tent all day. I sent the old Sherpa who fell sick straight down again. He had come to me in a very low state and with a confused look on his face, bringing all his belongings. High time he went down! The weather only stayed good till eleven o'clock. Then it deteriorated into a fearful storm all night. Moravec called it "the Pitiless Mountain". Very soon I shall believe it myself.'

6 April

Fantastic masses of fresh snow, at least three feet of it. Our equipment dumps have disappeared. Of the last batch only the big drum is now visible. Must do something. Put something on top of the drum and flags on that, for this snow is going on. There's a carton of millet biscuits somewhere under the snow out there. Cigarettes for our plucky Sherpa.

'Over to the drum and back (just a stone's throw). It took an hour. The snow is bottomless.

'Suppose an avalanche came all the way down those 8,000 feet? We are quite a long way away. But a powder snow avalanche might make this our last resting place. We should hear the thunder of it, see the sky go dark above us, and be blown away, tent and all.

'The wind is screaming, the snow rattling on the tent cloth, piling up higher all the time. You can feel it with your hand on the side wall. Cold.

'Terribly cold. The tent fabric grows lighter. The light of a pale moon. Up there, quite incredibly, the White Mountain, white, all white in the moonlight, soaring above delicate, shimmering mists. Uncanny, but magically beautiful. I called Ernst to look at it.

'What will happen tomorrow, if the sun gets on to those slopes above us?'

7 April

'A golden light through the fabric of the tent. The sun. No more wind. We heard Yeti buzzing in and landing. No movement anywhere. No sound.

'I built a protective wall and a wedge-shaped windbreak. Ernst and Nawang Dorje dug the vanished material-dump out of its covering of snow.'

8 April

'I told Ernst it looked like a break in the weather. No Yeti today. Once again we had to scrape the hoar-frost (it forms inside the tent during the night to a two-finger thickness). If you don't scrape it off, you get a snowfall in the tent as soon as it gets warm. Often there are tassels of frost hanging down on threads. In the evening there is a marvellous flashing and glittering inside the tent, in the light of our miner's lamps. Makes you think of Christmas, somehow.

'By eleven o'clock clouds had come up and a strong wind had risen from all directions. The break in the weather had arrived. The gale howled and snow rattled on the fabric. It went on till evening. (This was the notorious Dhaulagiri weather with its nerve-racking regularity, and we were getting to know it at first hand.)

'At midday I cooked omelettes, peas and bacon.'

9 April

'Only the tip of the Sherpa tent is still visible. From it Nawang Dorje emerges like a mole. The gale gets fiercer and fiercer, shaking the tent as it screams across it. We feel sure that an unprotected tent would have been blown away long ago. Anything up to 200 mph. The strip of light overhead gets narrower and narrower.

'Had to shovel the snow out of the tent. Didn't notice that my toes had lost all sensation. Not till a bit late, by which time they had sustained slight trouble. At midday Nawang and I cooked mushrooms, noodle soup and sausages.'

Just a few diary entries, written by the light of a forehead lamp in our glittering ice palace, in the night, at 18,700 feet. Written when I was alone with my thoughts, with the storm, with my companion at my side; written when I found it impossible to sleep. Jottings full of hope on the one hand, uncertainty on the other. For even if there was the aircraft, here we were served up on a silver salver in the clouds; literally in the clouds, and a long way from the earth's good floor. We had no radio-link, no supporting camp below us; not a soul between us and the Kali Valley, 10,000 feet away down there. Here, on our white platform, we were living as lonely and isolated a life as if we were on the moon. Here, with a huge white summit looming overhead, and only Yeti to provide an invisible bridge leading back to the world of men.

Saxer's Tour de Force

Our little plane came up again and again – sometimes from far away Pokhara out there beyond the Annapurna peaks, sometimes only from the Dapa Col out of sight behind Tukucha Peak, the expedition's first springboard. The material piled up in our depot and we were acclimatising rapidly. Sometimes we even sang – with due pauses to get our breath back – some mountain-lay or other, accompanied by my ubiquitous guitar.

Then, suddenly, came the black day when for long moments we feared it was all up with us.

Yeti had landed once again. There was a great deal of snow, but everything was normal otherwise. We helped with the unloading, did our rocking act, gasping for breath and looking like Father Christmas, ducked down and watched Yeti move off, though the tail didn't seem to lift properly. Down over the snowy rim of the saddle went our little craft, as usual, into the cauldron beyond … But this time it didn't zoom up. again. Full of foreboding, we followed its track to the rim of the saddle. Then we saw Yeti hanging at a slight angle on the slope down below. The tail-ski had never got clear of the snow and Yeti had failed to 'unstick' !

Saxer left us in no doubt as to the seriousness of the situation. It was only a hundred yards to the crevasses and séracs. We should have to stamp out a 'runway' – and a first class one at that – to give Yeti a chance of getting airborne. If it didn't take off in that short distance, it would finish up in the big crevasses ahead.

I never saw Ernst Saxer so determined. As he said, this was the only possible chance. If it failed, that was the end. We all worked like demons – Forrer and I, Nawang, Saxer, Wick; and Peter Diener, who had been flown up for a short visit. We tramped up and down the slope, knee deep in snow, panting and choking, till one or other of us had to lie down; we all gave everything we had, as we stamped out a runway at close on 20,000 feet. Finally the surface was smoothed with a pair of skis. Saxer jettisoned all but the essentials, heaving everything that weighed anything out of Yeti. A penny for his thoughts, as he looked at the ice of the séracs and crevasses, shimmering blue just ahead down the slope!

He decided to take off alone, full throttle at the séracs in front. A matter of only a few yards. We realised he was risking his life. Well, we should soon know the answer …

I had flattened out the last bit with my skis again and was coming up again when they signalled down that Ernst wanted to take off. I uttered a heartfelt prayer. The engine was roaring; the others were hanging on to the struts. The Yeti was off, hurtling down – rat-t-t-t – over the finely ribbed runway, down the slope, straight for the crevasses. Fifty yards: still on the floor. Forty: for God's sake lift! Thirty: and there, just short of the chasm, the skis separated from the surface, and – scraping over the séracs by inches – Yeti was airborne.

Saxer had pulled it off! I had tears in my eyes as I watched. It had been a damnably narrow squeak. I shall never forget standing there watching Yeti roaring flat out towards the crevasses, with Ernst's head looking small in the cockpit, and the skis still … still … still glued to the snow … and then, just before the runway's end, lifting clear … Ernst, man, what a performance!

Our friendship lasted for years, till he crashed, flying in his own mountains, in Switzerland.

But on that day, 10 April, 1960, Ernst Saxer, jet fighter and glacier pilot risked his life and saved our only link with the valley and the world outside – our Yeti.

6,000 Feet of North-East Spur

The three of us, Ernst Forrer, Albin Schelbert and I, were alone on our ladder to heaven, with four Sherpas in support; but we carried just as much as they did. Nothing stirred in our lonely world, except a big jet-black raven, which put in an appearance every now and then on the North-East Col.

We had suddenly been transformed into a lightweight expedition, cut-off in its advanced base; for the flight which had brought Albin up turned out to be the last. Since then, not a sight or sign of Yeti; not on the following day, nor the next, nor the third. There we were, waiting in vain.

They were probably doing running repairs, as had already happened once. One of these days Yeti would be here again, bringing up the rest of the expedition and equipment. Yes, but when? This time it seemed to be something more serious. We could do nothing up here but wait and see …

On the other hand, what would become of our intended ascent of the spur? The storms heralding the monsoon could break as early as mid-May, possibly even sooner. If we didn't put in some good, hard work on the mountain before the others came up, all our chances of reaching the summit would be gone.

So, we three, acting as a small, light group of the kind I had already experienced – without Sherpas – on Broad Peak, now tackled our mountain: an expedition consisting of only three climbers and four Sherpas, and again, as on Broad Peak, rejecting the use of oxygen. This 'Assault Party', at first with the Sherpas as porters, later on its own, forced its way higher and higher up the spur, and after long weeks of battle with the cold and the gales, established all the high-altitude camps up it.

Meanwhile, our fellow members on Dapa Col, forming the second and larger group of the expedition, left high and dry by Yeti's default, had reached the North-East Col on foot, and managed, with much toil and sweat, to ferry most of the remaining material up to it by way of the 'French Col' and the Mayangdi Glacier. In the course of this toilsome operation, they established two new camps: a base camp on the floor of the Mayangdi Glacier's trough at 15,400 feet and an interim camp on the ascent from there to the North-East Col, where our aircraft base was thus suddenly transformed into the expedition's camp II. So our plateau in the clouds had been fitted with a ladder from below. We had gone 'conventional'.

Yeti's disappearance from the scene had, incidentally, played havoc with the excellent-planned and ample provisioning of the expedition. As a result, one party was continually cooking different varieties of noodles and pasta, while hungering for chocolate and fruit juice; while the other could no longer stomach the sight of chocolate and gradually spooned up their rice with diminishing enthusiasm. (Albin, our vegetarian, dreamed of cornflakes and finished up by eating meat.)

The complete reversal of the basic plan fell hardest on Adam Skoczylas. Instead of being by now where he longed to be, on the great white ridge, he found himself saddled with the job of leading a column of coolies all the long way up from Pokhara, along the Mayangdi Khola – an endless valley crawl, which meant for him an even longer postponement in acclimatisation than the others were faced with on the transmigration from the Dapa to the South-East Col. Meanwhile, down in Pokhara itself, Max Eiselin, the leader of the expedition, joining Saxer and Wick, was occupying himself exclusively with Yeti's troubles.

We only learned what had happened when our colleagues came up from the Dapa Col during the first days of May. On 13 April a burst cylinder had forced Saxer to crash-land at Pokhara. Where in these parts could one get a replacement engine quickly? Nowhere, but there was one coming – coming from Europe! Three weeks later, on the very day of our first summit attempt, 4 May, Yeti was in the air again. However, it looked as if the Gods had no great affection for our gay little butterfly; for on the very next day, it crashed, from no great height, while taking off from the Dapa Col. It was a freak of ill fortune – for the same type of aircraft later on proved itself highly reliable in regular use in Nepal – the grip of the thing called the 'Cloche' had come clean away in Saxer's hands. It was not all bad luck, though; for the pilot and copilot made their way, uninjured, on foot to the valley, although Yeti was a complete write-off.

Meanwhile, Ernst, Albin and I – suddenly isolated by a stroke of fate, with our Sherpas, high up in that white wilderness – were pushing on up the spur, a totally committed trio.

Better still, during those days of humping loads in furious storms with our Sherpas, we discovered that two of these sons of the Himalaya, displaying exceptional enthusiasm, were distinguishing themselves beyond all expectation. In short that our summit, for which we were expending such efforts, was 'their' summit too. Nima Dorje and Nawang Dorje, showed themselves genuine and completely competent rope mates, with whom we became firm friends. Nawang, the tireless, we already knew from our days in the storm-swept tents on the North-East Col; Nima, the younger of the two, ever ready to help, always cheerful, had accompanied Herbert Tichy on one of his lengthy treks through Nepal.

The spur was steep, and it was difficult. Ernst, Albin and I meant to make our first attempt on the summit without Sherpas. Soon, too, we thought, for we managed, as early as 15 April, to establish a camp on the lower slopes of the ice wall, just to the left of the crest of the spur. It was at 21,650 feet, tucked in under an impressive, slightly overhanging ice step, the size of a family dwelling house, which guaranteed our tent community adequate protection from gales and avalanches. We were delighted at this first success – spur camp I, 2,800 feet higher up than the yellow fabric blobs of our base camp, far away down there on the snow of the saddle.

And now to establish our next support camp, above the ice wall, as soon as humanly possible. We were brim full of energy. The very next day we pushed on up to nearly 23,000 feet, finding on our way the first traces of the previous expedition, a whole stair rail of fixed ropes, which we dug out for the most part. We were full of hope that we would be able to establish spur camp II, above 23,000 feet, on the following day. But now, day after day, following a few bright early hours, the famous 'Dhaulagiri weather' struck, with gales and blizzards, which at times assumed terrifying proportions …

20 April (all four Sherpas; supplies brought up from the col)

'Went with the Sherpas. Got to the crest of the spur where we met a very cold wind, which became a gale. Bursts of sunshine in between. Dhaulagiri frowned down on us out of huge veils and banners. Hands and feet cold. Climbing a torture. Gale increasingly furious. The Sherpas in despair. Nawang shouting: "My foot finish, sahib!" It was terrifying. I said: "Drop your loads and get up to camp I", but nobody was sensible enough anymore to take any notice. Couldn't feel my own fingers and toes myself. Still, the only hope lay in help from camp

I. I was almost all in as I forced myself upwards … shouting,. screaming … Sherpas dark lumps in a white snow cloud. Ernst and Albin didn't hear me. Knee-deep snow. On all fours towards the end. At last they heard me, and started down. All they found was the loads, the other two Sherpas had already turned tail. Nima Dorje arrived. Pulled him up by his arm. Then Nawang, resting his face and arms in the snow again and again. Outside the tent, the tempest went on roaring over the ridge.'

Time and again we started up the ice wall from our shelter; the storms hunted us back to our place of refuge every time, often before we had got halfway up. All there was to show for our labours were a few material depots fixed to ice pitons. It was now impossible to find the fixed ropes under a layer of hard-blown snow, and we gave up looking for them. That was the state of affairs when, on 27 April, we embarked on a decisive assault, determined this time to succeed. Once again we ran into appalling weather, but this time we did not turn back. At 22,800 feet, on a narrow pitch, where it was just possible, we dug our tent and ourselves into the mountain's flank. We christened it emergency camp II. Two days later we moved from that uncomfortable spot to a hardly less airy perch just below the remnants of the tents of a camp the Austrians had established the previous year. We had done it at last. On 29 April our spur camp II was in being, at 23,150 feet. It had taken us a fortnight to defeat the ice wall.

On 1 May I went up to reconnoitre the 500-foot rock cliff immediately above. I found it very difficult and everywhere extremely exposed, but there were serviceable fixed ropes from the year before all the way up it. I worked my way up very carefully. Suddenly, at an almost vertical pitch, only some fifteen feet below the crest of the ridge, there was no fixed rope. I deliberated a while, then climbed it un-belayed and dumped the tent I had brought up with me at the top. At that moment I noticed that a menacing grey front was moving in. I only got back to the uppermost fixed rope at the second attempt. While taking a short breather there, I looked down the face's unbroken sweep of nearly 7,000 feet into the depths, where during the last few days tiny dots could be seen moving up towards the North-East Col – our colleagues from over there, 'outside.'

The first priority up here was to get a fixed rope hanging down that pitch !

The next morning was gloriously fine. The distant view all around us was clearer than we had ever seen it. It was possible to distinguish the farthest peaks in the Transhimalaya. Annapurna seemed quite close. We all agreed: this was summit weather. Now, we only had to establish one more camp as quickly as possible. Then we could have a go …

It was after midnight, so it was already 4 May, as we lay in our tent at 24,450 feet, dozing or sleeping. I woke up at a quarter to three.

What with dressing, breakfast and the rest, time simply raced away. By the time we got outside the tent, the sun was just rising – there was a riot of gorgeous colour out there, a marvellous view, but the cold was terrific. When I touched my crampons my fingers burned like fire and I let go again in a hurry (in the evening I noticed that even so slight a contact had raised a blister on my finger; later on, it turned black and fell off).

We roped up and moved slowly off, along a band of rock towards the right, till we found a somewhat awkward place at which it could be surmounted. But the snow which succeeded it was deep and rotten, and we made pitifully slow progress. Ought we to take to the crest of the ridge instead? It looked most uninviting, with flakes and humps up above us, separated by broad couloirs. Still, there was no alternative – so, up on to the ridge …

We were up at 25,000 feet. We were now able to look down on the long, sloping hanging glacier which falls down and across the whole North Face at this point, only a few hundred feet below the summit ridge. The rib we had been climbing petered out, to be followed by another very steep couloir. The condition of the snow up here was no better; we were forced to toil laboriously up the flaky rock at one side of it. When we were within measurable distance of the first summit in the ridge overhead, the weather gradually turned grey. We were used to that, but it might, after all, not … on we went. After a short snow-crawl on all fours, the angle eased off again.

All of a sudden we were stuck in thick fog. In spite of it, we recognised at once where we were; for rising out of the abyss on our left we could see the vague shape of a huge white ridge, while, not more than fifty feet above us, there was a sharp little snow summit, with nothing above it but grey mist. We had reached the junction point of the North-East Spur and the South-East Ridge, at a height of about 25,600 feet.

Should we press on? By now we could see absolutely nothing. The weather had disintegrated completely.

Although it was only midday, we decided to retreat. One cannot trifle with Dhaulagiri. As we were going down, it cleared up for a moment; we could see blue sky, and the surrounding peaks. We dithered briefly, but then the clouds closed down on us again and we soon ceased to regret our decision to withdraw, for the weather turned foul beyond words. The wind raged and it snowed hard. At times we had great difficulty in finding our way down. Finally, we reached our tent safely, and crawled into it with all possible dispatch. We had had enough for one day.

While we were massaging each other's toes and fingers, we drew up a balance sheet of our first attempt on the summit. It had taught us two important lessons. First, the apparently easier route over the hanging glacier and steep snow slopes was impossible, the only way lay up the ridge itself. Secondly, it was essential to establish a bivouac camp as high up as possible, so as to ensure reaching the summit in spite of what the 'Thaulagiri Weather' might do. The summit had to be climbed before the almost inevitable midday break in the weather.

Meanwhile, the first requisite was a couple of days' rest and recovery at base camp on the col.

'Dhaulagiri, Sahib, Dhaulagiri'

Back at the col, we now had the company of our teammates from 'over there', whom we had not seen for such a long time; there was much to talk about. Some of them were already at work on the spur in an effort to acclimatise to higher altitudes as quickly as possible, for they knew that time was running out. The monsoon storms might break any day now, and it was essential to use every moment of good weather.

On 9 May Ernst, Albin and I, with our two trusty Sherpas, Nima and Nawang, started up the spur again on our second drive for the summit, taking with us the good wishes of all those remaining down at the col.

I knew from our experience on a no-less-difficult mountain, Broad Peak, where on the first day of both our summit attempts we had climbed nearly 5,000 feet from base camp and still been able to climb again on the following day, that our present very fit party could tackle the 7,300 feet to our camp above the ice wall here. So we leap-frogged the intervening camp.

We felt in wonderful form after our rest days down below and everything went as I had foreseen. We got straight up to our spur camp II (now transformed into the expedition's camp IV, counting from the lower base on the Mayangdi Glacier) at 23,150 feet. There we found Peter Diener, who told us that the three Valaisian members of the expedition, Michel Vaucher, Hugo Weber and Jeanjacques Roussi, had gone on up that very morning to the next camp above, with a view to acclimatising there. Although he had not yet got properly used to the altitude, he asked us to let him join us on our bid for the summit, and we agreed. Then we settled down to some much-needed sleep.

Next morning, 10 May, we went on up to camp V (24,450 feet), where the three Valaisian climbers were occupying the tent we had pitched there during our first attempt. Fortunately we had now brought two tents up with us, so there was a solution to the accommodation problem. That night nine of us slept in three two-man tents, pretty close quarters, but not impossible. We had, in any case, been used to uncomfortable nights for weeks past, and this one was no exception; the outer sleeping bags soon turned to icy tubes owing to the hoar frost, which continually formed on the lining of the tent walls.

11 May brought with it a difficult problem. What would happen if we took one of the three tents with us for our intended bivouac camp? Suppose our unpredictable Dhaulagiri, instead of yielding the prize of its summit, forced us

to a dramatic retreat, and we had to abandon the tent up there? That would mean coming down to a camp with only two tents to house nine men – some of whom might well be frostbitten or utterly exhausted. It was a question which had already ruffled tempers yesterday, let alone this morning. In the end Michel, Hugo and Jeanjacques understood the situation and agreed to go down to the next camp and fetch up the tent whose absence might be so fatal. They started down at about 11 a.m., but failed to turn up again; it was only later that we knew the reason. Michel had been taken ill on the way down and they had consequently been forced down to the col.

On the 12th, after another day's climbing in an icy gale, we succeeded in establishing the bivouac tent, according to plan, at about 25,600 feet, in a snow cranny roofed over by a massive rock.

We thought the night of the 12th/13th would never end. The six of us squatted, crouched, and leaned against each other, all jammed together in our two-man tent. It was a long drawn out torture, and we hardly slept a wink. From time to time a flicker of conversation would break out, the invariable topic being the lack of space and the general discomfort. Albin, for instance, was bent double between the tent staves and the roof, with no means of stretching his legs, because the space was occupied by his neighbour. Nima Dorje had – comparatively speaking – the best place, close to the entrance. In the middle of the night Ernst and I asked him to make some tea, knowing how anxious he always was to help. Not this time, however; and suddenly – doubtless upset at being disturbed – he horrified us all by walking out and lying down in the open, where the temperature was at least –30°C. None of our entreaties could persuade him inside again till morning – when he came in, not one atom the worse for his night out in the cold.

Morning came as a deliverance for us all.

Getting our boots on at such close quarters took ages and racked our nerves, but we finally dragged our stiff limbs outside the tent. All the view around lay clear and, so far as we could tell, the day promised to be fine. The morning sun gilded Annapurna – the Nilgiris, now appreciably lower – Tukucha Peak and all the unnamed five- and six-thousanders stretching away into the Tibetan distances. I was filled with a great joy: the summit, only 1,300 feet above us, would fall to us today …

We roped up, put on our crampons and started slowly upwards, breathing deep at every step; for we were climbing without oxygen. As on the day before, I went with Nawang Dorje, that splendid type, tireless and always equable. Today there was joy written all over his face, because he was going to the summit; he kept on laughing and showing his flashing teeth. Out ahead, Ernst and Nima were moving slowly up towards the deep, dark blue sky, while Albin and Peter, intending to follow a little later, were still at the tent. I carried my 16 mm cine-camera in my breast pocket, for I meant to shoot some film on the way up and, in particular, on the summit.

Step by step we made our way up the snow crest, which was at times so narrow that, for safety, we had to plant our feet at right angles to it. Immeasurable depths fell away directly below us: 7,000 feet to our right, and to our left, at our very toe caps, we looked 13,000 feet down the South Face to a small glacier and low, greenish-brown foothills. We were left in no doubt that our path lay very high above the world.

Ernst was now stopping at the end of every rope's length and belaying Nima up to him; a false step here would have been fatal. Halfway up the ridge to the subsidiary summit, Nawang and I took over the lead. Very soon a step, with rock penetrating the snow, involved us in the utmost care and some precarious belaying. This was followed by a flatter sector of mixed rock and snow. The air grew appreciably rarer. We were climbing at the 26,000-foot level.

To avoid continual halts to get our breath back, I now throttled down our pace to well below what was possible. 'We go slow now, very slow,' I told Nawang, who seemed surprised at first, but soon got the idea.[1] Shortening the rope and climbing simultaneously, we hardly ever had to halt; and our even, leisurely pace made it possible to pick out the best line between boulders, snow patches and slabs, our steps never having to deviate more than a yard. As a result, we made much more rapid progress than before, in spite of the increasing altitude.

What would the summit be like? Nobody had ever seen the rock flakes on the arête from close at hand, and we wondered whether they would be easy or difficult. I soon noticed that the subsidiary summit was not a projection at all, but a mere kink in the crest of this huge ridge. Full of excitement, I looked beyond it. There it was, Dhaulagiri's summit! Between us and it, the back of a ridge covered in slabs, rather like the tiles on a roof, swung gently across to a solitary *gendarme*, beyond which there was a steep rise to a sharp, white summit, which one might have taken at first sight as the highest point; but beyond it there lay a notch, followed by a rocky step, which did not look exactly easy, and might possibly be a shade higher than the white peak. It must be the summit, because the humps and flakes of rock beyond it obviously fell away on its far side. We were standing at not less than 26,300 feet, so there were only four to five hundred feet more to go. And we still felt pretty good.

What fantastic luck we were having, too, with the weather! Though more and more cloud was building up below, it was exceptionally still up here; there

---

1 This intentional, drastic lowering of the tempo, almost down to 'slow motion', produces an unbroken sequence of movement and rest combined; it is a little difficult to achieve at first – but soon brings relaxation and great conservation of energy, largely because of the regular rate of breathing which results. In my opinion it is the most efficient method of progress at and above the 26,000-foot level. – K.D.

was practically no wind at all. We sat down, got something to eat out of a ruck-sack and gazed at the surrounding prospect. Annapurna was still visible; the white triangle of Tukucha Peak almost submerged down there. Alas, more and more clouds were banking up

Down in the depths, 10,000 feet below us, incredibly far off, lay the 'French Col'. That was where it had all started, ten years before …

And today? A sixty-mile-an-hour gale might just as well have been scream-ing across these fringed slabs of roof-tiling, interspersed by broken fragments, which almost looked as if they had been arranged in stripes. Yet, not a breath stirred. You had to say it out loud to yourself before you could believe it: today 13 May, the daemons of the storm were sound asleep!

I was happy beyond words at the marvellous way things were – so unexpectedly – going. Nawang's eyes, too, were shining and he was smiling all over his dark face. Ernst and Nima were no less thrilled when they came up and saw the summit. They sat down next to us. Then we moved on again, slowly ascending the easy slabby ridge, turning the *gendarme* on ledges without the slightest dif-ficulty; but the steep snow slope beyond, up into a notch, was a breath-taking business. We were now once again on a narrow crest of snow straight above the South Face, up which clouds and mist were advancing. Albin suddenly joined us in the notch and explained that Peter was following a little way behind.

Gradually the tension increased. We could no longer see the summit, but it could not be far now. I knew we had to deal with the white peak first, and on the sharp arête leading up to it we had to exercise the utmost caution. We belayed from a stance on its first steep surge, then Nawang, moving with exem-plary assurance, and I went on again simultaneously – mostly one on either side of the crest, so that we had an automatic belay. We were soon on the white peak, and we could see that the next projection really was the summit – not more than 200 to 150 feet above us!

Untrodden rock, with mist swirling round it …

Something changed at that instant.

I heard Albin next to me, saying: 'Man, am I enjoying myself!' I asked him to go on ahead, and filmed him as he slowly moved up towards the summit.

On we went. A difficult boulder, plumb on the crest of the ridge, barred our way. As I pulled myself up by a small ledge – the only available hold – I said to myself: 'A Grade IV pitch, for full measure!' ; and I thought of Albin who had just done it all on his own. I brought Nawang up on the rope. Only a little way to go now!

We traversed along a band, rather like a narrow path, moved out to the left for a short distance, up about six feet more – and Albin and I were shaking hands on the spacious summit. Nawang followed immediately, and we were soon joined by Ernst and Nima.

Overjoyed, we embraced one another, patted each other's backs …

We had been battling with storm and tempest for a whole month on this mountain, determined to get to the top, sustaining setback after setback, coming back at it again and again … and now, at last, we were here, on the summit.

It was 12.30 p.m. The ascent had taken just four and a half hours. The weather was still calm and fine, with hardly any wind. An in-comparable feeling of peace and security lay upon us …

Great, bulging towers of cloud came rising like columns from below, swelling to cloud castles high in the sky, now enveloping us, now clearing to let us see down to the 'French Col', Tukucha Peak, the North-East Col. From between the cloud curtains, too, appeared the magnificent range of the Dhaula Himal, a little to the right of the curiously flaked and humped ridge of our eight-thousander, which stretched far away ahead.

We hoisted our pennants, among them my own country's colours, bright on Dhaulagiri's summit. The ice axes and hammers we had brought up with us included two we had found on the way up in the camps of the 1959 pioneers. Our thoughts went back to the long battle for this peak; to Heini Roiss and Francisco Ibanez who gave their lives for it, and to all the others who had fought so long and hard … the summit was theirs, just as much as ours.

Presently Peter arrived and we all shook him by the hand. His performance had been an exceptional one, for he was markedly less well acclimatised than the rest of us.

Somewhere down in the depths, a thunderstorm was rumbling, the sound of the thunder-claps coming up faintly, almost imperceptibly. A painful prickling sensation of our scalps warned us that, here too, the air was becoming strongly charged with electricity and we started down without further delay.

It was about 5 p.m. when we got back to our top camp. We were very tired, but inexpressibly happy at the knowledge of our success. As we sat in our tent, with tea running comfortingly down our throats, Nawang looked at me, grinned broadly and said: 'Dhaulagiri, Sahib … Dhaulagiri.' I knew just how he felt, and nodded back. Yes, Dhaulagiri … a marvellous word to hear spoken.

Ten days later our teammates Michel Vaucher and Hugo Weber repeated the ascent to the summit, starting from camp V and dispensing with a bivouac tent.

Then we went down – endlessly down, deeper and deeper down – 20,000 feet lie between the summit and the silver ribbon of the Kali Gandhaki – down into the valleys where men live, into Nepal's greenery. It was like being born anew. Grass, trees, rain, villages, rivers. We sang and drank *chang* in honour of our peak, as we strolled in leisurely fashion out towards Pokhara. Orchids bloomed, parrots played about, in the forests. And then we heard a cuckoo! Nawang, noticing my surprise at hearing that familiar sound, laughingly explained its meaning. 'Don't go up !' it meant; 'don't go up into the mountains – you stay here!' At least, he added, that was what the girls at home in Sola Khumbu said it meant, with a tell-tale gleam in his dark eyes.

'Cuckoo!' So that was it, then. 'Cuckoo!' Dhaulagiri shone white through the branches from high up in the sky.

Three of our party got married almost as soon as they got home.

Whenever I think of Nepal, the view from the Gorapani Pass – the 'Horse-water' Pass – leaps to my mind.

The summit of the pass is jungle covered; lianas trail from the dark branches. Pale mauve flowers blossom in the moss that clothes the trunks. Tree ferns grow between them. And at the highest point on this immemorial road you will find prayer flags hanging.

As we were toiling up to the summit of that pass, close on 10,000 feet high, I saw Dhaulagiri once more. It was in the early morning. There it floated, utterly divorced from the earth and weightless as some mighty cloud.

Om Math Padme Hum – Om Math Padme Hum – *engraved on a stone tablet –* Om Math Padme Hum.
  Over and over again.
  Oh, thou Jewel in the Lotus!'
  The prayer of those who worship Buddha. Just a prayer.

This stone tablet here comes from Nepal; from the foot of Dhaulagiri – from one of the stone monuments one continually meets by the wayside, fashioned out of the mountain's slate.
  'Oh, thou Jewel in the Lotus!'
  Somebody who wanted to use that form of prayer engraved the letters of those words and laid the tablet there, next to all the others bearing the same inscription.

It is supposed to be unlucky to remove one of those prayer tablets; no native of Nepal would ever even think of doing such a thing. One of the climbers on the 1959 expedition had brought this one home with him.
  Later he began to have misgivings. One day he brought it to me, which was a sensible solution.

Om Math Padme Hum – just a prayer.
Sometimes it seems to come sounding right out of the stone.

18   Herbert Tichy

I looked at Herbert Tichy's postcard: a black and white photograph of flowers, grass, rocks, at whose feet great rollers were breaking in clouds of spray. Some island or other. 'This is what it looks like here,' he wrote; 'very impressive and noisy. The mountains here are steep and crumbling. I got up to a peak nearly 13,000 feet high, with a wonderful view, but very cold. So you are really working on your book? There are 7,000 islands; one of them must be the perfect subject, for it is high time I wrote another book ...'

I had no idea where the island, or this mountain, from which the postcard came, might be. There was no clue to its whereabouts, no date on the card; but the island existed, with its high mountain, its lush vegetation and its storm-tossed sea. When Herbert came home, he would tell me about it. Or he might even write a book about it. It might still not explain exactly where the island lay; the important thing would be that, somewhere, it existed. When Herbert unfolds a tale, space and time become subservient to another dimension.

A leading cartographer once wanted to translate one of Tichy's eventful journeys through a little-known region of the Himalaya into the terms of a map; all he succeeded in doing was to produce a sketch map full of question marks. He simply found it impossible to transfer Herbert Tichy's hidden dimension into the scale in which map makers work – a complete tribute to the integrity of both conceptions.

In the accompanying text, the well-known compiler of a Himalayan Chronicle grudgingly growled out a few complimentary remarks about the wonderful powers of observation of human customs and the skill with which this geologist-errant portrayed them. (Actually his thesis for his doctorate, a study of the Himalaya, was the end of his programme as a geologist and the start of his career as an author.)

A great deal has been written about Tichy's life, so I will not try to do so. We are friends; so it is of no importance what we studied, where we went or how those years passed. The important thing is that we met.

It is almost true to say that we met long before we came to know one another –for Herbert wrote books; and when I began to read about his years in China, about his pilgrimage to the holy peak of Kailas, about the hair-raising journey by motorcycle to India, I realised more and more that here was a man who wrote about things I knew, though till then far less clearly. And I realised, too, that I really knew the man who wrote those words, although I had never seen him.

That is how, strangely enough, it turned out when Kurt Maix took me to see him. And after that? We have never been on an expedition together, nor shared a journey. When Herbert is away for a year, somewhere on the globe, he may write me a letter or a couple of cards; but when I go to Vienna to see him, it makes no difference whether a year or a month has elapsed. We talk all through the long afternoon, seeking the purpose of all this journeying hither and thither, of life itself, of lecture tours, of being with other people; recalling the Himalayan peaks and skies. Very often we fail to find an answer.

I am sure every reader knows the importance of whom one meets – and that is why I have written these lines; for Herbert Tichy has clarified many things for me, if only by making me aware of what was previously unclear. He belongs in my life's orbit.

I know that in many ways we are very different people. I am a climber, while Herbert would never climb a mountain face as an end in itself. This wanderer over the earth's surface says he is no climber; but that did not prevent his strolling up to above 26,000 feet, through tempest and icy cold, towards the wide Himalayan sky, even to the white dome of Cho Oyu. With only a Sherpa for company, he climbed higher and higher on that mighty Tibetan peak, Gurla Mandhata, without ever getting to the top –but because he had seen it he understood the Sadhu, deep in his meditations, to whom the summit belongs.

One should never describe anyone else's room, because it is his personal kingdom, every corner of which can contribute its aura. So I will only describe the floor of Tichy's – that generally unused plain, to which we Europeans merely accord a sterile existence, that empty space between desk, divan and chest, whose unreality we, at best, try to disguise with a resplendent parquet or a colourful carpet. (Though children have long known its true value and have, without restrictions or inhibitions, converted it to a private world of their own.) In Asia, too, the floor is part of the living space and – coming back now to Herbert – everyone who writes books knows what a splendid place it is for scattering around the chapters of a manuscript, photographs, drawings, one's letters, maps, and mementoes of a journey; while the owner of the floor quietly surveys it all from on high, with the eyes of a traveller in space looking down on the earth's surface. .I think it is a modern concept, though it may be a very ancient one –and certainly one no 'lady of the house' would willingly accept. Herbert, however, is a bachelor; and he who has trodden the floors of Asia, is an adept at floors.

It is impossible to talk about Herbert without recalling his quiet sense of humour. On his way back from the holy peak of Kailas in Tibet – he had made his journey to and around it dressed as a pilgrim – devout peasants of the locality kissed his feet and those of his native companions. 'No joy for us,' said Tichy, 'but certainly none for them, seeing that we had been on the march for several weeks.'

Herbert is tall, about six foot, fair-haired and very quiet. His stride betrays the many months of wandering through the valleys, over the passes and ridges of the Himalaya. I suppose he is about fifty, but I don't know, for there is about him a quality of agelessness. He has spent much time in Asia, going back again and again –sometimes for a few months, once, in China, for seven years. He always came home –to Vienna, to Nepal, to people living under unnamed ranges, or at the edge of the sea in the far north of Alaska –it didn't matter, he was at home anywhere where people were at home.

What happens to a man who has grasped in its entirety one truth, and then another, and another? He will wander the earth till the end of his life –where to, none can say.

The poet Wang Wei wrote:
'The Earth is everywhere the same
And eternal, eternal are the white clouds …'

Herbert journeyed on, with two Lamas he had met on the way, southwards. He wanted to get to the south of the clouds.

I went to Vienna.

Herbert was happy and radiated his pleasure. He had been in Africa for a year. No, he had not been lonely. He talked of the life down there and the people he had met. I asked him if he planned to go there again.

Two years later I was in Vienna again.

Herbert was unhappy. We talked about life, a whole long afternoon – all to no avail, for we could not change the things we talked about: they were hard facts. Still, it was better to have talked again.

Six months later I stopped at Vienna on my way to a lecture in Budapest. 'I think I must get away somewhere,' said Herbert.

When I saw him again, a month later, his trunks were in the middle of the room, packed and ready.

'When do you leave?'

'In a month's time.'

'Where to?'

'I don't know yet, exactly. Might be Formosa… might even be Japan.'

We sat by those packed trunks, smoked a cigarette, drank a glass of whisky, to wish his journey well.

I called him up three weeks later. Herbert had gone. I had a card from Formosa, with greetings on it. How long will he be away? A year, two years? Nobody knows, not even Herbert himself.

One of these days he will be back in Vienna, as if he had left only yesterday.

That is the man who said to me, when I went off to climb Dhaulagiri: 'Come back safe. But even if you don't, I wish you joy!'

19 Eighteen to Eighty-One: Finals and a Police Sergeant

I have passed my finals: my finals – I have passed them: my finals are – past!

My clothes are clinging to my body. I am dragging one foot, because I have only one shoelace in one shoe; the other must be somewhere in the police station. My tie looks like a corkscrew. And I could embrace the whole world – even that fat police sergeant. For I am a diploma'd Lecturer in Commerce. At last!

No more swotting! I'm free again – isn't life wonderful? Wonderful rain, proper, gorgeous, beneficent, torrential rain, running down all over one's face. Isn't life wonderful?

A few years ago, at the University of Commerce, Vienna, these had been the reflections of a grant-aided student lectureship candidate: 'I am a mathematical genius, only it doesn't always show itself, because I always make mistakes in my arithmetic. Still, I belong to the higher IQ levels – I am a mathematician, not a reckoner. Arithmetic today is done by *machines*; mathematicians are the *men* of the future ...'

This stupid business of arithmetic. Just practice stuff, fit only for morons. Anyone can learn it, if he goes on long enough. Why do I always get the wrong answer? I gave a groan.

'My friend,' said the soft voice of an obvious head bookkeeper in the making, by my side. 'It is because you haven't had enough practice.' I said nothing and continued to stare at the example in front of me. 'I'll tell you what to do,' he went on, patiently and helpfully (by now he looked exactly like a doctor prescribing a medicine): 'You just take a bit of paper every day and do ten of these reckonings.' He took a piece of paper and, as I regarded him sceptically: 'Just watch,' he said, enthusiastically. Then he wrote down the figure eighteen and draw a vertical line down from it. 'Let us take eighteen as an example ... now you multiply it by two ... then the result by three ... and so on, up to fifteen.'

'Don't you think nine would do?' I interposed.

'All right, up to nine then,' he said, with an indulgent smile. 'And now you start dividing, first by two, then the result by three, and so on, up to nine. If you haven't made a mistake, you get back in the end to the figure eighteen. You do ten such reckonings a day – in addition to your others, of course ...'

I said, 'thanks' and gave a deep sigh. I remembered that kind of uncongenial task from the days of my o-Level exams; about as useful as fifty knee-bends after the shrilling of the alarm clock in the morning (stated in mathematical terms = + five minutes' lie-in).

Finally, I said: 'It wouldn't be the least use – I should just go on making mistakes.' You go on doing it until you don't make mistakes any more,' he said quietly, with a slight grimace. So we were back where we started – just stupid practice maths; didn't I know that commercial arithmetic was something for dolts? Why was the chap smiling so knowingly? He was beginning, somehow, to get on my nerves ...

I packed up my bank accounts and went to a coffee shop. So, I was supposed to fritter a quarter of an hour of my time away, simply to start from eighteen and get back to eighteen again? Give me a piece of paper... I needn't have worried: my result was seventy-three.

I did it again. Twenty-six. Well, anyway, I was getting nearer.

I got it right the third time, and thought it over for a while.

All hope was not lost, then. In any case, the finals weren't till April.

Just for the record: the paternal state takes great thought for Lecturers in Commerce. It wants them all to be practical people. So it prescribes eighteen months of practical sales or bookkeeping experience before they take their finals. I forgot a great deal during that time – perhaps others didn't suffer the same way, but I did.

I turned up with the gloomiest forebodings. I passed in bookkeeping, business correspondence, pedagogics (a 'V.G.' for that!), the theory of business management ... I went down in arithmetic like a bomb. So did some of the others, not that that cheered me up any. Anyway, my time in Vienna was up: from now on I would do a bit of desultory study in arithmetic, so as to take the beastly subject again, from a discreet distance. For, in the interim, I had found – well, I was going to say a 'career' – I had become a climber! My life had begun to include lecturing, going far afield on expeditions, visiting the mountains. I lectured on the Alps and the Himalaya in Austria, Italy, England and Switzerland – my journeys were often long and marvellous; and I got to know a great many people. Then I got married – and still I hadn't passed my finals – at least, not in that confounded subject, arithmetic.

I would have taught already, but I said to myself: until they have let you pass in commercial arithmetic, you will not teach. There may be two points of view, I'm sure. I personally don't regret those years in the least – it was so definitely the life I was meant to live; and so many other people shared it with me.

But now let us take another flying visit to Vienna.

The next 'finals' were due in a few days.

I sat in the front row, taking up what is scientifically known as a 'showerbath' position. For our professor set much store by attendance at his lectures. There he was, looking around, looking at me … and I heard him saying: 'Once I had a candidate who came regularly all the way from Linz to hear me lecture!' I bowed my head guiltily; I only came from Salzburg and by no means regularly.

Unfortunately, no luck again, that time … but it went much better than the first attempt – I was only *just* ploughed. Ruefully, I had to admit that this just wouldn't do, the way I was playing it; study by remote-control wasn't the right answer – in spite of the notes a kindly nun had made for me. There was always something to distract me: mountains, lectures, everyday life. Unfortunately, a man cannot do only the things that give him pleasure – even if that is his real life.

One day I took the great decision: it has to be! I must say farewell to wife and child and go to Vienna, in deadly earnest, for two months.

Over my desk there was a framed calculation based on eighteen.

I studied like mad. Foreign exchange, calculation, current accounts, arbitrage – really quite interesting subjects. All the same, I was still making occasional arithmetical mistakes. But this time I felt much more confident.

The night before the viva, I sat in a lecture room just under the roof of the University of Commerce. Here there were very few people, and there was at least peace and quiet. The view from there extends as far as the Prater. There was someone sitting a row in front of me, his head propped on his head. He was doing arithmetic. Suddenly he hurled his exercise book away. 'Wrong?' I asked, sympathetically. 'Yes – again!' he said.

'My friend,' I said, 'that's because you haven't had enough practice. I'll tell you what to do. Take the figure eighteen as an example, and then you …'

It so happened that police sergeant Pomeisl was stumping his normal beat that evening in the suburb of Hietzing. Actually, he had nothing to do with the figure eighteen; but fate had decreed that we should meet on the morrow, over quite a different figure, just a quarter of an hour before the deadline for my viva. Of course, I didn't know that this evening, when I went for a nice walk, sure that at last everything would go well next day …

The clink of arms! The hosts marching to the decisive battle. Varus … Arminius of the Cherusci … an adding machine … I had slept badly. Oh, it's only that damned alarm clock!

… Hell! That's what happens when you lie in for only five minutes. Out you get, quick!

Houses went racing past, dark tunnels shut their cavernous jaws. The Vienna *Metro* went clattering and rattling along, first above the city, then under the city; the jolly old Vienna *Metro*.

It wasn't going nearly fast enough for me. Tense as a wire, I sat there, looking at the second hand of my watch, as it went round and round. Seven-thirty. My viva was at eight – oh, yes, I shall just make it. Not a minute to spare, though. I wondered whether the other chap was there already – there were to be two of us … armies on the march, the outcome could not be delayed now, the muffled sound of drums, the field of battle lay close ahead.

I hoped the other one wasn't too bright. (What an egoist you are!) Of course, I wanted him to pass – I just hoped he wasn't too bright. I mean: there were only two of us. If one of us boobed, that would be a fifty per cent failure. One really mustn't be as hard-hearted as that …

'Hietzing!'

Quickly, hop out! There's the tram, on the other side of the road. Don't let it get away, right under your very nose. I know the light's red; but I can't help it. Got to get across! Cars … very skilful, I am … there. I am safely in the tram. Somewhere in my subconscious – the sound of a whistle … not surprising, with all this traffic …

No sign of the tram starting. I'm not a Viennese; how was I to know it was a terminus? Heavens, time was running out, after all; a quarter to eight! Where on earth was my reminder-notice with the conversion figures on it?

'That's 'im!' A tough, short, rose-red police sergeant was peering into the tram. At me? Why at me?

'Out wiv yer!'

'Me?'

'Yus, you! You can't take no rise out o' me. Didncherear me whistling like mad? Cross on the red, you did. Outcher comes – !' He was as red as the traffic light.

'I hope it won't take long … I was outside in a flash, pulling out my wallet. You see, inspector, I've got a viva. Quick, tell me what the fine is …'

'Ten schillings.'

Curse it, I hadn't any change. One, two, three, four schillings … not enough. A fifty-schilling note.

'Here's fifty schillings,' and I handed it to him. The conductor was boarding the tram.

'Ten schillings! … ain't got no change.' Hell and damnation!

'Please keep the fifty,' I begged. have an all-important exam – they are waiting for me. I'll fetch the change later!' The driver was getting aboard.

'P'raps I'd better get yer change now. Don't want no leftovers. Goin' inter shop fer change – then I gets ten schillings and don't owe no one nothing.'

'All aboard!' shouted the conductor; the tram bell clanged.

'No!' I shouted to him. Tye got to catch this tram and I'm going to (the board: my viva!). You can keep my passport (I *must* catch it). Keep the fifty schillings, the lot (what else could I do?) – but I *must* go on this tram!'

'You stay where y'are. You're under arrest!'

Everything began to go round and round, melting, wavering. Oh, no, not that – a whole year wasted! Perhaps never in such good form, ever again! No, not that! The tram was moving off – oh God, be merciful. The tram was moving on – merciful God … the tram … the sergeant … the Board … my viva. Tram, board, viva … *tram*!!

I was hanging on the step, my hands tight-gripped on the rail. The tram – despair, struggle, triumph …

The law was hanging on to my coat-tails. At the back of me. Useless. Good cloth this … but my police-friend wasn't a lightweight. However, I have strong hands. Of course, the strongest party concerned was the tram.

Something had to happen soon. I couldn't let go, now. I heard a seam rip. Titanic forces at work. I hung on desperately. So did he …

It turned into a superhuman display of strength, in which the tram was considerably involved. Seeing that my clothes were made in Austria and were therefore top quality goods, and taking into account that while I am no giant, I am no weakling either, the odds against the arm of the law were three to one, and the tram – a good strong product of Semmering – won the national lottery.

All of a sudden, I found myself free. I drew a deep breath of relief. My viva was safe!

Safe, for a few yards … surely not, surely not that?

There was a screeching, which cut deep into my soul – the trumpet of the day of Judgement … the tram was braking, coming to a halt. This was the absolute end; I dared not turn round.

Very soon he had hold of me, panting, his face traffic-light red. 'Now, Y'come along of me!' he said, winding my tie round his arm. In front of all those people, too. I was being marched off. *Finis*!

I tried to explain things a bit. I was almost sorrier by now for him than for myself. He was covered in dust – through measuring his length in the road – so tight had his hold on me been. I couldn't have foreseen that – in any case, I couldn't have let go …

In a towering rage, he marched me off to the police station.

It was after eight o'clock.

There was a telephone at the station. I rang the board up … I was in police care … would be late …

'Have you been involved in a street accident?'

'No – not directly (what could one say?).'

'Then be quick about it.'

Dear Lord, how much longer would they want me here?

Police sergeant Pomeisl was there again (we were beginning to know one another). Again he wound my tie round his arm. 'Taking you to the district police station,' he announced.

Marched by the tie through respectable Hietzing, I didn't mind a hoot about the people: I minded a great deal about my viva.

By now he was only holding on to my coat. Should I chance it again? No – a sideways look reminded me that my sergeant had something of a Russian tank about him – yes, just that.

Officialdom was in full stride.

Another room, larger this time, with two officials in it. There was a telephone … I rang up the board.

'I'm afraid it'll take a little time. I have to clear one or two matters –'

'All right. But you'll have to be here in an hour at the latest.'

God willing, I would be.

'Sit down,' said an official, opening a book. He was tall, fair, polite, concise. 'How much money have you?' I counted it out. What on earth was all this about?

'Any offensive weapons – such as a pocketknife? Put any pointed articles on the table.' This was ridiculous. I wouldn't hurt a fly. All I want is to take my viva. I asked what this all meant. Politely and concisely, the official remarked: 'And now your shoelaces and your tie.' … Something was beginning to dawn on me: goodbye, viva!

'I forgot a tin-opener. I could cut a wrist artery with that,' said I, bitingly, and dug savagely into my pocket (I am not very keen on *recherché* cooking). This was really the adjectival limit! Goodbye, viva!

One last hope. The station superintendent. I want to see the superintendent. Now –!

I summoned up all my powers of persuasion and gave him my version of the dilemma. It worked; he understood me … Proceedings suspended. My hour's grace was nearly over. The officer was concise, but not unfriendly. He had grasped what was at stake for me.

Of course, in the event, Pomeisl had only done his duty. (After all, what would happen to us in Austria if everyone who was in a hurry crossed on the red?) But the officer did more; he let me go in time for my viva!

I ran like a hare. The rain came down in torrents. I ran gasping round the blocks, then past trees, then two more streets. I made my appearance before the Board pale, breathless, soaked to the skin. Joy unalloyed! They were still there, and I was here.. Water dripped from my suit on to the parquet floor. Weren't they even annoyed with me? On the contrary, they were quite concerned about my state. 'But you can't take your viva like that; you are quite worn out!' they said. I sensed a great wave of sympathy – and I could have hugged friend Pomeisl. The police, I thought, your friends and helpers; I had them to thank for it. Out loud, I said: 'Of course I am fit to take my viva, I am used to great exertions; but (with a little bow) if the gentlemen of the board would be kind enough to give me five minutes, to sit down and collect myself – ?'

Not only did they give me five minutes, but they passed me with a 'Good' …

Commercial arithmetic is a wonderful subject. A year or two later I made a submission to the directorate: … I should be glad if, in the next syllabus, I could be allotted as many arithmetic classes as possible. For some reason or other I feel I have a special aptitude for the subject.' (And Susi, my new calculating machine, was a great help.)

The mills of justice grind slowly, but they do grind – not always a comfortable thought. In the end, my lawyer succeeded in getting the case transferred from Vienna to Salzburg. That was much more convenient; the court was in the next street.

There we were in a panelled room of the county court: the presiding magistrate, the public prosecutor, defending counsel, all in black robes … and, in the middle, on a slightly lower level, the defendant.

I was frankly anxious – you never know what may not happen. There was a picture of Justice hanging on the wall. I heard the words: You are charged, under paragraph 81 of the Act, of having offered open violence . ;

'81 … that's a wrong result', I thought.

'But, honestly, I couldn't have done anything else. If I had let go, I should have fallen on the back of my head, which is very dangerous; for, as everyone knows, looked at from any angle, the head is by far the most important part of the body … '

I was acquitted.

One more thing. I received a (not unexpected) official letter. On the – the day of – at Hietzing, during the performance of sergeant so-and-so's duty –' Pomeisl is a pseudonym – the officer's tunic suffered damage, for which you are duly held responsible. You are therefore required to pay a compensatory sum of S.50; in words, schillings fifty.'

I have learned something: always keep some change in your wallet.

Part 4

20 The Break-Even

A rending and a splintering, as when a tall tree falls. Fear; stabbing pain … I go hurtling through the air, impelled by some ungovernable force. My leg! Oh, you – *your* leg! One ski had bored deep into the ground. No! Oh, no! Bone fragments, splinters … I can see nothing, but I know well enough … searing pain …

I had had it.

… there was the tail end of a ski in front of my eyes, the heel of a boot under my knee … that heel belonged to me. So my leg must be twisted 180 degrees. I was on the point of passing out – thoughts: at least you have been on Dhaulagiri and Broad Peak … searing pain … fragments and fragments … this was it … I had had it …

My brother-in-law Herbert and someone I didn't know dragged me to a hospital. I lay on a table while the doctors examined me. A rotational fracture, they pronounced.

'Are you on National Health?'

'No, private.'

'Too bad – in that case we haven't a bed for you at the moment … God almighty! I was carted to another hospital, where there was room.

That day set its mark on three years of my life – years of hope, despair, doubts whether I should ever be able to go back to my mountains. Just a rotational fracture – not normally of any great account. Yet Bruno Winstersteller, who does Grade VI climbs on one leg, lost his that way; Carlo Mauri went limping around for years. It is possible to learn endless patience, to grit one's teeth, to live and see things differently, to hope and hope and hope …

Even I could do that. In my case, callous refused to form where the broken ends of the bones had been set against each other, at least for a long time, and then not much. Finally, after six months, at first on my back with my leg in an elastic sling, later in a long plaster, they discharged me. Gingerly I put my weight on that poor little leg, grown thin and wooden as Pinocchio's, stiff in the knee and ankle, and half an inch shorter. Would it bear me?

At first it seemed to. I tottered my first hesitant steps, began to take long walks, got back on to rock. It was a very odd leg, but it held together. I even took it, treating it with the greatest solicitude, up the South Ridge of the Noire.

Then I went to the post office where, with the feeblest of little reports, it broke again.

On my back once more; more plaster ...

In spite of all, the period I spent in hospital was no all-time 'low'. A man who cannot walk a single step, who lies permanently fettered to the same spot, with the same window, the same wall before his eyes, lives a totally different life. He sees right through everything, transcending space and time, in a dimension not achieved by the swiftest voyager through space. Suddenly he realises what a wonderful thing it is just to see the branch of a tree; and that others suffer pain more abominable than his own ...

Only, one cannot stay in hospital for ever.

The break-even ... is the moment in the course of a business venture when it shows neither profit nor loss. The business goes on, has no need to go into liquidation, but is unable to plough anything back; it simply maintains its entity. The only justification of its existence is the provision of its services ..

I had taken up a teaching post in business management at a school outside Salzburg – a decision undoubtedly influenced by the disaster to my leg.

Not an easy decision to take for one who had lived 'free' to the age of thirty, without a 'boss', without a timetable drawn up by someone else; but also, of course, without security. To such a one it is damnably difficult to adopt what is called a 'regular routine', which provides that security at the expense of everything else. Yet, there comes a day when you ask yourself: 'What have you actually achieved?' And with the question comes the sudden feeling that only a 'normal career' is a career at all – and so you take a job.

It was autumn, and I was listening to the end-of-the-holidays address to the pupils:

'... to pick up your work again gladly and with strength renewed ...'

All the same, the first year went well, and so did the second. I had my problems and dealt with them; after that, everything ran calmly along the same smooth track; and each year I was a year older and would be a year older each year – nothing else changing en route – till I was due for my retirement pension. I really enjoyed teaching; but my thoughts centred more and more on the knowledge that no pleasure, no improvisation, can permanently mitigate the monotonous burden of increasing regularity.

Ours is a ridiculous existence. Almost everyone today is a cog in an invisible machine, consisting almost entirely of bosses and employees. The boss is a lonely type. He is entirely pre-occupied with the morale of the workers in his business and the improvements required by that business; with bids, enquiries, turnovers. He nearly always ends up in splendid isolation – for few are they who bare their hearts to the boss …

And the employee? He watches everything being rationalised and does his own rationalisation: trying to 'achieve a definite end with the slenderest means' instead of – and this is how the boss sees it – 'the greatest possible end with the means available'. Can the gulf between these concepts ever be bridged? Twenty-four hours are twenty-four hours for both men; the machinery is the same machinery. Is it possible, none the less, to garner enough satisfaction from that kind of daily round? I marvel at the imagination of those who think they can. But many fall by the wayside; they stick to their jobs and, gradually, their spirit grows rectangular – like the television screen, the container, the office bench, and their own bottoms, sitting on that bench. In fact, like the whole huge rectangular machine! But it is never too late for anyone to get up and go – for freedom of thought is always his, if he really wants freedom. And, above all, if he can still recognise the point where he has 'broken even'.

Just a day, a grey day – any day in the curriculum. I might have only five periods, or seven; in between them, gaps in the timetable, as in any occupation. I sit there, thinking and looking out: 'window periods', like the air-spaces between the window gratings. There they are, and they are no use to one. What have I done? What should I do? Security … a living … but time is passing; the sun circles in its course. There is a despairing entry in my diary: 'How much longer can I stand it?'

My young charges have no idea how I feel; we get on splendidly together. By now I have rationalised my work so well that I have a great deal of time in which to think – ample 'window periods'. What am I to do?

I shut the next eight months away out of sight, waiting for the freedom of my next mountaineering expedition. But is that any solution? Time rotates slowly across the whole year, like the perforated dial of a musical clock, and there, day after day, one sits, between three pips of the mechanism, waiting for one's hour to strike. Perhaps I could write a book in those pauses? No, I have no feeling of freedom between the cogwheels of that clock.

And so I went on thinking and thinking: what am I to do? At times I tried to forget everything and to live just for the day. It was a kind of solution … but for how long?

Then I found another. I told myself I would do one more year, and then go to a forestry school – a highly improbable pipe-dream. But now I knew that there was a term to my time here, and that made all the difference. Suddenly I felt that it did not matter greatly whether it was one year or two; what did matter was that I was not going to end my days here. That day I felt more free than for a long time past; I felt that school was a happy and sunny place, and my colourful tribe in great good humour. I managed to work in the business economics and financial aspects of a Himalayan expedition – not excluding the abominable snowman. In the evening I, the non-skittler, went with my class to a skittle-alley, and for the first time in my life took all nine. We discussed our various problems and – *Gaudeamus Igitur*! – were thoroughly happy. The whole world lay open to us – yes, to them and me, too.

Nothing could upset me very much at the school after that day; for I knew my days were numbered.

It was Christmastime. My class had presented me with an eight-armed octopus made of black wool, with red eyes, inscribed: 'For our Yeti, on all steep climbs.' *I* was the Yeti, the snowman. I, who had told them I believed in it, who had seen photographs of its tracks.

I should hate leaving. We had all been bound together, as it were, by a common fate. But not by the one for me: not permanently. I had got to go, even though I did not know where to … perhaps to some underdeveloped country?

I had spent five whole years of my life here …

We celebrated the end of term; my class was leaving. It was a mixture of addresses, champagne, happy faces, the holiday atmosphere, gaiety. The blonde Elisabeth – spokeswoman for the whole 'mixed' class – handed me a huge black cube. 'For our Yeti,' she laughed, and all the others grinned.

'Hm!' I wondered. 'What's all this about?'

I saw the glint of a catch and pressed it. Wumph! The lid flew open: a black ball, black as the very devil, leaped at me on the end of a coiled spring and swung backwards and forwards in front of my eyes. On it was 'A2', the name of my class. It was only then that I discovered what was written on the outside of the black box: … 'The Break-even'. … because I had spoken of it so often.

It forms a feature of my furniture now; it stands in the middle of my table. The impression it makes is part serious, part cheerful.

21 The Fourth Dimension

I found the same pale red flower, with four petals and a distinctive Bross at its heart, near the edge of a glacier in the Hindu Kush and on the shore of a Greenland fjord teeming with icebergs.

What had borne it round the world?

Suddenly you find a link between two distant parts of the world. Mankind does not even need speech.

Then there was Bianca. What I have to tell of her is not a love story. It is something quite different – something that lives among the grasses, between the waves of the sea at Duino and on the broad expanse of the Karst[1]. We called it the fourth dimension.

Love? I do not know if one can give the name to such an understanding as this. There is something more to it than that. And I believe it is something everyone is capable of finding.

The waves at Duino ... Rilke wrote there, in the old walled castle, and he saw those waves as they are still to be seen today – differently by each beholder, different in themselves according to the day on which they are seen, yet always the same incomparable insurge of curving wave forms, one overlaying the other.

There, below the old walls of the castle, below the trees and grasses that grow between the rain-eroded, skeletal limestone of the Karst, the huge twisted rock faces of the peninsula plunge vertical to the sea.

The cliffs sweep up some 300 feet. At their base break the waves which come surging in from far out and surge back outwards again, with diminished force, curving, overlaying each other. Sometimes too, when the wind has set the thousand particles of deepest blue in swirling motion somewhere far out there, they themselves stay there. When, in the end, their motion, overleaping thousands of other particles, reaches the coast, this time to impinge obliquely, thrown back by slabs and buttresses, on the curves in the rock face, and is flung back in the other direction from the caves, over-running itself three and four

---

1 The Karst is a broad limestone plateau, arid, scrub-covered, pot-holed, fringing the coast near Trieste. – Translator's note.

times, obliquely at varying speeds – the matchless spectacle is such that the watcher, looking down on it 300-feet sheer, would do well to hold on to something for support. And yet, at the same time, there is a concept he can grasp; and, if he does so, he will gaze and gaze, unable to tear himself away .

The fourth dimension. Not only time, but many mingling dimensions. There, in the depths below, in the rise and fall of blue particles.

Bianca is a big girl and her eyes are dark. She comes from Istria. Always something of an enigma – she is for the most part fearfully energetic, as if she might lose one minute's worth of life. Then again, she will be absolutely quiet – that is how she is. She has always a mass of things to do – her job, school, theatre; but when she climbs, rippling up the most difficult pitches with an incredibly natural lightness of movement – then she is quiet. Those are the two sides of Bianca. She can lead anything up to Grade VI, loves the mountains, the Karst and the sea; but she has no positive attitude towards the world – she says the difference is too great.

I had been lecturing in Trieste. I had spoken with enthusiasm of the mountains, looking up at my pictures on the screen – pictures of all the peaks I did not know whether I should ever be involved with again, because of my broken leg: not that it altered my love for them one whit.

Suddenly, there was Bianca facing me. She seized me by the arm, dragged me away through all the after lecture confusion. 'Come along, let's drink a glass of beer,' she commanded; but before we could really start talking, all our friends joined us: Spiro, Walter, Fioretta, Erich, Violetta, and the evening turned into a cheery Trieste party .

All the same, next day, in the evening, we had our tête-ä-tête talk. 'One shouldn't think ...' she proclaimed. I wondered how much thinking she had done, before arriving at that thought.

'I believe one should think ...' I countered. (I too had done a good deal of thinking.)

Between a 'yes' and a no lie all the dimensions of this world.

The waters gulped and gurgled between the stones, the smell of the sea rose up to us – the delicate pink of the jellyfish shimmered and pulsated, multi-coloured, the mussels gleamed bright and black.

The grasses of the Karst. Clouds, trembling in the summer air. Greenish-black seaweed, greasy and heavy, feeling out into the moving waters like fingers.

This – all of it – was the present.

We went on across the Karst, over the rocky ribs at the heart of the Duino woods, till we stood at the edge, high above the waves. There they were, deep, deep below us – so that we had to hang on, craning far out to look down.

Suddenly I said: 'Look – over there – can you see it? – the waves, running over each other – more and more ...?'

'How can it be?' she cried.

Waves ... waves ... more waves ... as we seemed to look into a gigantic globe.

'*E incredibile* – beyond all belief!' she breathed.

It was overpowering. We squeezed each other's hands.

The movement continued, sweeping over the transparent blue deeps with a compulsive regularity; cones of waves, of dimensions overlaying each other; a whole fine-spun web of time, unbelievably close-woven, pressing inwards from all directions. For long moments I felt that we were levitating at the heart of it – free of all contact with the ground beneath our feet.

'*La quarta dimensione*,' said Bianca. The fourth dimension. Or was it the fifth? Was it ours, or not only ours, but belonging to others as well? If so, to how many? Today it belonged to us, or we belonged to it. The difference was quite meaningless.

'It is ours,' she said, 'let us call it that and keep it so.'

We kept it so.

I have often wondered what it is that draws so many people to water. For there are countless numbers who watch the waves.

One day, suddenly, I realised something which started a new experience, into an unknown realm, into a line of thought more exciting for me than even a great voyage or climb. It suddenly dawned on me that time is only a part, perhaps only an expression of that higher dimension – even though time in itself is an unimaginable concept, so huge that none of us can understand it. Yet suppose one could grasp its meaning and, all unknowingly, most clearly of all just when one looks at the water and sees the waves over-running each other?

Over-running ...

I have tried hard to solve the enigma.

I am standing on an enormous vertical slab of rock. From far away out there the waves come rolling in to break against the rocks at my feet and then roll away again in the opposite direction ... lines that come, lines that go. The moment of impact against the cliff is a fact ¬the 'now' – the present time. Looked at in this way, the next wave, just rolling in, brings the future; and the one thrown back outwards and receding, carries away with it the past. Successive waves represent the more distant future or the more distant past, and they are exactly superimposed; everywhere the past is rolling over the future, or the other way about. And they meet at the same point.

Is it such a fanciful vision? I do not think so. I can see the waves rolling farther and farther back towards the horizon, see the past meeting the future as it rolls in towards it, see that somewhere beyond that horizon the most distant past must meet the most distant future.

But then, the earth is round, isn't it?

Suppose it were completely covered by the sea and I were standing alone here on this slab, which springs from the ground like a shield, then that most distant past would come rolling in at my back, break against the rock and immediately hurry away, as the most distant future, towards the horizon, growing 'younger' – more immediate – till it came round again and broke, in front of me, at my feet – as the present.

That can only mean that here, on the slab beneath my feet, separated only by that thin sliver of rock, and approaching from both sides, the present and the remotest future – which, again, is born of the remotest past – meet one another.

Time encompasses even space.

And now some mountaineering friend will bang me on the head with my book. For my next question is this: what happens if the slab – the Stance – suddenly subsides, to be drowned in the waters – an alarming suggestion ... ?

Then, of course, the waves of the most distant past would, in that instant, sweep over you and your immediate present, just as the immediate future merges into the most remote. The very stance of your existence would have disappeared. Two eternal orbits would be turning in opposite directions.

Would they do so – sustained by divine tension? Or would they cancel each other out in a mutual Nirvana? Would all waves then roll in from one direction only? Would some new rock spring from the ground? Would you, as one who knows how to swim, be made eternal, or, as a materialist, drown out of hand? Or are you yourself the breath of one of those orbits?

I see a spider roping itself down from the ceiling on its exiguous thread. I love this earth of ours.

Something makes the blue particles of the waters ripple.

What makes them?

They do it.

What makes them?

They do it – whensoever the wind falls anywhere on the broad surface of the sea.

22   Ordeal by Fire

The Aiguille Noire is a magnificent peak. Sharp as a sword she cleaves the sky. Or a huge black sail.

The mountain exacts the ultimate from the climber, just because of its size. All its routes are steep and long. Even the East Ridge, a Grade III climb, is not easy. The other ridges, South, West and North and the West Face, are huge, exciting climbs, Grades V and VI, on firm granite. Few are they who can climb any of these in a single day. No, it is not easy to reach the tip of that sail, high in the sky, up in the clouds; but that is what makes it so splendid – a dream peak.

And then, suddenly, something can happen which leaves you shaking every time it comes to memory.

For on some days the Aiguille Noire can transform itself, all of a sudden, into a terrible ship. And then, having battened down, beyond all means of escape, whomsoever she has lured on to her fatal deck, she sails away through timeless time with him on board, spewing electricity, shuddering under the hammer blows of the lightning, which races to earth down her steep sides, on every hand.

What then of him who is caught on the rocks of her summit? He sits at the heart of the storm centre of some strange planet; trapped in the deadly labyrinth of invisible forces, whose laws he knows not; the victim of vindictive furies; shaken by shock after shock; faced by a black question, whose answer is beyond his comprehension; unable to do anything about it. And so he is borne headlong, farther and farther through time, among the screaming clouds at the tip of that sail. Or, rather, perhaps, on an electric chair of gigantic proportions.

We ourselves have to thank blind luck and the strength of the bond between us all for our safe return to the world below ...

Later, Bianca told her story:

'There were six of us on the South Ridge, climbing happily, light-heartedly, because the sun was warm and we were all friends together. Far below, the Val Veni shone green, dotted with the gay colours of the tents on the camping site, a joy to look at. I felt like a new being, thinking of the lush, warm grass and the pleasure of treading it barefoot when I got down there again. I looked at the shining blue and white cataract of the Fresnay Glacier, and up at Mont Blanc. And, although this was my first time on this granite wedge of ours, I felt as if I had always known it. I would have been content to go on like this, moving upwards, gazing about me, for timeless ages, submerged in that sea of light under the taut, deep sky.'

I was climbing with Tona, behind the other ropes. We had not been to the mountains for a long time and we were glad to be back, even if my bad leg was still troublesome. Actually, I was disappointed about it, but, I thought, this was, after all, only the start; and I was happy in the knowledge that we were all together here on the ridge, and that it was I who had brought them here. Tona, her long fair hair escaping from her helmet, happily gripping the holds in the good granite, climbing up and up, handhold and foothold, along the 'Way of the Film', whose sequences we had once so laboriously edited. Terenzio – 'the Voice' – who had seen the film projected, and was now seeing it live. Mario, his partner, on this huge ridge for the first time. Walter and Bianca, shouting down cheerfully from above.

There we were, each of us experiencing the ridge in his own way, thinking his own thoughts; but our hands used the same holds, we enjoyed the same sunshine, and we were united by the bonds of friendship.

It was my third ascent of the South Ridge, and it was a marvellous day; I found new variants, recognised the old pitches, thought of Wolfi and Franz. Finally, we bivouacked on the third tower, the Pointe Welzenbach. It was a luxury bivouac; two comfortable granite beds, with clean little table-like slabs. We looked up at the vertical upthrust of the Pointe Brendel and the Pointe Bich. Above them glittered a thousand stars.

Towards evening, next day, we were close under the subsidiary summit, climbing on two ropes: Tona, Terenzio and Mario on ahead, Walter, Bianca and I about 300 feet behind.

Let Tona take up the tale:

'We had dealt with the difficult pitches of the Pointe Bich and knew we were quite close to the summit of the Noire. The subsidiary was just at the top of the next couloir. It was almost dusk, and we were moving quickly, for we intended to bivouac somewhere on the normal descent from the summit after crossing it. The sky had been wonderfully clear in the morning; but now it was being invaded by masses of cirrus, strangely shaped and fantastic in colouring: flowers, fishes, dragons … We ought to press on, for the weather would certainly be bad tomorrow. The clouds were coming in from the west, and we, on the south-east face of the mountain, watched them dissipating, as if by magic, just above our heads. And then, one of them failed to dissipate'.

There was an uncanny silence; it was suddenly dark, as a gigantic fish swam across the sky. Down in the valley the lights were going on: it was eight o'clock. Time to find a bivouac site. Could we still catch the other up?

Suddenly we lay under an inexplicable threat, descending directly on us – a kind of tension, an invisible curtain, closing in all about us, closing inexorably down on the black rocks of the subsidiary summit …

A streak of fire split the firmament. There was a crash, which nearly lifted us off our feet, a hissing roar, as if a tidal wave were sweeping down the rocks, a fearful impact … right through our bodies it ran … the elements shook, in us, all around us … for long seconds chaos reigned … an electric salvo on an unprotected column …

The air echoed with shouts. 'Quick, on to that ledge!''Get down off the ridge!''The ironmongery – get rid of it!'

Then the next bludgeoning blow fell, in blinding light, with a rending crash. The distorted faces, the bowed figures of Walter and Bianca …

The whole ironmonger's shop came rattling down the rope to me on a karabiner. A nice present! Hell! Into a rock cranny with it, somewhere. Dynamite in my hands …

Hailstorms, another blinding flash, another hammer blow. The clatter of falling equipment, up above. A shout? My heart gave a stab. The others must be close under the summit up there. Great God – Tona … why weren't we together?

There was no way up to her.

Walter, Bianca and I, and the bivouac bag. We held hands. More crashes . Tona, Mario, Terenzio – suppose . ?

'What is it, Kurt?' asked Bianca.

'Tona – '

The thought of that was worse than my fear for myself. Suppose?

'Terenzio and Mario are with her,' she said.

No way up. There, on the next pitch, millions of volts were racing to earth down the crest. No way up; no way back. Each successive crack went rumbling down the crest of the ridge with the crazy speed of a runaway train.

Dear God … there is nothing I can do.

Tona, again:

'And then one cloud failed to dissipate. A rumbling blow struck and shook the face. "Lightning," said Terenzio, calmly.

'We bundled the pitons together as quickly as we could; sent every metal object flying down the face. We were almost at the summit, but who would risk crossing it at this moment? I put my down jacket on. It was almost pitch-dark.

'I felt a whiplash crack in my back; my head was enveloped in flame. Hildegard! I thought: My Hildegard! Again that flame, another explosion, and I knew no more … Terenzio's face appearing out of the darkness, smiling. God knows why smiling: "Are you all right?" At all events, the three of us were alive, crushed hard against the face.

'It was snowing now. Thirty feet above our heads, the tongues of lightning were racing down the ridge. A crash to each lightning flash. We tried to cover ourselves with the bivouac bag. I couldn't move my right leg; it was quite numb. (Struck by lightning, of course.) Terenzio helped me. Mario was shattered, overwhelmed, behaving strangely. We stood upright all night long, for there was nowhere to sit, on that face.'

They had all three been struck, by various branches of that flaming shaft of lightning. It leaped into their bodies from the rock or out of the air, sweeping their faces and their clothing, running to earth through the soles of their boots. Tona had two burn-holes the size of florins in the palms of her hands, a larger one in her right ankle – burnt right through her sock – one of her bootnails was blackened. Mario had a similar wound in his back, Terenzio in his foot; his shoulder, like all their clothing, was punctured by innumerable barbs of lightning. The storm raged unbroken from 8 p.m. till 2 a.m. None of them knew then that it was only the beginning: that eight more thunderstorms were to follow, during thirty more hours. They killed five people in the Mont Blanc group.

Again Tona:
'We stood upright all night long … It was still snowing next morning, but the thunder had stopped for the time being. It was high time to quit our over-narrow stance, so we tried to make our way up the ridge overhead. The air was saturated with electricity; the rock was crackling with it. Our movements disturbed its equilibrium; a discharge exploded into light around us and a ball of fire went rolling down the ridge.

'We roped down a little way, till we reached a small ledge, just large enough to house the three of us, jammed close together. A great boulder gave us protection from the direction of the summit. We used snow to heighten our protective cover, till we were in a little niche.' [It was not till then that they noticed their dark purple burns. Tona's leg slowly recovered sensation.]

The thunderstorms succeeded one another, close on each other's heels. We tried to make ourselves as small as possible, to reduce ourselves to nothing, to disappear altogether.'

They were panic-smitten lest they should be struck again. Wouldn't it ever let up? Had the sun vanished for ever? It went on snowing, there were more lightning flashes, and still the snow fell. A whole day passed; another night. Their faces were caked with ice, great shudders racked them. How much longer?

Were they going to die here, waiting in a niche, a few feet below the summit? In the end, that is what they came to believe.

Two of our friends, Gino and Silvia, overtaken by the storm, had managed to retreat, just in time, from the Innominata ridge of Mont Blanc ....

They looked up at the Aiguille Noire, dazzling white, piercing the clouds like a sword – armour-plated, ethereal, a mountain from some other world, a huge glittering sail.

Suddenly the thought halted them in their tracks: hadn't Walter and Bianca, Kurt and Tona, Terenzio and Mario planned to – ? Could they still be up there? Oh, no – not that!

But they *were* still up there, they *must* be; two Englishmen, who had just managed to escape from the storm on the Noire, confirmed it. Gino and Silvia raised the alarm, rang through to Spiro dalla Porta in Trieste, managed, in the end, to get in touch with Walter Bonatti...

There was no hope of getting to the summit of the Noire in that storm – it would be sheer lunacy to try. The lightning would kill anyone on the ridge. But Walter Bonatti bit his lip and looked at Gallieni, standing by his side, remembering the tragedy on the Pillar Fresnay, which they had both survived: the endless days of that storm, the fearful lightning flashes, the attempt to get down to the valley – which only he, Gallieni and Mazeaud had reached alive. The other four had all died, of exposure and exhaustion, one after another ...

'Hell! It looks just the same as it did then for us!' said Gallieni.

Bonatti knew it, too, but he did not hesitate to mount an immediate rescue-operation. Meanwhile, Spiro had driven over from Trieste with a group of friends – one of them, Dumbo, just home after seven years in Africa ...

The summit of the Noire went winging, white, white from head to foot, into the dark, hurrying cloud wrack. It looked uninhabited, uninhabitable by man.

On the crest of the ridge above our heads, the storm continued to rage – a dull, regular noise, only occasionally waxing and waning. The precipices below us shone bright in the pale light of the flashes. White all over, snow and ice plastered on every crack and cranny, the protuberances disappearing under a white pall.

Another detonation; the blast of it went through us as if we were a single body, and we groaned. This might have been the North Face of the Eiger in midwinter, under a network of electricity – escape? The lightning flashes tore along the crest, down the gullies around us, everywhere, hurtling down from the summit, a deadly network. If we got up, that would be it; if we didn't, what then?

The snow kept on falling, piling up deeper and deeper. Everything around us was flattened out by it. Even ourselves. Every moment, survival was becoming more unlikely, even if we escaped being struck by lightning.

And what about the others? All we knew was that they were just beyond the subsidiary summit. We had heard their voices, so we knew they had survived the first storm. But, directly after the fearful crash generated by their movement, the second storm had come racing in. They were on their own, as we were on our own. We could only think – were they still alive? I didn't want to think, I only wanted to hope. Yet I had to think …

And what of Walter and Bianca, here with me?

This is what she said, later:

'I wanted to say something to my friends, but they were so motionless and silent, shut into themselves, each in a world of his own. Sol didn't disturb them.

'It was I who had wanted to do the climb, and I knew that something like this could happen. I had come with my eyes open, and this must have all been decreed by time and fate. And now it had happened.'

The snow weighed heavy upon our bodies, now.

'To die is as natural as to be born … why did we find that simple fact as terrible as it was absurd? Perhaps, because it is logical when you only think of it, but becomes absurd when you experience it …' Another thunderstorm came rolling in.

'No, we shall never get out of this alive.'

It had cleared for a moment. There was snow everywhere, the summit wintry-white. Beneath our feet lay the green of the valley, 7,000 feet below. Something out of the distant past: the Val Veni.

Look, way down there, an aircraft, skimming the ridges! Was it searching for someone – us?

A strong north-west wind was chasing clouds across all the peaks. It was thundering again behind Mont Blanc. The plane droned on across the ridges and was lost to sight. Walter was sobbing; he was the worst hit of our trio, having been struck glancing blows off the rock, on his shoulder and head. He was wearing a *portafortuna,* a charm, around his neck, a little gold charm; but we didn't profit by it till later on.

'Here comes the next one,' said Bianca, looking through a hole in the bivouac bag.

Rumbumbum … it came rolling in, exactly at our level, at the speed of a train. Clouds like phantom ships, black, convulsed, mocking, feeling round with dark arms that grew and then dissipated. Every atom of rock around us was alive, moving, disintegrating. The notion shot through my mind that we were water, a cone of water, rising up from the earth below – no wonder the lightning made use of it, I thought. We held hands hard. 'This is a nasty one,' said Walter. Then there was cloud around our peppered bivouac bag, and, for a time, silence.

'**********, oh!' a moan, a flame and a shock, driving through every muscle of our bodies. That was a near thing! Plumb into the ridge next to us, on the rocky head of the Bich. And now what?

Now? … nothing. We held hands.

Now? …. nothing. You …

Now? … nothing …. the rocks …

Silence, silence, silence. But the lightning must come! What lightning? The next one, of course. Locked hands; mine, Bianca's, Walter's, tight-pressed in one another's …

'*Xracks huiiiiiiii .*' We were still alive …

'*… pflob … dump … xssss,*' said the spirit-voices. Each flash was different. Electro-shocks, lifting us up, every time. Were they driving us mad? No sleep …

There was one thing I have never quite understood to this day – in the end, I was enveloped by a sense of completely relaxed confidence, which included death itself. It may sound ridiculous, but I continued to make tea, and again tea. Just in case the thunder chose to stop some time; but also in case it lasted too long for us to survive it. I thought of Tona, hoping that she was still alive; I thought of a safe return to the valley and a resumption of life, down there. I also thought how it might be our fate to stay up here and never see each other again. All the same ….

I made tea … and I made tea … it was the only thing I could do to keep a flicker of energy alive in us – even if it was to no purpose.

Gradually we began to believe we were becoming part of the snow and the rock.

Tona, once more:

'The fourth day dawned. The sky was grey; but, at last, it was quiet. Mario took the lead, as we started off, moving slowly and safely.

'We heard voices … they were here … Kurt … We looked at each other, and smiled. The six of us were together again, and we knew, then, that we should get down.'

We went on down the East Ridge. Snow fell again, in heaps. We were mere animals now, capable of standing anything. Utterly weary, utterly resigned and patient. There was no other way, in spite of the cold and our failing limbs. One thought kept us going: we had traversed the summit, the lightning had stopped, there was one more day –tomorrow – to get through, then we would be back in the land of the living again. A fourth bivouac night; then one more day to get through!

I made tea, hot tea, and again hot tea.

Wallop! A snow slide had buried Walter and Bianca in their bivouac bag. Light, cold powder snow. For the umpteenth time, the bivouac bag shook itself like a dog.

'Tea! Tea coming up!'

Faint sunshine, driving mists. For a moment we could see the towers on the South ridge, before cloud closed down again. We attempted a sort of Indian dance, to get warm; breathless, we abandoned it as soon as started.

It was a good thing there were so many of us. We were a unity, slowly feeling its way down to earth, obeying its dictates, slowly and unflinchingly. Each of us, when he had to do something – actual climbing, belaying – was on the job; between times he retired into some spiritual vacuum. I noticed it myself: every time I was not safeguarding the rope or feeling for the next handhold, I dreamed of green fields, sunshine, its warmth on my skin. Actually, it would not have been painful to slip away into a twilight sleep – without a twilight, it would be – but we none of us wanted it. We would still get down below the snow line today, down into the broad saddle, where the East ridge starts, perhaps even farther down than that. We were not scared by the thought of yet another bivouac – it couldn't compare for horror with the last three. And it would be far down the mountain; there might even be some grass. And, now, it had, at last, turned fine …

Shouts? Surely, shouts? Someone was coming up from the depths. Was it really Walter Bonatti? Yes, it was Walter – down there on the snow-clad slabs – and someone else. I roared back at him, overcome with delight.

'Siete tutti – are you all there?' he was asking from down there.

'Siamo tutti, e salvi! Yes, all of us, all well!' (Even if that wasn't absolutely true – the lightning had stabbed three of us – but, for the time being ….)

Our spirits shot up. Movement, life stirred afresh.

Suddenly, I felt indescribably weary.

Nothing excels the guides' technical skill in bringing a party down a skein of good. fixed ropes. At each piton I greeted another familiar face. Cosimo … Bertone … farther down, Gigi Panei. We gripped hands. Everyone, including those who waited down in the valley, Spiro, Aldo, Dumbo. Hands, and more hands …

We were overwhelmed with a sense of blissful security, comfort, gratitude … and sheer amazement, to have come back from that other world, down from that utterly different world.

Nobody may have noticed it, but once we were down in the meadow, we felt ourselves in the heady ambience of an angel world. I am sure there were those who thought: 'How can they smile, after what they have been through?'

That was precisely why we could.

23 Higher than the Eagle Soars: Hindu Kush

'Hindu Kush – what on earth's that?' Ten years ago most climbers would have asked the question, furrowing their brows; for that marvellous mountain range lay for many years in the shadow of the Himalaya and Karakorum. Though its summits rise to 23,000 feet and more, there are no eight-thousand-ers, so nobody noticed them.

In Britain's days of colonisation, a few surveyors had penetrated those deeply carved valleys. Troops gazed up at the peaks; British soldiers in the south-east, Russian Cossacks from the north-west. A British officer, Younghusband, even reported a clash with a Cossack squadron, which was cheerfully pushing on into Afghan territory, after the Russian annexation of the Pamirs. Finally, towards the end of last century, the narrow corridor of the Wakhan was constituted as Afghan territory, thus separating the two major powers from direct contact.

The wheel of time turned; after the Second World War, India and Pakistan emerged as independent nations and Chitral, in which stand the highest sum-mits of the Hindu Kush, is today part of Pakistan. Yet the main mass of the range lies in Afghanistan, cutting .through that country roughly from south-west to north-east; its wall of white peaks finally providing, to the south of the Oxus, which flows through the Wakhan, the frontier with Pakistan.

The Hindu Kush were already of importance in ancient times. They then bore the name of Parapomisus – meaning 'higher than the eagle soars'. Greek and Mongol armies bore down over its passes, and the caravans bringing the precious silk from China followed the course of the Oxus.

It was not till 1960 that climbers were to be seen passing through the Wakhan. Now the number of smaller or larger expeditions following the old silk route grows steadily every year, on their way to the summits of the Hindu Kush.

Others again came from the south, by way of Chitral. There were a few early incursions, real pioneering enterprises, such as the attacks by British officers on Istor-o-Nal, 1929 and 1935 (Colonel Lawder) when it was very difficult to get porters, the local people being afraid of mountain ghosts. Later on there was the daring and successful Norwegian attempt in 1950 on Tirich Mir (25,263 feet and the highest peak in the range) and the ascent of Saraghrar also more than 23,000 feet high, by Fosco Maraini and his very large expedition in 1959. After that there began a real 'tribal-displacement' of Germans, Poles,

Japanese, Austrians and, not the least among them, again British and Italians. More and more climbers were fascinated by the savage mountain world of the Hindu Kush, by the tales they heard from those who had been there, by the pictures of mighty faces and ridges, sharp summits, raging torrents, which had to be crossed, secluded valleys, upland villages whose inhabitants were simple, friendly folk. The Hindu Kush had been 'discovered' and, within the space of a very few years, there followed an invasion almost impossible to keep under review.

My father, who had out of sheer personal interest involved himself in recording the events in this area – he has since been made an honorary member of the Himalayan Club – was soon the only person who really knew which summits had been climbed and which still offered a prize, where the most interesting objectives could be found, and how to get them. The paradox being, of course, that he has never been to the Hindu Kush. None the less, the walls of his room were covered to the ceiling with photographs of this world of glorious mountains: so he 'must have been everywhere'. With the advent of spring, not a week passed without some intended expedition appearing on his doorstep, wanting to know 'everything'. They left for their appointed target armed with maps, sketch maps and all the information they needed ...

What seems to me the most important feature is that they were mostly small undertakings, adventurous even in the matter of the outward journey; three or four climbers who just got together and said: 'Let's go!' People who might, for example, buy an old postal bus in Germany, drive all the way in it, and sell it when they got there (to be seen plying on some out-of-the-way route today). People who obtained a permit to go as far as a village called Langar, and then proceeded to march the whole length of the Wakhan corridor because, at the other end of it, they knew there was another hamlet also called Langar. People who never reached their destination; people who, after travelling thousands of miles, had to watch their wrecked car being hoisted out of a ditch by camels, and towed away.

Definitely, this was the evolution of a new 'race' – the men of the Hindu Kush. Their characteristics: a strong taste for adventure, very little money, love of a gamble – the whole thing often rested on the turn of a card. If you are prepared to start out in an old car to cover 12,000 miles, there and back – half the distance round the world – and then to climb a mountain, and a high one at that – you have to be fairly happy-go-lucky and self-reliant.

We certainly were ...

I will only try to sketch a brief picture of some of our experiences; they must needs be incompletely portrayed. I have been there twice, and I shall be going there again. I shall certainly have to write a book confined entirely to the Hindu Kush. One could write so much about them, quite apart from the things that happened to me personally.

'Inshallah' – in three four time

A car, decorated with a large international 'A' for Austria, goes bumping through the Lut desert, on three cylinders: … *ta tata … ta tata… ta tata…*

It belongs to us – Franz, Tona, Herwig and me – though Franz, who did the Peuterety ridge with me is not with us; he will be coming out by air.

We others are driving to Pakistan in the firm's own delivery van (we are a kind of Tirich Mir Co. Ltd., only without Articles of Association) with 1,000 pounds of luggage aboard. The expertly stowed cases are covered by a couple of sorbo mats, on which we sleep, by turns, as the journey continues, day and night, without a break.

Who was this Herwig? He was the comfortable antithesis to the uncomfortable rhythm of our engine. Franz had introduced us to this strongly built road-construction engineer from St Polten, who had a fair knowledge of cars and machinery generally. So long as Herwig was happy, our expedition went rolling merrily along.

Ta tata … ta tata … ta tata

It was he, too, who had christened the car 'Murl'. As he said, an old car has a personality and deserves a name. 'Eh, Murl?'

I turned the fan on, and a succulent aroma of coffee came streaming in, accompanied by a furnace-like blast of heat. Coffee from real coffee beans – it isn't every car that can produce an atmosphere like that! No, our:(at present) three-cylinder model was unique. It had delivered coffee for 60,000 miles and was now in retirement.

Ta tata … ta … tata … ta tata…

Why just Murl? Well, in Austria it is a favourite pet name for those large flying beetles that make a buzzing noise, as well as for small, shaggy dogs; also, it sounds as round as a worn-out tyre, and so familiarly Austrian – like the present rhythm of our engine … *ta tata … ta tata …*

There was no element of haste about our progress – no doubt we should get there in due course. Tona drove by day, Herwig by night, and sometimes during the day as well. And I – I had as yet no assignment, for owing to so much mountaineering, I had so far neglected to pass my driving test. That was still to come, before our second trip. Meanwhile, I salved my conscience with the good intention of carrying more rucksacks than the others, when we got there.

Herwig was very good company, always calm and equable. We often sang – all through the night – it helped the driver to keep awake, a highly desirable objective. My guitar came in very handy, for our portable emitted nothing but oriental *'Jaiii, jaoooo, jaeee'* – liable to send the man at the wheel to sleep. When everything else failed, I just reminded Herwig of the dealer in Vienna who sold him Murl. That woke him up instantly.

When the morning sun climbed lemon-yellow out of the desert, Herwig knew his stint was finished, and Tona took over at the helm. Then the whole scene would gradually change colour. The pleasant early warmth swiftly increased to searing, blinding heat, which shook the ground into vibrating waves, making it impossible to touch the van's roof or to set a bare foot on the floor, even for an instant. It was July, the hottest time of the year. The country-side would change to a leaden hue, then rusty-brown, then yellow. We wondered what colour it really was.

There were plains, ridges of sandhills, mountains, and a vast emptiness …

The desert is a magnificent thing. I would never have believed it could offer so much to marvel at: the occasional oasis, an unexpected green field with a couple of trees, then suddenly in the midst of the sand water.

Rain has become an old-time fairy tale. Of course, such a thing exists, but it has grown impossible, here, to visualise what it is like, rain? A figment of the imagination, a dispensation of fantasy, remote. remote, remote … And yet, we were continually surrounded by wide mirror-like sheets of water, out of which rose bright yellow dunes, like flowers, quivering, floating, rising and falling, and then again suddenly taking on firm outlines; acquiring as we drove towards it hard reality, rising out of the solid ground which, a short time ago, was water. And then, behind us, where we had been driving, there stretched another wide, mirror-like expanse …

All sorts of other things, too. During a brief halt, I found in the sand what I took to be a feather; but it wasn't a feather, it was the seed of some plant, with a slightly tilted corkscrew-like thread under it – the wind had carried it far overland and screwed it firmly in the sandy ground.

That same wind, allied to the blown sand, acts as nature's blasting operation on the quartz surface of the sun-scorched rocks, which lie scattered around. Generally they exhibited the same larger or smaller wave formations as the wind conjures into the desert sands.

There were few creatures to be seen by day. At night, we frequently saw scorpions and spiders in the beam of our headlights, and jerboas scampered across the eternal washboard pattern of the ground – as familiar to us for many days now as the zebra stripes on hard asphalt. Only, to this one there was no end, as it rattled and shook and bumped together the packing-cases, the van and ourselves. We dared not exceed twenty-five miles an hour; our Murl would have taken umbrage.

One learned to be patient, as the savage spires of mountain ranges filed past in slow-motion, set one behind the other, like stage-scenery; brown, grey, blue, changing colour according to their distances and the time of day.

I even found time to sleep, occasionally.

Where had we got to? Oh, I remember, not very long ago we had enjoyed one of the most moving moments of the whole journey. After a thousand miles of desert tracks, sand, boulders, and a few oases, an amazing phenomenon had popped up out of the limitless wastes – a triangle mounted on a post. The nearer we drew to it, the more incredible it seemed: a traffic sign in the desert. 'Drive left,' it commanded.

'Drive to the left from now on: you are in Pakistan.' (In the Pakistan deserts one drives to the left, you see.) We danced around that lonely shield as if it were the Golden Calf, and when we were worn out with laughing, Herwig delivered a ceremonial address from the depths of his beard and his soul. 'My friends,' he said beaming, 'we shall get to the Hindu Kush, and we shall see our native land again. *Inshallah!*'

And so we drove out of the Persian desert into the desert of Pakistan. We had arrived. 'Drive left …'

Had we really arrived, though?

Ta tata … to tata … to tata …

For some time past we had been proceeding in three-four time. To start with, our Murl had been relatively modern, and normally functioned on four cylinders; but since a certain halt it had lost contact with the rhythmic haste of this day and age …

Ta tata … to tata …

This desert was a very odd, dark one. Was it the Thalab, or still the Lut; nobody knows where, in these parts, the boundaries lie? There was no longer any sign of life, except for a few stems sticking out of the black sand; they were dried-up and you could count them. Black desert, black rocks, black sand, and on the far horizon black mountains – the no-man's land between Persia and Pakistan. It was a week since the last car had passed this way.

It was then it happened. We had just had one of our halts – if we didn't stop fairly often, the oil in the engine would start to boil and lose its lubricating properties. Lords of all we surveyed, we had spread our tablecloth on 'our' road, laid our blanket in front of the wheels of the van (Bedouin are also know to take advantage of the shade thrown by their camels), and Tona was dividing a melon. We sat gazing into space, thinking of the snowy dream peaks, of the limitless time at our disposal, the vast expanse of the landscape around us, utterly content with the world.

However, when we wanted to move on, our Murl refused to budge an inch. 'We'll soon fix that,' said Herwig and went to fetch his toolkit. It was late in the day, the sun had dipped into the desert in a riot of colours, and Tona began to boil some soup. No need for alarm; this was by no means the first time Murl had declined to start.

This time, though, it seemed to be more serious. 'Damned nuisance!' growled Herwig. 'I shall have to take the engine down.' What on earth was the good of that? I merely said, 'oh yes'; but my knowledge about motors had once again been enriched. In the meantime, dusk had fallen, and a wind as hot as the breath of a baker's oven kept on coming from the north in isolated gusts …

'I mustn't let any sand get into the engine when I take it down,' said Herwig, adding: 'We'll all have to screen it.' He had suddenly become as serious as a surgeon before an operation. We were greatly impressed, and the wind in the silence of the desert had all of a sudden assumed unnatural proportions. As quickly as we could, we confined the area where Herwig was lying underneath the van with the backrest from the bench seat, blankets and other things.

Here we were, in no-man's land …

I tried to raise the morale of the party with a wisecrack. 'We have provisions for four weeks,' I said.

'Yes, and seventy litres of petrol in the jerrycan,' came Herwig's sarcastic rejoinder from underneath the engine. Tona didn't say anything; we were each of us holding a blanket round the space in which Herwig was working, as he lay on his back, his miner's lamp on his forehead, drawing a deep breath every now and then, his toolkit by his side. We carried out his orders, handing him whatever he asked for – hoping with the bleak hope of a man at death's door in the skill of a Barnard. Perhaps the situation was not quite so dire. Our water supply was sufficient, with care, for a week – possibly ten days, we reflected as we spooned up our soup. The engine still refused to work. In the middle of the night, some hours later, Herwig succeeded in eliminating one cylinder, thus allowing the other three to function. 'It's the only chance,' he said. I think we fell on his neck for joy.

Saved! We could drive on – at any rate till we met our first steep hill; and the next mountains we should meet were near Quetta. We would be coming across people before then …

Ta tata … ta tata … ta tata …

Flat wadis stretched away to the south. Somewhere over there lay a salt lake.

A dancing dot appeared on the horizon; not a car, surely? No, for there was no dust cloud. It stopped dancing and revealed itself as a house; then, as a cube adjoining some rails, here in the midst of Pakistan's boundless plain – in short, a railway station!

An ancient, weather-beaten, turbaned station master presided over it, and there were hordes of children. 'My sons!' he explained, proudly. We presented him with a bundle of marker-pennants, and the desert was soon ringing with all the sounds of the hunt.

We asked him if we could ship our van to Quetta by train. He shook his head, informing us that special papers were required for that – but, of course! – and a special type of wagon; and in any case – excuse me, did we hear you correctly? – the next train wouldn't be going for a fortnight, no …

Oh well, we thanked him and re-embarked in our Murl. We looked back and saw the children waving their pennants, and we waved back.

There seemed to be more of them than ever.

We came to the pass. Murl refused, on the very first rise. So we parked by the roadside and adopted hitch-hike techniques – one thumb in the direction we were going, the other on Murl. Traffic was relatively heavy hereabouts – there was a car almost every hour or so.

Then, an Arabian Nights fairy tale – a lorry came along! (I ask forgiveness for the historical paradox; but the history of this kind of lorry must be colourful and rich in fantasy; its voyaging circuitous and exciting for an ordinary mortal – I have no doubt that the Khalif himself would have allotted an extra night to its story, had Scheherazade only known about it.) There was every kind of decoration, in all the colours of the rainbow, on that lorry: landscapes, faces – and, of course, the firm's telephone number. The warlike, turbaned figures of its two drivers might have come straight out of some ancient tale. With the aid of a rise in the ground, we succeeded in driving Murl, by way of two planks, up into the lorry. Then we ourselves climbed up in to the roomy driving cabin and installed ourselves alongside the man at the wheel.

The place looked like a living room. There he was, bending over his hookah, and nodding to us. And when he started up, the windscreen rattled and rang and danced, with the glass beads, spangles, tiny bells and fringes that hung there, rather like the forehead finery of some elephant in a fairy story, moving at every step or, I should of course say, at every swell and fall in the road. Herwig was beaming with delight, the corners of his mouth tucked up into his beard. 'My friends,' he pontificated, slightly varying his favourite theme, 'we shall get to the Hindu Kush yet!' – and this time he omitted the *Inshallah!*

Trrrrrr … the lorry in fourth gear, and the turbaned one tearing hell-for-leather over everything, including the undulations in the ground. We might have been forgiven for losing all sense of vision and sound, but one thing we could still hear was Murl bouncing about behind us….

Two hundred miles to Quetta … *Inshallah!*

The rest of the story – how there was no hump in the ground to enable us to get our Murl down out of the lorry again, how it nearly finished up in the bed of the river, and a few other similar trifles – is recorded elsewhere.

Dertona Peak

At this point, I propose to tell the story of a single climb on that first reconnaissance trip of ours. It bears the name of an Italian city and also Tona's, according to how you read it. Dertona Peak – which we climbed together. Since the

Tortona Section of the Club Alpino Italiano had sponsored our expedition, and since the Latin name of that little city – whose enthusiastic climbers are to be found in every continent – was Dertona, the choice of the name for our mountain seemed doubly appropriate. She herself had originally opted for Hildegard Peak; but as the government would certainly have refused to sanction our daughter's name for a summit in the Hindu Kush, we dropped the idea.

It is not permissible nowadays cheerfully to label peaks in the Himalaya with people's names; though there was a time when you could. For instance, in Nepal there is a Gyaltzen Peak, so named because a Scottish Women's expedition wanted to leave a permanent memorial to the devotion and skill of their Sherpa Sirdar. In the Hindu Kush, too, there are a few peaks named after cities, such as the Picco di Teramo, Citta di Milano and others; beyond all doubt, a Munich party achieved the ultimate with Koh-i-Batzenhäusl! It depends on the government in power whether those mountains will be allowed to keep the names given them in so happy-go-lucky fashion.

Hayat üd Din, our high-altitude porter, had come with us to the foot of the lovely pyramid, rising above the end of a great glacier coombe, four hours from camp. The snow was very deep all the way to our ice-plastered peak, in the centre of the Ghul lasht Zom group, whose summits bore some resemblance to the Lyskamm. (During the whole of four weeks, we had only five really fine days.) Yet, in spite of the depth of the snow, we had the delicious feeling that every step we took was on untrodden ground.

It is always interesting, too, to discover how wrong existing sketch maps can be; the explorer of new ground derives from this source a deeply human satisfaction, difficult to describe in scientific terms (though it is well-known that science and truth approach one another ever more closely). Only very great scholars should get swollen-headed about such matters. At all events, with regard to the as-yet untrodden Ghul lasht Zom group, there were a great many discrepancies, and we enjoyed them.

Hayat trudged on ahead, carrying both our rucksacks. This blue-eyed steinbock-hunter from Shagrom had the strength of a bear, besides being a charming and sympathetic character. (He was almost as good at carrying rucksacks as I am; indeed he might have been my brother.) He was unaffected and always ready to help, too; and candid to the extent of one day bringing us Sahibs, without any trace of embarrassment, a bowl of hot water and making it clear, beyond any risk of misunderstanding, that washing was a good and healthy practice. Out there in Shagrom, in the Tirich Gol valley, below those steep and gigantic debris slopes which threaten to swallow everything up, he owned a field or two and a hut. We never saw his wife, even veiled; she must be very beautiful, for his children had something about them quite different from the others in the valley.

At the foot of the snowy face, Hayat shook hands with us, looked up at the rocky summit of our 20,000-foot peak and started on his journey back to camp. He would probably have liked to come with us, but it was out of the question. While we were roping up and getting everything ready, Tona told me how she had taken him up to a little peak, 19,000 feet high, just above the camp; the 'Viewpoint' – with a lovely view down on to the curving streams of the glacier, with the 25,000-foot crests of Tirich Mir and Istor-o-Nal opposite. Hayat had enjoyed it immensely, singing and laughing, and continually indicating that he had never been so high up before.

I was wallowing my way up, on all fours. The best description of what I was doing is to equate it with the activities of a mole. For I was boring my way up that exceptionally steep snow face, straight up it, exactly like one of those delightful little beasts. Tona said I looked like Father Christmas. Well, there was no better method here; it was quite impossible to talk about breaking a trail. At places, the snow – all of it freshly fallen – was up to our middles. So much for Gerald Gruber's wonderful Hindu Kush weather; how dared he advertise the range as a permanent fine weather paradise! I could only hope it had been snowing as hard on him, over there at the foot of Buni Zom, as it had on us for the last few days. 'Geri', as they call him in the more intimate Hindu Kush circles (he has visited the range five times, and once drove the 5,500 miles from Graz to Peshawar in six days; though – this is not unusual among Hindu Kush drivers – he maintains a discreet silence about the fate of the first expedition's vehicle) must surely have choked every time he thought of us watching the snowflakes whirling down and remembering his weather forecasts.

Tona shouted up to me: '*Guarda* – look!' and pointed up to the ridge of Ghul lasht Zom, curving white into the blue sky.

She was right – there they were, Herwig and Franz, two little dots, unbelievably small and unbelievably high up, there on the white ribbon of that ridge, close under the sky, moving almost imperceptibly towards the summit.

'Isn't it splendid?' I said to her. 'Two summit successes on the same day!' She smiled and nodded her agreement – '*si, e vero!*'

She looked charming: her small straight nose under her fur cap, her delicate mouth, now muffled in a scarf, and the joy of the climb – her climb – shining in her eyes. 'Let's go!' she said, and this girl called Tona – this strange combination of softness, energy and drive, of unselfishness and toughness – began to plunge energetically up through the snow again. She had rarely climbed a peak with me; mostly she stayed at home when I was climbing. But today we were climbing a six-thousander, together. And I could see how happy she was.

We were up at last on the ridge, a continuous chain of undulations, like the glossy belly of a snake, winding its way up to the summit. Snow, mostly, but some polished ice, too. There was a difficult spot where I had to use two ice pitons. Close to us a spur fell away into the depths to where, fully 10,000 feet below, to the south-west there was a shimmer of green fields and streams; the Arkari valley. Beyond rose a sea of five-thousanders.

Our track up the ridge looked like a pearl necklace, as we drew near to the summit; we were now close to the 19.700 foot level.

'*Aspetta un po* – wait a minute,' came Tona's request. Yes, air was thinning rapidly. She waved up to me, her mouth open, gasping for breath, signalling to me not to move on yet. I waited. That gesture of her hand – it reminded me, suddenly of the concourse at the railway station in Milan, dark and grimy. Sure – what greater contrast could there be to the white world of peaks and glaciers around us here, outshining everything.

Then I knew why. It was the same movement of her hand, that brief, shy, half doubtful, swift waving motion, twice repeated; exactly like at Milan's railway station, when we had first come to know one another and I had so often had to say goodbye, only to come back again and again ...

What a wonderful day this was, today, with the peaks cradling everything in a white mantle of resplendent snow!

There were only a couple of rope's lengths to go now, with Tona taking the lead. Through the thin mist beyond the ridge rose a mighty fluted wall, like some wonderful panelling of white linenfold. There it stood, opposite us, higher and deeper than our mountain; and now the sun was shining full on it.

One more rope; then we should have to be careful, at the white rim up there. I spotted an excellent belaying point in the sweep of the ridge, which was part snow, part rock. 'Stop at that boulder,' I told her. 'Right. Are you coming up?' Yes, at once! She had looped a belay round the rock and seen me safely up. Only a few feet more now: that wavy crest of snow just above us, that was the summit. 'Look out for cornices,' I advised, when she started off again and I watched her every moment, as I let the rope run through my hands. However, there were none, for firm rock lay beneath the snow. There she was, on top. She turned and looked down at me, smiling. Yes, there she was, on her summit. *Ciao!*

Dertona Peak, 20,000 feet: Hildegard's peak: my peak: her peak. It belonged to the Tortona Section, to our friends, the mountaineers, and of course, the mayor and all the chemists – in fact to everyone in Tortona.

We laughed and embraced. *Ciao!* Then we thought again of everyone to whom this mountain belonged. Only, today, it belonged, first and foremost, to us.

The summit consisted of two snow domes of about equal height, with steep sides. It was a perfect arrangement for photographing each other with our various pennants, which we proceeded to do extensively. The green Reifenstein one, with its edelweiss, the one my dear old climbing friend 'Schorsch' had given me, the purple of Tortona, the sunshine gold of the Munich Berglanders, and again that one from Bruno and his little town on the slopes of the Appennines; finally – for the young skiers – the Mickey Mouse of the Topolinos. Exposure after exposure.

While we were busy photographing, great gusts of wind kept on coming up from below, covering us with glittering clouds of ice darts, against the blue of the sky or the pale drifting mists. Gradually, the cold penetrated our clothing and we moved down a little to seek shelter and enjoy a summit snack. We hadn't had a bite all day – we had simply forgotten about it – and now it was only a trifle; for the wind was eddying ever more strongly, and it was getting uncomfortable. Clouds of snowdust began to envelop us, and the ridges of Ghul lasht Zom were hidden from sight. It was already five o'clock, and time to be going down.

After an absolutely endless descent, we rejoined Hayat ud Din at about midnight. 'Tona Sahb! Kurt Sahb!' he cried, joyfully and obviously much relieved after his long wait. 'Tona Zom?' he enquired, shaking us by the hand. Yes, we had been to the summit. He dragged us into the tent; the thermos of tea he handed us tasted marvellous. 'What a treasure you are, Hayat ud Din!' we told him. He smiled. We wondered if he had understood? Of course, he had; he understood almost everything. Then he laid his head against his hands at an angle, looking at us enquiringly. Yes we nodded, back, definitely – sleep! We were dead dog tired.

We seemed to be sinking into a great void through drifting mist and white, shimmering snow.

When Herwig and Franz came back from Ghul lasht Zom, after a bivouac at 19,700 feet, we indulged in a tremendous victory celebration. The level of Franz's cognac bottle sank considerably, till we remembered that there were still other peaks to climb. Franz had not been with us very long. A few days earlier he had come, with the precious bottle in his rucksack, up the vast expanse of the Upper Tirich Glacier, like a voice crying in the wilderness, as he tried to locate us. He had followed us out to Pakistan by air and his further directions for the rendezvous were simple: Upper Tirich Glacier. So he had had to do a good deal of shouting and was pretty hoarse by the time we eventually met; but – a point greatly in his favour – that bottle had remained untouched. A man of character, we agreed.

'Chin! Chin! Four against Tirich Mir!' we toasted Franz, and as he described his long journey on foot and we told him of our adventures in the desert, the hoarseness gradually left his voice.

Yes, there was plenty for the four of us to do: the various white summits of the Ghul lasht Zom group, reconnaissances into remote, untrodden corners of the broad Tirich Glacier, our seven-day long attack on the huge spur of Tirich Nord, nearly 7,000 feet high – days packed with adventure, during which we were not always together but still formed a united party. We all loved Hayat ud Din and hated parting with him; likewise Aja Chan, that friendly old man who suddenly turned up at base camp with a basket full of apples, to pay a call on Hayat (Shagrom, his village, was three days away down there). The apples were a present for us.

Our time ran out all too quickly, and now we are at home again, going to our jobs every day. When, each morning, I put on my shiny town shoes, I think of Aja Chan climbing around in my fur boots, which I gave him as a farewell present; going out, maybe, into the bitter winter cold of the Tirich Gol to have a chat with Hayat, before he goes off to shoot a steinbock. While I go to catch my bus.

At the University of Milan they are busy estimating the age of one of our blocks of granite and preparing thin polished specimens. Oh yes, and in a backyard in St Pollen there stands a lonely coffee delivery van, rusting and philosophizing about old age. Nobody ever disturbs its rest, and there seems no great danger that anybody will do so in the near future – for it remains unsold.

There were a few things before that which I should like to touch on briefly before closing this chapter – the memory of our eventful journey home, and of a Viennese butterfly collector to whom we owe it that we and our Murl ever got home at all, in spite of a war, a typhus-quarantine and a broken-down engine.

As to Herwig, I believe that if we had only had one good cylinder left, he would have laughed as unconcernedly as ever into his beard, taken everything to pieces again, and made such a good job of the single one that the others, or at least half of them, would have thought better of it. Still, it was a very good thing that we ran into that Viennese collector of butterflies – Azad Vartian.

A great surprise awaited us when we emerged from the high valley; there was a war on – between Pakistan and India. We kept on seeing heavily bearded and often very elderly volunteers leaving their valleys and heading for Peshawar, carrying drawn swords and age-old flintlocks. They gestured fiercely as they listened to the news about the fighting bombs on Peshawar, tank-battles in the frontier areas. Next thing, we ourselves came within an ace of a bombardment, in Peshawar's bazaar. I don't know now what the outcome would have been, had not a policeman with a drawn pistol appeared at the critical moment and rescued me – for the crowd took me for, well, anything but an Austrian. There was nothing for it but to clear out. We spent the night sitting up with Hugo Kruschandl, the manager of Dean's Hotel, all of sixteen stone and a prince among men.

It was an unforgettable night: aircraft overhead, in front of us a whisky bottle to make do for the non-existent air-raid shelter, and Hugo telling us the story of his life ... next day we were in Afghanistan. With the Khyber Pass behind us, we washed off the obligatory coat of camouflage (two buckets of water mixed with dirt and emptied over Murl). Murl, by the way was running in 4/4 time; but not for long. One night he went into a steep decline on to two cylinders – miles from the nearest habitation. And then the clutch started to misbehave. We trembled at every rise in the ground, ready to jump out and push. Finally, after a spectacular effort on the part of the whole crew, Murl stuck in a hollow; the opposing slope was too steep for us. It looked like the end. As we stood wiping away the sweat and panting, Herbert spoke. 'My friends,' he said, 'we shall see our homes again – *Inshallah!*' It did not sound very convincing.

Murl was on his way again.

We were a splendid 'rope'. Our rescuers were Azad, a dealer in carpets, and his wife, an artist; but their real passion was for Afghani-stan's gaily coloured butterflies – they even bred them in their car. Azad knew the valleys of the Hindu Kush well, and was worth listening to on the subject. We were a happy party, bumbling across the plain at 15 to 20 m.p.h., united by a rope between their vehicle and ours. How suddenly one's view of life can be completely changed!

I quote from my diary: 'No trouble with Murl. The bumper is standing up to it and the rope is in good condition. Our greatest problem, whenever we got to an oasis is: where do the caterpillars find leaves to live on?'

Two years later I was back again. It was a unique expedition, during which I climbed more high peaks than in any previous enterprise. Renato Cepparo, writing in Scarpone called it the world's smallest expedition'. It consisted entirely of me, the leader and solitary member of the 1967 Austrian Hindu Kush Expedition'.

The preparations were simple and successful. Once again I designed an impressive headed notepaper to full efficiency, and this time I was helped by considerable experience. There was another recognised Hindu Kush enterprise that summer, precisely the same as my own; it was the '1967 German Hindu Kush Expedition', for it came from Germany and consisted solely of its leader, Dietmar Proske. We did most of our climbs in each other's company, but – hardly knowing each other as yet – remained basically independent. Many of the larger expeditions cast somewhat sceptical glances on us two Chitral hikers – for we were, like most of the visitors to the Hindu Kush during the last few years, mere tourists. During that summer, the tourists' bagged four six- and three seven-thousanders, including the highest peak in the Hindu Kush. They also garnered the first complete circuit of Tirich Mir, a great many moments of doubt and uncertainty, untold hours of delight and, in sum, a tremendous experience.

The North Face of Tirich West IV

There are many who say I have a weakness for north faces: how right they are!

When, on the afternoon of 2 July 'Didi' Proske and I stood on the summit of Ghul lasht Zom's southern summit, it was not only his first six-thousander, but also a fantastic 'presentation plate' for us to stand on and survey hundreds of peaks all around us. The finest prospect was to the south-east, where, directly opposite, the summits of Tirich Mir shot skywards.

There was a banner of cloud hanging on the very top of the main summit. Below it lay a whole gallery of precipices anything from seven to ten thousand feet high. There were rugged buttresses, slabs, hanging glaciers, all the way up to 24,000 and even to the summit's 25,263 feet. What a challenge!

We turned our attention to the north face of the farthest of the western summits. It is a little lower than the other three in Tirich Mir's western group, but it is the most impressive and carries its own quote of 24,073 feet. It forms the cornerstone of that gigantic wall, perhaps best comparable with the Grandes Jorasses, for in each case there is an immense granite face, interrupted by buttresses, on whose crest rises a row of separate summits relatively close to one another. Here the height of the summits increases in a south-easterly direction, towards Tirich Mir itself. West III, a corniced white crown of snow, can only be a few feet higher than our No. IV from which it is separated by the deepest saddle in the whole comb. West II, a sharply ridged summit eventually leads to the highest point in the crest, which also bears a quotation of 24,427 feet. It can best be reached from Tirich Mir's north-west col, which it overtops by a mere 800 feet.

If the big Czech expedition besieging Tirich Mir took the route over that saddle, it would surely not miss the chance of so adjacent a first ascent. We looked down; far below, fine-drawn as a hair, ran the trail the porters had beaten between the Czech camps, all the way up the glacier, till it made a wide curve around the rocky base of West IV and disappeared behind it in the direction of Tirich Mir.

Every day, they must have seen the ramp stabbing up into the lower half of the face, giving access to it; but they must also have seen what lay above it. So we felt sure our fortress over there was safely ours, and we need not worry. Safely? We might find we couldn't get up it, when the time came ...

I watched the snow banner on Tirich Mir's summit and wondered how long it would take the Czechs to get up there.

After a reconnaissance into the Anogol and the ascent of another six-thousander, we both felt in sufficiently good form to warrant an approach to our unknown wall and try to establish from close quarters the details which still remained unsolved in spite of binoculars; for many pitches looked different according to the point from which we were observing them and the time of day. Things that seemed possible one day looked quite impossible the following morning. Meanwhile, we had acclimatised splendidly, thanks to the continual humping of heavy loads.

I am leaving it to Didi to give his own account of his first ascent of a seven-thousander:

We had originally intended to climb the mountain with a larger party; but when the team did not show up in our area as planned, we had to readjust things for the two of us. To be honest, this huge 24,000-foot lump of granite, so difficult to survey from a distance, did not look exactly a sitting target for a two-man team.

The first thing we did was to establish a new assault camp, at 19,350 feet on the southern arm of the Upper Tirich Glacier, specially sited at the foot of our Tirich West IV. With the assistance of Musheraf Din, our only porter, we lugged more than 200 pound of equipment and provisions from our lower base camp to the new site, more than 3,000 feet higher up, in a forced march lasting eight hours. Musheraf then went down to Shagrom in the valley, with instructions to come back and meet us in fifteen days' time.

We started our climb on 31 July. Kurt and I each humped a forty-five pound rucksack over disgusting pinnacle ice to the start of a broad ice couloir. Our objective was the great ice balcony, a long, narrow plateau in the midst of the steep face at about 20,700 feet. And this 1,300 foot couloir was the easiest way to it. After five hours under the drudgery of a forty-five pound burden we reached the top of the couloir. There we dumped our loads and went down again. Next day we went through whole procedure again, with one difference: this time we stayed up there.

We managed to pitch our two-man tent at the beginning of the balcony, in the lee of a protecting tower of rock. A special luxury at this camp I was the "ice lake", two yards long and mostly frozen over, which almost always spared us the tedious chore of melting snow. Unfortunately, this amenity involved a descent of 150 feet; we tossed up each time to decide who was to go down and whether this was to be late in the evening or in the bitter early morning cold.

As soon as we had the tent in position, we went on along the sloping. balcony; presently it levelled out and broke away vertically to the Lower Tirich Glacier, far below. Opposite us, the northern face of Tirich Mir towered in all its immensity. We, from our fantastic vantage point, were the first to see this aspect of that mighty wall.

The route ahead of us looked savage to a degree. The whole dauntingly steep north face of our own mountain was cut across by numerous superimposed veins of granite, from vertical to over-hanging, many of them 100-feet high, separated by ice patches or roof-like, outward-sloping black slates. The whole constituted a geological contact, full of surprises and problems for us who wanted to climb it. We scanned it for a long time through binoculars, searching for ribs or gullies by which to penetrate those granite veins.

One thing was greatly in our favour: this year the weather in the Hindu Kush had been uninterruptedly fine, and we felt we could reckon on continued luck with it for the days to come. (Kurt thought that, in the conditions he met in 1965, we should never have got even as far as this.) The risks attending a possible forced retreat were sizeably reduced, in the circumstances.

'Starting from camp I next day we both carried thirty-five pound loads along the plateau and, beyond it, up a steep snow-slope in the face. Our intention was to lay down a depot of material on the face above at a distance of six hours from our first high camp.

'Everything was fearfully steep, hereabouts. On the very first traverse of the dark walls of slate we made very slow progress; one hold after another went clattering down into the abyss as soon as we put any weight on it, and it was almost impossible to use a piton. Overhead lay more than 3,000 feet of unexplored face …

'We managed it in due course, and were able to work our cautious way upwards rope's length by rope's length. Our morale rose appreciably. The granite veins we had to cross did not present any exceptional difficulties in spite of great altitude, the loads which weighted us down and our great thick boots; though there were one or two Grade IV pitches. It was afternoon when we laid down our depot at about 21,800 feet. Up till then we had not found a single level spot in the whole face large enough to house even a bivouac tent; and now there was barely room to stow our equipment. Our descent to camp I was considerably easier, for we had marked the sector with pennants. The following day was spent in carrying more rope and provisions up to the depot. Our preparations were complete: we were ready to move up to the next storey of our granite castle. On 4 August, lightly laden, we climbed up to the depot. Once there, we had to lift a mass of material into and on to our rucksacks. Further progress was slow. Our intention was to go straight for the summit without a break.

'Just above our heads, everything was cut off by a vertical yellow barrier; we should have to traverse.

'It was a traverse full of dodgy passages: a sharp ridge, to be turned first to the right, then to the left, deep ice gullies and bands of granite barring the way. On this face, the question is always whether, and more especially, where one will find a way up, so little of it can one see ahead at any given time. That traverse from right to left of the precipice, with its ups and its downs, must have been fully a quarter of a mile long. Finally, with the aid of pitons, we mastered a very strenuous Grade IV pitch and reached the lower rim of a hanging glacier. One particular moment of that traverse lives vividly in my memory; as

I was strapping on my crampons, the huge block on which I was standing suddenly began to move – I just had time to get off before it went down the face.

'The sun was low in the sky as we now came to the upper part of the face, which consisted mainly of ice slopes and granite buttresses. We had hoped it would be easier to find a place for our little bivouac tent here, but our optimism was premature. Darkness fell, and we had to settle for a crevasse in the hanging-glacier. In it – remaining roped, of course – we were able to put our tent up, if somewhat uncomfortably, on a snow bridge. The work of hacking-out and levelling took all of two hours; during that time, in spite of circulation tablets, we said goodbye to our fingers and feet, and it took a long time and much effort before we got them back again.

'The cold – down to minus 30 degrees C. – was in fact the greatest problem we had to deal with during the whole undertaking. We had the very best equipment available (boots, clothes, food, medical aids), but somebody will have to invent even better ones!

'We had very little room in the tent, but the night was still a thousand times better than one spent in a bivouac bag. Everything we didn't actually need we hung from ice pitons all around outside the tent, to prevent it going down the mountainside, for the surroundings were everywhere smooth and sheer. Fortunately, the darkness prevented our seeing how far things fell away below us – for we were at the very rim of the hanging-glacier.

'In the morning when we made tea and the sun eventually reached us in our perlon home, we were subjected to the inevitable drip-bath, for the condensed ice on the lining melted or peeled off on us. To add to the joys of this "camp", a strong wind blew up; bringing, through the thin wall of the tent, a most unacceptable chill just where it is most uncomfortable to the man lying on the outer side. All through the next day, our dearest wish was to find a place for a comfortable camp.

'So on 5 August we struck our bivouac tent and went up the ice field in a strong wind, feeling very hopeful, though the gale continually whipped ice-needles in our faces. After two hours there was not much left of this hope. Our thoughts were just going back to that camp II of ours, with its "comforts", when, at about 23,000 feet we found a splendid camp-site in a big, roomy crevasse, complete with a roof of ice over it and full protection from the wind. Even in that "ice-palace" with its fine panoramic view of the world below, we never unroped ; for here there were just two alternatives – stay on, or come off ...

'On the 6th we set out for the summit. The weather was lovely, though we suffered a great deal from the intense cold and the wind – not unexpectedly above 23,000 feet on the north side of our mountain. After every rope's length in steep, cold powder-snow we had to swing our feet vigorously to restore a vestige of feeling in them.

'We traversed upwards to the left for a long distance, below a wall of polished granite, till we came to a steep slope of hard ice which seemed to end in the blue sky itself'.

'The drop below us was prodigious – we looked down sheer on to avalanche cones 7,000 feet below on the floor of the Lower Tirich Glacier. Our hearts were beating high in our throats. Every stride was taken with the utmost caution, with that breath-taking abyss beneath our feet.

'In the middle of all this verticality, a little island of rock invited us to rest and brew some tea. We were dying for a drop of something hot.

'After that tea-halt everything seemed to go twice as easily. We even began to take an interest in photography and I suddenly felt much as I would have done on a fine day climbing the north-west face of the Wiessbachhorn at home. Nor was our delight unjustified; for, as things turned out, the exit from this narrow ice slope was actually the key to the summit, and we had found it first time. Whereas from down below, even with strong binoculars, we had never been able to establish whether, or where, there was a way through these vertical walls of granite and the rock towers below the summit. Though we had tried from various viewpoints, it had all remained, till now, a matter of conjecture.

'And now, suddenly, we were standing on a little shoulder, from which – to our relief and suppressed delight – we could see, close in front of us, the top part of the West Face and, just above it, the spiny crest of the summit!

'A couple more ropes lengths up the slope, in sunshine, zig-zagging between enormous boulders lifting from the snow – we were breathless with altitude, excitement and impatience – then a last tower, a huge monolith, barring the ridge like some sentinel, frowning down upon us … and at about 3 p.m. we were on the summit.

I was overjoyed, for it was my first seven-thousander.'

That is how Didi saw it. I will take up the thread again. Darkness was falling by the time our long descent brought us down to our comfortable camp in the crevasse. On the following day we got down to camp I, at the 'ice lake. Our two-man tent looked as large and spacious as a room. That very evening it began to snow; the phenomenon was so unusual that we could hardly believe it. We realised that our summit would now be unclimbable for days to come, and rejoiced all the more at having done it just in time; also that we were safely back down here …

On 9 August, ten days after our first ascent to the 'balcony', we climbed down to base camp with a mass of stuff on our backs. Our descent was rather like a ballet performed by two elephants.

24   An Apple on Tirich Mir

Little Masaaki was laughing and his dark eyes, set in a round sunburnt face, were dancing with joy. 'Very lucky,' he said; 'very happy,' and laughed again.

We were 'very happy': we hugged each other and patted each other's backs. Then we got out the pennants, which we had made of paper and bright red sticking-plaster stuck together: one red, white and red, the other displaying on its white background a big round blob of red plaster – the sun of Japan. I had to bend down a little to lay my arm round Masaaki's shoulders for the summit photograph Didi was trying to take – Pat and Patachon on the summit of 'Pyramid Peak', maybe? We had swopped the symbols of East and West in our hands. 'Cheers!' 'Yes, very happy.' And Didi pressed the shutter.

Masaaki Kondo was the Jonah of the Japanese Tirich Mir Expedition, but at that moment nobody would have known it. He was delighted to be standing on a summit, even if it was only the modest P 6778 (22,238 feet), already climbed by the Czechs. Besides which we were a happy party and the whole thing was only a day's outing from our highest camp to date (21,300 feet), our advanced assault camp for Tirich Mir.

During the descent, with the rocks and the clouds already turned to gold, Masaaki kept on looking up at Tirich Mir's summit (25,263 feet). His friends, who had started out some days before, must be somewhere up there. They had left him behind because, right at the start of proceedings, he had fallen sixty feet into a crevasse down on the Tirich Glacier, cracking a rib, and suffering other injuries. So they had thought it better to attempt that high summit without him. His rib was still hurting him, but having to be left behind hurt much more.

The Czechs had gone down in the meantime. They had climbed Tirich Mir by the North-West Col and Ridge, and also taken the first of the West summits from the col. From that saddle, they reported to the Japanese, they had taken twelve hours up and down for Tirich Mir, and ten for the other peak. They had left a tent up there on the col at 23,800 feet. They explained that it was terribly cold and stormy up there, which we had no difficulty in believing. Even on fine days, clouds might roll up in the mountain in the middle of the day, completely enveloping it – one could not doubt for a moment that then things were pretty unpleasant, and a sojourn in those regions, up there, not exactly an attractive proposition. When the peak emerged in the evening, it was often freshly powdered white. According to the Czechs, the ridge climb from the col to the top offered no great technical difficulties, but there was a vital key point on the ascent from the forward assault camp to the col at about 23,000 feet: a 250-foot chimney, Grade IV, with a possible Grade V pitch in it. We kept on looking up through the glasses: the chimney looked exactly like that.

For the moment I meant to wait for the return of the Japanese summit party. So there was our modest little tent, planted next to the comfortable spread of sunshine-golden perlon and bamboo of the Japanese camp. In it we could sit in comfort with the amiable, elderly Takahashi, the lively Nishina, and Masaaki, cheerful in spite of his setbacks – five of us on mats around the humming tea kettle, talking about Japan and Europe, about mountains and a thousand other things. We acquired a taste for Japanese seaweed, pudding, coffee and whisky; and I sponsored an almost perfect Trieste fish soup, made according to a secret recipe of my own, which I should not care to publish. They also got to like smoked ham and noodles; but not even oriental politeness could bridge the gap to my camp special rice pudding.

The summit party should have returned by now, but there was no sign of them, except a slender trail on a snow slope to the right of the col. They had left the walkie-talkie sets down here in order to minimise weight, and Nishina was beginning to get worried. In the circumstances I decided that we ought to make our own summit push at once; we could take the radio along and one or other of us could report back, if anything was wrong.

Unfortunately, Didi's insides had failed to stomach the mixture of western and oriental diets. It might be days before he was all right again and nobody knew better than he that you have to be fighting-fit to climb a difficult peak, falling short by only 1,000 feet of being an eight-thousander. At first we could not think what to do; then, suddenly, we thought of Masaaki. He might like to? ... *Would* he just! Of course, he wouldn't be able to carry a heavy pack – he pointed to his chest, shook his head and made a slight face, but smiled, as he almost always did. But I had seen how well he could go, he was fully acclimatised and, above all, he was such a good sort. On the previous day, he had come up with me to about 22,600 feet in the direction of the big chimney. We had left some food and a special thermos of tea hanging on a piton for the descending party. I had also imparted some Austrian ice-technique to Masaaki, the only difficulty being that his English was limited to about twenty words; however, he cheerfully said 'yes' to everything, and then did the exact opposite. He also greeted my occasional Austrian swearwords with a smile and an amiable 'yes' – so we got on splendidly.

Our sudden decision involved the necessary preparations, so it was not till about noon that we were ready to take leave of our friends. It was, of course, late to be starting out for one of the high seven-thousanders, but we pinned our hopes on reaching a little projection below the chimney, which might take our bivouac tent. We stuffed our pockets full of small, green Shagrom apples, which Didi and Musheraf Din handed us out of the tent, as they wished us good luck. Then we were off.

We reached the projection – it was at about 23,000 feet – towards evening. On either side of it steep couloirs shot down through the vertical buttresses of granite. I climbed another ropes length up the steep one on the left-hand side, hoping to find a better site for our tent at its edge; but every apparent step turned out on close inspection to be smooth and sheer. So I fixed one rope and quickly returned down it to the projection. Not any too soon, for it was too small for our tent, and there was work to be done. The Japanese had sat the night out here – and I had no taste for that.

We went at the brittle rock with our ice hammers, building two bays out into space at the sides, where it was too narrow; of course we were belayed as we worked. Our worst headache was getting the tent up – we had to fix some of the pitons directly underneath it, others out to right and left. Finally we got the two poles, which turn the perlon-tube into a tent, fixed, and pushed in two three-foot lengths of sorbo for a floor. Then followed the trapeze act of getting inside. At last we lay head to foot, gasping for breath, in our contraption and got some rest. The projection, plus our engineering work, was just large enough for the two of us, but we didn't dare to move much. In any case, it was nice to be lying still.

I had put one of my boots, with the cooker laced up inside, between my head and the rock face. It worked, and a couple of lumps of ice melted slowly for a fine cup of Tokyo coffee. Through a little spy-hole we looked down on Pyramid Peak, pale in the moonlight.

We got up rather late. It took quite a time to undo everything and get it packed. Just as we were at last ready to start up the couloir, so as to get to grips with the chimney, which started immediately above – a dark, forbidding rift – a lump of rock came clattering down, making us jump for cover. Then we heard a voice, someone shouting, high up above. We answered. It was the Japanese, coming down.

An hour or two later we were all sitting together on boulders and ledges at the bivouac place. They were tired and depressed, having failed to reach the summit, though by only a short distance, defeated by the cold and the wind. Fortunately all four were well and had escaped frostbite. During the tea session I fixed two of the long Japanese ropes, to facilitate their descent; that would enable them to get down almost to our depot, after which there were no serious difficulties on the rest of the way down.

Later, when Masaaki and I were stuck in the big chimney, the sun was already pretty low in the sky. The fixed ropes helped a little but, unfortunately, they were very elastic and I had a forty pound rucksack on me. It was a horrid struggle. I swore and banged in another piton, while the ropes – stretched by the recent roping-down manoeuvres of the descending party – were now quite useless for my purposes. Darkness fell slowly.

I had found a stance in a niche, and the ropes were serviceable again, thank goodness, for I needed them. There was a short crack, its lower part overhanging, just above me. Two pitons were here; this must be the Grade V pitch. I wished I knew what the English for *Zug!* was, so as to get a lift on the rope; but then Masaaki probably didn't know either. I latched on and tried it on my own. I had almost got there, when I realised I couldn't quite do it; I gasped and fought to gain an inch. That blasted rucksack! Nothing for it but to retreat. I tried to bang in a piton, on which to hang my pack; it went ringing away. In the poor light I managed to find a crack, and the next piton held. As I was getting free of my rucksack, I heard a sudden clatter below me …

'Look out! Stone!' I roared down.

It went banging from one wall of the chimney to the other.

'Masaaki!'

'Yes.'

Everything was all right, then.

Without the rucksack it was quite a different matter; but it was dark by the time I got up. We were now above 23,000 feet. We could only go on by the light of Masaaki's 'searchlight'. That was in his pack.

This necessitated a lengthy manoeuvre. First, Masaaki had to come all the way up to the niche; then I had to get my rucksack up over the bulge below me, only a few feet, but a fearful effort; then Masaaki's rucksack and finally Masaaki himself, up from the niche, to join me. He seemed perfectly calm and collected, in spite of the darkness and our exposed position, which was very encouraging. We disentangled the ropes by the friendly light of the lamp; I kept my own, much the weakest, in reserve. Then the light went probing up the slabby face to our left and its cone revealed, right above us, a projecting flake of rock in a kind of groove; and there was the fixed rope, coming down it. This was another Grade IV problem and a pretty tough exercise, with one's feet against the slabs and the rucksack 'backing-up'. But now there was a shimmer of white, and things began to ease off. I have no idea how long it took before we got on to the snow slope .

The moon was up now, and though we were in the shadow of the rocks above us to the right, we could see well enough, our fingertips assessing the slope of the snow; we had put the lamp away.

We belayed from stance to stance. It was crushingly cold, and the one who was waiting shivered and counted the moments till the next reviving 130 feet of movement. We could have put on more clothing, but neither of us had the drive to unpack a rucksack. All we wanted to do was to get up another couple of rope's lengths. Up to our left there was a rock comb leaning against the night sky. The col must be just above us. Everything became clearer; we were out in the moonlight now, and we felt much better.

Who can judge distances in these places? First of all we said: just two more rope's lengths – but it was always more. Then, suddenly, I realised it was only one more. In the silence of the moonlight, the wind above us was hissing over the snow crest, powdering us with cold dust. We stamped hard into the wind-pressed snow, our crampon points grated on hard ice, and out of the pother of snowdust there loomed a dark mass, a flapping structure of stuff, planted on this loneliest spot on earth: the tent the Czechs had left behind.

We were very glad that it was still standing and we should not have to use our own. The wind was howling across the little saddle, protected by a short three-foot high ice barrier, slanting in sideways and giving scanty shelter. The tent was in a bad way – one stay gone and the entrance torn open; it fluttered like some black ghost. I managed to insert a stay … and we couldn't get inside soon enough.

We tied the entrance up somehow, and there we sat in a welter of cast-off tins, bags, equipment, powdered here and there by snow, which had forced its way in through a couple of holes in the tent wall. It was midnight, at 23,800 feet; but, at least, we were under cover.

We were separated from the gale outside by a single layer of cloth, on which the wind pressed, ballooning it far inwards because of the lack of tension, filling the air with a murderous rattling, shaking our heads mercilessly as we sat there; but it was a biggish tent and we were able to move away from the billowing wall. We cooked a bit, having discovered a bag of Czech biscuits, tidied things up and settled down. Wearing a fleece jacket you can feel comfortable even in an ice shanty – one which has been erected by the hand of man, at that.

I had long ago realised that, having Masaaki Kondo with me, I was not at all alone. 'Masaaki!' I said, 'Tomorrow: nothing! After tomorrow … summit!' He laughed. 'Now sleep,' he said. And that is just what we did.

It was dark and 19 August had already begun, the day when we were to attempt the summit. The cooker was humming. We had found two extra thermos-flasks; we were going to fill the lot with pudding, tea, Ovo, then we could really get going with the sun's first ray. We started up a second cooker, so as to have a meal now. The hours went by and the big yellow tent-sack-full of snow slowly emptied.

We had taken a long rest yesterday and then reconnoitred the route. First over to the left, eastwards, across the hanging-glacier on the north side; but that way up to the saddle between the east and main summits, with which I had, for special reasons, flirted with from down below, looked very long and would mean hours of hard work on tough, blue ice. There was some of this terribly tough stuff just above the tent, barring access to the North-West Ridge; but we had found a way to turn it by circling to the east, and the ridge itself, from what we had seen yesterday, was good. We still could not make out how the Czechs had gone on up above. Perhaps we should find a solution satisfactory to ourselves. Perhaps the West Face? The upper part had looked very good, but we were separated from it by a deep gully; maybe we could get on to it higher up. Actually, the route I had reconnoitred in 1965, when Tona, Herwig and I caught our first discoverers' glimpse into this corner, ran over the lower part of the West Face and then up the South ridge. (Someday someone will do it, as well as the traverse of all four of the West Peaks, a huge climb. We at least proved that it is possible.)

Today all those high crests would sink far below us.

The icy gale kept on, though slightly less intense. Everything in the tent was frozen, and little heaps of powdery, fine snow had collected under the holes in the rim of the tent. Every now and then the entrance blew open. Outside, the tension was now better, in spite of the missing pole. Yesterday, we had fixed dark lenses and face-scarves to our ski-goggles – which we had in addition to ordinary glacier glasses. Under our helmets, the masks were more reminiscent of space travel … but the icy bombardment was grim …

We could make do with a couple of hours of sleep, later – cooking was, at the moment, much more important. In any case one doesn't sleep properly. Every nerve and sinew was concentrated on the coming day, as if it were the only day ever. Indeed, for the time being, it *was* the only day.

The question was would Masaaki's crampons stay on. Yesterday, on the reconnaissance, they had come off several times: a problem of his outer-boots. Could we dispense with them? No, neither of us. Meanwhile we had adjusted the crampons. I had sustained slightly frozen toes on Tirich West IV; I didn't want them to get properly frostbitten this time. So I had found a solution: I wrapped a sheet of sorbo round the whole boot, pulled the stuff-bag over it and then, using a little force, strapped the crampons on over the lot.

One thing we must not, repeat not, forget: to take one of the two cookers along. Otherwise, we were ready. We had drunk to satiety, and the three thermoses – one of them for the climb – were full. Now for a short nap …

The day was blue and clear. We had reached the ridge by the way we had pinpointed yesterday; at present it was easy, a snow crest of no great steepness, decorated with great boulders, around which the wind had shaped deep, semi-circular hollows. Days ago, from the base, we could see the track of the Japanese summit party, just here, high above. It all seemed a long time ago …

Masaaki and I went on up the ridge, towards the summit; slowly, very slowly, much more slowly than we were capable of going, but keeping the rhythm of our breathing absolutely even. My thoughts went back to Dhaulagiri: seven years ago Nawang Dorje and I had approached the summit in exactly the same way. I had told him: 'We go slow, very slow, now!' And so we had gone on up ... one step – and breathing ... another step – and breathing ... a shorter step, because it was steeper now – and breathing ... then a zig-zag – and breathing ... never stopping altogether – and breathing. In an hour Nawang Dorje and I had got to 26,000 feet, all by ourselves, and not excessively exhausted; and there we sat down and waited for the others. They weren't any less good than we – we simply used a different method. Where does the limit lie for a man? It is all a question of 'how' – that is to say, of technique – of self-reliance and, of course, a combination of both. It is a basis which anyone can find, but not till then will he reach the limits of his capabilities, or the ability to approach them – and then only if fortune gives him his chance.

So now, on Tirich Mir, we went slowly upwards – in the end, when it got steep, in a ludicrous pattern of zig-zags. By taking this long way, we mastered the human body's fallibility, never stopping, with the least possible exertion. Masaaki and I, going on up. Today we would be standing on the summit – if we did everything the right way ... and I would see to it, every moment of the way, that we did. For fortune had given us our chance.

The wind had almost dropped, except when a sudden gust howled through the crags of the Czech ridge. We had reached the arete, which consists of rough, somewhat unstable blocks, from the north, by way of the face, on to which we had made a traverse. Our rhythmic progress was now at an end, and we belayed one another from one stance to another. We were already on a level with the first of the West Peaks, something like 24,600 feet, having started out at eight o'clock, and it was now ten. There were still 700 feet, more difficult now, to the summit. A porridge carton and a red silk pennant marked the place where the Japanese had turned back after their bivouac in the icy gale. Far down in the valleys we could see a few little tatters of cloud. It was a grand day.

The peaks shone clear around us and beneath us, almost all below our own level now. In the depths the curving glaciers snaked their way down, repeated again and again by the yellowy-white and black lines of their moraines. Directly below us, the granite buttresses of the north group shot up, crowned by the white crest of Tirich Nord, but even that was far, far below us. Far over in the thin mists of morning ranged Afghanistan's myriad peaks, Koh-i-Bandakor dominating them all. There lay the Arkari valley, with Ghul lasht Zom, Noshaq and Istor-o-Nal soaring above. We had to press on, but which way?

The ridge of unstable boulders did not look attractive. I looked across to 'my' west face; once we were across the couloir just ahead of us and up the wall beyond it, the going would be perfect. There we could resume simultaneous movement, step by step, till we hit the South Ridge, and then on up its soft back, rather like an enormous roof of snow, to the summit. That's what we would do!

Crossing the brittle couloir proved tricky. It was a V-shaped, deeply scored gully, very steep, its bed only a few feet wide and filled at the bottom with snow. For safety's sake I fixed a piton, but the whole thing was not more than Grade III. The rock cliff was no more difficult; once up it we allowed ourselves a short rest at the rim of the West Face. The way up to the South Ridge lay clear …

We reached it at about midday, after a long ascent over fine scree, little patches of snow, and boulders, straight through the upper sector of the west face. Our attention was attracted by a few lightish-coloured stones; dark tourmaline had overlaid them with a network of shining suns. My mind was by now completely at rest: we would get to the top. So we sat down for half an hour on a big flat stone at the edge of the South Ridge's broad white crest, ate a small meal and emptied the thermos. Wherever we looked now, our eyes travelled out over an endless sea of cloud. It was rising very slowly, but it was still far, far below us. And there, sitting next to me, was none other than the Jonah of the Japanese party – Masaaki – smiling.

Every now and then a hint of green showed through some hole in the cloud carpet – a hamlet, 16,000 feet below. We had kept two apples for the summit, all these days – little green things which Musheraf Din, so eagerly awaited, had brought up to base camp the last time he went down to Shagrom. I decided I would leave mine up there on the summit.

Why do I have such luck on mountains? I do not know; all I know is that, at that moment, I was very grateful.

Yet, there's a question mark over all such matters …

We went on again. Though the summit was probably no more than a hundred 150 feet higher, the ridge had become almost level, so it would take time to get there. That didn't bother us – this strolling, high above the clouds, was marvellous. To our right, on the eastern side, I detected a cornice bordering our way, but the whale back on which we were moving was broad and there was nothing to force us out towards it.

The ridge flattened out … at 1 p.m. we were standing on the white dome of the summit. Tirich Mir was ours.

What can one say? Masaaki looked at me and said: 'Very lucky ..

We hugged each other.

A page of Masaaki's diary with a hole, held before his chest … became the red gleaming sun of Japan.

What was there left for Didi and me to climb after I had done Tirich Mir? Obviously, nothing. But we were greatly attracted by a different kind of adventure: the crossing from the Tirich Glacier into Gazikistan, and then on into the Arkari valley. And after that, why not skirt Tirich Mir's southern flanks and come back into the Tirich Gol to rejoin our porter friends at Shagrom? Our baggage could in the meantime be taken there, along the normal route, by some men led by Musheraf Din and stored in his hut. All around Tirich Mir: the prospect of strolling from village to village, with its white summit ever and again lifting a new aspect above the valleys, was highly attractive.

It was on 25 August that Didi and I started out from 'Koncordiaplatz', the name I had given, for private use, to the junction of the Upper Tirich Glacier's three arms. Once again we climbed over the scree slope to the left of the icefall that bars the way to the Anogol[1] and pitched our bivouac tent in the afternoon on the 'water lily moraine', close to the provision-dump we had with such wise foresight established there during our last reconnaissance (where, below a face with massive stratifications I had found rock fragments full of crinoids). The following day produced an unpleasant surprise; the pinnacles of ice in the upper basin of the glacier had grown considerably, and were now chest-high. We stumbled and cursed and fell about for hours, pushing a way through them, with Anogol Zom always before our eyes, but never appreciably nearer. In the end, we decided to steer as far as possible towards its east face, and to climb there; but before we could do that, we had to get through pinnacles of ice taller than ourselves. It turned into a veritable battle with these apparitions.

By evening our tent was up on the ridge at about 19,000 feet. Over a white fence of pinnacle ice we could look down into Gazikistan.

The next evening brought us sheer delight: flowers and grass, at the rim of a small tarn, which had formed between an old edge-moraine and the slope of the mountains, at about 13,000 feet. We had been on the march almost the whole day, climbing and making our way down and down; in the end to find the scent of grass and flowers. We slept out in the open, under a wide sky. What a lovely world this is!

For the next two days we were plagued by hunger – contrary to expectation there was no sign of human life here in Gazikistan – but we silenced it with wild rhubarb and onions. At first there was no kind of a track, and unstable scree slopes made progress impossible at places. I chose an upper route, following a steinbock trail; while Didi climbed down to the glacier. So we went on for hours, with anything from three-to six-hundred feet of differential between us; while from time to time one or other of us would shout that it was 'better here'.

---

1 Anogol means 'valley of the pass', though there is no sign of any crossing of this glacier nowadays. – K.D.

In spite of niggardly rhubarb rations, I started to undertake an excursion on to the Upper Gazikistan Glacier, where I collected some geological specimens from its retaining wall. This also gave me the opportunity for a clear study of the 'crossing' from the Anogol into upper Gazikistan. This consisted of a pretty lofty ice slope, which a climber could manage, maybe a Sherpa, but certainly not a local man without mountain equipment.

Till now, no expedition or reconnaissance had undertaken any of these crossings into Gazikistan. Even the inhabitants differ in their opinions. Judging by what we had seen, any such crossing must have been a very long time ago, for certainly nobody came up here nowadays. Yet what is the explanation of Musheraf Din's story: that long, long ago, people with horses used to cross from Afghanistan to Shagrom by way of the Anogol? Was it simply a legend? We had looked everywhere: nowhere had we seen even the possibility of such an 'extreme' route for horses. Even taking the alterations in the glaciers into account, the thing remains a riddle.

Didi, who had had to wait six hours for me because of my 'diversion', was rewarded by the spectacle of my trying to jump the full-flowing glacier-torrent between us, and – my leap curtailed by my heavy rucksack – falling right into it; it cooled my enthusiasm for 'diversions' for some time. That night we slept on sand under a thorn bush and dreamed of chapattis. We got them next day in that never-forgotten Arkari valley.

We were back with mother earth; and it was like a fairy tale. At first there were just a boy and a girl standing on the path, their great eyes full of wonderment; then a bearded man came hurrying up, pointing enquiringly, asking where we had come from and shaking his head in unbelief. However, when we said 'chapattis' his astonishment at our 'bisi Tirich Mir' soon turned to swift sympathy, as he patted us on the back and led us to his hut. We sat on the grass under two tall trees, whose branches bent, as the wind rustled through their leaves. An old man appeared, and a woman with a small child; she looked at us with marvellously clear eyes before departing, presumably to prepare the chapattis. It all seemed to us like a miracle. And the bearded man took down from the tree an age-old match-lock muzzle-loader and related with many words and gestures, how he had brought a steinbock down with it in Gazikistan. On the following day he came along with us as a porter.

Down at Arkari, we learned that two climbers had met their death on Tirich Mir. Next day, we met their companions and were given fuller details: they were the two Carinthian climbers, Hans Thomaser and Fritz Samonigg. They had set out for the summit on 19 August – just as we had done – quite unknown to us, be it said, and from a much lower camp than ours, on the other side of the mountain. At about 22,000 feet they had disappeared into the clouds – into that same sea of cloud on to which we had looked down and which, as it spread and spread, had that same day brought us a snow-storm and some critical moments in the choice of our line of descent. They were never seen again.

During the following days, as I watched the clouds continually mounting the flanks of that huge white peak, I kept on wondering whether our friends had reached the summit.

But the clouds keep their secret, and in any case, how would the answer alter anything?

There is a question mark hanging over all things.

25   360 Million Years

Here in my hand I hold an unknown creature, which lived 360 million years ago. Its fossil still exists.

Three hundred and sixty million? I took a sheet of paper and tried somehow to get hold of the very idea. The thing was unbelievable; it sent shivers down my spine ...

If I took a single forty-inch step every day, I would cover roughly 240 yards in a year. So in the thirty-six years of my life I would have gone five miles, and might expect – taking an optimistic view – to cover another four, or a little more, before I die. But if I wanted to go back to the time when this 'animal' I am holding in my hand was alive, I would – taking the prescribed single pace a day – have to cover a distance of 49,275,000 miles; in other words, farther than from this earth to Mars, or more than halfway to the sun – on foot.

One step a day for 360 million years ...

In my hand lies a fossil, a thing that was once – unimaginably remote from me – alive.

Yes, farther from me than the orbit of Mars.

Nobody knows what this thing I am holding is, for no such living creature exists any more. It is one of the oldest, an inhabitant of the Devonian Sea, on whose bed waved whole forests of water lilies.[1] In those days the first amphibians were invading the land which had already succumbed to ferns, shave grass and licopodia. There were cuttle-fish and crabs, corals and mussels, strange types to some extent, but all identifiable today. And here, in the calm waters of a sea, whose surface the waves once ruffled, here where now cloud-topped mountains stand; here, between the delicate shapes of fronded sea-stars – those creatures so like 'miniature palms', for they look like plants, and have even been given the name 'water lilies' – lived an absolutely unknown 'thing', unique and fascinatingly beautiful in its formation, about which nobody has the slightest notion

Receptaculites Neptuni DEFRANCE, the scientists have named it. A resounding title for what? For a rare 'receptacle', about which no one is quite sure

---

1 Crinoids. – K.D.

whether to class it as an animal or a plant. It appears to be several separate creatures, arranged in a marvellously regular pattern, enclosing a spherical space. No one has any idea how 'the thing' lived and functioned; but there it was – it existed.

It must have been a shallow sea which covered the original ground, where nowadays a track runs up to the 13,000-foot saddle of the Owir An; by its side there are still today single corals, countless stems of water lilies, from the dawn of the earth's history.

I looked up at Tirich Mir, itself an instant in time. As Tona and I pushed forward along the southern arm of the Upper Tirich Glacier, we had seen revealed one of the great snapshots in the geological history of the earth – the 3,000-foot high intrusion of the Tirich Mir granite into the primeval black slate in the enormous plane of Tirich Mir West IV's western face. It was a whole chaos of light-coloured arms clawing into the dark slates, prising them apart, breaking them into clumps of strata – there were even great separate fragments, bigger than a row of houses, swimming like lost things in the weathered brown mass of the original bedrock, once a fluid fiery mass in the tertiary period. They looked like dark lumps of sugar in dough. There they had remained unassimilated – for the granite had 'frozen' at that moment. A snapshot clocked, 3,000 feet and more of it in height; the last sequence in a film shot millions of years ago.

You do not need to be a geologist to be impressed by it. It is an adventure from which, once introduced into it, you cannot escape. Tona and I regarded the Tirich Mir area as our own province. She was a qualified geologist; for me it was a serious though passionate hobby. Tona had made the first geological sketch map of the mountains in this area. I broadened it, taking in a wider sweep, measuring strata, fetching samples, as yet not available, from remote corners. Nobody can imagine how delighted I was when, suddenly, on that lateral moraine of the Anogol Glacier, at about 16,500 feet, I came upon the stems of water lilies, and at last the possibility of establishing the age of those dark layers moved within reasonable reach.

We were on the first complete circuit of Tirich Mir. My companion was a young native from the Arkari valley, Didi in the meantime had gone to Chitral and I pushed a fossil – a sea lily stem found at the edge of the path below the Owir An – under my companion's nose. 'Look at that!' I said. He smiled, but shrugged his shoulders. I couldn't help thinking of the well-known Himalayan geologist whose porter took a very individual view about carrying 'stones'. When they reached their destination and the professor opened the case (which weighed the right amount) he found that its contents were ordinary stones from the bed of the last stream they had crossed. I understand that the porter had by then gone home.

When, after two hours, I was still breaking up boulders, my companion finally took such a waste of time amiss and pointed up to the saddle of the pass. However, we had not gone a hundred yards, when I suddenly discovered these rare, scarcely ever seen creatures. They were beautifully circular, their pattern like some prehistoric jewellery. If they were corals, they were certainly very unusual ones. I had never before seen the base on which they lay, nor the surface – almost like a pineapple, or rather like a lepidendron, and yet not like that either. Some bryozoon, perhaps. Perhaps, after all, corals. Yet, a very special kind of coral …

Till this day not a soul knows how to classify these 'beings'. Only nine times have they been found anywhere in the world, only two of these in Asia. The nearest site where one has been found lies 600 miles away in Persia, the next nearest as far away as Western Australia. When I found mine, I at once felt sure that it was something extraordinary, and under the critical gaze of my porter packed all the marvellous looking but somewhat heavy fragments I could lay hands on into my rucksack. (And, of course, not into *his* bag …) Then we strolled on towards the top of the pass and a new aspect of Tirich Mir, or of the clouds gathered about its crest.

'Higher than the eagle soars …'

I shall go back there again; many times, I rather suspect.

Part 5

26   Three Words From Greenland

Tässa ... Susa ... Imaka ...

It is snowing. I am standing at my window in Salzburg, looking down on the rubble of the Salzach, with its big round boulders. The flakes go whirling by .

A book grows rather like a snow crystal. One doesn't write it from start to finish but, in greater or less degree, all at the same time – a bit here and a bit there; some of the star points grow big, others remain rudimentary, some of them cut into each other – irregularly, as a snowflake forms, though it, too, follows its own laws.

The dry smell of the rope, the river and its stones down there, the echo of a Greenland song – that is why my book is not in chronological order; for everything is of the present, held in the moment when thought captures it. At times I have tried to preserve a chronology, so as to give the reader a picture of time's passage; but I have only succeeded in the broadest sense. So the jumble in these pages is not meant to be of time, but just as it comes to mind, now linked by strands of time, now suddenly timeless again. And for that reason, this book will never be a neatly rounded whole – but it reflects a reality, which I am sure is not mine alone.

The echo of that song from Greenland – I hear it all of a sudden, and suddenly, in the midst of the city's densest traffic, Greenland is there, the great open spaces, the silence; until the next bus rumbles past. Or again, in the far Hindu Kush, by the rim of whose glaciers blow the same pale red flowers as blow on the shores of the iceberg-cluttered Greenland fjords, I remember an evening when the cheerful native porters stamped in rhythmic unison on the ground, while Hayad ud Din, Musheraf, or Neap, clapped time with their hands till the air above the camp fire trembled as if an iceberg were overturning. There they danced an uninhibited dance, like Greenlanders, to a tune, which my old guitar – four times broken and five times stuck together again – had transported from the northlands, just as if it were a song of their own. None of them knew a Greenland word, no one understood '*uchlok navok tachererpok sekinek*' , nobody had any idea that it was all about the sun and the thunder of the icebergs ; but they sang, and they clapped, and Greenland was there, though only I knew it. The fact that it was all in the past did not upset me. '*Tässa*' and '*Susa*' – Greenland was there. And would be again. '*Imaka*' – 'perhaps'.

Those three words are common in Greenland, and one hears them repeated every day. They are a sort of philosophy for those dwellers under the perpetual day and the long night of many months.

Greenland is an island. Geographers allot it to North America, politicians to Denmark. Basically, it is something quite unique; a kind of continent, on which human beings live, as hardly anywhere else on the earth's surface, in the midst of an all-powerful nature – and know it. It is peopled by roughly 30,000 souls, the population of a provincial town; yet so large is this island that, if laid out across Europe, it would stretch from Scandinavia to North Africa. The habitable ground is narrow, a coastal hem; the settlements lie at great distances from one another, with no road links, on the fringe of the ice cap, at places 10,000 feet thick, which almost covers the island in its entirety. When you look above the Greenland peaks, the sky behind them is not blue like ours, but white – the *inlandsis*; higher than almost all the mightiest peaks in the island; it seems illimitable, and the loneliness of the traveller in this immensity of the white, sky is unmeasurable, terrifying and compelling.

Fridtjof Nansen, Robert Peary, Alfred Wegener …

Winter in Greenland. The polar night endures for months; the nearer to the Pole you are, the longer it lasts. Icy cold and darkness reign, lightened only by the coloured glory of the Northern Lights, the moon and, at long last, by the reflection of the returning sun. A European is especially hard hit by the isolation from the world without. And the sea remains frozen long after the sunlight has come back. It is not till late in spring, rather the beginning of summer, that the supply vessels from Denmark fight their way, slowly, slowly, through the coastal ice. This is not so everywhere; but even in the south-west of this gigantic island, where, in the orbit of a branch of the Gulf Stream and mostly this side of the Polar Circle, the greater part of the 'towns' lie situated (Godthaab, the biggest, has 5,000 inhabitants), where living conditions are a little more favourable, a foreigner must love Greenland (or a fat salary) greatly before he can be persuaded to spend more than one winter there. And what about the Greenlanders themselves? They say their winter is lovely beyond compare. The foreigner, thinking perhaps of the endless journeys by sledge, can hardly understand that. The Greenlander just smiles: for him Greenland, in the grip of its long winter, is 'his' Greenland; even more than in the brilliant summer, when, under a flood of light, there is a universal explosion of green, with the sun continually circling the heavens, flowers of every hue show their bright faces, often springing from soil lying only inches deep over the smooth, polished rock below. Greenland – in truth the green land – as the Vikings found it, at the turn of the tenth century, on their incredibly daring voyage in their long boats, under Eric the Red. Green Land, as today's climber experiences it, flying in for a short visit from Copenhagen or Los Angeles, or coming by ship up the fjords, to reach unclimbed peaks on the rim of the ice cap; and returning home, ere ever the twilight of winter's approach descends on the land and the sea stiffens in the grip of the first frost.

… There, below the aircraft's wing lay Iceland; the broad ice field of the Vatna Joku, fringed by a carpet of cloud, greyish-black lava streams, then green, much green, overlaid with grey; brightly coloured extinct volcanoes, red, yellow, ochre, dark brown; then clouds again and the darkness of the sea. That was Iceland. We were flying at 31,000 feet, almost at the speed of sound – Bruno, Pigi, Silvio, Mauro, Carlo and I. We represented the Greenland Expedition of the Tortona Italian Alpine Club, and had all been together before, in Africa. Our objective, the peaks of the Qioqe Peninsula far up the west coast, beyond the 71st parallel; great unclimbed mountains – only Mauri, Guaico and Ghiglione had ever visited the place, six years before, and had climbed wonderful Perserajoq.

How much longer? Look: little, sharp lumps of sugar, close together on the dark sea surface below the clouds – drift-ice! We glued our noses to the windows – we could only be a matter of seconds from Greenland.

There it was – the east coast! A spiky wilderness of peaks, rising sheer out of the sea – behind an armour-plating of enormous floes. Blue fjords with millions of white dots on them, gigantic rivers of ice winding down to the sea, mountains and yet more mountains. The east coast, with its armour of floes, held for the greater part of the year in the icy grip of a cold stream from the north.

We could not tear ourselves from the windows; looking down to where, now, the shadow of our aircraft and its vapour-trails was etching a black line across fjords, cloud-layers and peaks, as we drew ever nearer to the gigantic ice cap. That streak which had grown in a matter of seconds – could that really be us? – was tearing across crevassed glaciers, jumping the very next moment, quicker than a heartbeat, from summit to summit, finally touching the last isolated crags still able to penetrate the ever-growing armour-plate of the ice – the so-called *nunatakker* …

Interruptions of blue-green lakes formed by the melting waters, miles broad. Then blinding brightness. White; nothing but white. So stark, so dazzling that it hurt the eyes. Light without outlines. During the next hour of the flight two passengers went snow-blind. I could only detect faint contours down there through doubled glare-glasses. Wavy contours …

Inlandsis. The great white desert. Enormous, indescribable.

We flew 500 miles across it.

Sondre Stromfjord: the jet-strip close to the edge of the ice, on the west coast, at the start of the fjord of the same name, 130 miles long: a civil airport, sprung from an American base. And that is what it still is, though one may not see much of the installations, mostly underground, any more than of the other military posts which one hears are partly buried beneath the cuirass of *inland-sis*. We touched down.

We touched down. A reindeer was taking a walk on the runway, followed soon by an Arctic fox. Presently a jet took off for Los Angeles.

When would our helicopter arrive to take us to Egedesminde?

'Well, why don't you make an excursion to the inland ice today – it's very fine. Meanwhile we will do our best. You might be able to get away tomorrow; if not, the day after. Don't worry too much; you are in Greenland now, you know ...' the fair-haired Dane gave a laugh. So the sun circled round the wooden huts – twice ...

The red bus, seating twenty-eight, whose big shovel-bladed rotors whirled in the air as it slowly settled down, buzzed like a giant bumblebee.

Then we were off. After two infuriating days of waiting (that is what one would have said in Europe: here they just shrugged their shoulders and said the single word, *susa*). For a moment I thought of Asia, whence these Greenlanders originally came from, and of its timelessness, as we swept across the land at 130 m.p.h. in our red 'et-chopper'. I was told later that there are precisely three of these flying buses in all Greenland. One was always undergoing maintenance. The other two – well, there was a flight-plan for them ...

Brilliant, bright green. Low humps, rock, grass, fjords. Hundreds of lakes – in the distance, the inland ice. A river with great, uncontrolled loops. Sand. Greyish-green reeds and mosses. Grey-green water ... Violet-hued, milk-coloured, deep blue water! Each lake a different colour. Bright light: everything clear and sharply defined. Ice flakes on the water, a fine webbing of ice on the next lake. Another fjord. Islands, and more islands. Unpretentious, on one of them, lay our Egedesminde, with icebergs like toy dice in front of it. Like ships – no, much bigger ...

We just escaped being made very unhappy that day at Egedesminde. The captain of the *Tikerak* explained to us, calmly and amiably, that he had never heard of us, his ship was full and that he would be very pleased to take us on his next trip, which would be in a fortnight. In a fortnight!

And what about our telegram from Italy? Damn it all! Some agitated moments ensued. We had to deal with heads no less tough than the iceberg-scored timbers of the ship. We did it at the top of our voices, using the whole range of the vocabulary, and we kept at it relentlessly. After all we were an Italian Expedition, and an official one at that! No, nothing could persuade us to go ashore from the *Tikerak* of our own freewill! And that telegram, where was it? Next morning everything was still as inconclusive as before ...

We leaned on the rail as the ship headed northwards, leaving Egedesminde in her wake. Bruno thought solemnly of all Tortona's famous deeds of heroism, while we cleared our throats, and stood stiff as tall statues in the strong breeze, looking with resolute mien into the wind.

The wooden hull of our ship went bobbing up and down. Icebergs, innumerable ice blocks went past. The sea was a bluish-black and there were white horses on it. Above it, under a pale sky, lay the ridges separating the fjords, brownish-grey, topped by a little snow. Soft and far they stretched, merging into one another.

Our good ship *Tikerak* was built for just such journeys as this. Round, all of wood, slow, comfortable. In Greenland language her name means: 'who comes for a short visit'.

The helmsman, a Dane, came to Greenland fifteen years ago, got caught up in it, and has been steaming along this coast, year by year, ever since. He kept on telling me proudly of his lovely Greenland daughter, whom he was going to take back to Denmark for the first time; she had just turned fourteen. He was pale, rather sloppy, looking more like some kind of an office-wallah somewhere. I wondered how many icebergs he had had to miss in the fog, in his time? He was a quiet man, and his every second word – when not actually talking about his daughter – was susa, which means, 'don't worry about it'. I have him to thank for that word.

The sky above our mast was deep and dark. There was a whole flotilla of icebergs ahead. Then – a heap of little dots, a cluster of gaily coloured dabs along the shore, jolly, every kind of colour. Little wooden houses. A 'town'.

They were all of a pattern. There was a church (for both faiths) a school, various buildings of the KGH – the Royal Greenland Trade Department – a fish-processing factory, maybe, a small supermarket, even a motorcar for the two miles of road. It is very rare nowadays to find one of the old Greenland peat-igloos alongside the gay little wooden homes.

' … *Uchlok navok tachererpok sekinek pavanilo uchloriak kaamavok* … To our ears, it sounded like a *conversazione* among wild ducks in the reeds. Karen, Eva and Louise were royally amused at our efforts to master the secrets of wild duck talk, or rather to learn one of their Greenland songs by heart. It was quite a job. We captured the notes on the guitar; Louise wrote down the words; Karen produced a sort of translation. Karen was a delightful child, casting smiles or oblique glances from slanting Asiatic eyes; blue they were, and her round face was framed by two long reddish-brown plaits. The buxom Louise had pencilled eyebrows; she was dark as they come, like an actress in an

Eskimo film. Eva evinced something of the jolliness of a young, female seal. Karen was a beauty of rare quality, though. Later, when my second daughter was born, I gave her that name, a piece of Greenland, to keep.

As it happened, we found out afterwards that the tune originated somewhere in Canada. Gaily strung together, with Greenland words, the song was a portrait of this coast: an entity which the timbers of our ship also embraced. People, met together by mere chance, utterly different people, each with his own goal in life, yet, under Greenland skies, constituting an entity. An ephemeral circle, to which each of them, if only by his presence, contributed something.

There was the old professor of geography from St Andrew's University in Scotland; a quiet man, who returned every year, for many years, to Greenland, to the unknown island off the west coast. There he had discovered a petrified forest, and was working on a map. He was mostly to be found leaning on the rail, alone. He was glad to be here again, and told me that he now had with him the material for setting up a small, permanent research but at the perimeter of the native settlement on the island.

There was tall, black Michel, a sympathetic type, speaking fluent French, even understanding the Greenland tongue. He had been living on the island for two years, in one place or another. Greenland's only Negro, he was apparently working on a book. He liked it here, this possessor of all the vitality of Africa, all the charm of Paris – on this bleak coast, where one was responsive to charm. He really wanted to go to Thule, to the last of the racially pure Eskimos, but had not been granted a permit. It was from him that I, the new boy' in Greenland, learned that *ab* and *namek* mean yes and no. Also the meaning of the continual *imaka*, which means 'perhaps', and often sounds like a Greenland version of *inshallah*! (As in: our ship will turn up in three days, *imaka*' – perhaps: God willing …)

I got to know the first officer, at midnight one night – it was of course daylight – as I wandered about the empty deck, my guitar under my arm. Suddenly I was confronted by this Dane with a huge, bushy beard. Very soon three of us, he, the helmsman and I, were sitting over beer and Danish ham in the cookhouse, guzzling like savages. Presently I reached for my guitar. When I started my song from Trieste, the bearded one leaped to his feet, banged his fist on the table and beamed with delight. *'Trieste – oh, bella Trieste!'* He stood there, bulking like a wardrobe and sang, full-throated. Trieste. Outside, the icebergs were bobbing. Then he explained that he had been there for a day, some years ago.

Mountaineering he held to be sheer lunacy …

Green is the emerald and its fire burns fiercer than ice. Mette's intelligence was ice-cold – a green laser-beam; a computer with the heart of a twenty-year-old girl. It was extraordinary; when she said anything, it was almost impossible to find an answer. She had come to Greenland for the winter. When I got back from the mountains of Qioqe I met her again at Umanak. She was off to Nepal next. I have never seen her since.

She told me much about the Greenlanders. She made me understand that our sojourn here was only a short visit, and I envied her the freedom of the great winter lying ahead of her – an experience barred to me.

On went our ship. Christianshaab, Jakobshaven, Qotligssat ... new faces came aboard, old ones were missing. Yet, for a definite time, each of them belonged to the day's round, simply because they were on board.

Upernivik, Umanak ... the journey lasted four days. Actually, it was always the same day.

Diary:

Jakobshaven, ashore. The big fjord, spewing out thousands of icebergs. Up the hill ... How low the sun stands in the sky ... Utter stillness. The sea glints yellow. The rocks are rounded and firm. We go on up.

'The children find a bird. Joy! So many little hands reaching out, stroking, squeezing it ... it will die. Love ...

'We turned to go, and they wave to us: *Farvel – farvel – farvel* ... the flowers, the crosses, the moss. The icebergs.

"Tomorrow it will be dead – and it is love."

The ship will be leaving soon.'

We came to Umanak on a dark, rainy day. A handful of houses on an island, consisting almost entirely of one great sharp-peaked mountain, winging up more than 3,000 feet straight out of the waves. Many, many icebergs. A tiny harbour. And Pedersen waiting for us, here at the starting point of our expedition.

'*Ragazzi, siamo arrivati* – here we are boys!' It was midnight, at the peninsula Qioqe. The mountain walls were dark in cloud, and it was raining. The bow of our small boat grated on shingle. Out we jumped, Bruno first, then the rest of us and the two Greenlanders, come to help us unload the heavy cases, labelled Qioqe. There was nothing to be seen in the filthy rain.

Pederson had brought us the sixty miles from Umanak, Pedersen, the resident agent of the government and the angelic helper of all expeditions. This man had already spent ten years in Greenland – oh, for his gift of complete relaxation! Everything in order: we, our cases, everything, safely on the rocks, in the teeming rain. The Greenland men pushed off from shore, laughing, pointing a finger to their foreheads: mountaineering, what a joke! One of them, a great bear of a Viking, the others short, dark, Mongolian types. '*Arrivederci!*' We waved, Pedersen raised a hand, the red boat shuddered and disappeared among the shadowy icebergs. We were to be here for weeks, all alone on the great, unpeopled peninsula. '*Arrivederci,* Pedersen!' Don't forget us …

This filthy rain! Quick, boys, up with the tent!

Our base camp was just twenty feet above sea level. The sun came breaking through the clouds. Up there, 6,000 feet up, one marvellous peak, then another …

Qioqe: a veritable Piz Badile, a pyramid of a mountain, gently curving ice peaks, like in the Bernina; a great wall, not unlike the Jorasses. And then an unbroken succession of peaks …

Qioqe. We spent weeks there, but months would not have sufficed. How infinite can a range of mountains be?

The peninsula reaches out thirty miles from the rim of the inland ice towards the Baffin Sea. A huge fjord to the north, another to the south; to the west, beyond the deeply indented arm of a fjord, the mountainous island of Upernivik, uninhabited, as is all the realm of Qioqe. A huge glacier, flowing down from the ice cap, ceaselessly calves icebergs into the forty-mile long north fjord; it is the some in the south. And then there are the peninsula's own glaciers. These do not all reach down to the fjord; but from 'Three Fjord Peak' the ice avalanches thunder down, airborne for 5,000 feet, on to the surface of the sea. More icebergs …

Floating archways; a giant's boot; Monte Rosa – really, it looked just like Monte Rosa; a hat; a giantess's comb, shimmering, full of fine teeth; patches of green, blue, yellow light; crystals glittering in the light of the low sun; ships; castles, often 300 feet long … all of them moving slowly down the fjord, or back up it, at the dictates of the daily current. We kept on seeing some of them, like Monte Rosa and the comb, over and over again. Others disappeared. Then there would be thunder, tremendous in the silence, as a berg suddenly disintegrated, or some colossus, higher than a house, lost its balance and, with the noise of a dying beast, began to turn over in the water, as chunks broke away or the whole edifice burst into pieces. Often, then, the great waves engendered by the dissolution pictured other fantastic images, as the thing tottered to destruction .

Qioqe, with its huge walls, shining yellow, sheer from the water's edge, mirrored below – 5,000 feet and more they shoot up from the sea. 'Ultimate problems.' Grey flanks. And, higher still, peaks running up to nearly 8,000 feet …

'Ultimate problems?' These have always existed, everywhere; but who thinks of them here?

My thoughts turn to the moon's overpowering landscape. Huge brownish-yellow craters against the blue, white-rimmed sky of the earth. Utter loneliness. Craters, mountains. Who would even think of climbing a face, there? That is too vast a landscape; and movement there is different, strange …

Something similar happens to the visitor to Greenland. In a boat, he moves over submerged valleys, glides past mountain walls, as in a dream, from one peak to another. Here they are, all the time, everywhere, the mountains. They have climbed down into the sea. Mountains and sea, fused in one another, in front of your eyes. This unity of height and breadth transforms the mountains; they are more omnipresent, stronger.

As the sun circles they never cease to vary their expression. A wall? Just part of a mountain, a trait of its face.

Everything here becomes more substantial, constitutes a unity. The rock-faces of Qioqe, gleaming yellow. Pale red blossoms with a cross at their heart. Strata of black tourmaline, thick as your arm. Red granite; yellowish-grey lichens. Knuckle-deep moss. The dark, white-flecked carpet of the harebell meadow. Icebergs. Glimmering muscovites. The bright light of day; the muted yellow light by night. The sharp black shadows thrown on the fjord walls by the opposing peaks. Silence. Blue-green beryl crystals. Green ones? Emeralds? High excitement, fully justified from the human standpoint. However, the mighty pressure of the mountains has crushed them.

Shimmering bodies of many small fish, swarming to the surface like one body; a few big ones ... We could not get them to bite. They played with the float, nibbled happily at the lead. We only caught one. Innumerable screaming gulls. Dark green water plants. Layers of cyanide in the rock, shimmering a whitish-blue, like ice. And the icebergs ...

I went out while the others were still asleep. It was a fabulous morning, that first one on Qioqe. I was avid to know what it all looked like behind the barrier of dark blocks, piled up perhaps, one fine day, by a landslide from 'Three Fjord Peak'. I found a valley there, leading from this western shore towards the interior of the peninsula. It was the only way, for great mounds of slabs went plumbing into the sea on either side of our base camp.

What kind of a valley – would there be cliffs in it, too? I moved on up, over a soft cushion of moss. It was a paradise. Deep and soft, like a carpet, underfoot. Lichens at every step, flowers; and among them the landslide's enormous boulders. It was a broad upland valley like those at home among the 10,000-foot peaks – yet I was not 700-feet above sea level. Knuckle-deep moss, rust-brown peaks, streaked with fresh snow, ice slopes thrusting to the blue vault, endless humps of moraines. All of it unexplored, untrodden till this day. I was content, happy. Here there would be plenty to do.

Was that a partridge? Or a pheasant? It was certainly a big bird, mottled black and brown, with a long neck ... just like a picture in the cookery book. It was just two yards away. Trustfulness personified, it laid its head on one side and gave me a searching examination. No, this one had never seen a human being before! It was not till I got within three feet that he gave a little hop and stood, reluctantly, aside.

A partridge, eh? I am the first human being, thought I, the first in paradise; and that naturally connotes certain responsibilities. Happily, and with the lofty feeling of one who has exercised great renunciation, I went farther into paradise, the first human being ...

There, cut into a boulder in front of me, stood that word Imaka' –'perhaps'. At first I could not grasp it. What, here? I stood there as though turned to stone. Was that a date – just a fortnight ago? I, Adam, the first man ever, breathed heavily. But – who?

'Eva – Hans,' I read. I swallowed hard.

But how was it possible? Umanak was sixty miles away. Qioqe uninhabited – hadn't Pedersen told us so? That hadn't bothered Eva. Suddenly I was look-ing at the region with different eyes – from the mountaineering angle, I told myself, the peninsula remained unexplored.

On my way down to camp I came upon another inscription. 'Eva-Knud', it ran. (My reconnaissance report began to assume a universal interest. During the many days we went on the peninsula, we went deeply and variedly into what Eva looked like ; unfortunately, it all remained obscure – she never materialized.)

I had noticed something else: we had landed on the wrong side of the gla-cier tongue. Up its trough, every way was blocked, from here, by a deep gorge. Later, we erected a kind of emergency crossing in the icy water – the 'bridge' – built of slabs of rock. It took a long time. The gulls screeched and laughed 'he–he–he–he!' at us. They are laughing at us,' declares Mario, dragging rocks around (he is an insurance director).

At first we had nothing to laugh about. What distances! Heavy carries, recon-naissances – miles long – towards the centre of the peninsula. Moraine hummocks – up and down, up and down, down and up – then ice. Camp I at 1,400 feet; camp II at 3,300. The central glacier was a chaos of crevasses; gaping cracks full of water. The snow bridges were so sloppy that one was prepared to see them cave in if one only looked hard enough. We began to wonder whether we would ever get to the centre of the peninsula, as Carlo and I crawled over the snow, on all fours, during our first attempt. That is the great handicap at this time of year: there is no frost at night and, under the sun that never ceases to circle, the glaciers seem to be visibly disintegrating into water, snow-slush and again water. There is no safe climbing 'daytime' ; only near the summits do conditions improve.

'*Avanti i mei prodi!*' – onwards, my heroes! This was Bruno's stock exhortation. Definitely a memory of Tortona's famous history goes everywhere with him – Tortona, the 'strawberry city in the Apennines. Bruno was the originator of our expedition, the inspiration of everything undertaken by the Tortona Section of the CAI, but most of all a fire-cracker of ideas and humour. He is a doctor, and had served in Russia during the war. He wore a fierce red sou'-wester, and we called him Nansen. And it was he who climbed weighed down by bundles of tents, cases and gunny bags. Like the others, Mauro, the insurance director, assured us that he had never spent a leave to match this one. He was our unconscious humourist. At Copenhagen, with a deadpan face, he had wanted to declare his *Corriere della Sera* as our fourteenth item of baggage, because we had thirteen and he was superstitious. Meanwhile we still survived; though one day, horror written on his face, he discovered that we had pitched our base camp plumb on the burial ground of a long-vanished Greenland settlement.

Carlo – we called him 'Il Mulo' – said little and carted much. He was a patient man, married, and a sculptor. He deserved a hero's monument, rucksack and all, in the main square. He carried more than anyone else.

Pigi was the best groomed of us all: even in Qioqe he looked like an Italian. Seeing that he was the second doctor in the party, obviously nothing could happen to us.

All the same, something did happen. High up in the dangerous central glacier's chaos of crevasses, a snow bridge collapsed under Silvio, pitching him headfirst into the deep, water-filled rift and dis-locating an arm. The united efforts of Pigi and Bruno got it back again, but for Silvio, unfortunately, this meant *finis*. Next time Pedersen came, he went back with him. Would we ever get to the centre of the peninsula, with the glacier 'running against us' like this? We had quite enough by the time we did …

'Avanti i mei prodi!' Bruno's eyes were bright with excitement at the overpowering impressions showering down on us. We were just 300-feet below the summit of Three Fjord Peak – the last 300 feet before it would be ours. We had finished the traverse of the hanging-glacier's rim – that hanging-glacier from which the ice avalanches break away 5,000-feet sheer into the fjord. Now we could see down to the water, a breath-taking downward glance – deep and far below, dark as the dark-blue heavens, pointed with dazzling white stars, yes a heaven in itself.

I stood bemused, rooted to the spot, looking at that white-starred, blue expanse.

They were icebergs of course. One of them capsized, and the distant roar of thunder came rolling up from the abyss. Out of this world … if one could only stay here for ever. Astonishing what feelings every manifestation of heaven can awaken .. .

'Up, my heroes!' On again, up. Mountains and more mountains, grey, blue, white, all around. With a shout we pushed a ski-stick, with its pennants, up into the Greenland sky. We had climbed our first peak. We shook hands, hugged each other, laughing, full of joy.

Here we stood on the north-western cornerstone of Qioqe, at our feet the mighty north fjord, forty miles long; and nearly 6,000 feet below our toe-caps lay the wide mirror of the sea. A whole Eiger North Face! But this one was yellow, with vertical walls. And, over there, in the north – *sneepyramiden*! The outlines of a huge peak 1,500 feet higher than ours. Then the sharp needles of Upernivik, the mountain walls of Qioqe. And deep indented arms of fjords ...

We christened it Three Fjord Peak. A day of days, this. And the knowledge that night would not fall on this peak of ours gave that lofty, exposed place an indescribable air of friendliness and security. Under the slowly circling sun, we spent six hours up there.

Another capsizing iceberg, somewhere – that roar breaking the limitless silence, ever returning out of the peace of the blue heavens, surprising every time, yet familiar, often sounding like a sudden thunderclap from the sun itself. It is as much a part of Greenland's long day as the hooting of cars is in our own. Could there be a greater contrast?

Lower and lower moved the sun, northwards now and closer to the horizon. The mountains changed their faces, the shadows lengthened, warmer grew the tints ... Sea! Dazzling light! Black icebergs floating in the blinding gold of the waters. I closed my eyes. 'Yes – we will stay a while longer .

Today, when any of us thinks back to the Peak of the Three Fjords, what he sees is that incredible sky, below him.

The stones came rolling and rattling down. We were high above the ice plateau at the heart of the peninsula, on the central peak. It is a huge, regularly shaped mountain, the highest or second highest in Qioqe, about 7,600-feet high. We were pushing on up the west face, with bivouac equipment on our backs, Carlo, Pigi and I; we moved over steep, crumbling gullys, and rock cliffs which hung, overlapping, above us. We talked in whispers, for fear of dislodging falling stones. There was a rumbling, crackling crash ... 'Take cover!' And again. 'That's because you coughed,' said Carlo the silent, tersely. That disintegrating face is 2,500 feet tall, and quite a thing for the nerves; cat's climbing, on velvet paws, always ready to jump. We zig-zagged up the confusion of grey and rust-red rock, where things could at any moment spring so suddenly to life. We took a breather on a shoulder of rock. It was evening; once again the sun was circling northwards. There was a castellated ridge above us. Should we take a short nap?

What an illimitable, universal thing is mountaineering here in Greenland – made for men of the daytime and men of the night! Anything is possible, all the time. I lay in my sleeping bag in the sun, out in the open. Pigi crawled into the red bivouac tent and Carlo, after smoking a cigarette, followed him. I woke up towards midnight, when the sun stood low and the light had turned yellow. It was an extraordinary scene. So we decided to climb our peak by night.

Midnight, an ochre sun. We climbed. The towers on the ridge were like cardboard cut-outs; we watched our own shadows moving against glaciers that glimmered yellow, themselves stroked by long shadow-fingers. The sun disappeared behind a cloud-bank and everything went blue and cold.

At 6,500 feet we took to our down jackets and climbed on. Slowly the peaks sank away below us and the view grew wider, embracing *sneepyramiden* pyramids to the north, far across Upernivik's rock-teeth to the soft outlines of the hills in the Nugssuak peninsula, far to the south, farther even than Umanak. The fjords stabbed darkly into the land. Out to the east there lay an unnatural whiteness – the inland ice. There was tough, smooth ice close to my face. And now there was the cornice of a ridge; just below it, I was within an inch of falling into a totally unexpected crevasse.

We got to the top at 2 a.m., and named it '*Picco Centrale Gabriele Boccalatte*', in honour of that great Tortona climber who fell while climbing the Triolet. Our altimeter showed 7,700 feet. Before us lay the SUdfjord, deep in the dusk, and the shimmering domes of Alfred Wegener-land, looking as if someone had poured yellow whipped cream over them. A broad glacier flowed down to the sea. From its front, clean-cut as by a knife, a newborn iceberg was slowly floating out into the south fjord …

Would climbing – mountaineering – *downwards* be a crazy idea? If you have an objective the 'greatest nonsense in the world' knows no bounds of restraint. There was the Südfjord: there was the sea.

Suppose we were to cross all the ranges, all the glaciers of Qioqe right down to the sea, at the far side of the peninsula? My companions looked at me in astonishment; seconds later they were patting me on the back – what a splendid notion – *Che idea!* let's do it! It would be the first ever traverse of Qioqe! So, while Bruno and Mauro set off on a reconnaissance to the north-east, we climbed, heavily laden, up into the central glacier's criss-cross of crevasses – Carlo, '*Il Mulo*' , fully living up to his nickname, Pigi and I, carrying smaller 'sentry-boxes' on our backs.

Far out ahead of us stretched the white, untrodden plateau that was the peninsula's heart, with thin lines – hidden crevasses – drawn on its bright surface. We thought of Silvio and his crippling fall; the snow was soft and watery, here too; no frost to harden it by night. For all the magnificence of central Qioqe spread around us, those hidden crevasses left us with an uncomfortable feeling. One cautious stride after another, along an avalanche cone. Was that a stream I could hear – the gurgling of a –

… Stream? Oh yes, it was a stream all right, gurgling noisily, 150 feet below my dangling legs, at the bottom of a crevasse. I clung to the lip of the fissure, jamming myself into the snow, fighting to keep upright, pressed down by my heavy pack, beneath me the void. Not a damned thing to be found, to give me a foothold! In the end I found some support, somewhere, and stayed motionless on it for a matter of seconds; then, very carefully, I rammed in my axe, Carlo tightened the rope and I heaved myself sideways out on to the flat snow of the glacier, where I lay for a time, gasping for breath. Thanks, Carlo: a lucky getaway! I could easily have gone dangling down there, for the first time in my life.

The plateau seemed to go on for ever. We broke through more than once. It was not till evening that we came to a broad snow saddle, with great ice peaks above it; a breach flanked by towers like skyscrapers. Ahead, where it fell away steeply into the depths, lay grey mists. Could the sea be somewhere down there? We waited six hours on a rock rib at the saddle's edge, before the view cleared. There was the sea, 4,000 feet below us – the Südfjord.

Immediately, came the doubts. Could we climb all that way down, and then all the way up again? We had no boat, and there is not a living soul in the Südfjord. A few hundred feet below us, the glacier appeared to have been chopped-off abruptly; there must be an enormous ice cliff down there. Much, much farther below, a brown snake of moraine poured out of a deep, steep-sided cauldron, on its long way down to the sea. Over it all presided a marvellous mountain, a peak such as one finds in the Andes.

Our objective was that sea down there.

At camp III, Pigi was all growls; he didn't think we could possibly do it. All the same, we said, let's go as far as we can, and then we can see what still lies ahead. Carlo thought we could do it. We decided to leave the tent here at 4,400 feet.

We managed it. For nine hours we climbed and clambered down rock pitches, ledges and ice; lower down still, over the rubble of the moraines. Then – we ran the last hundred yards down to the shore, plunged our hands into the waters of the Südfjord. Everything about us was green, there were flowers everywhere – and that lovely coast was ours and ours alone for a whole hour. Delighted, we built a big cairn, strolled along the water's edge. Exactly where the glacier stream cascades into the. sea, we hoisted our pennants on a couple of boulders in the foaming brown water, to celebrate the first traverse of Qioqe. Our joy knew no bounds.

We were plagued by raging hunger; our provisions had run out., After a short bivouac a few hundred feet up from the sea we were climbing again. 'The second traverse of Qioqe!' growled Carlo, usually so silent, as we worked our weary way up towards the last tin of pork up on the saddle. We threw a longing glance back at the Andean peak … After thirty hours on end, we waded, more dead than alive, through the ice-cold water of the stream between us and base camp. Where the hell had that 'bridge' got to? The gulls mocked us overhead.

Curiously enough, the bridge was there next day.

'Apples! Have some apples!' cried Bruno, very excited. We were busy packing up, after a terrific celebration, during which we loosed-off all our remaining signal-rockets. 'Do eat some apples!' said Bruno, in a voice full of entreaty. Thereby hung a tale. Bruno had ordered them from Pedersen, who brought them. Fifty kilos, to replace the miserable five I had bought at the expensive luxury store of the KGH in Umanak. We fell upon them; in due course we chewed more slowly, finally just every now and then – at the North Pole even New Zealand apples lose their charm. 'You don't know how good apples are,' said Bruno, chewing ostentatiously and determinedly, and we thought of Pedersen, who would soon be here; it was a matter of honour that the load of apples he had delivered should have disappeared by then. How could Italians in Greenland fail to eat apples! But Bruno didn't get through them, so we hid them in a packing case, where Pedersen immediately discovered them. 'Oh, look!' he said, with a grin, 'an apple!' and bit into one with enthusiasm. 'We haven't had any in Umanak for three weeks,' he remarked. 'You bought the lot.' Bruno heaved a sigh, and we tried to keep a straight face. And I blinked into the sun and considered that we were certainly the most important expedition on the west coast that summer, seeing that a whole town had been apple-less on our account.

The boat lurched forward. Qioqe faded astern. The peaks; the lovely lake, not marked on the map, discovered by Mauro and Bruno; the central plateau; the vertical walls of the fjord, and oh, a great many other things. Qioqe … *'Tässa'*. What had been, had been …

And now, I am bitten by a mosquito – a fact I forgot to register in my base camp chronicle. Even that insect belongs to 'Eva's' paradise. *'Susa'* Not to worry!

There was a yellow sunflower in a pot, against the background of a huge blue-and-white iceberg, framed in the window behind it; there was just room for that plant, growing a little crookedly. Then there was a polished, green tomato on the stem of a tomato plant, in another flowerpot. All in front of the same bluish-white, icy background. The iceberg was bigger than the church, bigger than half of Umanak. 'Those are my window plants, my garden!' said Mrs Pedersen, moving affectionately towards one of the tomato pots. 'There are five now.' She smiled as she passed her hand over one of the shiny tomato spheres in front of the iceberg. I nodded. We were to leave next day, on board the fast-steaming *Kununguak*. Fragments of conversation, in Italian, rose from the back of the room, and I heard the name 'Milano' … envy you your window,' I said. She laughed. Then she said: 'Somebody once grew a cucumber in the window on Disko Island, but that wasn't easy.' I kept on looking at the odd garden under the crooked sunflower, and thought how the day when we would not bat an eyelid for a *pomodoro* lay close at hand. I looked straight through those green leaves and that blue ice to thick forests of trees, meadows full of green grass, fields of waving corn ...

And I had no enthusiasm at all for what I saw. I wanted to stay here.

Had I contracted a form of Greenland sickness? ... The Pedersens had been here ten years. Ten whole years in Greenland: A handful of plants set against an iceberg. Those meaningful tomatoes: a fenced-in sunflower, reared with difficulty. Ten years! Ten years of winter gales and darkness; of people living at the rim of the ice, for whom the ice and icebergs lurk outside their front doors, cold and pitiless. Greenland, grim, vast, icy and overwhelming – where every feeling, even love, has to be outsize, or perish. Where light is really light, and shadow really darkness. Greenland, and its long night. The green and yellow polar lights, magic curtain in the void of space, covering the whole sky, moving, waxing and waning, fusing in iridescent changes, fading to pure green light in the ink-blue of the night, mysterious – and then, darkness again. The sun, returning out of the night, at first for a few minutes, later for an hour out of the twenty-four – until, in the end, it never sets all day. Greenland: a petrified forest and a 10,000-foot thick wedge of ice ... I put the stone I held back on Pedersen's table top; its structure was still that of the wood.

Now he was telling us about his sledge journeys, hundreds of miles long, about the people in the tiny hamlets ... Ten years. Not everyone who lives in Greenland loves it, but many of them cannot bear to leave it. Pedersen loves it. He didn't say much, but what he did say amounted to something. Not that I needed its message – Greenland already had me in thrall.

I stood on one .of the town's granite knolls, watching the Kununguak sail away. My companions of the expedition were aboard her, and I was thinking of them, returning home without me. I was thinking of home. 'I shall sail on the *Tikerak*,' I told myself. 'Later on.'

'*Uchlok navok tachererpok sekinek*' ... the day runs down and dies.

There was a pack of dogs, howling. Karen was walking her little brother by the hand. A father was upbraiding his son ... 'You codling, you!' A Greenlander, chewing at the roadside, offered me a slice of raw whale-fat – the best cut, close under the skin – so I sat down by him and we chewed fat. I played '*Uchlok navok*' on my guitar and he told me a long story in his native tongue. 'Ab,' said I – 'Yes!' I expect it was something to do with the whale. We shook hands.

An Italian paper printed: 'Diemberger continues his researches in the polar regions.' But I was living in Umanak and on the Nugssuak coast, the proud possessor of a Greenland song and perhaps twenty words of the language ...

Umanak, ab, namek, imaka, tässa, susa, ichli, uvanga, sermerssuak, kuja-nak, tikerak, kajak and more still ending in – ak.[1]

We hunted seals; sailed along the coast. '*Kassuta tamasa – skol!*' We understood one another. And something inside me fell away: something which had to some extent prevented my being myself. I counted each day as just one more, rejoicing in the clarity of things, the colours, life itself as they impinged upon me – that Greenland clarity for which there is no descriptive word ... vast, inexorable and – certainly, for one person utterly harmonious.

'What, you here?' said the computer. It was Mette, standing on the pier, wearing Mette-expression number one – a little meditative behind her glasses – a green iceberg, on a surprise visit from the Isle of Disko. 'Yes, it's me,' I said, concealing my pleasure at seeing her again, with some difficulty. 'I'm still here for a few days – this is my "winter".' The iceberg shook the long reddish-brown mane on its head: 'I never thought I should set eyes on you again,' it said. Then suddenly she, Mette, that abstraction of a fantasy, smiled. 'Splendid!' she said. 'Let's have a good time ...'

Sledges on roofs, dogs, kayaks, little villages, Greenlanders, a whole community of life; so many children, so many dogs, so many fishes. The wooden racks for drying fish. The all-pervading smell: everything here smells of fish and dogs. It doesn't bother one much anymore; one smells of them oneself.

The dogs are ravenous – ten to fifteen of them to every house. In summer they are not fed; they have to forage for themselves. They devour everything. That is why the fish are hung up so high, and even the kayaks are on stands. Mette knew a great deal about that coast. 'There are no cats or chickens in Greenland,' she told me: 'the dogs would have eaten them long ago. There is a cock and a hen at Jakobshaven, behind a fence, of course; the dogs sit outside the enclosure ...' And the dogs will eat even one's camera case, if one puts it down, I knew. They kill the dogs, when short of fur, often by strangling them, because the pelt is warmer and the hair stays erect, then.' Thus spake Mette, looking, as usual into the water.

An iceberg was moving past, semi-circular like a theatre, wave-washed completely hollow inside, gulls occupying the dress-circle and the upper-circle. 'There are very few polar bears left,' she went on, 'except far up in Thule. It's news in the Jakobshaven paper, when one gets shot.' Another berg went dipping past, one of those with slices hewn off it – to provide drinking water.

---

1 Later, in Basque country, hardly believing my eyes, I came upon similar words ending in – ak. Just chance? Then I learned that the language was as old as time itself – 'knife' was 'sharpened stone', cave drawings showed ice age reindeer. Is there a connection – starting in Asia – between the Pyrenees and Greenland? It is worth thinking about. K. D.

Many villages get it that way, especially in the winter, that long darkness during the sea is hard-frozen, the inhabitants build huts on it and fetch their fish up through a hole in the 'floor'.

Mette and I were as different as the hills and the sea are, here. We would often go into a village by widely divergent ways; then we would meet and tell each other what we had seen – or else say not a word.

There was a village called Niaciornat. The women were rolling casks up into the barns from the beach, for the winter. At Qaersut, the Danish flag was hoisted – I mean it! – in honour of our visit. The mayor, a friendly great sea-bear of a Dane, had an enchanting Greenland wife. The atmosphere was Japanese ... As the fishing-smack sailed on, a Greenlander chanted the melody of *'Im Frühtau zu Berge'*. He had heard it just once, and memorized it ...

They are musical – dance like dervishes – these Greenlanders. A party can last two whole days. In spite of the tough conditions in which they live, they are unbelievably light-hearted. Their gaiety can be noisy; yet it can be so quiet that you can hardly hear it. As at Niaqornat in the evenings.

'... It was only today that I understood. Here, alone with it all, when I was among the old fishermen's huts, below the rocky hill – it must have come to me then. When I could only hear my own footsteps, and found myself alone with the peat-walled huts, the people behind their windows, and the dogs . .

No one will ever be able to reveal the secret at the heart of Greenland.

We were on the ridge of a tower on the Umanak Mountain. Gorgeous climbing; but rain had driven us back. Then the rain stopped.

Below us lay the sea. We sat throwing little stones down into the twilight-blue inlet, caught between red-streaked rocks. They hit the surface of the water with a 'Click!"Click!' There were great rectangular boulders on the seabed, like drowned books. There was another 'click' on the surface as the next little stone went tumbling into the depths, swinging gently through the water, then lay still. Like seconds of time.

We didn't get to the top,' I said, the rain –'

'Ab,' said Mette, which means 'yes'. She smiled; it was lovely. This was her first climb.

'Shall we have another go?'

'Namek,' said Mette, which means 'no'.

'Click'. Another little stone, swerving its way down, coming to rest. 'Click!' ...

'In a couple of centuries we could throw the whole mountain into the sea,' said Mette.

Mette stayed on Disko till March. Then she went away, somewhere.

On the day after my arrival at Egedesminde, the *Tikerak* caught fire. It started in the engine room, out there on the high seas. The fire gradually enveloped the whole ship. Au Egedesminde stood on the shore, watching the spectacle. The timbers cracked, the hull shivered. Huge flames, the crashing mast, a sea yellow under the midnight sun, a shower of sparks – the good old *Tikerak*, that was.

Next day I met the helmsman. He had a pair of shoes in his hand and a card-board box under his arm. I tried to find words. 'Oh, it's you, is it?' he laughed. You know, we shall get a new ship – next year. Susa: don't worry about it.'

'*Farvel*,' I said. He started to go, then turned and added: 'don't forget to look me up in Denmark. That's where I'm going now, with my daughter.'

The engines of the great jet hummed. There was a class of Greenland children on board, on their way to Copenhagen. Their school mistress was telling them about the myriad lights of the great city; but the children were very quiet, and one girl kept on picking a photograph out of her little handbag. The Danish schoolmarm sobbed: they all find it so terribly hard to leave their island; its only for them to learn a little Danish and see the country. They have given me a Greenland schoolmaster, to lend support during the flight. He was crying too, yesterday.'

The inland ice stretched endlessly below us. After that, leagues of cloud and sea. Then it gradually grew gloomier, a universal greyness closed down, hemming us in. Down we flew into an unfamiliar darkness, in which each day has a day, followed by a night.

Windbumps, rain ...

And a thousand lights: Copenhagen.

My daughter Karen was born in Milan. She is as fair as Tona, her head is as hard as a Greenland iceberg, she climbs everything, is happy, and has a name that comes from the west coasts. We love each other very much.

A telephone call from Bologna? Why, Bernardi! Bernardi is a journalist, ex-bank clerk, a warrior of the Spanish war – in which he was nearly killed. He is also Bologna's liveliest grandfather.

What's that? Greenland? Winter in Greenland? A publisher wants an article? Of course I'll come!

Greenland in the winter ...

'*Imaka* – maybe!'

27 Between the Gran Sasso, Salzburg and ...

The Gran Sasso d'Italia – the Great Rock. A melody sounds over the savage mountains of the Abruzzi: *'Vulessi fa venir pe un ora sola ...'* The villages are small, their houses huddle together, stone-walled. There are churches like fortresses, some of them with loopholes for firearms and battlements – relics of a bygone age. The people who inhabit that sterile land are simple and kindly folk ... *'e vola, vola, vola, e vola lu pavone, se stai col cuore buone, bon ...'* In wintertime you can hear the wolves howling below the Majella's peak. It is the very antithesis of anything a foreigner would expect to find in Italy.

I had driven all night, with my daughter Hildegard in her sleeping bag, next to me on the bench seat. I had told her: 'When you wake up with tomorrow morning's sun, we shall be at the foot of the Gran Sasso... .' This was to be her first mountain.

There was the sound of ice axes clattering against rock. The wind had conjured up ice crusts and snow flowers. 'Look, Papa!' cried Hilde. She had shed all fear, and was determined to climb. She was just seven years old. Karen was only two; I could still see her eyes, above her comforter, looking at me over the garden gate: *'ed io?"Domani – un altra volta.'* Later on, when you're bigger. *'Ciao!'* she said, raising her hand in farewell.

We were 8,500 feet up, the sun shone warmly above transparent blue veils, below which lay the countryside. While I took in the rope and Hildegard came nimbly up by hand- and foothold, Gigi, up above us on the ridge, sang the song of the Gran Sasso, from whose summit you can see the sea on both sides of Italy; while Bruno spoke of the 3,000-foot faces, of the mushrooms that grow in the colourful autumn woods down there, and how he, who lived at its foot, had often climbed the Gran Sasso. But today, he said, beaming all over his wrinkled face, was a special day; and it was obvious how happy he was to be guiding the blonde young princess up his own mountain. Once the drudgery of the snowy coombe at the bottom was over, she climbed happily and easily. 'Say, Papa, I like climbing much better than walking,' she said. And now she decided that she wanted to stick her head into the 'gun barrel', that black hole in the rock at 9,200 feet, a thing not even Bruno had ever done. What on earth for? But then Hilde had her own ideas; and while we were scrambling across to that dark cave, I recalled that the walls at home were papered with space pictures, the cat was called Neil; and Hilde, determined to prepare herself for a flight in space, could tell one all about NASA, the astronauts, the flights of the various capsules. It was quite a relief to remember that she had expressed a wish merely to cross Iceland with me on horseback …

'Papa, we are higher up than the Corno Piccolo,' she cried, her eyes bright with excitement. Soon we would be higher than anything else in the Appenines …

The light fell gleaming on the autumn mists far below. Gigi *was 'Me pareia the passu passu, se saliesse all'infinitu . .!'*[1] And today, when we four had the Great Rock all to ourselves, and Hilde was climbing her first mountain, it really did seem as if we were going up into the heart of the limitless blue sky.

Hildegard has decorated the walls of our home in Varese with countless space photographs – the Himalaya seen through the window of the Apollo capsule, an astonishing brown-and-white tapestry, fine-woven; the unruffled, dark curve of the ocean, with cloud layers above it; the cratered landscape of the moon, over which the earth floats like some deep blue soap bubble. And then, hanging on our walls in Salzburg, there is a picture of one of this earth's craters … the crater of the summit Tona had climbed – her own photograph of it – Kilimanjaro, the 'High Snow'. A mountain of ice slopes high above primeval forests, tree ferns, lianas, giant heather and lobelia; a summit of lava and ash. A summit reached by trails you have to hack out for yourself, or by existing tracks, far from the normal route – through the forest, up over the mighty slopes, thousands of feet high. And Tona had been to the top, by the western flank.

There, at the rim of the gigantic Kibo crater, her companions had decided to halt; so Tona had gone on alone. She wanted to reach the 'Ash Pie'. Step by step, in the thin air at nearly 20,000 feet, she drove herself on till, at last, she stood at the mighty edge of the inner crater and could see down into it. That foray, all by herself, up in the skies, high above all Africa must have been an indescribable experience; and Tona has never said much about it. But there are times when such an experience – one crowded hour of glorious life – can alter the whole course of one's existence. Now she is writing: a book about plants, and a children's story about the travels of a little fish.

Here I am in Salzburg, the festival city, looking out at the rubble in the bed of the Salzach and everything else one can see and share in the life going on all around: Mozart, the leaf of a tree and – the postman.

---

1 'Step by step into the Infinite.'

He brings greetings from Masaaki Kondo (memories of our Tirich Mir!); a postcard from Trieste – *saluti* from Spiro, Walter, Bianca, Fioretta. (Trieste, because of them, is my home from home.) A card from Ingher in Iceland, a place I have not yet managed to visit.

And here is a summons from the Association of Guides, for the following Sunday – yes, I will be there. For now I have yet another profession: guiding those who want to go up to the places where one becomes a 'different man' – and I enjoy doing it. Climbing a peak now has a new slant to it, even if it meant my being unable to carry out all my own plans, for sheer lack of time. (I cannot help thinking of Pierre in Paris, with whom I have for so long been meaning to do a big tour; and of Wolfi, now living in Pakistan.)

There is another postcard, too, from my ex-pupils. 'Greetings to our Yeti!' it reads ...

I had left the school. If I had gone on sitting there, looking out of that window next to the directors' office, I would never have written this book; now, I have been working on it for nearly a year, and I am enjoying being an author. I am no longer ruled by a timetable, though it means that life is more unsure and unpredictable, less smooth and easy. On the other hand, I am now sitting on the cover of the 'machine', having lifted myself off its basic 'plan' – only, now there was another 'machine' in front of me – a typewriter. There is no way of escape; we are born into a world of plans and machines, they control and decide our existence. It is a fact of life. Still, I can use my freedom by tapping away at the keys: 'make life more human, humanise yourselves, each and every one of you. Don't let yourselves grow square; don't computerise your minds as well as everything else.' And that is not addressed only to my pupils, who will one day be bosses and employees ...

Mountains, rock and ice – lovely shimmering ice. The lover of mountains must go to the mountains; otherwise he will cease to be a person, for others as well as for himself, and he will lose the very joy of life. But there are other things, too. I am watching a student preparing crabs for his collection (I take my typewriter all over the place with me in my car). The thought enters my mind that in a few milliards of years the sun will blow up and the earth will perish. What is the sense of it all? And yet, watching him, I find I have something to believe in.

I walked through the town, taking yesterday's rough pages to be copied out fair by a secretary, then back over the Monchsberg, high above the city. It is a good place for thinking, and I thought about what I had done so far and what I was doing. An idea occurred to me, and at home I wrote it on the wall – or rather, not on the wall itself, but on the snowfield of a huge photograph hanging on the wall: 'For whatever I do, give me the true measure it deserves ...'

Above the snowfield in that picture, soars K2, high as the heavens themselves. Where does that true measure lie?

To stand again above 26,000 feet ... *Imaka* ... perhaps. Certainly I will be going again – to Greenland, Nepal, the Andes. I must go there and live and discover things. Maybe make a book or a film of them; maybe just to live there a while and then come home – till the day arrives when I can take Hilde and, later on, Karen with me – wherever it may be that we go.

Rock, ice. Whenever I go up there the same miracle always happens: I feel as if that is where I was born. After twenty years of it, since the days of the lad who went crystal hunting ...

When I look up from the keys of the typewriter to the green-and-red bilberry leaves on the slope between the drooping larch branches, I see a limestone wall, bathed in sunshine ... a high wall: I have seen it for a long time, now.

Yes, I shall be going again; and when I do, I shall not have any more idea why, than I have ever had till this day.

28   Altamira

I was under the impression that I had written the closing chapter of this book. But now, again it has changed, this strange, unpredictable life, unforeseeable.

I had gone to Spain on a lecture tour. My journey took me in winter through that wide and wild country – the Spaniards themselves call it *Savache* – so different from the rest of Europe.

At Altamira I went below ground.

Those unforeseen vicissitudes … Though one may not always know it, everything one does has an effect – on you, on someone else. The earth is continually dying and bringing forth something new: simply … just as grass may do.

Rain was falling softly on Santillana del Mar. Here on Spain's north coast, between the Pyrenees and the Bay of Biscay, lies one of Europe's heaviest rainfall areas; totally different from the heart of Spain, where in winter the icy wind whistles over the *Meseta,* and in summer the air quivers above the dry ground. But here, there seems to be a springy green carpet spread over the land – so green, so dense, so lush that the rain strikes one as a miracle, bringing life from the sky; or evoking it from the earth – or both. The rain is so much an integral part of this country that it no longer arouses any feeling of discomfort. It is just a fact; and man has accommodated himself to it. The inhabitants wear wooden clogs, with three stilt-like projections at the bottom; for if you leave the damp cushion of the meadows, you can find yourself ankle-deep in mud. In the course of thousands of years, the water has hollowed-out caves in the limestone which, during the ice age, were the habitations of man. Many of them had been discovered, but who knows how many still lie beneath the surface, unbeknown to anyone? When you are driving across this hummocky land of the Province of Santander in your car, you notice, over and again, circular depressions, some of them funnel shaped, in the ground; under many of them there might be hidden caves, though probably not habitable ones. One would only have to dig down a little, to find out.

It was in 1868, on a green slope near Santillana de Mar, that a hunter sent his dog into a fox's lair. He could not know that he was standing that day a few feet above a vault, which was later to be known as the Cathedral of the Ice Age.

When the dog did not come back, the hunter started digging. That is how the cave was discovered.

Until that day, no air had touched the paintings in its roof; for the original entrance had been silted-up for time immemorial. Professor Herbert Kuhn, explaining the reason for the immaculate preservation of the pictures, for the strength and freshness of their colours, wrote: 'And so, since the Ice Age, no one had seen the pictures, no breath of air had touched them, the temperature had remained even through thousands of years; one could really believe they had been painted yesterday …'

They are pictures of animals, mostly bison, but there are others, too. Animals that lived here then; and, miraculously, alive in these paintings today as they were then.

Was it the 'cult of the chase' that moved men to decorate the vault with the animal life, which populated those meadows – and maybe, at the time, those woods – of the hillocks of this coastal strip? Or was it an artist's sheer pleasure in painting: the urge to reproduce, to express life – and death?

Time and again, today, men go down below ground to Altamira; and when they come out again into the light of day, they seem bemused, overwhelmed. Altamira beggars description. If I should presently try to share the impressions of a visit, I know it can only be a feeble attempt. I can only hope to give a faint idea of what I experienced that day.

Anyone intending to go there should do so in winter. For then there are few visitors and it may be his luck to have the cave to himself, or be alone with just one person with whom he would care to share it. And then, in the silence of the cave, thousands of years will fade away and he will find himself able to identify himself, at its primeval springs, with the spirit of that human being who immortalised his vision on the roof of the vault with a paintbrush – as if it were himself, who had just come in from outside – he himself, that human being.

There is a road which leads from the continent of perception to an island of reality, outside. The road is intuition, the bridge, art. Where does it lead –?

Altamira is the bridge built by the art of the Ice Age.

The vault is flat, some twenty yards long, ten wide, so low that there is no difficulty in touching the rock of the roof with one's fingers. There can be no doubt that it was the shrine of some cult. The living quarters were apart, for there are several rooms in the cave. During the excavations, they found tools, made of stone and bone; flat mussels from the nearby sea, as large as plates, with holes bored in them … and little round mussels to act as containers for the colours, some of them with the paint still in them …

The animals painted on the roof are from three to six feet long, with smaller ones in between; but, as you look up at them, you are quite unaware of these dimensions. There are bisons, a running boar, a doe at rest, a horse, then more bisons. Some of the beasts are shown, rearing high into the air, in mortal combat. Others are static, beautifully at rest – all incredibly exciting. Some are overpainted – a new painting over the older, more faded one. Faded, or rubbed out? How many years between the two paintings – centuries, perhaps? I am no scientist; I have only my own way of recognising something, of trying to put myself in the mind of the being who painted this or that picture. This takes no cognizance of time.

I think that many of the pictures are closely connected: I could specify them, but that is of no great importance here. There is one master who has spread the quiet shape of a bison over a shallow depression in the roof – almost in relief, concave. And here another bison – I think, from the same hand. But there, a very different matter – a wild, forceful character, who sought the circumference of the circle, in an effort to burst forth from it with his powers of expression; this one has composed of his brilliant surfaces, his economical, effective dark strokes, a dying bison, laid on a projection in the rock. In frantic movements, red and black, the beast bursts the bounds of space, of his own red-and-black space ...

The animal is incredibly expressive.

'There are three of these pictures on rock projections here – don't you see the similarity?'

'I think they are in the same style, springing from the same thought, but not from the same hand.'

In the dull light, the ochre paint flames red. The beast remains dumb. 'I think the same man did them.'

We remarked that the difference was irrelevant and sank back into contemplation of the pictures.

I was sitting somewhere, writing. Everything was still there, before my eyes. I wrote in chopped-up sentences, just as they came ...

A few notes, on bits of paper in the glove locker of the car. Written, not in Altamira, nor even in Santillana del Mar, but somewhere along the road.

Unnecessary, perhaps ... it is all there for anyone to see ... Why, then ...?

All the same I have attempted it. There were those scraps of paper, my separate impressions on them, almost indecipherable ... but perhaps the entirety was there?

Altamira! bigger ... recognisable ... but still possible to capture, but ... for moments, for only a moment. It links us with eternity. 10,000 years, vanished at a stroke. It is the present time. The idea which motivated the brush, no not the brush; the hand which wielded the red chalk. Not the hand either, but the thought: 'How shall I draw this line, this reflection of my inner spirit, before my eyes, life, bursting the bounds of space, passing into death – immortal?' It dies, it lives as never before, I see it …

A sound of dripping in the cave, in the silence.

The Idea has come.

He wanted to perpetuate what he had seen. The beast, life, death. Red and black, the strokes go winging, the ruffled mane, the tensed muscles. He himself – the very beast itself. Up there on the roof, above me. You.

The grass grows. A dog looks along the street. The naked being, waiting, running, thinking. The bird sings; a voice. It lives, and chatters. No madness. No death. A thousand beings behind it … hundreds coming after. Perhaps.

Life. Death is unimportant. It is life that matters. Everything that has ever been, still exists.

That is the thing to know …

Life. Death is unimportant, a natural thing, inevitable. Life, a moment of existence. Why? Because of love. Being … all being. It is life that matters.

It endures; time is of no account.

The houses dissipate into thin air. The floor beneath my feet is his floor. The floor of the hillock above his cave. The trees are the same trees – a moment in the present – hundreds of trees, the past behind them. It is all here: the green knolls all around, the undulating contours of the horizon. Down in the depths under them, forests, and the beasts they house. Tomorrow one of them will die, … I am alive. We shall be leaving tomorrow. The aurochs, the bear, the stag, the doe. The forest. Tomorrow.

The floor beneath my feet. The horizon. Houses. God. The grass that grows. A few trees. A picture painted on the rock. An idea …

We live for a moment. That is a fact. My thanks to you, Beloved. Even if I didn't thank you, it would still be a fact. Just a day.

We stood outside the cave, looking at the grey sky, a few trees, the house that holds a museum. Should we go in? What for? Later …

'I'd like to be alone for a few minutes.'

'Yes – so would I.'

We walked over the meadows of Santillana del Mar, those meadows like a great green carpet, under a grey sky. We wandered up a path, then down again, back and forth, purposeless – everything was everywhere, where it has always been.

There was a small, low built Romanesque church and we went over to it.

A few hours later I was driving – unconsciously or by design? – at fifteen miles an hour – through the hillocky landscape …

'I felt it for a moment – the real thing – but only for a moment; when I tried to find it again, I couldn't.'

I know it. I sense it. It is the real thing. You knew it, too.

We had left Altamira far behind, and it was still there.

Everything is everywhere, where it has always been ...

I drove on, over the wide *Meseta*, alone; the road ran straight as a die through that immense landscape. I was in the grip of a wild joy. I sang, to drown the gale that kept on buffeting the car.

Everything is everywhere, where it has always been ...

The sierras stood white in the distance – did an ancestress of mine perhaps dwell somewhere on an arid mountainside, like those? – the distant Sierras ...

Dazzling sunlight! There was sand blowing through the air; grey-green, dishevelled olive-copses; greyish-red, terraced hills in the wandering circles of light. It was like in the desert.

Everything was everywhere, where it always had been ...

The gale had ripped round clumps of plants out of the soil; they rolled away across the *Meseta* tumbling oddly; continuously, like a *perpetuum mobile*; round clumps, cartwheels ... the wings of the car rattled. My good old *Giovanna*, with nearly 120,000 miles tucked under her bonnet; rusty and battered ... (I wonder, shall I ever learn how to park properly?)

Everything is everywhere, where it has always been ...

Pot-holes, a curve ... dancing miles ... spots of light; the branches rustling ... I sang at the top of my voice, out of a full heart.

... it exists.

By the way, Lovell, after circling the moon, decided to stay on earth. Be it noted: *after* –

... after?

The author, heavily laden, in the Valais in 1955 and leading on the classic Fox/Stenico route (grade VI) on the Cima d'Ambiez, Brenta Dolomites, in 1954. Wolfgang Stefan took this picture of one of the steep and solid wall pitches high on the face ... 'It was a gigantic freeclimbing pitch, then; I wonder whether it still is?' The Fox/Stenico route (1939) was enthusiastically commended to them by Cesare Maestri as one of the best Dolomite climbs. © Diemberger Collection

The author with Wolfgang Stefan after their rapid (storm-lashed) ascent of the Eiger Nordwand in 1958. Photo: Albert Winkler. © Diemberger Collection

The Direttissima through the North Face of the Koenigspitze (Ortler Alps) was lead-climbed by the author in 1956 (partnered by Albert Morocutti and, regarding the ice overhang – the Giant 'Meringue' – at the top of the Face, also by Hannes Unterweger and Herbert Knapp) in the days before modern ice tools. The first third of this crux involved aid-climbing using long ice pitons but the upper part was a struggle through sugary ice. This first ascent led to an invitation for Kurt to join the Broad Peak expedition. © Diemberger Collection

Using a steep approach from the Godwin-Austen Glacier at 4,900 metres (a previous attempt having approached by the Broad Glacier) the climbers placed and stocked three camps, a process that provided an ideal training and acclimatisation programme. Here Hermann Buhl, makes a supply trip to Camp 2 (6,400 metres). These were the slopes that Diemberger and Tullis descended after their avalanche escape in 1984. © Diemberger Collection

Diemberger and Buhl were tackling Chogolisa's South-East Ridge when a sudden storm forced a hurried retreat. In a near whiteout, unroped, with Diemberger leading, they groped back along their fading tracks. Near the cornice edge, Diemberger felt the snow give way and swiftly bounded to the right, whereas Buhl was less lucky. Later the storm cleared and the author took this photograph of the tracks leading to disaster. © Diemberger Collection

Tona Sironi Diemberger after surviving a direct lightning hit near the summit of the Aiguille Noire in 1963. The lightning, not conducted by her helmet, skimmed her forehead, went into her hand, burnt her heel and sock and took its exit by a nail in her boot's rubber sole. Tona, the author's first wife, remains a keen climber and a close friend, and translates all his books into Italian. © Diemberger Collection

Hermann Buhl portrait. © Diemberger Collection

The Peuterey Ridge of Mont Blanc – the finest ridge of the Alps. The complete traverse of the dark Aiguille Noire, the partially ice-covered Aiguille Blanche and up to the white Dome of Mont Blanc consists in a sequence of difficult climbs and descents along the edge of this great ridge and was first filmed by Kurt Diemberger and Franz Lindner in September 1958 for five days. The skyline of the traverse has a total length of eight kilometers – hardly to imagine – if you sit in a car! © Diemberger Collection

The Peuterey Ridge of Mont Blanc (seen here from the Grandes Jorasses) is the author's favourite alpine climb. The Aig. Noire (the pointed peak on extreme left) is best climbed by its classic South Ridge. A long series of abseils then lead down the North Ridge to the Dames Anglais. The Aig. Blanche is traversed and then a grand finale is provided by the majestic ice slopes and ridges of the highest mountain of Western Europe. In 1958, partnered by Franz Lindner, the author filmed this great alpine classic and later won the main prize at the Trento Film Festival. © Diemberger Collection

The north-eastern aspect of Dhaulagiri with the North-East Ridge (the first ascent route) in the centre, the East Face to its left (climbed in 1981, alpine-style, by a Franco/Anglo Polish quartet) and the dangerous South-East Ridge on the extreme left (climbed in 1978 by a large Japanese expedition – with four fatalities). The Pear Route takes the shadowy slopes on the right. © Diemberger Collection

Dhaulagiri's North Face. The much-tried route up the pear buttress (far right) was not completed until 1983. The North-East Ridge is the left skyline. The central rock face succumbed in 1994. © Diemberger Collection

From the south Dhaulagiri assumes it most majestic presence. This huge face, first tried in 1977, has been climbed by indirect lines by Polish (1986) and Yugoslav (1981) groups (neither reaching the summit). In 1988 a Czech trio made an alpine-style ascent by the South-West Pillar on the left. The South-East Ridge (Japanese, 1978) is on the right. Photo: Leo Dickinson. © Diemberger Collection

The final scenes during the first ascent of Dhaulagiri. © Diemberger Collection

'My father has made me a great gift: a brand-new hamp rope; I am happy!' Kurt at the age of 17 on the Untersberg above Salzburg, his first rock climbing Eldorado ... © Diemberger Collection

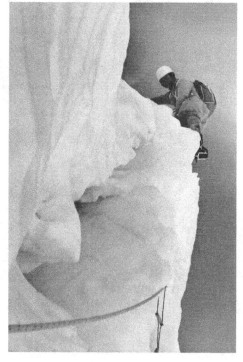

'Up and over the icy overhang of the Aiguille Blanche de Peuterey, the crux of the North Face'- Kurt in another adventure after the earlier traverse of the great integral ridge of Mont Blanc ... © Diemberger Collection

Hermann Buhl at his second first ascent of an 8,000 metre peak, standing on top of Broad Peak on 9 June 1957 ... In the background Gasherbrum IV catches the last rays of the sunset. © Diemberger Collection

Kurt, high on Broad Peak, taking a picture towards Chogolisa, photographed by Hermann Buhl, several days before they went to this mountain. © Diemberger Collection

der Salzburger Wimpel auf dem Gipfel des 8250 m hohen DHAULAGIRI

Kurt Diemberger

Kurt Diemberger (left) and Albin Schelbert on 13 May 1960 on the summit of Dhaulagiri (with four others, not in the picture) at the first ascent of this mountain. They did not use oxygen and for Kurt it was his second 8,000 metre peak.
© Diemberger Collection

Hermann Buhl, famed throughout Europe after his Nanga Parbat ascent in 1953, leaves Salzburg station, en route to Genoa, and thence by ship to Pakistan. Accompanying him are Kurt Diemberger and Fritz Wintersteller (plus Marcus Schmuck, not illustrated), sprucely dressed in trilby hats and gaberdine mackintoshes, the norm in the late 1950s. © Diemberger Collection

Hermann Buhl on the summit of Broad Peak on 9 June 1957. In the background, Gasherbrum 4 catches the last rays of sunlight. © Diemberger Collection

Buhl's plan was for four well-trained alpinists to tackle an 8,000 metre peak without porters in a lightweight Westalpinstil push. Here Buhl recuperates at Camp 3 (6,950 metres), the final camp before the summit attempt. K2 is seen in the background. © Diemberger Collection

Buhl, slowed by his Nanga Parbat injuries, moving up the ridge above the col. © Diemberger Collection

Buhl working carefully along the corniced ridge of Chogolisa on 27 June 1957. © Diemberger Collection

297

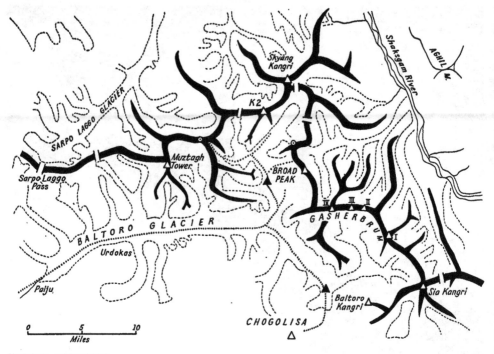

The Baltoro and Broad Peak.

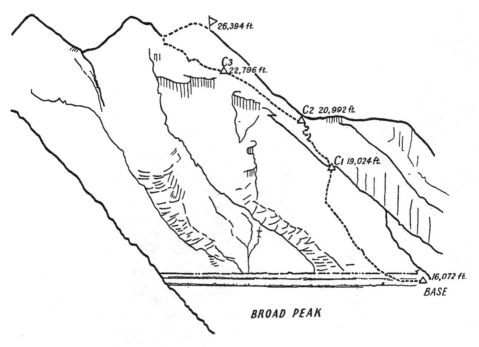

The Route on Broad Peak.

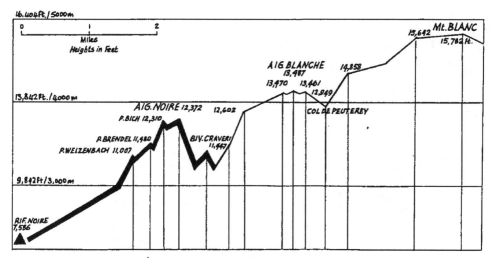

The Peuterey Ridge

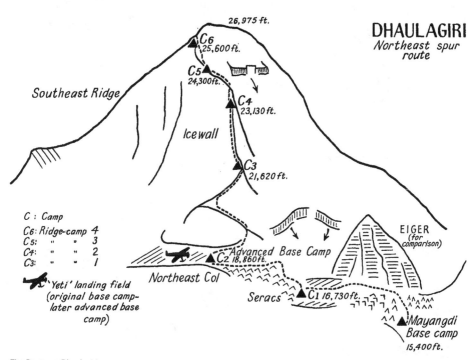

The Route on Dhaulagiri.

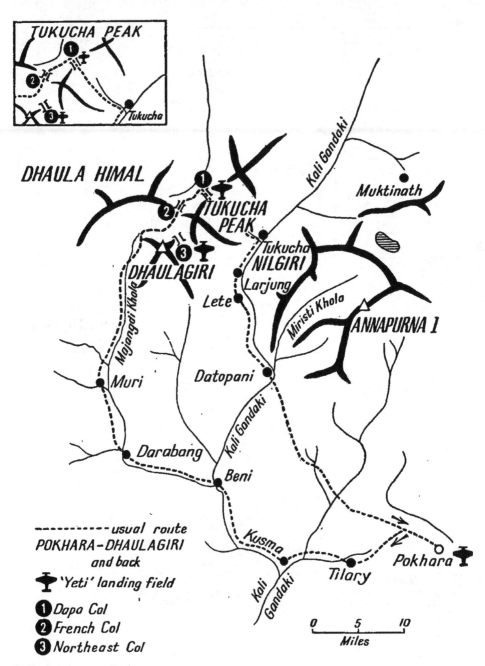

TUKUCHA PEAK

①
②
③
Tukucha

DHAULA HIMAL

①
②
TUKUCHA PEAK

③
DHAULAGIRI

Tukucha
NILGIRI

Larjung

Lete

Muktinath

Kali Gandaki

Miristi Khola

ANNAPURNA 1

Majangdi Khola

Muri

Datopani

Kali Gandaki

Darabang

Beni

Kusma

Kali Gandaki

Tilary

Pokhara

- - - - - - - usual route
POKHARA-DHAULAGIRI
and back

'Yeti' landing field

① Dapa Col
② French Col
③ Northeast Col

0   5   10
Miles

The Dhaulagiri-Annapurna Himal.

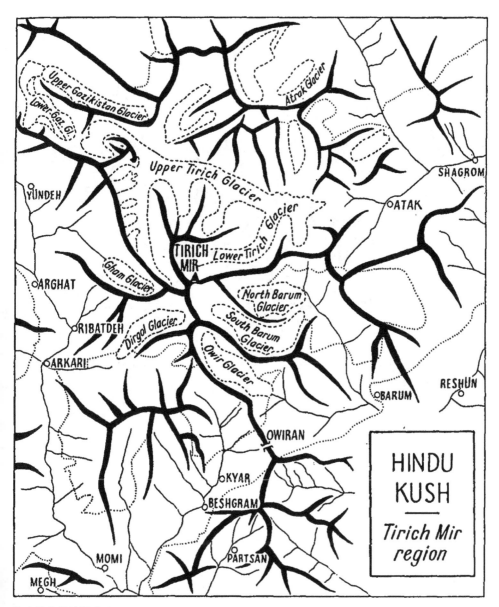

Hindu Kush: Tirich Mir Region.

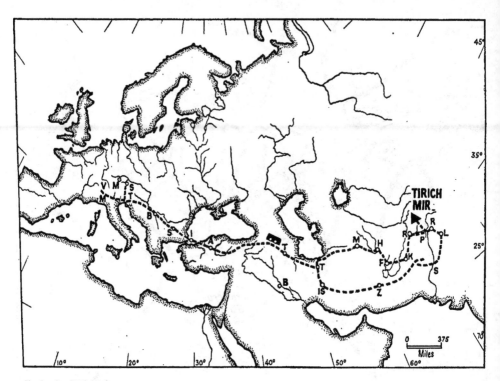

The Road to Tirich Mir.

Printed in the USA
CPSIA information can be obtained
at www.ICGtesting.com
JSHW012014140824
68134JS00025B/2404

9 781912 560035